KARL THE VIKING ™

VOLUME I
THE SWORD OF EINGAR

Karl The Viking
created by
Ted Cowan,
Ken Bulmer &
Don Lawrence

THE SWORD OF EINGAR

Serialised in **Lion**
29th October 1960 – 11th February 1961

Written by
Ted Cowan

Art by
Don Lawrence

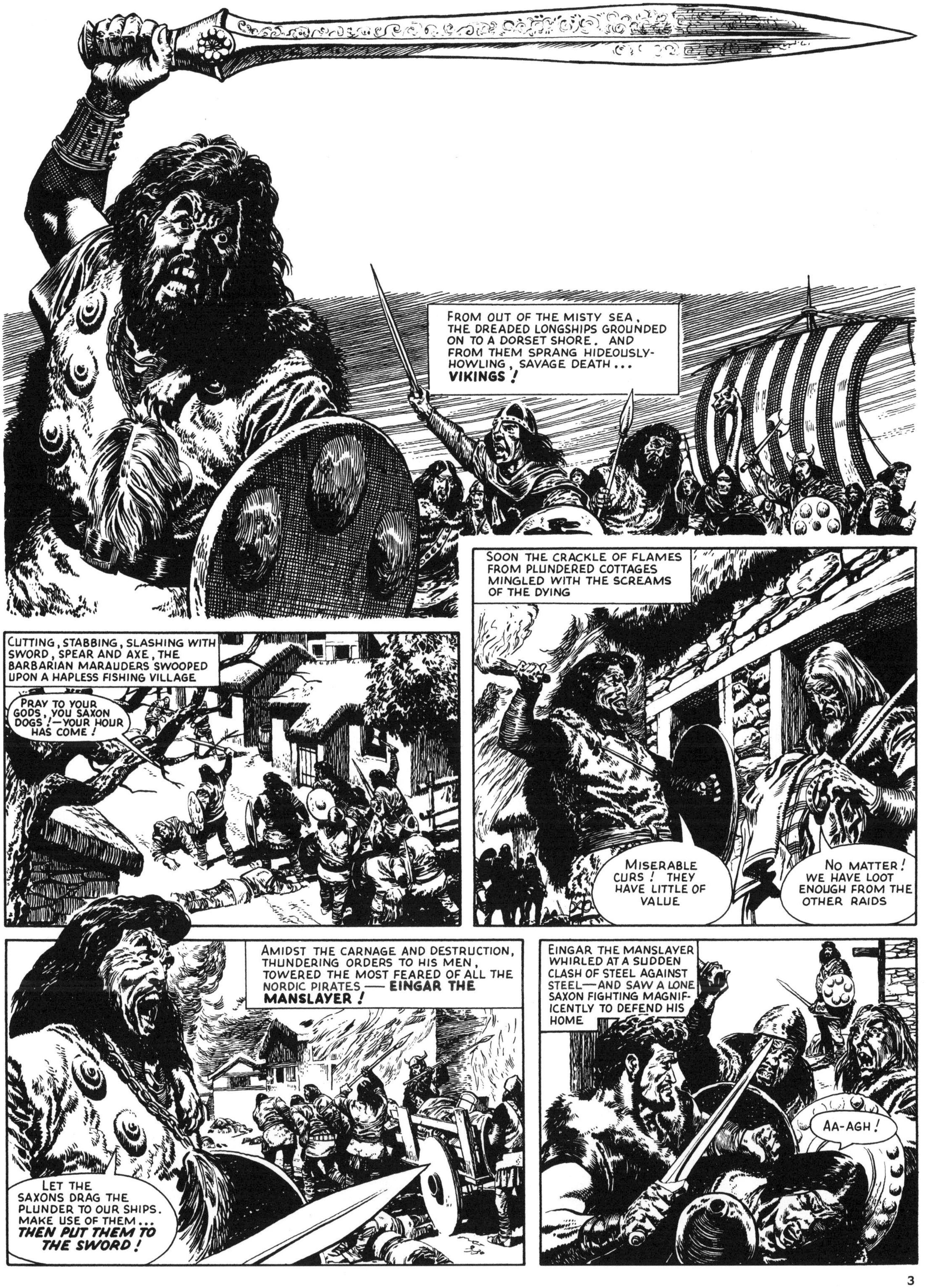

FROM OUT OF THE MISTY SEA, THE DREADED LONGSHIPS GROUNDED ON TO A DORSET SHORE. AND FROM THEM SPRANG HIDEOUSLY-HOWLING, SAVAGE DEATH... VIKINGS!
SOON THE CRACKLE OF FLAMES FROM PLUNDERED COTTAGES MINGLED WITH THE SCREAMS OF THE DYING
CUTTING, STABBING, SLASHING WITH SWORD, SPEAR AND AXE, THE BARBARIAN MARAUDERS SWOOPED UPON A HAPLESS FISHING VILLAGE
PRAY TO YOUR GODS, YOU SAXON DOGS! — YOUR HOUR HAS COME!
MISERABLE CURS! THEY HAVE LITTLE OF VALUE
NO MATTER! WE HAVE LOOT ENOUGH FROM THE OTHER RAIDS
AMIDST THE CARNAGE AND DESTRUCTION, THUNDERING ORDERS TO HIS MEN, TOWERED THE MOST FEARED OF ALL THE NORDIC PIRATES — EINGAR THE MANSLAYER!
LET THE SAXONS DRAG THE PLUNDER TO OUR SHIPS. MAKE USE OF THEM... THEN PUT THEM TO THE SWORD!
EINGAR THE MANSLAYER WHIRLED AT A SUDDEN CLASH OF STEEL AGAINST STEEL — AND SAW A LONE SAXON FIGHTING MAGNIFICENTLY TO DEFEND HIS HOME
AA-AGH!

WITH A ROAR OF MINGLED RAGE AND ASTONISHMENT THE VIKING CHIEF BOUNDED TOWARDS THE BATTLING FIGURES

HAVE THE GODS TURNED YOU TO WOMEN — THAT ONE SAXON WEAKLING CAN HOLD YOU AT BAY?

BY THE HALLS OF VALHALLA, EINGAR, THIS IS NO ORDINARY SAXON!

Then, howling his battle cry, the viking chief attacked — and the lone saxon's fate was sealed

AH! YOU FOUGHT WELL AGAINST MY CUBS, SAXON! BUT YOU CANNOT MATCH THE WOLF HIMSELF!

EINGAR DUCKED BENEATH A SWINGING SWORD SLASH.

INDEED THIS IS NO ORDINARY SAXON! HE FIGHTS LIKE A MAN — LIKE A VIKING!

Mercy had no part in the viking creed—not even towards respected foes. A split-second later, the valiant saxon was dead

YOU DIED WELL AND BRAVELY! THE GODS WILL FIND A PLACE IN VALHALLA FOR YOU!

The cottage door splintered under the smashing impact of eingar's bull-like shoulders

KILL EVERYONE! SPARE NOTHING THAT LIVES!

A VIKING SWORD SWUNG HIGH ABOVE A WOODEN CRIB — **THEN POISED AT EINGAR'S SUDDEN CRY**

HOLD! THAT IS THE CHILD OF A BRAVE MAN!

INCREDIBLY THE EYES OF EINGAR HELD A TRACE OF FEAR

WORDS FILL MY HEAD! STRANGE WORDS — AS—AS IF IT WERE THE GODS SPEAKING TO ME. THEY SAY I SHOULD SPARE THIS LIFE — THAT THIS CHILD SHOULD JOURNEY BACK WITH US

ABRUPTLY, HE CAME TO A FATEFUL DECISION

CARRY HIM TO THE LONGSHIPS! LET ONE SAXON WOMAN LIVE, THAT SHE MAY CARE FOR HIM DURING OUR LONG JOURNEY BACK!

AS THE PLUNDER-LADEN VIKING SHIPS SAILED FROM THE RAVAGED SHORE, THUNDER MUTTERED ACROSS A DARKENING SKY

BUT WAS IT THUNDER? OR WAS IT THE MIGHTY ODIN AND THOR RUMBLING THEIR APPROVAL OF EINGAR'S BARBARIC PROWESS?

OR WERE THESE VIKING GODS ARGUING THE FATE OF THE SAXON BOY-CHILD —

— THE CHILD WHO WAS TO BECOME KNOWN AS THE SON OF EINGAR THE MANSLAYER!

AND THAT NIGHT, IN THE GREAT FEASTING HALL, EINGAR TOLD HIS PEOPLE OF THE SAXON BOY CHILD

...AND THIS IS THE GREATEST OF ALL THE TREASURES I HAVE BROUGHT BACK WITH ME!

FOR THE GODS HAVE TOLD ME THAT THIS BOY IS TO BE A GREAT AND VALOROUS VIKING. HE IS TO BE MY SON! THE SON OF YOUR CHIEFTAIN — EINGAR THE MANSLAYER!

AND AS THE YEARS PASSED, KARL WAS TAUGHT MANY THINGS — PARTICULARLY HOW TO SURVIVE THE CRUEL ELEMENTS

EINGAR NAMED HIS SON KARL, AND HAD HIM RAISED IN THE HARSH, BARBARIC MANNER OF THE NORSEMEN. AND WHEN THE BOY HAD REACHED THE AGE OF ELEVEN —

NO — YET HE CONTINUES TO FIGHT ON! *THAT* IS THE THING THAT MATTERS!

YOUR SON HAS THE COURAGE OF A YOUNG EAGLE, EINGAR. BUT IT IS FIVE AGAINST ONE. HE CANNOT WIN!

THAT ICY WATER WOULD FREEZE *MY* BLOOD! HE IS TRULY THE SON OF EINGAR!

EINGAR TAUGHT HIM PROWESS WITH THE SWORD, AXE AND SPEAR

YOUR AIM IS GOOD, MY SON! ONLY I COULD BETTER SUCH A CAST!

AND IN HIS ARMS GREW THE SINEWY STRENGTH OF THE MOUNTAIN PINE

BY THE GODS, EINGAR, COULD ANY MAN BE PROUDER OF HIS SON? THAT IRON BAR IS AS THICK AS MY WRIST!

AND THEN CAME A GREAT AND FATEFUL DAY KARL, MY SON, YOU PLEASE ME IN ALL THINGS YOU ARE STRONG, HARD AND BRAVE—TRULY FITTED-TO BECOME CHIEFTAIN OF MY PEOPLE WHEN I DIE!

BUT AGE LEAVES YOU UNTOUCHED, FATHER. YOU ARE STILL THE WOLF—STILL THE STRONGEST OF US ALL. I CANNOT BELIEVE YOU WILL EVER DIE!

THAT IS YOUR HEART SPEAKING, MY SON, AND NOT YOUR HEAD! NO, KARL, I MUST MAKE SURE YOU ARE READY TO RULE—IN EVERY WAY! *THE TIME HAS COME FOR YOU TO GO A-VIKING!* WE SAIL TOMORROW!

EYES SHINING WITH EXCITEMENT, KARL HURRIED TO BREAK THE GOOD NEWS TO THE AGED SAXON WOMAN WHOSE LIFE EINGAR HAD SPARED SO THAT SHE COULD CARE FOR HIS SON

...AND SO TOMORROW I BECOME A MAN, AFREDA! TOMORROW I SHALL SAIL ACROSS THE GREAT SEAS, TOWARDS STRANGE LANDS AND MANY BATTLES!

I KNOW HOW YOU HAVE LONGED FOR THIS, KARL. BUT I CANNOT REJOICE FOR YOU... FOR I AM FILLED WITH A STRANGE FEAR!

IN THE DIM LIGHT OF THE RAIN-FILLED DAWN, THE VIKING FLEET ASSEMBLED, AND KARL TRIED TO EASE AFREDA'S TROUBLED MIND

HURRY, MY SON!

I SHALL COME BACK, AFREDA! IT IS TRUE THERE WILL BE BATTLES. BUT I AM NO WEAKLING

IT IS NOT THE BATTLES I FEAR KARL. IT IS SOMETHING MUCH WORSE—SOMETHING STRANGE—EVIL!

A FEW MINUTES LATER, THE OARS THRUST AGAINST THE SHORE, AND THE GREAT LONGSHIPS SAILED INTO THE TOSSING WATERS

PAY NO HEED TO AFREDA'S FEARS, MY SON! IT IS NATURAL SHE SHOULD WORRY, FOR YOU ARE GOING WHERE SHE CAN NO LONGER WATCH OVER YOU!

PERHAPS YOU ARE RIGHT, FATHER. YET SHE IS A STRANGE WOMAN—AND SHE SAYS HER DREAMS HAVE BEEN FILLED WITH FORE-BODING!

FOR DAYS THE VIKINGS GRAPPLED WITH RAGING SEAS, AND AFREDA'S FEARS WERE FORGOTTEN

THEN THE LONGSHIPS' KEELS GRATED ON TO A FOREIGN SHORE... AND BEFORE THE VIKINGS STRETCHED THE NIGHT-SHROUDED HILLS OF IRELAND

THE CELTS' TOWN IS NOT FAR FROM HERE

I REMEMBER IT FROM EARLIER DAYS, EINGAR. BY THE SWORD OF ODIN, THERE WILL BE RICH PLUNDER FOR US!

SILENTLY THE MARAUDERS MOVED INLAND, TO WAIT BELOW THE CREST OF A HILL OVERLOOKING THE SLEEPING, UNSUSPECTING TOWN

SOON IT WILL BECOME LIGHT, AND THE FOOLS WILL OPEN THE GATES TO LET OUT THEIR CATTLE

THE BLOOD-RED FINGERS OF THE DAWN REACHED INTO THE SKY. THE TOWN GATES OPENED, AND—

—KARL THE BRITON HAD BECOME KARL THE VIKING!

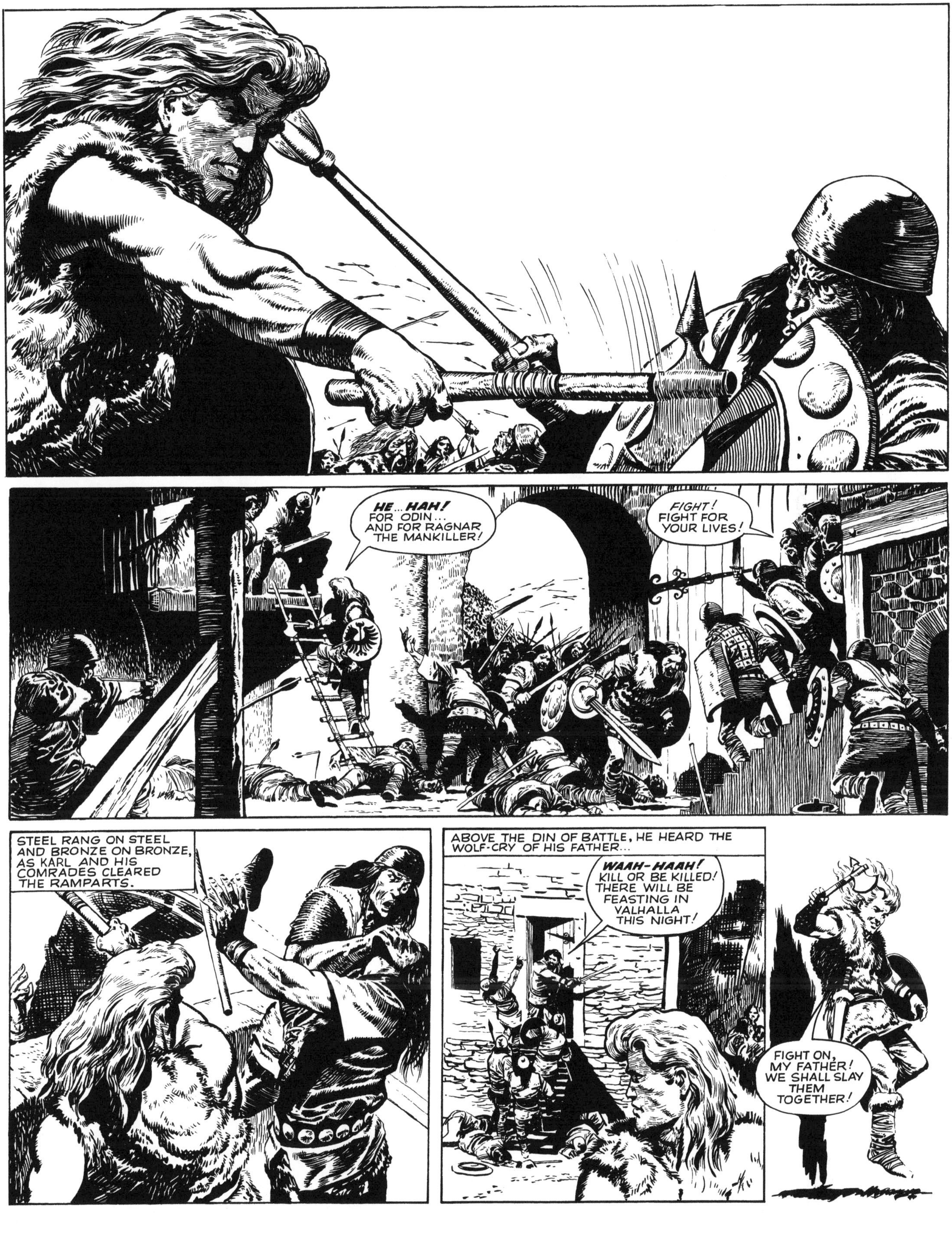

HE...HAH! FOR ODIN... AND FOR RAGNAR THE MANKILLER!
FIGHT! FIGHT FOR YOUR LIVES!
STEEL RANG ON STEEL AND BRONZE ON BRONZE, AS KARL AND HIS COMRADES CLEARED THE RAMPARTS.
ABOVE THE DIN OF BATTLE, HE HEARD THE WOLF-CRY OF HIS FATHER...
WAAH-HAAH! KILL OR BE KILLED! THERE WILL BE FEASTING IN VALHALLA THIS NIGHT!
FIGHT ON, MY FATHER! WE SHALL SLAY THEM TOGETHER!

BACK TO BACK, FATHER AND SON FOUGHT LIKE WOLVES AT BAY...

AA-AAGH!

HO! HO! SEE HOW RAGNAR'S CUB SHOWS HIS TEETH!

AAAGH!

WHEN ALL RESISTANCE WAS STAMPED OUT, THE LOOTING BEGAN...

VIKING CURS!

WHAT'S THIS? ONE OF THEM STILL ALIVE? CUT HIM DOWN!

A CRUEL GRIN SPLIT RAGNAR'S FEARSOME FACE...

NO... LET HIM LIVE TO GAZE UPON THE TOWN AS WE BURN IT TO THE GROUND!

NO, FATHER!

LET THE TOWN STAND, FATHER! THE CELTS ARE INDUSTRIOUS PEOPLE. THE FEW WHO REMAIN WILL REPAIR THE DAMAGE... IN A YEAR OR MORE, WE CAN RETURN AGAIN!

... AND LOOT IT ONCE MORE! THERE IS WISDOM IN YOUR WORDS, MY SON. VERY WELL, THE TOWN WILL BE SPARED, AND THERE WILL BE NO MORE KILLING!

THERE IS A CUNNINGNESS IN MY SON THAT YOU WILL NEVER FIND IN A TRUE-BORN VIKING!

THERE IS MUCH HE CAN TEACH US... LIKE THE FOLLY OF CUTTING DOWN A TREE FOR THE SAKE OF ONE CROP OF FRUIT!

SEEKING FURTHER PLUNDER, THE SEA-WOLF HORDE MARCHED INLAND...

TWO DAYS... AND WE HAVE FOUND NOTHING BUT FOREST AND BOGS!

OUR LUCK WILL CHANGE!

DAYLIGHT WAS FADING WHEN THEY CAME TO A STONE CAIRN...

IT IS THE GRAVE OF AN IRISH CHIEF. SUCH MEN ARE BURIED WITH ALL THEIR RICHES!

SILENCE ... AND THEN PROTESTS... FOLLOWED RAGNAR'S WORDS...

MIGHTY RAGNAR... DO NOT DISTURB YONDER GRAVE! IF THE STONES ARE REMOVED THE SPIRIT OF THE CHIEF WILL BE FREED TO DESTROY US ALL!

THRUSTING HIS WARRIORS ASIDE, RAGNAR MOUNTED THE CAIRN...

YOU TALK LIKE FRIGHTENED WOMEN! RAGNAR FEARS NEITHER MAN NOR SPIRIT!

AND THEN IT CAME... A CHILL WIND FROM OUT OF THE DARKENING WEST..

THIS IS NO ORDINARY WIND... IT CHILLS MY VERY HEART!

RAGNAR! THE SPIRITS ARE ANGRY!

LET US FLEE FROM THIS ACCURSED SPOT!

NAMELESS DREAD FILLED THE FIERCE DANISH SEA-RAIDERS. AS THEIR LEADER, RAGNAR THE MANSLAYER, LAID HIS HANDS ON THE TOMB OF A LONG-DEAD CELTIC CHIEF, AN UNEARTHLY WIND HAD SPRUNG UP...

RAGNAR, YOU HAVE RELEASED A SPIRIT FROM THE TOMB!

IT SEEKS VENGEANCE... IT WILL DESTROY US ALL!

RAGNAR STROVE TO HIDE HIS OWN TERROR FROM THE MEN, BUT IN HIS HEART HE WAS GLAD TO LEAVE THAT ACCURSED SPOT...

BACK TO THE LONGSHIPS... THERE IS NOTHING MORE FOR US HERE IN THIS LAND OF BOGS AND MIST!

THE WIND DIED DOWN TO AN EERIE MOAN, AND NIGHT BEGAN TO FALL...

HE DID A GREAT WRONG TO THE SPIRIT OF THAT DEAD CHIEF, AND I FEAR WE HAVE YET TO PAY FOR IT!

CEASE YOUR CRAVEN WHINING, SIGURD!

AND THEN THEY SAW THE WEIRD FIGURE AGAINST THE SKYLINE...

AAAGH! LOOK!

IT WAS AN OLD WOMAN...

IN GREED YOU DID DEFILE THE TOMB OF KING RAUNACH, WHO WAS SLAIN BY OTHERS OF YOUR ACCURSED BREED. FOR THIS WRONG I LAY A CURSE UPON YOUR HEADS!

WITH A ROAR OF FURY, RAGNAR BOUNDED UP THE HILL WITH BLADE RAISED ALOFT...

YOU WILL NEVER AGAIN SEE YOUR OWN LAND!

OLD CRONE, MY SWORD WILL PROVE THAT YOU ARE MORTAL!

BUT... SHE HAS GONE... VANISHED LIKE A WRAITH!

COME AWAY, MY FATHER... LET US NOT MEDDLE FURTHER WITH THE BEINGS THAT HAUNT THIS PLACE!

A DAY'S MARCH BROUGHT THEM BACK TO THEIR BOATS... AND THEIR SPIRITS REVIVED...

WE BID FAREWELL TO THIS ACCURSED LAND... AND SAIL EASTWARDS TO THE SHORES OF BRITAIN!

I PRAY THAT WE NEVER RETURN HERE AGAIN!

AND YET, RAGNAR COULD NOT FORGET THE WORDS OF THE OLD WOMEN...

ONLY TO YOU WILL I CONFESS, MY SON, THAT THERE IS FEAR IN MY HEART. THE CELTS ARE STRANGE PEOPLE, WITH POWERS BEYOND OUR UNDERSTANDING. I THINK, INDEED, THAT WE SHALL NEVER SEE OUR OWN LAND AGAIN!

RAGNAR'S GRIM FOREBODINGS BEGAN TO COME TRUE THAT SAME NIGHT... A GREAT STORM FELL UPON THE LONGSHIPS.

AT LAST ONLY RAGNAR'S OWN SHIP REMAINED ABOVE THE TORTURED SEAS...

WE ARE DOOMED, ! WE ARE DOOMED... ALL OF US!

AT DAWN, THE SKY CLEARED... AND THEY WERE ALONE...

ODIN MUST BE WATCHING OVER US!

PERHAPS IT WOULD HAVE BEEN BETTER IF WE HAD DROWNED WITH THE OTHERS!

DIMLY THROUGH THE MIST THEY SAW LAND...

DARE WE VENTURE ASHORE, RAGNAR? SO FEW OF US?

WE HAVE NO CHOICE... OUR WATER IS ALL SPOILED, AND THE FOOD ALL GONE. WE HAVE TO LAND!

SLOWLY, THE STORM-BATTERED LONGSHIP CREPT TOWARDS THE UNKNOWN SHORE. AND FROM THE CLIFFTOPS A HORDE OF HIDEOUSLY-PAINTED WARRIORS WATCHED... AND WAITED FOR THE KILLING!

THEN, THEIR BODIES HIDEOUSLY
PAINTED WITH BLUE WOAD, SAVAGE
PICTS POURED DOWN A TERRIFYING
HAIL OF WHISTLING DEATH

FORWARD!
ATTACK THEM!
THIS IS OUR
ONLY CHANCE!

IF EVER WILD NORSEMAN COURAGE
WAS PUT TO GRIM TEST IT WAS THEN —
IN THAT TERRIBLE, DEATH-DEFYING
CLIMB

FIRST TO REACH THE CLIFF EDGE WAS KARL,
THE SON OF EINGAR THE MANSLAYER

AND HIS EARS RANG TO THE BLOOD-
CURDLING SCREAM OF A LEAPING, KILL-
HUNGRY PICT

WITH HEAD AND SHOULDERS HANGING
OVER THE DIZZY DROP, KARL FOUGHT
FOR HIS LIFE

AT THEM,
MY WOLVES!
HEW THEM
DOWN!

KARL'S POWERFUL
LEG BENT BACK
UNDER THE
BODY OF THE
SAVAGE—THEN
STRAIGHTENED

11

KARL'S SWORD SLASHED DOWNWARDS...THEN HE SAW ANOTHER VIKING IN MORTAL DANGER

KARL! HELP ME!

SWIFTLY KARL SNATCHED UP A SPEAR, AND HURLED IT WITH TERRIBLE ACCURACY. BUT THE PICT'S DEATH CRY HAD DROWNED THE WARNING TWANG OF A BOWSTRING

KARL!

THE SON OF EINGAR WHIRLED ABOUT — BUT TOO LATE

STRUCK SENSELESS BY THE SLASHING IMPACT OF THE PICT ARROW, KARL STAGGERED BACKWARDS — OUT OVER THE CLIFF EDGE

THE BATTLE BETWEEN PICTS AND VIKINGS RAGED ON. THEN EINGAR LOWERED HIS BLOOD-RED SWORD

THE SAVAGES RUN! THEY ARE BEATEN!

BUT OTHERS ARE COMING, EINGAR! MANY, MANY MORE OF THEM!

THE VIKING CHIEF WOULD HAVE BATTLED ON. BUT A SWIFT GLANCE AROUND TOLD HIM IT WOULD BE HOPELESS

WE ARE TOO FEW NOW TO FIGHT THE SAVAGES. ENOUGH VALIANT VIKING HEARTS HAVE BEEN STILLED THIS DAY. RETURN TO THE LONGSHIP!

AS THE VIKINGS SCRAMBLED DOWN TO THE SHORE, EINGAR REALISED THAT KARL WAS NOT AMONGST THEM

KARL! WHERE IS MY SON?

IT SADDENS ME TO TELL YOU, MY CHIEF — BUT KARL IS DEAD! I SAW THE ARROW STRIKE HIS HEAD — AND HE FELL TO HIS DEATH

A SHUDDER RAN THROUGH EINGAR'S BODY, AND THE FIERCENESS FADED FROM HIS EYES. GRIEF HAD WOUNDED THE VIKING WOLF MORE TERRIBLY THAN COULD ANY SWORD

IT — IS THE CURSE OF THAT WITCH UPON ME THAT HAS DONE THIS. FAR RATHER HAD I DIED IN BATTLE THAN THIS

COME, EINGAR. IT DOES OUR DEAD NO GOOD FOR US TO DELAY HERE. COME — BEFORE THE SAVAGES ARE UPON US!

BUT AS THE VIKING LONGSHIP PULLED AWAY — OTHER EYES SAW THAT KARL WAS STILL ALIVE — HIS FALL CHECKED BY AN OUT-JUTTING CLIFF GROWTH!

BUT KARL HAD NOT BEEN KILLED... AND NOW THE WILD PICTS BORE HIS UNCONSCIOUS BODY AWAY FROM THE BATTLEFIELD

REACHING THEIR VILLAGE, THEY THREW THEIR CAPTIVE AT THE FEET OF THEIR CHIEFTAIN

IT IS GOOD THAT ONE OF THE ENEMY STILL LIVES. FOR IT WAS THESE MEN FROM THE SEA WHO SLEW MY FATHER

WITH CRUEL PATIENCE, THE CHIEFTAIN WAITED FOR KARL TO REGAIN HIS SENSES. THEN —

IT WAS A SPEAR THAT CLEFT THE HEART OF MY FATHER. IT IS FITTING THAT THIS OFFERING TO HIS SPIRIT SHOULD DIE IN THE SAME MANNER!

KARL KNEW THAT DEATH WAS INEVITABLE. BUT STRONGER EVEN THAN THE FEAR OF DEATH WAS A VIKING'S DESIRE TO DIE FIGHTING

O, VIKING GODS! SEE! I DIE A WARRIOR STILL! MAKE VALHALLA MY REWARD!

AA—AGH!

AND THE PICT CHIEF SCREAMED WITH AGONY AS FLAME SEARED HIS FLESH!

A HOWL OF RAGE ROSE FROM THE SAVAGES. BUT AS CLUBS, SWORDS AND SPEARS ROSE INTO THE AIR—

NO! HE SHALL NOT DIE SO EASILY! DRAG HIM TO THE TEMPLE AND DELIVER HIM TO THE PRIESTS!

NIGHT PASSED. AND WHEN THE FINGERS OF DAWN SHAFTED THROUGH A STONE ARCH, BATHING KARL IN A BLOOD-RED GLOW —

ALL ABOUT HIM IN THAT EERIE GLOW, THE ASSEMBLED PICTS PROSTRATED THEMSELVES BEFORE THEIR PAGAN PRIESTS

A WILD CHANTING FILLED THE AIR... BARBARIC... FRIGHTENING!

ABRUPTLY THE CHANTING CEASED, AND THE PRIESTS POURED EVIL-SMELLING FLUID OVER THE CAPTIVE VIKING

WHAT EVIL IS THIS? IF — I COULD ONLY — GET MY HANDS FREE, YOU DOGS!

THUNDER RUMBLED IN THE SKY AS A SILENT PROCESSION WOUND ITS WAY ALONG A ROCKY PATH

I HEAR WAVES BREAKING! THEY ARE LEADING ME BACK TOWARDS THE SEA!

THEY REACHED THE SHORE, AND AS KARL'S HANDS WERE STRETCHED ABOVE HIM, THE CHIEFTAIN LAUGHED AND POINTED TO A ROCK POOL IN FRONT OF THEM

HOW YOU ARE GOING TO WISH YOU HAD DIED BY MY SPEAR, NORTHMAN! *FOR SEE WHAT THE PRIESTS HAVE INSTEAD FOR YOU!*

THE CHIEFTAIN SPOKE IN A LANGUAGE THAT KARL COULD NOT UNDERSTAND. BUT HIS POINTING FINGER MADE HIS MEANING TERRIBLY CLEAR...

AND KARL GASPED WITH HORROR AS HE STARED DOWN INTO A ROCK POOL —**WHICH SEETHED WITH CLAW-CLICKING CRABS!**

THEN CAME A GREAT SHOUT, AND KARL WAS SWUNG OUT OVER THE FROTHING, CRAB-FILLED POOL

THAT STUFF THEY POURED OVER ME! IT IS DRIVING THE CRABS TO A MAD EXCITEMENT! I AM TO BE EATEN ALIVE!

THEN —

NOW! LOWER HIM... SLOWLY!

THE ICY WATERS CLOSED OVER KARL'S FEET — AND OVER HIS ANKLES! AND ABOVE THE ROLLING THUNDER, HIS VOICE ROSE IN A DESPAIRING CRY

O, MIGHTY ODIN — GIVE ME COURAGE! DON'T — LET — **AA-AGH!**

AND AN INSTANT LATER IT SEEMED THAT HIS PLEA HAD BEEN HEARD. FOR A GREAT LIGHTNING FLASH SCARRED THE STORM-BLACK SKY, CAUSING THE GATHERED PICTS TO MOAN AND SHRIEK WITH FEAR

AA-AGH! WE HAVE ANGERED THE SKY GOD! FLEE!

AND WITH AN EAR-SPLITTING CRACK AND SUDDEN STENCH OF SULPHUR, THE LIGHTNING SHAFT STRUCK DEEP INTO THE TOWERING CLIFF

THEN PULVERISING, BODY-CRUSHING DEATH SLID AND HURTLED DOWNWARDS —

— AND SCREAMS ROSE AND DIED IN THE TERRIFYING ROAR AND RUMBLE OF FALLING, SMASHING ROCK!

THE YOUNG VIKING HURTLED WILDLY THROUGH THE AIR AT THE END OF THE ROPE AROUND HIS WRISTS AND FELL HARMLESSLY INTO SOFT SAND —

A GREAT BOULDER, FLUNG FROM THE CLIFF FACE, BOUNDED AS IF IT HAD LIFE OF ITS OWN ... AND THE SON OF EINGAR WAS FLUNG FROM THE TERRIBLE CRAB POOL

— WHILST BEHIND HIM, THE CRUEL ROCKS STILL RAINED DOWN UPON BODIES CRUSHED AND ALREADY BURIED FROM SIGHT!

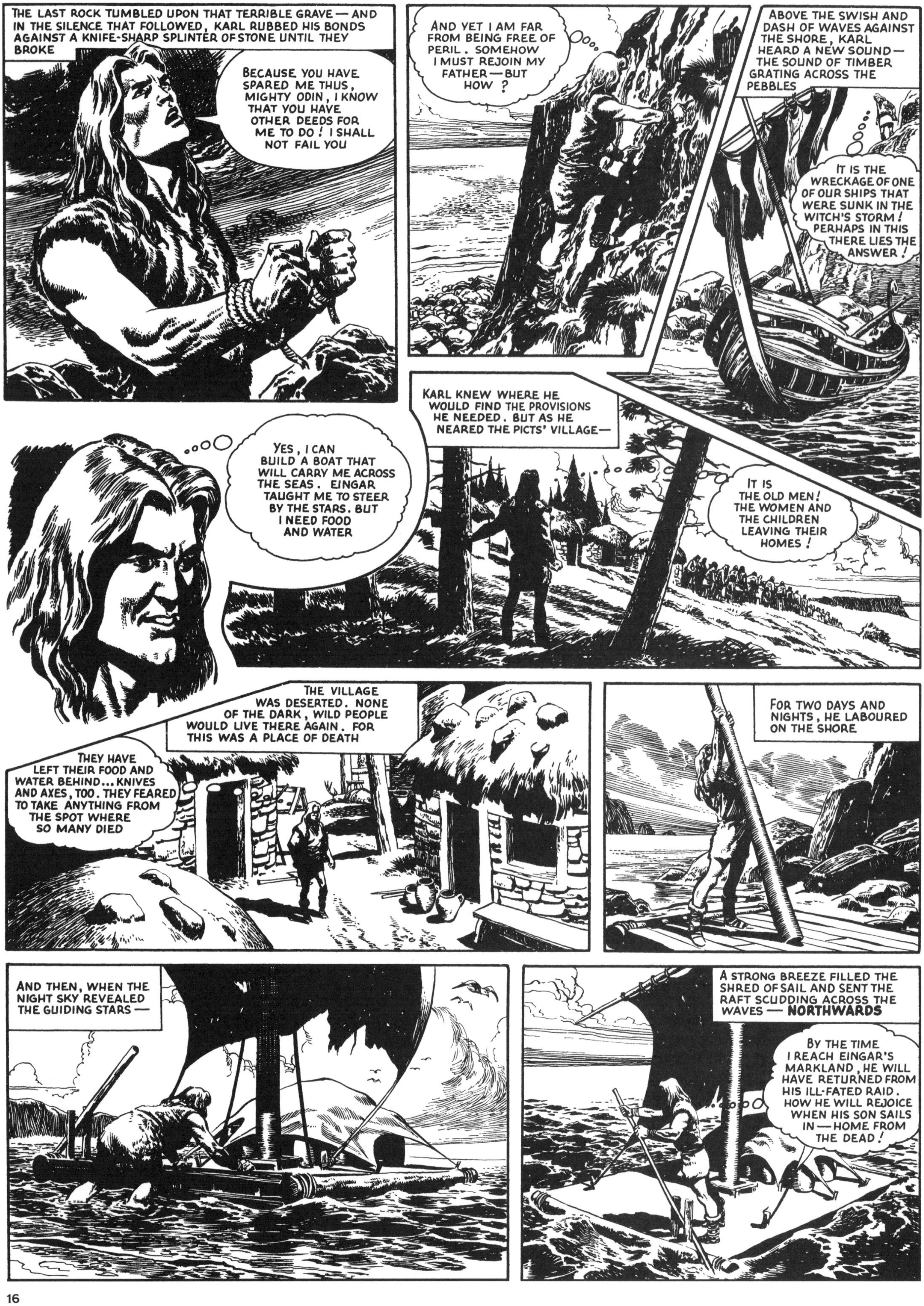
THE LAST ROCK TUMBLED UPON THAT TERRIBLE GRAVE — AND IN THE SILENCE THAT FOLLOWED, KARL RUBBED HIS BONDS AGAINST A KNIFE-SHARP SPLINTER OF STONE UNTIL THEY BROKE
BECAUSE YOU HAVE SPARED ME THUS, MIGHTY ODIN, I KNOW THAT YOU HAVE OTHER DEEDS FOR ME TO DO! I SHALL NOT FAIL YOU
AND YET I AM FAR FROM BEING FREE OF PERIL. SOMEHOW I MUST REJOIN MY FATHER — BUT HOW?
ABOVE THE SWISH AND DASH OF WAVES AGAINST THE SHORE, KARL HEARD A NEW SOUND — THE SOUND OF TIMBER GRATING ACROSS THE PEBBLES
IT IS THE WRECKAGE OF ONE OF OUR SHIPS THAT WERE SUNK IN THE WITCH'S STORM! PERHAPS IN THIS THERE LIES THE ANSWER!
YES, I CAN BUILD A BOAT THAT WILL CARRY ME ACROSS THE SEAS. EINGAR TAUGHT ME TO STEER BY THE STARS. BUT I NEED FOOD AND WATER
KARL KNEW WHERE HE WOULD FIND THE PROVISIONS HE NEEDED. BUT AS HE NEARED THE PICTS' VILLAGE—
IT IS THE OLD MEN! THE WOMEN AND THE CHILDREN LEAVING THEIR HOMES!
THE VILLAGE WAS DESERTED. NONE OF THE DARK, WILD PEOPLE WOULD LIVE THERE AGAIN. FOR THIS WAS A PLACE OF DEATH
THEY HAVE LEFT THEIR FOOD AND WATER BEHIND... KNIVES AND AXES, TOO. THEY FEARED TO TAKE ANYTHING FROM THE SPOT WHERE SO MANY DIED
FOR TWO DAYS AND NIGHTS, HE LABOURED ON THE SHORE
AND THEN, WHEN THE NIGHT SKY REVEALED THE GUIDING STARS —
A STRONG BREEZE FILLED THE SHRED OF SAIL AND SENT THE RAFT SCUDDING ACROSS THE WAVES — NORTHWARDS
BY THE TIME I REACH EINGAR'S MARKLAND, HE WILL HAVE RETURNED FROM HIS ILL-FATED RAID. HOW HE WILL REJOICE WHEN HIS SON SAILS IN — HOME FROM THE DEAD!

IT WAS A LONG AND TERRIBLE VOYAGE, IN WHICH LONELINESS, HUNGER AND RAGING SEAS TESTED TO THE UTMOST HIS STRENGTH AND DETERMINATION

BUT AGAIN IT SEEMED AS IF THOR AND ODIN WERE PROTECTING THIS ADOPTED SON OF THE GREATEST OF THE VIKINGS. FOR THE DAY DAWNED WHEN KARL SAW THE MISTY PEAKS OF EINGAR'S MARKLAND

WHAT STORIES SOON WILL RESOUND THROUGH-OUT THE FEASTING HALL! BUT EINGAR MAY NOT HAVE YET RETURNED FROM HIS ILL-FATED EXPEDITION

AS HE SAILED NEARER, HOWEVER, HIS HEART LEAPT, FOR TIED TO THE MOORING BANK WAS A LONGSHIP

IT IS EINGAR'S LONGSHIP! SO HE HAS RETURNED SAFELY! BUT—BUT WHERE ARE THE PEOPLE? I CAN ONLY SEE ONE FIGURE!

THE FIGURE WAS THAT OF AFREDA — THE OLD SAXON WOMAN WHO HAD CARED FOR KARL SINCE BABYHOOD. SHE AWAITED HIM ON THE SHORE. IN HER STRANGE WAY SHE HAD KNOWN THAT HE WAS COMING

AFREDA! WHAT TROUBLES YOU? I WAS HOPING FOR JOY AT MY RETURN—NOT GLOOM!

YOU KNOW WELL I REJOICE THAT YOU ARE BACK SAFE, KARL. BUT THERE IS GREAT ANXIETY HERE IN EINGAR'S MARKLAND!

"THAT IS THE ONLY LONGSHIP THAT HAS RETURNED—EINGAR'S! THERE WAS ONLY ONE MAN INSIDE IT. AND HE IS DYING FROM WOUNDS!"

"BUT WHAT OF EINGAR? WHAT HAS HAPPENED TO MY FATHER—AND ALL THE OTHERS?"

KARL THRUST HIS WAY THROUGH A THRONG OF VILLAGERS WHO WERE GATHERED ABOUT A STILL FIGURE IN THE FEASTING HALL

"YOU AND HARALD ARE THE ONLY TWO TO COME BACK TO US, KARL!"

"WHAT NEWS IS THERE OF EINGAR?"

AT THE SOUND OF KARL'S VOICE, THE DYING VIKING RAISED HIS HEAD

"KARL! KARL! WE THOUGHT YOU WERE DEAD, TOO!"

"TELL US ABOUT THE OTHERS, HARALD. IS EINGAR ALIVE?"

THE WOUNDED MAN SEEMED NOT TO HEAR KARL'S QUESTION. HE BEGAN TO MUMBLE DELIRIOUSLY

"THE FATE OF US ALL WAS SEALED—WHEN EINGAR ROBBED THE CELT'S TOMB. THAT OLD CRONE'S CURSE—"

"CURSE! WHAT IS THIS HE SPEAKS OF?"

"HUSH, SKURL! I WILL TELL YOU LATER"

THEN HARALD'S EYES OPENED AND BECAME FIXED UPON KARL'S. HIS VOICE ROSE TO A CRY

"ALL DEAD—ALL BUT YOU! THE OLD CRONE'S CURSE WAS UPON ALL WITH VIKING BLOOD IN THEIR VEINS. NOW, YOU ALONE LIVE—BECAUSE YOU ARE NOT TRULY A VIKING, BUT SAXON BORN—AA-AGH!"

AND WITH THAT LAST GASP HARALD FELL BACK AND DIED

AN ELDER TURNED TO KARL

"THEN YOU, KARL, AS SON OF EINGAR THE MANSLAYER, BECOME OUR NEW CHIEFTAIN!"

"NO! I CHALLENGE THAT!"

ORLAF WAS EINGAR'S HALF-BROTHER. WITH ONE HAND HE POINTED RESENTFULLY AT KARL. WITH THE OTHER HE PUSHED FORWARD HIS OWN SON, SKURL

"YOU—A SAXON—HAVE NO RIGHT TO BE OUR LEADER! WE ALL HEARD WHAT HARALD SAID WITH HIS DYING BREATH—THAT HE WHOM EINGAR CALLED HIS SON HAS NOT A DROP OF REAL VIKING BLOOD IN HIS VEINS! NO! IT IS I WHO SHOULD RULE. BUT I AM TOO OLD. THEREFORE, I SAY THAT MY SON INHERITS THE RIGHT TO CHIEFTAINSHIP!"

FOR A MOMENT THERE WAS A STARTLED SILENCE. THEN A FIERCE ARGUMENT ECHOED THROUGHOUT THE GREAT FEASTING HALL

"ORLAF IS RIGHT! WE SHOULD NOT BE LED BY A SAXON!"

"FOOL! DEEDS SPEAK LOUDER THAN MERE BLOOD! KARL IS MORE VIKING THAN ANY OF US HERE!"

"LISTEN! HEAR WHAT I HAVE TO SAY!"

THE HIGH, ANCIENT VOICE OF A RESPECTED ELDER—FAMED FOR HIS WISDOM—STILLED THE DIN

"ARE WE CHILDREN THAT WE TRY TO SETTLE THIS VITAL ISSUE IN SUCH A MANNER? HARALD DIED BEFORE HE COULD TELL US WHAT TRULY HAPPENED TO EINGAR THE MANSLAYER AND HIS MEN! NONE OF US CAN BE SURE, EVEN, THAT OUR LEADER IS DEAD!"

"SO I DECREE THIS! KARL AND SKURL SHALL EACH TAKE A LONGSHIP AND FORTY MEN. LET THEM SAIL AT ONCE—AND SEARCH TO DISCOVER IF EINGAR IS DEAD OR ALIVE! IF HE IS DEAD—THEN WHICHEVER ONE BRINGS BACK THE SWORD OF EINGAR THE MANSLAYER SHALL BE CHIEFTAIN!"

AND SO, IN THE BLEAK AND RAIN-LASHED DAWN, THE QUEST FOR THE SWORD OF EINGAR BEGAN...

KARL GLANCED ACROSS AT HIS RIVAL—JUST IN TIME TO SEE THE EXPRESSION OF STARK, MURDEROUS HATRED THAT CONTORTED SKURL'S FACE!

By the end of that first day, a strong wind had carried the Viking ships swiftly across the sullen waters — deep into the North Sea

Both Karl and Skurl had decided on the shortest route to Britain — even though it meant the risk of wild gales and fogs

Seldom did Skurl's glittering eyes leave the figure of Karl standing in the other ship. And when he overheard two of his own men speaking, his face twisted in a spasm of hatred

IT COULD TAKE A WHOLE YEAR BEFORE WE FIND OUT THE FATE OF EINGAR. BUT I'LL WAGER IT WILL BE KARL WHO BRINGS BACK THE SWORD

THE CHIEFTAINSHIP SHOULD BE MINE BY RIGHTS — NOT AN ACCURSED SAXON'S!

The voyage continued uneventfully through the night, with the longships cutting fast and cleanly through a strangely-calm sea. But in the dawn light Karl saw a dense wall of mist rolling towards them

FOG! SKURL, WE MUST MAKE MORE DISTANCE BETWEEN US, OR WE MAY COLLIDE!

Karl saw Skurl's longship swing farther away. Then, as the first clammy tendrils of fog reached out for them, he took over the great steering oar

I WILL STEER HER, IVAR. YOU KEEP WATCH AHEAD OF US

IT IS THE BEST WAY, KARL. YOU HAVE THE STRONGEST ARM — AND IT IS ESSENTIAL THAT WE DO NOT DRIFT OFF COURSE

In the other longship, Skurl also decided that he would be steersman — but for quite a different reason

 As the dense fog concealed his movements, Skurl shifted the steering oar slightly — easing his craft over to where the muffled splash of oars marked the position of Karl's longship

THIS FOG IS A FORTUNATE THING — FOR ME... BUT NOT FOR YOU, SAXON KARL!

Inch by inch, Skurl cunningly swung his longship off course until —

LOOK OUT!

Screams of pain and shouts of terror merged with the hideous sound of splintering wood as the heavy prow of Skurl's longship smashed through the thinner side of the other vessel

And as the shattered longship tipped on to its side, Vikings were hurled into the green, deep sea

Some, weighted down by weapons and chain mail, sank like stones into the depths. But the strongest struck out desperately for the side of Skurl's craft

HELP! SAVE US!

KARL MUST HAVE STEERED OFF COURSE! REACH DOWN WITH YOUR OARS — HELP THEM TO CLIMB ABOARD!

Karl was amongst those who had survived the impact. But as he looked up, he saw death plainly written on Skurl's face

YOU! I HAD HOPED YOU'D BE AMONG THOSE ALREADY DEAD!

SKURL! YOU DID THIS — PURPOSELY!

Then Skurl's oar struck down, cruelly, murderously

SKURL, DON'T — UUUUGH!

DIE, CURSE YOU!

Again and again Skurl stabbed with the oar — until Karl's unconscious body drifted away into the fog. Then —

THERE ARE NO OTHERS HERE! ROW AHEAD — WE MAY FIND SOME MORE!

Because of the concealing fog, none of Skurl's men had witnessed Karl's fate!

But the son of Eingar was strong and hard. The icy chill of the sea quickly revived his senses, and his groping hands found floating timber

He called for help — but no one answered. Then, through a sudden hole in the fog, he saw why

THEY DIDN'T HEAR ME! THEY'VE LEFT ME BEHIND!

Skurl's ship was now little more than a dot on the distant horizon — and Karl was alone, drifting helplessly in the limitless sea!

THE FOG PASSED WITH THE COMING OF A NEW DAY. AND SOON KARL'S THROAT WAS PARCHED WITH A RAGING THIRST THAT LESSER MEN COULD NOT HAVE ENDURED

HOW LONG HE DRIFTED UPON THAT TERRIBLE SEA HE HAD NO WAY OF KNOWING. WHEN AT LAST A FISHING BOAT SIGHTED HIM, KARL WAS UNCONSCIOUS

LOOK! THERE IS A MAN OVER THERE!

A SURVIVOR FROM A WRECKED FISHING BOAT, PERHAPS! BUT HE APPEARS TO BE DEAD!

THE SAXON FISHERMEN GUIDED THEIR CRAFT ALONGSIDE THE STILL FIGURE. TENDERLY THEY LIFTED HIM ABOARD

HE IS MUMBLING STRANGE THINGS — AND IN OUR OWN TONGUE!

HE IS NOT DRESSED LIKE A SAXON! WE MUST RETURN WITH HIM TO THE VILLAGE, FOR HE IS CLOSE TO DEATH

SEVERAL HOURS LATER KARL WAS CARRIED ASHORE. AS THE VILLAGERS PEERED CURIOUSLY AT THE STRANGER RESCUED FROM THE SEA, AN OLD WOMAN BARELY STIFLED A GASP OF SURPRISE

NO! IT CAN'T BE! I MUST BE MISTAKEN!

WHOEVER HE IS, HE NEEDS TO BE NURSED AND CARED FOR IF HE IS TO LIVE

I WILL DO THAT. HAVE HIM TAKEN TO MY HOUSE

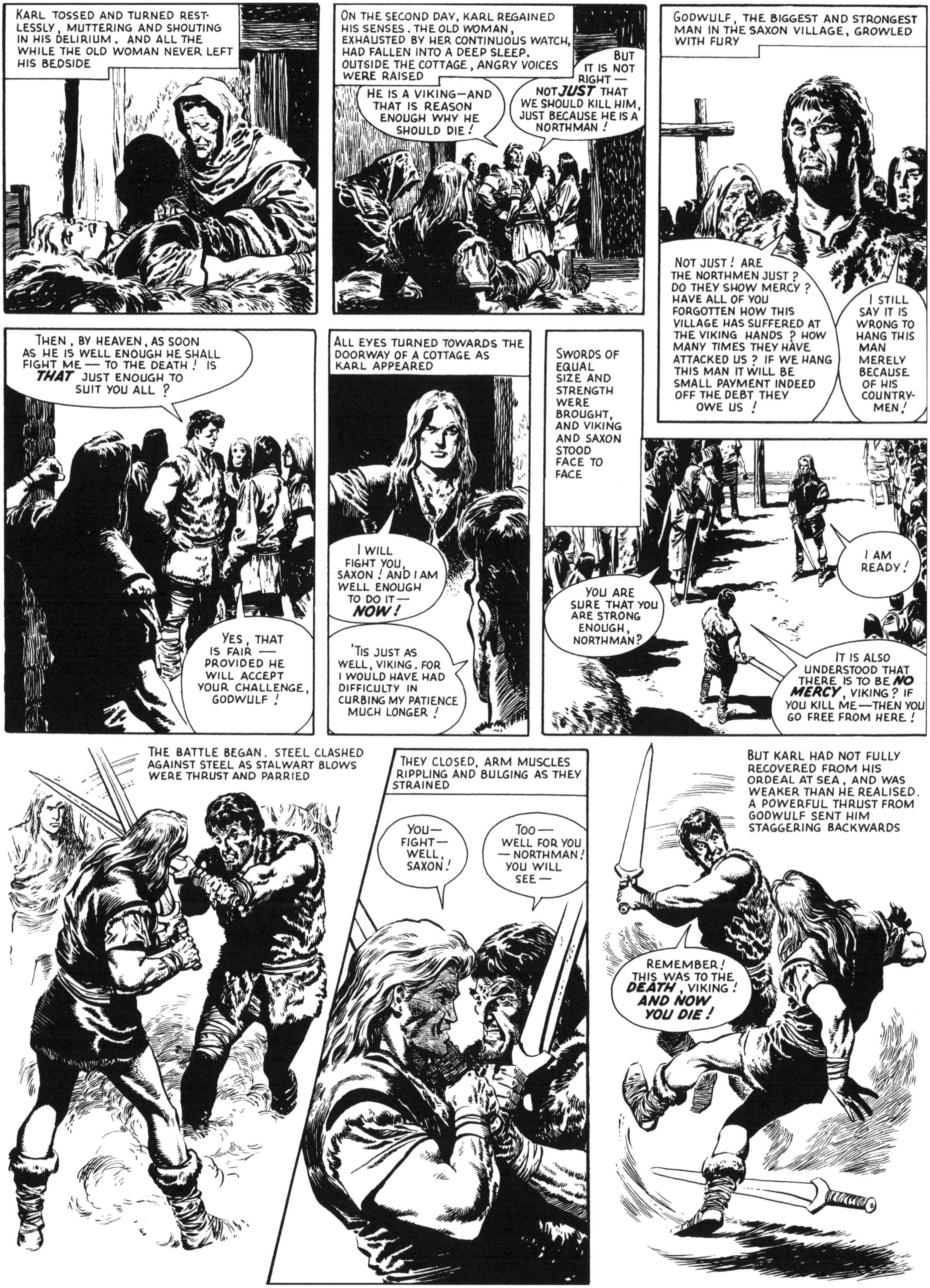
KARL TOSSED AND TURNED RESTLESSLY, MUTTERING AND SHOUTING IN HIS DELIRIUM. AND ALL THE WHILE THE OLD WOMAN NEVER LEFT HIS BEDSIDE
ON THE SECOND DAY, KARL REGAINED HIS SENSES. THE OLD WOMAN, EXHAUSTED BY HER CONTINUOUS WATCH, HAD FALLEN INTO A DEEP SLEEP. OUTSIDE THE COTTAGE, ANGRY VOICES WERE RAISED
HE IS A VIKING—AND THAT IS REASON ENOUGH WHY HE SHOULD DIE!
BUT IT IS NOT RIGHT— NOT JUST THAT WE SHOULD KILL HIM, JUST BECAUSE HE IS A NORTHMAN!
GODWULF, THE BIGGEST AND STRONGEST MAN IN THE SAXON VILLAGE, GROWLED WITH FURY
NOT JUST! ARE THE NORTHMEN JUST? DO THEY SHOW MERCY? HAVE ALL OF YOU FORGOTTEN HOW THIS VILLAGE HAS SUFFERED AT THE VIKING HANDS? HOW MANY TIMES THEY HAVE ATTACKED US? IF WE HANG THIS MAN IT WILL BE SMALL PAYMENT INDEED OFF THE DEBT THEY OWE US!
I STILL SAY IT IS WRONG TO HANG THIS MAN MERELY BECAUSE OF HIS COUNTRYMEN!
THEN, BY HEAVEN, AS SOON AS HE IS WELL ENOUGH HE SHALL FIGHT ME — TO THE DEATH! IS THAT JUST ENOUGH TO SUIT YOU ALL?
YES, THAT IS FAIR — PROVIDED HE WILL ACCEPT YOUR CHALLENGE, GODWULF!
ALL EYES TURNED TOWARDS THE DOORWAY OF A COTTAGE AS KARL APPEARED
I WILL FIGHT YOU, SAXON! AND I AM WELL ENOUGH TO DO IT— NOW!
'TIS JUST AS WELL, VIKING. FOR I WOULD HAVE HAD DIFFICULTY IN CURBING MY PATIENCE MUCH LONGER!
SWORDS OF EQUAL SIZE AND STRENGTH WERE BROUGHT, AND VIKING AND SAXON STOOD FACE TO FACE
I AM READY!
YOU ARE SURE THAT YOU ARE STRONG ENOUGH, NORTHMAN?
IT IS ALSO UNDERSTOOD THAT THERE IS TO BE NO MERCY, VIKING? IF YOU KILL ME—THEN YOU GO FREE FROM HERE!
THE BATTLE BEGAN. STEEL CLASHED AGAINST STEEL AS STALWART BLOWS WERE THRUST AND PARRIED
THEY CLOSED, ARM MUSCLES RIPPLING AND BULGING AS THEY STRAINED
YOU— FIGHT— WELL, SAXON!
TOO— WELL FOR YOU — NORTHMAN! YOU WILL SEE —
BUT KARL HAD NOT FULLY RECOVERED FROM HIS ORDEAL AT SEA, AND WAS WEAKER THAN HE REALISED. A POWERFUL THRUST FROM GODWULF SENT HIM STAGGERING BACKWARDS
REMEMBER! THIS WAS TO THE DEATH, VIKING! AND NOW YOU DIE!

AN INSTANT BEFORE THE SAXON'S SWORD FLASHED TOWARDS KARL'S HEART THERE CAME A DESPERATE CRY

STOP, GODWULF! WOULD YOU KILL SOMEONE OF YOUR OWN FLESH AND BLOOD?

MY OWN FLESH AND BLOOD! ARE YOU MAD, OLD WOMAN? THIS IS A *VIKING* DOG WHO IS ABOUT TO DIE!

IT WAS THE OLD WOMAN WHO HAD WATCHED OVER KARL AS HE LAY UNCONSCIOUS AND DELIRIOUS AFTER HIS TERRIBLE ORDEAL AT SEA

WHEN HE WAS BROUGHT TO THIS VILLAGE I FELT SURE I HAD SEEN HIS FACE BEFORE. BUT IT SEEMED IMPOSSIBLE — UNTIL, IN HIS TROUBLED SLEEP, HE SPOKE OF *EINGAR THE MAN-SLAYER* — AND *AFREDA!*

I WAS GOING TO QUESTION HIM WHEN HE REGAINED CONSCIOUSNESS. BUT I FELL ASLEEP FROM EXHAUSTION. IT IS LUCKY THAT THE CLASH OF YOUR SWORDS AWOKE ME IN TIME. FOR, GODWULF, THIS MAN YOU WERE ABOUT TO SLAY IS *YOUR COUSIN* — WHO WAS STOLEN AS A BABY BY THE VIKINGS!

BY THE STARS! CAN THIS BE TRUE?

I KNOW ONLY THAT I AM SAXON BORN — NOTHING ELSE!

THE LIGHT OF BATTLE FADED FROM GODWULF'S EYES. HE TOSSED AWAY THE SWORD THAT HAD ALMOST TAKEN KARL'S LIFE

NOW I CAN SEE WITH MY OWN EYES THAT WHAT THE OLD WOMAN SAID IS TRUE. FORGIVE ME, MY COUSIN!

IT WAS A FAIR FIGHT. YOU COULD HAVE KILLED ME IN MY SLEEP. BUT YOU CHOSE A JUST AND HONOURABLE WAY TO SETTLE OLD SCORES

HAVING RETURNED TO YOUR REAL HOME, YOU MUST STAY! HALF OF THE LITTLE I OWN IS YOURS, COUSIN

YES, STAY. HERE YOU WILL BE AMONGST YOUR OWN KIND!

YOU ARE GOOD PEOPLE, AND IN MANY WAYS I WOULD WISH TO STAY HERE. BUT I HAVE BEEN RAISED AS A VIKING — AND MY WAY IS NO LONGER YOURS

THEN, TOO, I MUST SEEK THE MAN WHO MADE ME HIS SON—RAGNAR THE MAN-SLAYER! BUT I PLEDGE YOU THIS—THAT IF I BECOME CHIEFTAIN OF HIS MARK-LAND, THIS VILLAGE WILL NEVER AGAIN SUFFER AT VIKING HANDS...

AND SO KARL LEFT THE PLACE OF HIS BIRTH AND JOURNEYED NORTHWARDS ALONG THE COAST ON HIS QUEST FOR THE SWORD OF EINGAR

IT WAS KARL'S PLAN TO QUESTION THE PEOPLE OF EACH VILLAGE HE CAME ACROSS IN THE HOPE THAT THEY COULD GIVE HIM NEWS OF EINGAR BUT EVERYWHERE HIS APPEARANCE PRODUCED A WAVE OF TERROR

A VIKING! THE NORTH-MEN HAVE COME AGAIN!

STOP! I MEAN YOU NO HARM!

FETCH YOUR BOWS AND SWORDS! DEFEND OUR HOMES!

THE FOLLOWING DAY HE WAYLAID A SAXON SERF RETURNING FROM HIS DAY'S LABOUR IN THE FIELDS

DON'T SLAY ME, NORTHMAN!

I HAVE TOLD YOU. I WANT ONLY YOUR CLOTHES IN EXCHANGE FOR MINE. AND BY THE LOOK OF THEM, YOU WILL BE GETTING THE BEST OF THE BARGAIN!

HAVING DONNED THE SERF'S CLOTHES, KARL STRODE ON

NOW PERHAPS THE VILLAGERS WILL SPEAK WITH ME... AH— WHAT IS THIS...?

FATE HAD LED HIM TO AN OLD SHEPHERD LOWERING HIM-SELF DANGEROUSLY OVER THE EDGE OF A CLIFF

AT KARL'S SHOUT HE PULLED HIMSELF SHAKILY BACK TO SAFER GROUND

MEN MUCH YOUNGER THAN YOU WOULD NOT ATTEMPT TO CLIMB DOWN THERE!

YOU SPEAK THE TRUTH. I AM INDEED TOO OLD FOR SUCH EFFORTS. BUT ONE OF MY SHEEP HAS FALLEN TO A LEDGE BELOW. I AM A POOR MAN, AND CAN ILL AFFORD TO LOSE IT

KARL HESITATED, THEN SWUNG HIMSELF OVER THE EDGE.

FAR BETTER FOR ME TO TRY, OLD MAN. EVEN IF YOU REACHED YOUR SHEEP YOU WOULD BE UNABLE TO CARRY IT UP AGAIN!

IT WAS A SLOW AND DIFFICULT DESCENT... AND BY THE TIME KARL HAD CLIMBED BACK TO THE TOP OF THE CLIFF, OTHERS HAD COME UPON THE SCENE.

IS THAT HIM? IS THAT THE NORTHMAN?

YES! SEE, HE WEARS MY CLOTHES!

THEN AS KARL LOWERED THE STRUGGLING SHEEP TO THE GROUND—

DO NOT ATTEMPT TO ESCAPE, NORTHMAN. IF YOU DO, YOUR DEATH WILL BE SO MUCH THE QUICKER!

THEY ARE EARL GYRTH'S MEN!

SOME DISTANCE INLAND STOOD THE GRIM CASTLE OF EARL GYRTH OF EASTUMBRIA

OUR MASTER WILL BE OVERJOYED TO SEE THE PRIZE WE HAVE BROUGHT HIM! HOW HE HATES THESE VIKING DOGS!

EARL GYRTH LOATHED TO BE DISTURBED AT HIS FEASTING. HE TURNED, SNARLING, FROM HIS LADEN TABLE AT THE SOUND OF FOOTSTEPS

GET OUT! GET OUT BEFORE I ORDER YOU TO BE KILLED! WHEN I AM EATING, I SEE NO ONE!

BUT—BUT, MASTER! I THOUGHT YOU WOULD WISH TO KNOW AT ONCE. WE HAVE A PRISONER — A VIKING!

BUT WHEN HIS SOLDIERS SEIZED THE YOUNG VIKING'S ARMS AGAIN, EARL GYRTH'S COURAGE RETURNED. HIS LIPS TWISTED IN A CRUEL, MOCKING GRIN

IS MY FATHER STILL ALIVE? YOU'VE GOT TO TELL ME!

KEEP STILL, NORTHMAN, OR I'LL DRIVE MY SWORD THROUGH YOUR CHEST!

INSTANTLY, THE EARL OF EASTUMBRIA'S EXPRESSION CHANGED. HIS EYES GLEAMED WITH CRUEL DELIGHT AS HE PONDEROUSLY PUSHED HIMSELF AWAY FROM HIS UNFINISHED MEAL

A VIKING! AH, YES, THAT IS DIFFERENT! YOU DID WELL TO BRING HIM TO ME! WELL, NORTHMAN, THIS WILL PROVE A SORRY DAY FOR YOU — A SORRY DAY INDEED!

BUT KARL DID NOT EVEN HEAR THE MENACING WORDS. HIS GAZE WAS FIXED UPON THE GLEAMING SWORD HANGING FROM EARL GYRTH'S WAIST

THEN THE SAXON NOBLEMAN'S PIGGISH EYES BULGED WITH SUDDEN FEAR AS — HEEDLESS OF HIS BOUND HANDS — KARL WRENCHED FROM HIS GUARDS' GRASP

THAT IS THE SWORD OF EINGAR YOU ARE WEARING! HOW DID YOU GET IT? WHAT HAS HAPPENED TO MY FATHER?

STOP HIM! KEEP HIM AWAY FROM ME!

SO EINGAR WAS YOUR FATHER, EH? AND YOU VIKINGS PUT GREAT STOCK ON BRAVERY. WELL, HE DIED A SCREAMING COWARD!

KARL'S EYES BLAZED WITH FURY. HE PULLED AND JERKED AT THE THONGS ABOUT HIS WRISTS

YOU LIE! THE MIGHTY EINGAR COULD NEVER BE AFRAID! IF MY HANDS WERE FREE YOU WOULD DIE FOR THAT INSULT!

I WARNED YOU, NORTH-MAN!

DON'T KILL HIM, CAPTAIN! WE WILL SEE IF HE IS BRAVER THAN THE DOG WHO BRED HIM. TAKE HIM TO THE BATTLEMENTS!

A GREAT STONE WAS TIED TO KARL'S ANKLES. THEN HE WAS PUSHED UP-WARDS TO STAND SWAYING IN THE WIND ABOVE A TERRIFYING DROP DOWN TO THE CASTLE MOAT

I HATE YOU VIKINGS MORE THAN I HATE THE DEVIL HIMSELF! SO MANY TIMES HAVE YOU PLUNDERED MY LANDS AND MY WEALTH AND EVEN DRIVEN ME LIKE A WHIPPED CUR FROM MY OWN CASTLE!

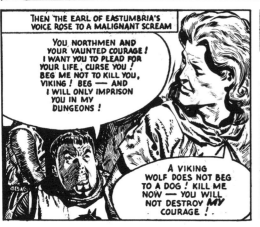

THEN THE EARL OF EASTUMBRIA'S VOICE ROSE TO A MALIGNANT SCREAM

YOU NORTHMEN AND YOUR VAUNTED COURAGE! I WANT YOU TO PLEAD FOR YOUR LIFE, CURSE YOU! BEG ME NOT TO KILL YOU, VIKING! BEG — AND I WILL ONLY IMPRISON YOU IN MY DUNGEONS!

A VIKING WOLF DOES NOT BEG TO A DOG! KILL ME NOW — YOU WILL NOT DESTROY *MY* COURAGE!.

THE SAXON EARL FLINCHED UNDER KARL'S STEADY, CONTEMPTUOUS GAZE, THEN —

PUSH HIM OVER — *NOW!* DROWNING WILL WIPE THAT SMILE OFF HIS FACE!

IT WILL BE A PLEASURE, MY MASTER

BUT EVEN AS THE CAPTAIN OF THE EARL'S SOLDIERS RAISED HIS HANDS TO PUSH KARL OVER —

AA-AGH!

WHO — WHO SHOT THAT ARROW?

TO THE SAXONS' DISMAY, THE CAPTAIN HURTLED INTO SPACE. AND THEN THEY SAW A SIGHT THAT CHILLED THEIR BLOOD

VIKINGS!

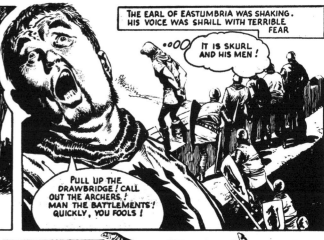

THE EARL OF EASTUMBRIA WAS SHAKING. HIS VOICE WAS SHRILL WITH TERRIBLE FEAR

IT IS SKURL AND HIS MEN!

PULL UP THE DRAWBRIDGE! CALL OUT THE ARCHERS! MAN THE BATTLEMENTS! QUICKLY, YOU FOOLS!

FOR PANIC-FILLED SECONDS EARL GYRTH HAD FORGOTTEN KARL. BUT NOW HE HAD JUMPED FORWARD, SWINGING THE SWORD OF EINGAR ABOVE HIS HEAD

BUT *YOU* — YOU WILL DIE NOW — BY YOUR FATHER'S OWN SWORD!

THE GREAT VIKING SWORD, HOWEVER, CLEAVED ONLY THE AIR. FOR KARL HAD LEAPT OUT FROM THE HIGH BATTLE-MENTS — AND AS HE PLUMMETED DOWN, HIS VOICE ROARED ACROSS TO THE WATCHING VIKINGS

SKURL, IT IS I! KARL! *THE SWORD OF EINGAR IS IN THIS CASTLE!*

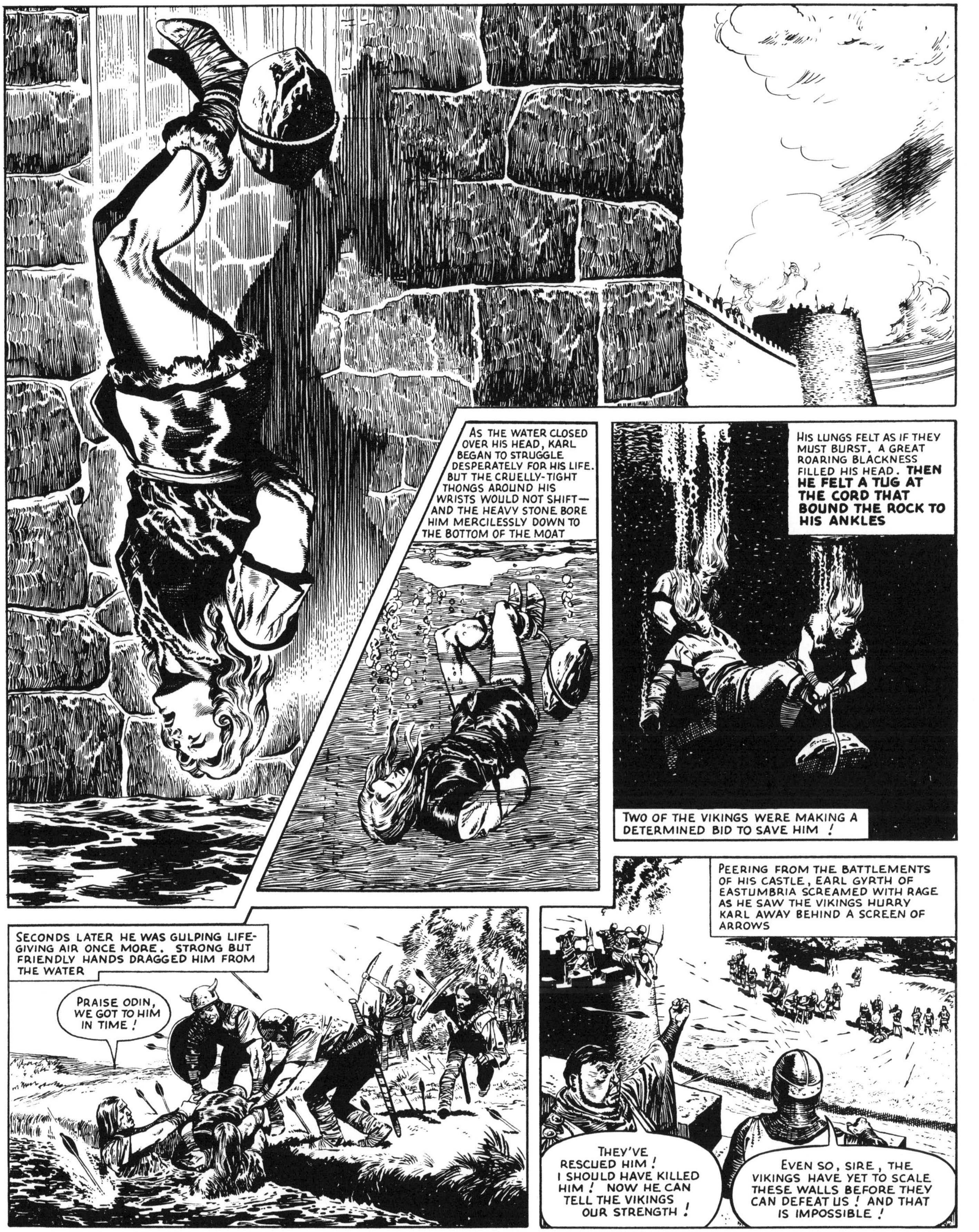

As the water closed over his head, Karl began to struggle desperately for his life. But the cruelly-tight thongs around his wrists would not shift—and the heavy stone bore him mercilessly down to the bottom of the moat
His lungs felt as if they must burst. A great roaring blackness filled his head. THEN HE FELT A TUG AT THE CORD THAT BOUND THE ROCK TO HIS ANKLES
Two of the Vikings were making a determined bid to save him!
Seconds later he was gulping life-giving air once more. Strong but friendly hands dragged him from the water
Praise Odin, we got to him in time!
Peering from the battlements of his castle, Earl Gyrth of Eastumbria screamed with rage as he saw the Vikings hurry Karl away behind a screen of arrows
They've rescued him! I should have killed him! Now he can tell the Vikings our strength!
Even so, sire, the Vikings have yet to scale these walls before they can defeat us! And that is impossible!

OUT OF RANGE OF THE SAXON ARROWS, KARL WAS BEING GREETED BY THE DELIGHTED NORSE WARRIORS

WHEN WE HEARD YOU CALL, WE THOUGHT AT FIRST IT WAS A GHOST! WE BELIEVED YOU DEAD!

WE LOST YOU IN THE SEA WHEN OUR LONGSHIPS CRASHED TOGETHER. HOW DID YOU GET BACK TO LAND?

IT IS A LONG STORY, AND I SHALL RECOUNT IT TO YOU LATER. BUT NOW WE HAVE OTHER THINGS TO DO!

THEN A COLD VOICE BROKE IN. KARL TURNED AND SAW HIS RIVAL FOR THE THRONE OF EINGAR — THE MAN WHO HAD TRIED TO DROWN HIM IN THE NORTH SEA — SKURL!

YES, YOU ARE RIGHT, KARL! IF, AS YOU SAY, THE SWORD OF EINGAR IS IN THAT CASTLE, WE MUST GET TO IT!

I SAW THE SWORD! THE FAT PIG WHO IS LORD OF THE CASTLE DARES TO WEAR IT AS IF IT IS HIS OWN!

KARL GAZED COOLLY AT THE BLAZING HATRED IN SKURL'S EYES

YOU AND I HAVE SOMETHING TO SETTLE BETWEEN US! BUT THAT, TOO, CAN WAIT UNTIL LATER. WE NEED EVERY MAN WE HAVE IF WE ARE TO TAKE THAT SAXON FORTRESS!

FOR THE TIME BEING WE WILL FIGHT AS COMRADES. BUT REMEMBER, KARL, THESE ARE MY MEN. I COMMAND THEM!

AN HOUR PASSED AND STILL THE VIKINGS HAD NOT ATTACKED. EARL GYRTH TRIED UNSUCCESSFULLY TO STIFLE HIS FEAR

WHY DON'T THEY COME? WHAT DEVILRY ARE THEY UP TO?

WHEN THEY DO COME WE SHALL BE READY FOR THEM, SIRE!

THEN, HOWLING THEIR BATTLE-CRIES LIKE BAYING WOLVES, THE VIKINGS CAME RUNNING INTO THE OPEN

HERE THEY COME, SIRE!

SEE! SOME CARRY WHAT APPEAR TO BE LADDERS!

ON TORE THE VIKINGS, BRAVING THE HAIL OF ARROWS THAT GREETED THEM

THOSE THAT REACHED THE MOAT-EDGE PLUNGED THEIR SLENDER LADDERS INTO THE MUDDY BOTTOM AND PUSHED THE TOPS TOWARDS THE TOWERING WALLS

CLIMB, MY WOLVES! LET US GET AT THEM!

I DOUBT IF SKURL'S PLAN WILL SUCCEED! BUT I WILL NOT HOLD BACK!

HIS SHIELD CLANGING UNDER THE IMPACT OF SAXON ARROWS, KARL BEGAN TO SCALE A SWAYING LADDER

AS MORE AND MORE LADDERS GRATED AGAINST THE CASTLE WALLS, EARL GYRTH'S CAPTAIN OF SOLDIERS RAISED HIS HAND HIGH

NOW IS THE TIME! NOW!

NEXT INSTANT, THE LADDERS WERE SWAYING BACKWARDS — SPILLING THE ATTACKERS INTO THE AIR!

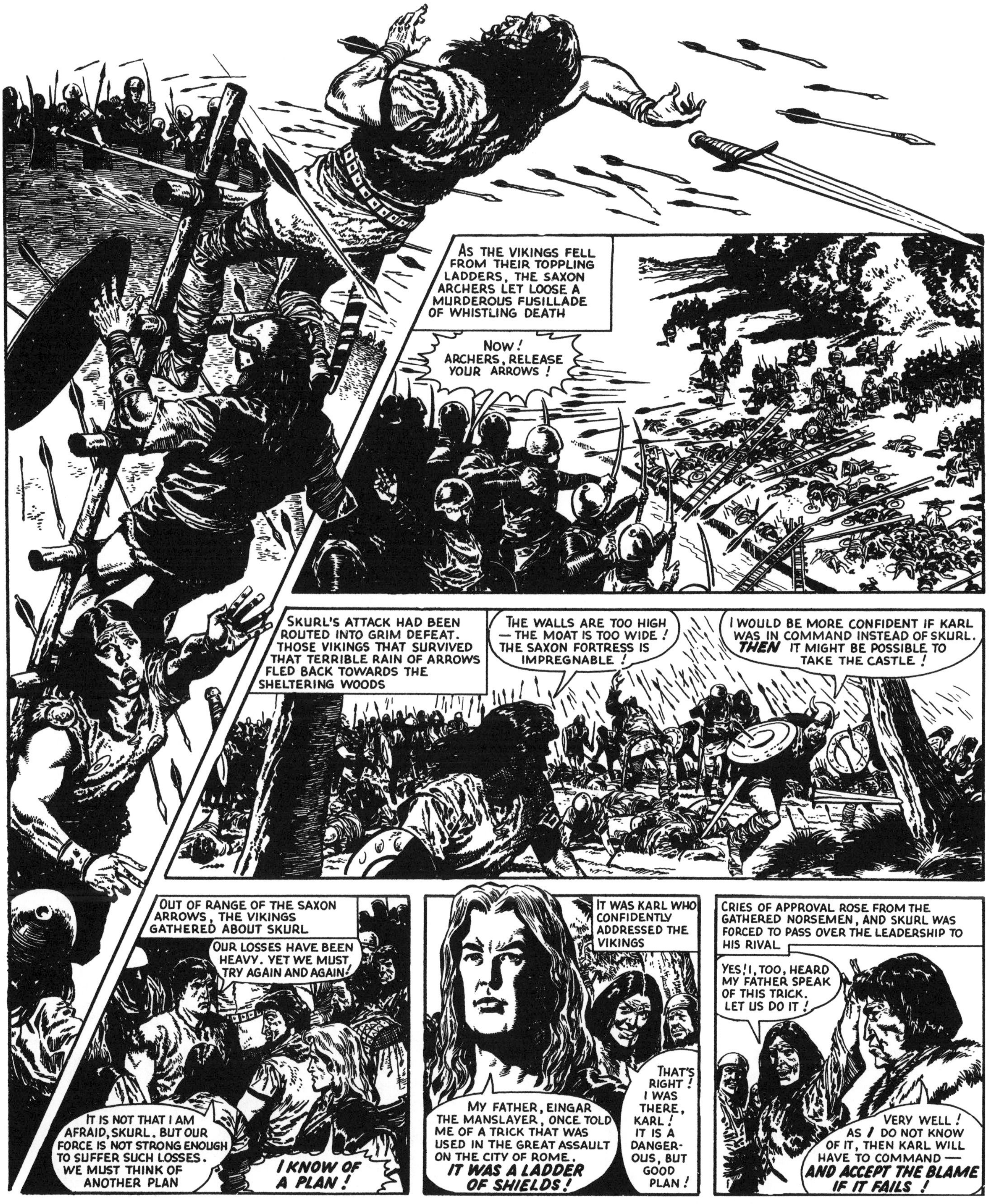

AS THE VIKINGS FELL FROM THEIR TOPPLING LADDERS, THE SAXON ARCHERS LET LOOSE A MURDEROUS FUSILLADE OF WHISTLING DEATH
NOW! ARCHERS, RELEASE YOUR ARROWS!
SKURL'S ATTACK HAD BEEN ROUTED INTO GRIM DEFEAT. THOSE VIKINGS THAT SURVIVED THAT TERRIBLE RAIN OF ARROWS FLED BACK TOWARDS THE SHELTERING WOODS
THE WALLS ARE TOO HIGH — THE MOAT IS TOO WIDE! THE SAXON FORTRESS IS IMPREGNABLE!
I WOULD BE MORE CONFIDENT IF KARL WAS IN COMMAND INSTEAD OF SKURL. THEN IT MIGHT BE POSSIBLE TO TAKE THE CASTLE!
OUT OF RANGE OF THE SAXON ARROWS, THE VIKINGS GATHERED ABOUT SKURL
OUR LOSSES HAVE BEEN HEAVY. YET WE MUST TRY AGAIN AND AGAIN!
IT IS NOT THAT I AM AFRAID, SKURL. BUT OUR FORCE IS NOT STRONG ENOUGH TO SUFFER SUCH LOSSES. WE MUST THINK OF ANOTHER PLAN
I KNOW OF A PLAN!
IT WAS KARL WHO CONFIDENTLY ADDRESSED THE VIKINGS
MY FATHER, EINGAR THE MANSLAYER, ONCE TOLD ME OF A TRICK THAT WAS USED IN THE GREAT ASSAULT ON THE CITY OF ROME. IT WAS A LADDER OF SHIELDS!
THAT'S RIGHT! I WAS THERE, KARL! IT IS A DANGEROUS, BUT GOOD PLAN!
CRIES OF APPROVAL ROSE FROM THE GATHERED NORSEMEN, AND SKURL WAS FORCED TO PASS OVER THE LEADERSHIP TO HIS RIVAL
YES! I, TOO, HEARD MY FATHER SPEAK OF THIS TRICK. LET US DO IT!
VERY WELL! AS I DO NOT KNOW OF IT, THEN KARL WILL HAVE TO COMMAND — AND ACCEPT THE BLAME IF IT FAILS!

AGAIN, A LONG SILENCE FELL UPON THE BATTLEFIELD. FROM THEIR BATTLEMENTS THE SAXONS WATCHED AND WAITED NERVOUSLY

IT IS POSSIBLE THE NORSEMEN HAVE ADMITTED THEIR DEFEAT—AND LEFT US!

NO—THOSE WOLVES DO NOT GIVE UP SO EASILY. SOON THEY WILL ATTACK AGAIN!

AND AS SOON AS THE WORDS HAD LEFT THE SAXON'S LIPS, THE VIKINGS EMERGED FROM THE SHELTERING TREES!

HERE THEY COME! ARCHERS, CUT THEM DOWN!

BUT THIS TIME THE ATTACKERS DID NOT RIP THE AIR WITH THEIR WILD BATTLE-CRIES. THEY RAN SILENTLY, GRIMLY —BEARING WITH THEM TWO HUGE TREE-TRUNKS SHARPENED AT ONE END!

AGAIN A BLACK CLOUD OF ARROWS WHISTLED FROM THE SAXON BATTLEMENTS

BUT STILL THE VIKINGS RAN ON, STAGGERING BENEATH THEIR HEAVY LOADS

MOMENTS LATER THE RUNNING ATTACKERS REACHED THE EDGE OF THE MOAT. MUSCLES BULGED AS THEY THRUST FORWARD, AND THE TWO SHARPENED TREE-TRUNKS SMASHED INTO THE WOODEN, RAISED DRAWBRIDGE— FORMING A BRIDGE ACROSS THE MOAT!

THEN, AT KARL'S RINGING COMMAND, VIKING BOWMEN LOOSED A HAIL OF ARROWS AT THE SAXON BATTLEMENTS

NOW IT IS YOUR TURN, MEN!

AND AS THE SAXON ARCHERS DUCKED, SHIELD-BEARING VIKINGS DASHED FOR THE LOG BRIDGE!

WHILE SIX OF THE BIGGEST, STRONGEST VIKINGS CROUCHED UPON THE LOG BRIDGE, SHIELDS HELD ABOVE THEIR HEADS, ANOTHER CLOUD OF ARROWS WHISTLED ABOUT THE SAXON BATTLEMENTS AND SIX MORE ATTACKERS RACED FOR THE CASTLE

AGAIN, ARCHERS! KEEP THE SAXONS' HEADS DOWN!

AGAIN AND AGAIN THE STRONGEST OF THE VIKINGS DASHED ACROSS THE BRIDGE—CLAMBERING UPON THEIR COMRADES' SHIELDS TO FORM A LIVING TOWER AGAINST THE CASTLE WALLS

THEN, LED BY KARL, SON OF EINGAR, THE REMAINDER OF THE VIKING ARMY THUNDERED THEIR ALLEGIANCE TO THE GODS OF BATTLE—AND CHARGED!

FORWARD, MY WOLVES!

FOR ODIN! FOR EINGAR!

VALHALLA!

NOTHING COULD STOP THAT WILD, MAGNIFICENT CHARGE! THE VIKINGS CROSSED THE LOG BRIDGE AND BEGAN TO SWARM UP THE TOWER OF SHIELDS—HACKING WITH SWORD AND AXE AT THE SAXON DEFENDERS

FOLLOW KARL—TO VICTORY!

As more and more Vikings got to grips with the Saxons, Karl glanced down and saw the winch that operated the castle drawbridge.

THE SAXONS COULD THROW US BACK EVEN NOW ... UNLESS ...

Using the Saxon ladder as a slide, the son of Eingar hurtled into action.

U-UGH!

Then, with sword swinging, Karl began to cut his way through the Saxons towards the draw-bridge winch. And as he fought, he raised his voice in a thunderous shout.

VIKINGS! IT IS I — KARL! CLEAR THE WAY FOR THE DRAW BRIDGE!

Karl charged the soldiers by the winch, the weight of his muscle-packed body scattering them on all sides. Then his keen sword-edge sliced through the thick rope.

VIKINGS — KEEP BACK!

ON THE OUTSIDE OF THE CASTLE WALLS, THE HUMAN TOWER HAD SCATTERED AT KARL'S WARNING WORDS. AS THEY STOOD BACK, THE GREAT DRAW-BRIDGE CRASHED DOWN

GET READY, MY WOLVES! SEE—THE GATES ARE BEING OPENED!

IT IS KARL! HE IS TRULY A CHIEFTAIN'S SON!

LIKE A FEROCIOUS, INVINCIBLE TIDE THE ATTACKERS POURED THROUGH THE OPENED GATES. SAXONS AND VIKINGS CLASHED TO A RINGING OF STEEL AGAINST STEEL. BUT IN SPITE OF THE BATTLE SURGING ABOUT HIM, KARL SAW THE GROSS FIGURE OF EARL GYRTH SCUTTLING INTO THE ENTRANCE OF A TOWER

THE FRIGHTENED PIG IS TRYING TO HIDE FROM US — AND HE HAS THE SWORD OF EINGAR WITH HIM!

KARL CHASED THE TERRIFIED SAXON NOBLEMAN UP THE WINDING STEPS OF THE TOWER—UNTIL EARL GYRTH COULD RETREAT NO LONGER

NO! DON'T KILL ME — PLEASE!

YOU SAID MY FATHER, EINGAR THE MANSLAYER, DIED A QUIVERING COWARD! IS THAT TRUE?

THE SAXON EARL WAS TOO TERRIFIED TO LIE AGAIN. AS THE FRIGHTENED WORDS BEGAN TO SPILL FROM GYRTH'S TREMBLING LIPS, KARL KNEW THAT HE WAS ABOUT TO HEAR THE TRUE ACCOUNT OF EINGAR THE MANSLAYER

NO! NO! I WAS LYING — TO—TO TORTURE YOU! YOUR CHIEFTAIN DIED BRAVELY—MORE BRAVELY THAN ANY MAN I HAVE SEEN. I WILL TELL YOU WHAT HAPPENED...

"THE VIKINGS' LONGSHIP MUST HAVE SUNK IN A STORM AT SEA. WE FOUND THE SURVIVORS WEAK AND SPENT, RESTING IN A NARROW PASS."

THE SAXONS COME! FLEE! I WILL TRY TO HOLD THEM!

"AND SO WHILE HIS MEN STAGGERED WEAKLY AWAY DOWN THE PASS, THE VIKING CHIEFTAIN FOUGHT TO PREVENT US CAPTURING THEM. IT WAS ONE MAN AGAINST FIFTY!"

AT HIM, YOU DOGS! IS ONE MAN TOO MANY FOR YOU? CUT HIM DOWN—KILL HIM!

HE FIGHTS LIKE A WILD BOAR AT BAY, SIRE. IF WE HAD ARCHERS WITH US IT WOULD BE DIFFERENT!

"WEAKENED THOUGH HE WAS, AND WOUNDED IN A DOZEN PLACES, THIS FIERCE VIKING FOUGHT ON. BUT EVEN THOUGH OUR DEAD PILED IN FRONT OF HIM, **WE WERE TOO MANY!**"

"HE WAS CUT DOWN TO THE GROUND, STILL FIGHTING, STILL SHOUTING HIS WILD BATTLE CRY AS DEATH TOOK HIM. AND IT WAS THEN THAT I NOTICED THE MAGNIFICENT SWORD IN HIS LIFELESS HAND."

I WILL KEEP THIS SWORD... IT IS MORE SUITED TO A NOBLEMAN THAN A VIKING BARBAR-IAN!

WE WILL GO AFTER THE OTHERS, SIRE. THEY SEEMED TOO WEAK TO HAVE RUN FAR!

EARL GYRTH'S STORY CAME TO AN END, AND HE TOSSED THE SWORD OF EINGAR AT KARL'S FEET

MY MEN CAUGHT UP WITH THE OTHER VIKINGS — AND KILLED THEM ALL! NOW — I HAVE TOLD YOU THE TRUTH. AND HERE IS THE CHIEFTAIN'S SWORD! SPARE MY LIFE!

SO MY FATHER DIED TO SAVE HIS MEN. HE DIED AS ALL VIKINGS WOULD WISH TO DIE!

BUT AS KARL STOOPED TO PICK UP HIS FATHER'S SWORD—

A-GH!

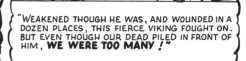

IT'S YOU — SKURL!

I MEANT THAT SPEAR FOR YOU, KARL! I WANT THAT SWORD—AND TO GET IT I AM GOING TO KILL YOU!

BUT BEFORE A MORTAL BLOW COULD BE STRUCK, THE RIVALS WERE FORCED APART BY THEIR FRIENDS

IT IS FORTUNATE THAT I SAW SKURL FOLLOW KARL UP HERE, AND GUESSED WHAT WOULD HAPPEN. THIS IS NO PETTY SQUABBLE — BUT A DUEL FOR THE RIGHT TO BE CHIEF...

KARL SHALL NOT BE CHIEF—NOT WHILE I LIVE!

WE HAVE FOUND THE SWORD OF EINGAR THE MANSLAYER — AND NOW WE CAN RETURN ACROSS THE SEA TO OUR MARK-LAND. BOTH OF YOU **WILL** FIGHT YOUR DUEL — IN TRUE VIKING FASHION, AND BEFORE OUR PEOPLE

SOME DAYS LATER THE VIKING WARRIORS WERE WITHIN SIGHT OF THEIR VILLAGE AT THE HEAD OF A WILD AND WIND-SWEPT FJORD

YOU WILL BOTH WAIT BY THE WATER'S EDGE WHILST I DISCUSS WITH THE ELDERS THE MANNER IN WHICH THIS DUEL SHOULD BE FOUGHT

THE ELDERS WERE A LONG TIME DECIDING UPON THIS IMPORTANT MATTER — AND DUSK WAS FALLING WHEN KARL AND SKURL WERE TAKEN ABOARD ANOTHER LONGSHIP

IT WILL BE FOUGHT THIS WAY. SEE, THE SWORD OF EINGAR IS BEING TIED TO THE MAST. ONE MAN WILL STEER THIS SHIP OUT INTO THE WATER, THEN HE WILL GIVE YOU EACH A SWORD—**AND SET LIGHT TO THE SHIP BEFORE HE RETURNS!**

SAY NO MORE, OLD MAN. WE UNDERSTAND. WE TWO SHALL FIGHT WHILST THE LONGSHIP BURNS. THE WINNER WILL SWIM BACK WITH THE SWORD OF EINGAR AND BECOME CHIEFTAIN. THE ONE THAT DIES WILL HAVE A VIKING'S FUNERAL!

AND SO — WHILST THE WHOLE VILLAGE WATCHED — THE SHIP THAT WAS DESTINED TO BECOME A BURNING FUNERAL PYRE FOR EITHER KARL OR SKURL WAS PUSHED OUT FROM THE SHORE

OF THE TWO, KARL IS THE STRONGER AND MORE SKILFUL SWORDSMAN. BUT SKURL'S DESIRE TO BE CHIEF HAS BECOME ALMOST A MADNESS WITH HIM

IT WILL BE A GRIM AND TERRIBLE BATTLE!

THE STEERSMAN SET A BURNING BRAND TO THE DRY TIMBER OF THE LONG-SHIP AND HELD OUT A SWORD TO EACH CONTESTANT

NOW I LEAVE YOU. I HAVE DONE EXACTLY WHAT WAS REQUESTED OF ME

THEN YOU HAVE DONE WELL — AND YOU WILL BE REWARDED!

AND AS THE STEERSMAN SWAM FOR THE SHORE, SKURL SCREAMED HIS HATE-FILLED BATTLE CRY AND LEAPT TOWARDS HIS RIVAL

HII—YAAH! I HAVE WAITED LONG FOR THIS. NOW I SHALL BE CHIEF-TAIN!

BUT YOU MUST KILL ME FIRST, SKURL! AND, BY ODIN, YOU WON'T FIND THAT EASY!

LIKE LIGHTNING, KARL'S SWORD SWEPT UP TO PARRY SKURL'S SAVAGE STROKE. **AND THEN CAME DISASTER**

IT **WILL** BE EASY, SAXON DOG. I HAVE MADE CERTAIN OF THAT!

MY SWORD-BLADE! IT—IT SNAPPED LIKE ROTTEN TIMBER

DESPERATELY KARL DODGED AS SKURL'S SWORD SLASHED TOWARDS HIS HEAD

I PAID THE STEERSMAN WELL TO GIVE YOU A SWORD WITH A WEAKENED BLADE. BUT WHEN I AM CHIEF, I SHALL HAVE HIM KILLED—AND THUS SEAL **HIS** TONGUE AS WELL AS YOURS!

YOU TREACHEROUS SNAKE!

THEN SKURL'S VOICE ROSE TO A HOWL OF TRIUMPH — AS KARL TRIPPED AND FELL SPRAWLING TO THE SMOKING DECK

NOW YOU WILL DIE!

BUT, AGAIN, IT SEEMED THAT THE VIKING GODS TOOK A HAND. FOR EVEN AS SKURL'S ARM DREW BACK FOR THE KILLING THRUST, A TONGUE OF FLAME BIT THROUGH THE ROPE THAT BOUND THE SWORD OF EINGAR TO THE MAST. **AND THE HEAVY BLADE TORE LOOSE!**

DOWN PLUNGED THE TERRIBLE SWORD. **AND—**

AAAGH!

WITH THE CRACKLE OF FLAMES LOUD IN HIS EARS, KARL PULLED THE BLADE FROM THE DEAD BODY OF THE EVIL SKURL. AND BEFORE HE LEAPT INTO THE WATER, THE SON OF EINGAR LIFTED HIS EYES TO THE NORTHERN SKY

EINGAR MY FATHER, WAS IT **YOU** WHO PROTECTED ME FROM DEATH? I SHALL NEVER KNOW THE ANSWER, BUT I SWEAR I SHALL STRIVE TO RULE YOUR PEOPLE WISELY — **AND TO BE A WORTHY SON!**

THEN KARL SWAM BACK TO THE MARKLAND THAT WAS NOW HIS...

IT IS KARL! KARL LIVES!

HAIL TO KARL, OUR CHIEF-TAIN!

... AND AS HE CLAMBERED ASHORE, THUNDER RUMBLED FROM THE CLOUDLESS SKY—AS IF EINGAR AND THE VIKING GODS IN VALHALLA WERE ADDING **THEIR** VOICES TO THE CHEERING OF THE VILLAGERS

V

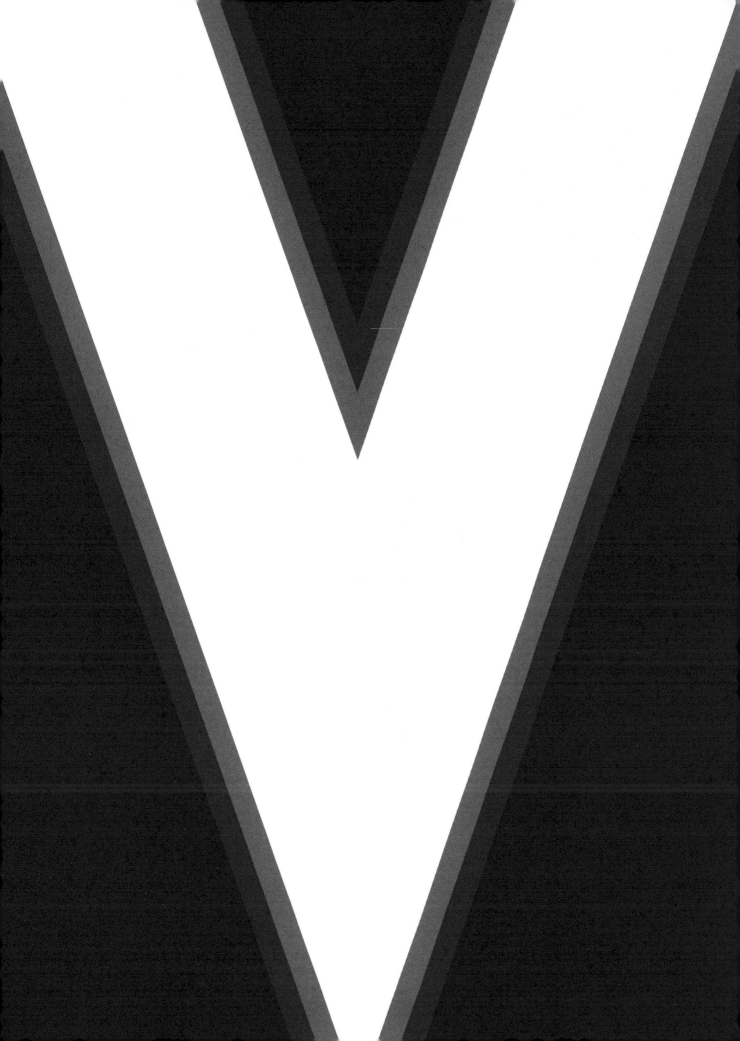

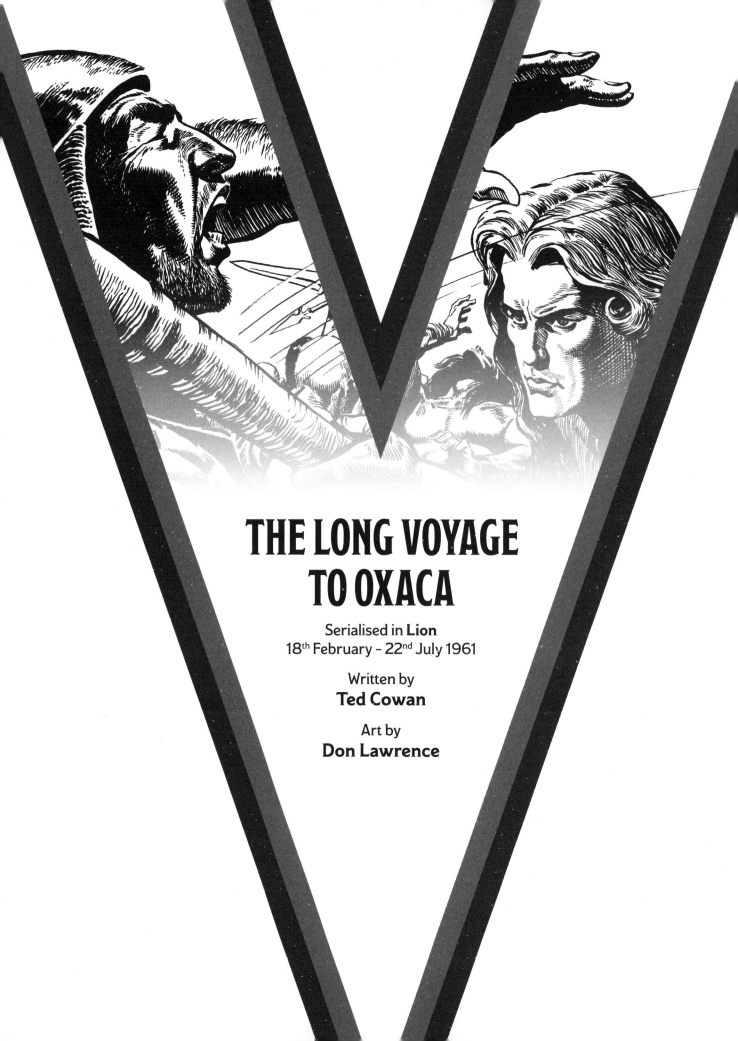

THE LONG VOYAGE TO OXACA

Serialised in **Lion**
18th February – 22nd July 1961

Written by
Ted Cowan

Art by
Don Lawrence

YET AS KARL LET FLY HIS ARROW, HE LITTLE REALISED THAT HE HAD STARTED THE FIRST OF A CHAIN OF INCIDENTS THAT WOULD PLUNGE HIM INTO ONE OF THE MOST STIRRING ADVENTURES IN VIKING HISTORY

KARL WAS NOT THE ONLY HUNTER IN THAT PART OF THE FOREST. DRIVEN FROM THE HIGH MOUNTAINS BY COLD AND HUNGER, A HUGE BEAR WATCHED THE YOUNG VIKING HEAVE THE DEER ACROSS HIS SHOULDERS

THEN, SCREAMING WITH FURY, IT BOUNDED WITH INCREDIBLE SPEED FROM CONCEALING TREES

BEFORE KARL COULD DRAW HIS SWORD, A MASSIVE PAW SLAMMED HIM OVER AND OVER LIKE A HUMAN NINEPIN

ALTHOUGH KNOCKED ALMOST SENSELESS BY THAT POWERFUL BLOW, KARL SOMEHOW MANAGED TO STAGGER TO HIS FEET. AND NEXT MOMENT, MAN AND BEAST WERE LOCKED IN MORTAL COMBAT

BUT EVEN AS HE FOUGHT SO DESPERATELY, KARL KNEW THAT ONLY A MIRACLE COULD SAVE HIS LIFE

YET UNSEEN HELP WAS AT HAND

WITH DEATH-DEALING ACCURACY THE ARROW BIT HOME. AND AS KARL STAGGERED BACK FROM THE TOPPLING WEIGHT OF THE DEAD KILLER-BEAR, HE GASPED WITH ASTONISHMENT AT THE TALL, THIN FIGURE OF HIS RESCUER

WHAT KIND OF MAN IS THIS WHO HAS SAVED ME FROM DEATH? NEVER HAVE I SEEN CLOTHES LIKE HIS. AND THE COLOUR OF HIS SKIN... IT—IT IS ALMOST RED!

THEN A NEW, TERRIFYING SOUND RIPPED THE WINTRY AIR — THE BAYING OF THE FOREST'S MOST FEARSOME HUNTERS, ATTRACTED BY THE SCENT OF THE BEAR'S BLOOD

WOLVES!

AGHAST, KARL SAW THE TALL, ELDERLY STRANGER DRAW ANOTHER ARROW

NO! YOU HAVE DONE ENOUGH! IF YOU SHOOT, THE WOLVES WILL SEE YOU! YOU WILL ATTRACT THEM TO YOURSELF. RUN! SAVE YOUR LIFE!

BUT IF THE OTHER MAN HEARD OR UNDERSTOOD KARL'S WORDS, HE PAID NO HEED. HIS ARROW FELLED THE LEADING WOLF — AND THE HOWLING PACK SWUNG IN HIS DIRECTION

FLEE! FLEE!

THE STRANGER'S ONLY REPLY WAS TO ATTEMPT ANOTHER SHOT WITH HIS ARROW — BUT TOO LATE

HE DELIBERATELY CHOSE TO SACRIFICE HIS LIFE—TO SAVE MINE! BUT I CAN-NOT STAND BY AND LET HIM DIE UNAIDED!

SECONDS LATER, KARL WAS AMONGST THE WOLVES, SLASHING RIGHT AND LEFT WITH HIS SWORD TO KEEP THE SNARLING KILLERS FROM THE STILL BODY OF THE STRANGER

THEN OTHER MEN BURST FROM THE TREES. THEY WERE KARL'S OWN VIKING WARRIORS

SEE! I TOLD YOU IT WAS THE VOICE OF OUR CHIEFTAIN!

WE ARE JUST IN TIME!

HUNGRY AND KILL-MAD AS THEY WERE, THE REMAINING WOLVES SLUNK DEFEATEDLY AWAY AT THE SIGHT OF THE DANES

KARL, ARE YOU ALL RIGHT?

YES, THANKS TO THIS BRAVE MAN I AM STILL ALIVE

BUT AS KARL KNELT TO LIFT THE STILL, THIN FIGURE —

KARL! LOOK OUT!

IN THE NICK OF TIME KARL HURLED HIMSELF TO ONE SIDE AS THE ARROW WINGED TOWARDS HIM

HE TRIED TO SLAY KARL! KILL HIM!

ANOTHER SECOND AND A DOZEN ARROWS WOULD HAVE RIDDLED THE MYSTERIOUS BOWMAN. BUT THE WOUNDED ELDER UTTERED A QUAVERING SHOUT

CHILANO! ALL IS WELL! THESE MEN DO NOT SEEK TO HARM ME!

THE BOWMAN PAUSED UNCERTAINLY — THEN HURRIED ACROSS THE SNOW TO THE WOUNDED MAN'S SIDE

YUCATEC, MY LORD. WHO HAS INJURED YOU THUS?

IT WAS THE WOLVES. THESE NORTHMEN SAVED ME.

BUT FIRST YOU SAVED *ME* FROM THE WOLVES! NOW WE MUST TAKE YOU TO MY VILLAGE SO THAT ALFREDA CAN TEND YOUR WOUNDS

AND SO THE WOUNDED STRANGER WAS BORNE BY THE STALWART VIKING TO THE VILLAGE AT THE EDGE OF A RIVER

HURRY, ALFREDA. FETCH YOUR HERBS AND CLOTH TO BIND THIS MAN'S WOUNDS!

WHO ARE THEY? I HAVE SAILED FOREIGN SEAS FOR HALF A CENTURY, YET NEVER HAVE I SEEN MEN DRESSED LIKE THIS

ALL THROUGH THAT DAY AND NIGHT ALFREDA TENDED THE WOUNDED MAN. BY MORNING HE WAS MUCH BETTER, AND KARL WENT TO VISIT HIM

I OWE YOU MY LIFE, AND I AM IN YOUR DEBT. ANYTHING I HAVE, OTHER THAN MY KINGDOM, IS YOURS!

WELL — IF YOU ARE SINCERE IN WHAT YOU SAY, THERE IS SOMETHING —

THE OLD MAN'S DARK EYES BURNED WITH INTENSITY

THEN NAME IT—FOR I STAND BY MY WORD. BUT TELL ME WHAT YOU WISH ME TO DO

AS YOU CLAIM YOU ARE IN MY DEBT—THEN I AM DESPERATE ENOUGH TO ASK WHAT I COULD ASK NO OTHER MAN. I WANT YOU TO TAKE ONE OF YOUR LONGSHIPS FAR, FAR BEYOND THE MOST DISTANT HORIZONS—ACROSS STRANGE SEAS THAT I AM SURE YOU HAVE NEVER DREAMED OF

CHILANO AND I COME FROM A MIGHTY LAND OF LIMITLESS FORESTS WHERE THE SUN GOD RULES THE PEOPLE FROM HIS FIERY THRONE IN THE SKY. FOR DAYS AND NIGHTS BEYOND COUNT WE DRIFTED IN OUR SMALL SHIP—UNTIL, A YEAR AGO, WE SIGHTED THE SHORES OF YOUR LAND

BUT WHY DID YOU SET OUT UPON SUCH A VOYAGE?

WE BROUGHT WITH US ONE OTHER PERSON—TIHUANA, A BOY WHO SHOULD RIGHTFULLY BE KING OF THE PEOPLE OF OXACA. IT WAS HIS UNCLE WHO SET THE THREE OF US ADRIFT IN A BALSA CRAFT, HOPING THAT WE WOULD DROWN AT SEA, FOR WITH TIHUANA DEAD HE SUCCEEDS TO THE THRONE. HE DARED NOT KILL US WITH HIS OWN HANDS FOR FEAR OF INCURRING THE WRATH OF THE SUN GOD!

I AM ASKING THAT YOU TAKE THE YOUNG KING BACK ACROSS THE SEAS, AND IF NECESSARY FIGHT TO REPLACE HIM ON THE THRONE OF OXACA. I AM TOO OLD TO UNDERTAKE SUCH A JOURNEY

I GAVE YOU MY PLEDGE, AND I WILL KEEP TO IT. BUT WHERE IS THIS BOY KING?

GRATITUDE SHONE IN THE OLD MAN'S EYES

HE IS IN THE FOREST—NOT FAR FROM HERE. WE LEFT HIM IN THE SAFETY OF A CAVE WHILST WE HUNTED FOR FOOD. CHILANO HERE WILL LEAD YOU TO HIM!

I WILL DO AS YOU ASK, MY LORD. BUT WE SHOULD WARN THIS VIKING THAT THE DANGERS WILL BE MANY AND TERRIFYING! WE MAY ALL VOYAGE TO OUR DEATHS!

AT THE OLD MAN'S REQUEST, CHILANO LED KARL DEEP INTO THE FROZEN FOREST

HOW IS IT THAT YOU SPEAK THE VIKING LANGUAGE?

YUCATEC LEARNT IT FROM AN OLD FISHERMAN WHO SHELTERED US. AND THEN HE TAUGHT ME AND THE BOY KING. THERE IS THE CAVE WHERE TIHUANA WAITS FOR US

TIHUANA, THE RIGHTFUL KING OF OXACA, WAS BARELY TWELVE YEARS OLD, BUT HE WAS EVERY INCH A RULER. HE LISTENED TO CHILANO'S ACCOUNT OF WHAT HAD HAPPENED. THEN—

IF YOU DO SUCCEED IN SLAYING MY TRAITOROUS UNCLE AND PLACING ME ON THE THRONE, YOU WILL BE WELL REWARDED, NORTHMAN. IN OXACA THERE IS PLENTY OF THE YELLOW METAL THAT YOU CALL GOLD. YOU CAN RETURN HERE WITH AS MUCH AS YOUR SHIP CAN CARRY!

THAT WILL INDEED PAY YOUR DEBT TO YUCATEC, EH, NORTHMAN?

THE FOLLOWING MORNING, JUST BEFORE BOARDING A LONGSHIP MANNED BY A PICKED CREW OF THE HARDIEST VIKINGS, AND PACKED WITH PROVISIONS FOR THE GREAT VOYAGE, ROLF SAID GOODBYE TO YUCATEC

I WILL DO MY BEST TO CARRY OUT WHAT YOU ASKED OF ME

TWO DAYS LATER THE LONGSHIP WAS BUFFETING WEST THROUGH THE ANGRY WAVES OF A MIGHTY OCEAN

FOR THIRTY DAYS THEY SAILED ON, WHILST THE SUN GREW STEADILY WARMER AND THE SEA MORE CALM. THEN, ONE NIGHT, CHILANO GAVE KARL A NEW DIRECTION

FROM HERE WE JOURNEY SOUTH, KARL, FOR THE LONGEST AND MOST DANGEROUS PART OF THE VOYAGE. KING TIHUANA, YUCATEC AND I MUST HAVE BEEN PROTECTED BY THE SUN GOD WHEN WE SAILED THIS WAY THE FIRST TIME... FOR THE LEGENDS OF MY PEOPLE SAY THAT IN THESE WATERS THE DARKEST DEMONS DWELL. AND THAT THERE ARE FEARFUL EVILS THAT NO MAN CAN ENCOUNTER—AND LIVE!

THIRTY DAYS PASSED WITHOUT INCIDENT. THEN, SUDDENLY, A WILD STORM AROSE

DAY AND NIGHT IT RAGED. AND WHEN IT PASSED, CHILANO THE GUIDE REALISED THAT THEY WERE LOST

MY CHART — IT MUST HAVE BEEN WASHED INTO THE SEA! AND THAT STORM HAS SURELY BLOWN US MANY, MANY MILES OFF OUR COURSE!

THEN ALL WE CAN DO IS TO CONTINUE SOUTH BY THE SUN — AND PRAY THAT WE SIGHT LAND!

THE SUN BECAME A MOLTEN GLOBE IN A BRASSY SKY, TORTURING THE VOYAGERS WITH ITS MERCILESS HEAT

OUR DRINKING WATER IS DRYING UP, AND WITH NO WIND TO FILL OUR SAIL WE ARE MAKING SLOW PROGRESS!

AT LAST THEIR PRECIOUS WATER RAN OUT, AND THE VIKINGS — STRENGTH SAPPED BY THE OVEN-LIKE AIR — SLUMPED OVER THEIR OARS THEN CAME A GASPING, CROAKING CRY

KARL! I SEE LAND!

SPURRED BY THE LURE OF LAND AND WATER, THE OARSMEN FOUND NEW STRENGTH. TWO HOURS LATER THEY WERE GAZING AT THE THICKLY-WOODED HILLS OF AN UNKNOWN ISLAND

I DO NOT LIKE THIS PLACE, KARL. I FEEL THERE IS DANGER HERE

DANGEROUS OR NOT, SOMEONE HAS TO GO ASHORE TO FIND AND BRING BACK WATER... AS WELL AS FRUIT!

BUT KARL SAW THAT HIS WARRIORS WERE WORRIED BY THE STRANGE SILENCE THAT HUNG OVER THE ISLAND

SOMETHING IS NOT RIGHT THERE. WITH ALL THAT JUNGLE WE SHOULD BE ABLE TO HEAR THE BIRDS

AND THE CHATTERING OF MONKEYS! BUT THERE IS NOTHING— NOT EVEN THE SIGHT OF A BIRD IN THE AIR!

ABRUPTLY, KARL CAME TO A DECISION. HIS MEN HAD DONE ENOUGH ALREADY— IT WAS NOT RIGHT TO ASK MORE OF THEM UNTIL THEIR STRENGTH HAD RETURNED

THEN I WILL SWIM TO THE ISLAND AND EXPLORE IT BY MYSELF. WHEN I HAVE FOUND OUT THAT NOTHING IS THERE TO HARM US, AND WHEN I HAVE FOUND WATER, I WILL RETURN TO THE BEACH AND SIGNAL YOU

TAKE CARE, KARL AND KEEP YOUR SWORD IN YOUR HAND!

KARL STRUCK OUT FOR THE SHORE AND SOON REACHED THE BEACH

THE CREW ARE NOT AFRAID OF ANY LIVING THING— BUT IT IS CHILANO'S TALK OF DEMONS THAT HAS UNNERVED THEM

LEAVING THE NARROW STRIP OF SAND, KARL STEPPED CAUTIOUSLY INTO THE TANGLE OF THE JUNGLE

NEVER HAVE I SEEN SUCH A FOREST AS THIS. AND MY MEN WERE RIGHT— THERE ARE NO BIRDS, NO ANIMALS! NOTHING BUT SILENCE!

BUT DEEPER IN THE JUNGLE KARL CAME UPON STARTLING PROOF THAT LIFE **HAD** EXISTED ON THAT MYSTERIOUS ISLAND

BY ODIN, IT IS AN ARROW! FOUR TIMES THE SIZE OF A NORMAL ARROW— AND MADE OF *IRON!* WHAT MANNER OF HUNTER WOULD HAVE THE STRENGTH NEEDED TO USE SUCH A WEAPON?

AT THAT MOMENT, BACK ON THE LONG-SHIP, ONE OF THE VIKINGS TURNED TO ANOTHER

I FOR ONE CANNOT LET KARL STAY THERE ALONE. WHAT OF YOU, ERIK? KARL SAVED YOUR LIFE ONCE, REMEMBER? WILL YOU GO ASHORE WITH ME?

I AM AFRAID, OLEV, BUT I WILL GO WITH YOU. FOR IT— IT IS TRUE THAT I OWE MY LIFE TO KARL!

MINUTES LATER THEY, TOO, WERE STRUGGLING THROUGH THE BREAKERS TO THE BEACH

THERE ARE KARL'S FOOTPRINTS. WE CAN CATCH HIM UP— HE CANNOT YET HAVE GONE FAR

THE TWO VIKINGS HURRIED THROUGH THE UNDERGROWTH, FOLLOWING THE TRACKS MADE BY THEIR YOUNG CHIEFTAIN. THEN OLEV NOTICED A MOVEMENT IN A CLEARING AHEAD

THERE IS KARL, ERIK. HURRY!

BUT NEXT INSTANT, ERIK SAW OLEV HURTLE VIOLENTLY THROUGH THE AIR — **AS IF THRUST BY SOME GIANT, UNSEEN HAND!**

AA-AGH!

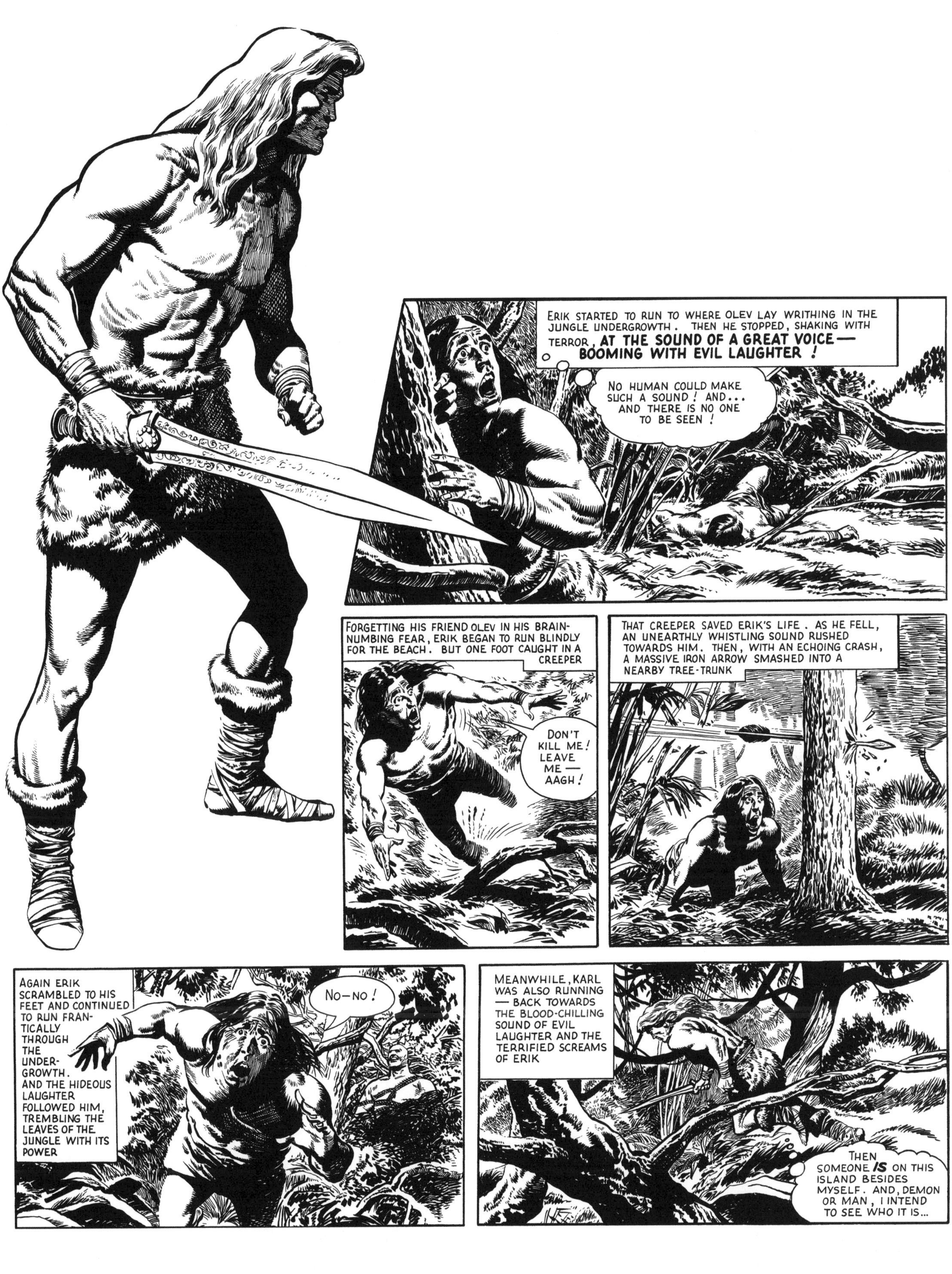
ERIK STARTED TO RUN TO WHERE OLEV LAY WRITHING IN THE JUNGLE UNDERGROWTH. THEN HE STOPPED, SHAKING WITH TERROR, AT THE SOUND OF A GREAT VOICE — BOOMING WITH EVIL LAUGHTER !
NO HUMAN COULD MAKE SUCH A SOUND ! AND... AND THERE IS NO ONE TO BE SEEN !
FORGETTING HIS FRIEND OLEV IN HIS BRAIN-NUMBING FEAR, ERIK BEGAN TO RUN BLINDLY FOR THE BEACH. BUT ONE FOOT CAUGHT IN A CREEPER
DON'T KILL ME ! LEAVE ME — AAGH !
THAT CREEPER SAVED ERIK'S LIFE. AS HE FELL, AN UNEARTHLY WHISTLING SOUND RUSHED TOWARDS HIM. THEN, WITH AN ECHOING CRASH, A MASSIVE IRON ARROW SMASHED INTO A NEARBY TREE-TRUNK
AGAIN ERIK SCRAMBLED TO HIS FEET AND CONTINUED TO RUN FRANTICALLY THROUGH THE UNDERGROWTH. AND THE HIDEOUS LAUGHTER FOLLOWED HIM, TREMBLING THE LEAVES OF THE JUNGLE WITH ITS POWER
NO—NO !
MEANWHILE, KARL WAS ALSO RUNNING — BACK TOWARDS THE BLOOD-CHILLING SOUND OF EVIL LAUGHTER AND THE TERRIFIED SCREAMS OF ERIK
THEN SOMEONE IS ON THIS ISLAND BESIDES MYSELF. AND, DEMON OR MAN, I INTEND TO SEE WHO IT IS...

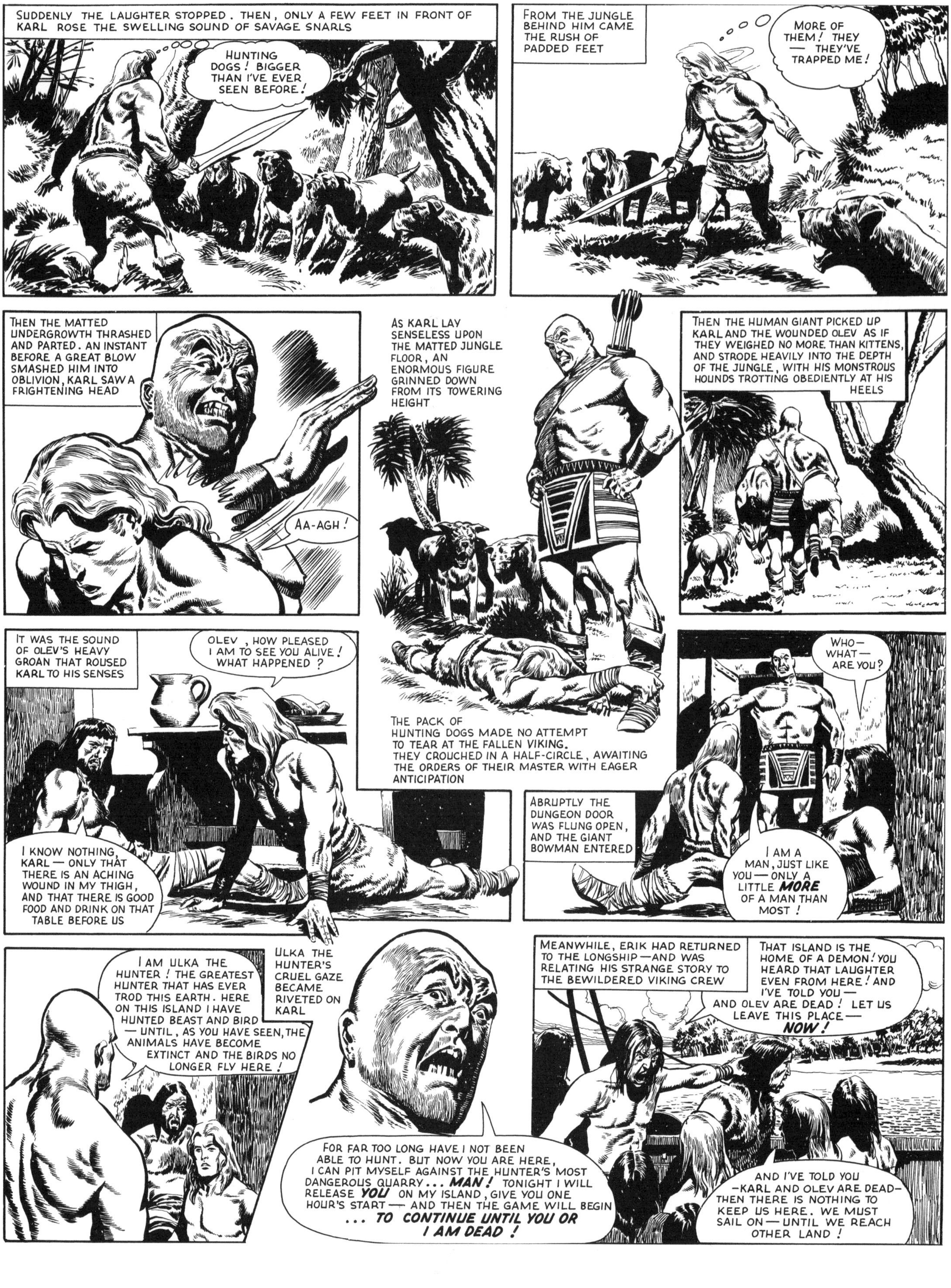

SUDDENLY THE LAUGHTER STOPPED. THEN, ONLY A FEW FEET IN FRONT OF KARL ROSE THE SWELLING SOUND OF SAVAGE SNARLS
HUNTING DOGS! BIGGER THAN I'VE EVER SEEN BEFORE!
FROM THE JUNGLE BEHIND HIM CAME THE RUSH OF PADDED FEET
MORE OF THEM! THEY — THEY'VE TRAPPED ME!
THEN THE MATTED UNDERGROWTH THRASHED AND PARTED. AN INSTANT BEFORE A GREAT BLOW SMASHED HIM INTO OBLIVION, KARL SAW A FRIGHTENING HEAD
AA-AGH!
AS KARL LAY SENSELESS UPON THE MATTED JUNGLE FLOOR, AN ENORMOUS FIGURE GRINNED DOWN FROM ITS TOWERING HEIGHT
THE PACK OF HUNTING DOGS MADE NO ATTEMPT TO TEAR AT THE FALLEN VIKING. THEY CROUCHED IN A HALF-CIRCLE, AWAITING THE ORDERS OF THEIR MASTER WITH EAGER ANTICIPATION
THEN THE HUMAN GIANT PICKED UP KARL AND THE WOUNDED OLEV AS IF THEY WEIGHED NO MORE THAN KITTENS, AND STRODE HEAVILY INTO THE DEPTH OF THE JUNGLE, WITH HIS MONSTROUS HOUNDS TROTTING OBEDIENTLY AT HIS HEELS
IT WAS THE SOUND OF OLEV'S HEAVY GROAN THAT ROUSED KARL TO HIS SENSES
OLEV, HOW PLEASED I AM TO SEE YOU ALIVE! WHAT HAPPENED?
I KNOW NOTHING, KARL — ONLY THAT THERE IS AN ACHING WOUND IN MY THIGH, AND THAT THERE IS GOOD FOOD AND DRINK ON THAT TABLE BEFORE US
ABRUPTLY THE DUNGEON DOOR WAS FLUNG OPEN, AND THE GIANT BOWMAN ENTERED
WHO— WHAT— ARE YOU?
I AM A MAN, JUST LIKE YOU — ONLY A LITTLE MORE OF A MAN THAN MOST!
I AM ULKA THE HUNTER! THE GREATEST HUNTER THAT HAS EVER TROD THIS EARTH. HERE ON THIS ISLAND I HAVE HUNTED BEAST AND BIRD — UNTIL, AS YOU HAVE SEEN, THE ANIMALS HAVE BECOME EXTINCT AND THE BIRDS NO LONGER FLY HERE!
ULKA THE HUNTER'S CRUEL GAZE BECAME RIVETED ON KARL
FOR FAR TOO LONG HAVE I NOT BEEN ABLE TO HUNT. BUT NOW YOU ARE HERE, I CAN PIT MYSELF AGAINST THE HUNTER'S MOST DANGEROUS QUARRY... MAN! TONIGHT I WILL RELEASE YOU ON MY ISLAND, GIVE YOU ONE HOUR'S START — AND THEN THE GAME WILL BEGIN ... TO CONTINUE UNTIL YOU OR I AM DEAD!
MEANWHILE, ERIK HAD RETURNED TO THE LONGSHIP — AND WAS RELATING HIS STRANGE STORY TO THE BEWILDERED VIKING CREW
THAT ISLAND IS THE HOME OF A DEMON! YOU HEARD THAT LAUGHTER EVEN FROM HERE! AND I'VE TOLD YOU — AND OLEV ARE DEAD! LET US LEAVE THIS PLACE — NOW!
AND I'VE TOLD YOU —KARL AND OLEV ARE DEAD— THEN THERE IS NOTHING TO KEEP US HERE. WE MUST SAIL ON — UNTIL WE REACH OTHER LAND!

THE NEEDLE-SHARP POINT OF ULKA THE HUNTER'S SWORD THRUST KARL OUT INTO THE NIGHT AIR. BEFORE HIM, THE THICK, SHADOWY JUNGLE STRETCHED BLACK AND MENACING BENEATH A DARK SKY. THEN ULKA SPOKE

GO, VIKING! STRAIGHT AHEAD YOU WILL FIND YOUR SWORD AT THE FOOT OF A TWISTED TREE. IT WOULD BE TOO EASY FOR ME TO HUNT YOU IF YOU WERE UNARMED!

AS KARL BEGAN TO STUMBLE DOWN THE NARROW PATH THROUGH THE TANGLED UNDERGROWTH, HE FOUGHT AGAINST A FEAR GREATER THAN HE HAD EVER KNOWN BEFORE.

IF I AM TO SURVIVE, I MUST KEEP CALM!

REMEMBER, YOU HAVE ONE HOUR, VIKING! THEN I SHALL HUNT YOU — UNTIL ONE OF US IS DEAD!

AS SOON AS KARL HAD DISAPPEARED INTO THE GLOOM OF THE JUNGLE, ULKA THE HUNTER SLAMMED THE DOOR OF HIS LAIR — AND STRODE TO WHERE HIS GREAT HOUNDS BAYED AND SLAVERED WITH EAGER ANTICIPATION

YES, MY PETS, YOU ARE HUNGRY — AND YOU SENSE THAT SOON WE ARE TO HUNT AGAIN! BUT THIS TIME OUR QUARRY IS TO BE THE MOST DANGEROUS OF ALL ANIMALS — MAN! IT WILL BE SPORT INDEED!

KARL FOUND HIS SWORD. BUT THE WEIGHT OF ITS KEEN-EDGED, STURDY BLADE BROUGHT LITTLE COMFORT TO THE YOUNG VIKING CHIEFTAIN.

WHAT GOOD WILL THIS SWORD BE AGAINST ULKA'S MONSTROUS IRON ARROWS AND HIS KILLER-HOUNDS? ONLY MY WITS CAN PRESERVE MY LIFE.

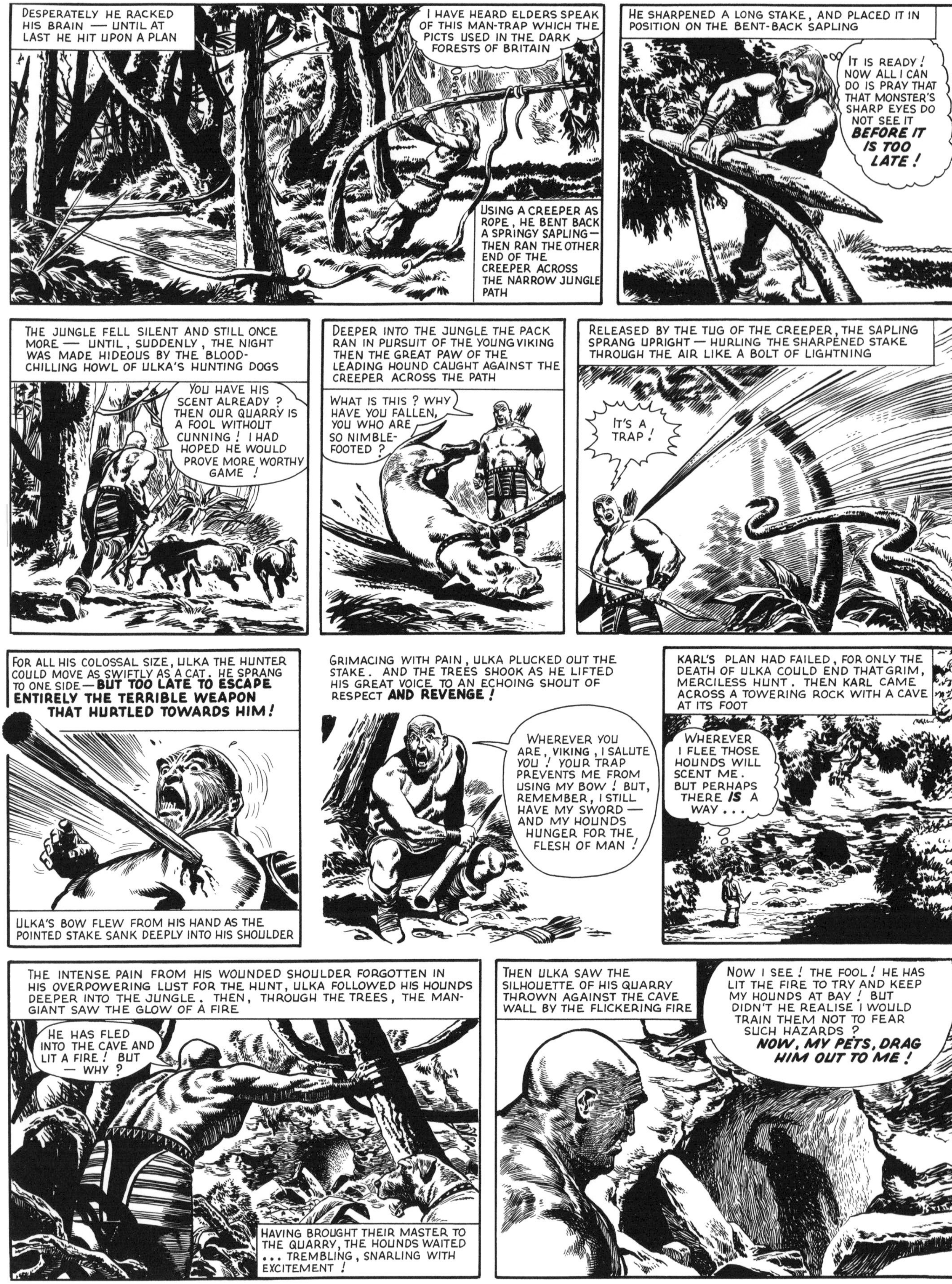

DESPERATELY HE RACKED HIS BRAIN — UNTIL AT LAST HE HIT UPON A PLAN
I HAVE HEARD ELDERS SPEAK OF THIS MAN-TRAP WHICH THE PICTS USED IN THE DARK FORESTS OF BRITAIN
USING A CREEPER AS ROPE, HE BENT BACK A SPRINGY SAPLING — THEN RAN THE OTHER END OF THE CREEPER ACROSS THE NARROW JUNGLE PATH
HE SHARPENED A LONG STAKE, AND PLACED IT IN POSITION ON THE BENT-BACK SAPLING
IT IS READY! NOW ALL I CAN DO IS PRAY THAT THAT MONSTER'S SHARP EYES DO NOT SEE IT **BEFORE IT IS TOO LATE!**
THE JUNGLE FELL SILENT AND STILL ONCE MORE — UNTIL, SUDDENLY, THE NIGHT WAS MADE HIDEOUS BY THE BLOOD-CHILLING HOWL OF ULKA'S HUNTING DOGS
YOU HAVE HIS SCENT ALREADY? THEN OUR QUARRY IS A FOOL WITHOUT CUNNING! I HAD HOPED HE WOULD PROVE MORE WORTHY GAME!
DEEPER INTO THE JUNGLE THE PACK RAN IN PURSUIT OF THE YOUNG VIKING THEN THE GREAT PAW OF THE LEADING HOUND CAUGHT AGAINST THE CREEPER ACROSS THE PATH
WHAT IS THIS? WHY HAVE YOU FALLEN, YOU WHO ARE SO NIMBLE-FOOTED?
RELEASED BY THE TUG OF THE CREEPER, THE SAPLING SPRANG UPRIGHT — HURLING THE SHARPENED STAKE THROUGH THE AIR LIKE A BOLT OF LIGHTNING
IT'S A TRAP!
FOR ALL HIS COLOSSAL SIZE, ULKA THE HUNTER COULD MOVE AS SWIFTLY AS A CAT. HE SPRANG TO ONE SIDE — **BUT TOO LATE TO ESCAPE ENTIRELY THE TERRIBLE WEAPON THAT HURTLED TOWARDS HIM!**
ULKA'S BOW FLEW FROM HIS HAND AS THE POINTED STAKE SANK DEEPLY INTO HIS SHOULDER
GRIMACING WITH PAIN, ULKA PLUCKED OUT THE STAKE. AND THE TREES SHOOK AS HE LIFTED HIS GREAT VOICE TO AN ECHOING SHOUT OF RESPECT **AND REVENGE!**
WHEREVER YOU ARE, VIKING, I SALUTE YOU! YOUR TRAP PREVENTS ME FROM USING MY BOW! BUT, REMEMBER, I STILL HAVE MY SWORD — AND MY HOUNDS HUNGER FOR THE FLESH OF MAN!
KARL'S PLAN HAD FAILED, FOR ONLY THE DEATH OF ULKA COULD END THAT GRIM, MERCILESS HUNT. THEN KARL CAME ACROSS A TOWERING ROCK WITH A CAVE AT ITS FOOT
WHEREVER I FLEE THOSE HOUNDS WILL SCENT ME. BUT PERHAPS THERE **IS** A WAY...
THE INTENSE PAIN FROM HIS WOUNDED SHOULDER FORGOTTEN IN HIS OVERPOWERING LUST FOR THE HUNT, ULKA FOLLOWED HIS HOUNDS DEEPER INTO THE JUNGLE. THEN, THROUGH THE TREES, THE MAN-GIANT SAW THE GLOW OF A FIRE
HE HAS FLED INTO THE CAVE AND LIT A FIRE! BUT — WHY?
HAVING BROUGHT THEIR MASTER TO THE QUARRY, THE HOUNDS WAITED ... TREMBLING, SNARLING WITH EXCITEMENT!
THEN ULKA SAW THE SILHOUETTE OF HIS QUARRY THROWN AGAINST THE CAVE WALL BY THE FLICKERING FIRE
NOW I SEE! THE FOOL! HE HAS LIT THE FIRE TO TRY AND KEEP MY HOUNDS AT BAY! BUT DIDN'T HE REALISE I WOULD TRAIN THEM NOT TO FEAR SUCH HAZARDS? **NOW, MY PETS, DRAG HIM OUT TO ME!**

DRAG HIM OUT TO ME, MY BEAUTIES! LITTLE DOES THE FOOL KNOW THAT YOU HAVE BEEN TRAINED TO LEAP THROUGH FLAMES!

BUT AS THE HOUNDS BOUNDED INTO THE CAVE, IT WAS NOT KARL THAT FACED THEM — BUT A CUNNINGLY-RIGGED DUMMY!

HIGH ABOVE THE CAVE-MOUTH KARL, THEIR REAL QUARRY, PUSHED AND STRAINED AT A MASSIVE BOULDER

MY PLAN HAS WORKED — SO FAR! ULKA'S HOUNDS ARE ALL INSIDE THE CAVE!

THE BOULDER SLID AND BOUNCED DOWN THE ROCK WALL, TEARING LOOSE AN AVALANCHE OF SMALLER ROCKS THAT COMPLETELY SEALED THE MOUTH OF THE CAVE.

DONE IT! NOW IT WILL BE HOURS BEFORE THOSE HOUNDS CAN DIG THEIR WAY OUT OF MY TRAP!

KARL GAZED ABOUT HIM AT THE STILL, SILENT DARKNESS OF THE JUNGLE — THEN TOOK A TIGHTER GRIP ON HIS SWORD

WHILST ULKA HAD HIS HOUNDS, I COULD DO NOTHING! BUT NOW — GIANT THOUGH HE IS — IT IS MAN AGAINST MAN! NOW IT IS MY TURN TO BE HUNTER!

BUT THE YOUNG VIKING SAW AND HEARD NO SIGN OF ULKA — UNTIL HE CAME ACROSS DEEP FOOTPRINTS NEAR THE EDGE OF A CLIFF

HE SEEMS TO HAVE TURNED BACK TOWARDS HIS LAIR

AS HE PAUSED KARL BOUND HIS SWORD TO A SLENDER STAKE WITH SUPPLE JUNGLE VINE, THUS FORMING A MAKESHIFT BUT DEADLY JAVELIN!

KARL, HOWEVER, HAD UNDERESTIMATED THE CUNNING OF ULKA THE HUNTER. FOR THE MAN-GIANT, IN SPITE OF HIS WOUNDED ARM, WAS AIMING A HUGE ARROW AT THE ONCOMING VIKING

I MUST GET TO HIM QUICKLY, FOR HE MAY HAVE **MORE** HOUNDS!

NOW I HAVE HIM!

A SPLIT-SECOND LATER THE GREAT IRON ARROW WHISTLED THROUGH THE AIR — AND A SCREAM OF AGONY TORE FROM KARL'S LIPS AS HE WRITHED INTO THE UNDERGROWTH

AA-AGH!

AGAIN KARL HAD OUTWITTED THE EVIL HUNTER, FOR HE HAD DODGED THE GREAT ARROW IN THE NICK OF TIME. UNHARMED, HE SPRANG UP TO FACE HIS ENEMY

NOW I HAVE BROUGHT YOU OUT INTO THE OPEN, MAN-GIANT!

YOU HAVE CUNNING, VIKING — BUT IT WILL SERVE YOU NO GOOD!

WITH A LIGHTNING-FAST, TREMENDOUS BLOW WITH HIS HUGE SWORD, ULKA SMASHED KARL'S SPEAR ASIDE AS IF IT WERE NOTHING MORE THAN A REED

AH! I HAVE UNARMED YOU, VIKING! NOW WHAT?

TRAPPED WITH HIS BACK TO THE CLIFF EDGE, KARL KNEW THAT ALL HE COULD DO WAS SELL HIS LIFE BRAVELY. HANDS REACHING FOR ULKA'S SWORD ARM, HE SPRANG

DIE I MIGHT! BUT NOT WITHOUT A STRUGGLE!

CALLING UPON EVERY OUNCE OF HIS STRENGTH, KARL STRAINED TO HOLD OFF ULKA THE HUNTER'S RAZOR-EDGED SWORD

THE ENORMOUS WEIGHT OF HIS OPPONENT SENT KARL TOPPLING BACKWARDS. YET STILL HE KEPT HIS GRIP

AS THEY CRASHED TO THE GROUND, THE LOOSE EARTH AT THE TOP OF THE CLIFF SHUDDERED — **AND BEGAN TO CRACK AND CRUMBLE!**

THE CLIFF! IT IS FALLING AWAY!

NEXT INSTANT, BOTH MEN WERE HURTLING DOWN TOWARDS THE GLISTENING SEA FAR BELOW

AND AS THEY CRASHED INTO THE WATER, OTHER HUNTERS ROSE HUNGRILY FROM THE GREEN DEPTHS!

STRUCK SENSELESS BY THE IMPACT OF HIS LONG FALL, KARL WAS CARRIED BY THE WAVES TOWARDS THE SHORE— WHILST BEHIND HIM, ULKA THE HUNTER'S HUGE LIMBS THRESHED THE WATER DESPERATELY

ATTRACTED BY THE LURE OF LARGER PREY, THE KILLER SHARKS SWUNG TOWARDS THE STRUGGLING, SPLASHING MAN-GIANT

THEY ARE ALMOST UPON ME! I CANNOT SWIM FAST ENOUGH!

THEN, GAPING, TEETH-FILLED JAWS OPENED AND SNAPPED. THE WATERS TURNED CRIMSON **AS ULKA THE HUNTER FOUGHT FOR HIS LIFE AGAINST HUNTERS EVEN MORE TERRIBLE THAN HIMSELF**

WITH A DESPAIRING CRY, ULKA THE HUNTER SANK BENEATH THE FOAMING SEA — AND HIS FIERCE EXECUTIONERS CLOSED IN

NOW THE SHARKS TURNED TOWARDS THEIR SECOND PREY —KARL! BUT AT THAT MOMENT —

THERE IS KARL! BUT... IS HE DEAD?

LOOK! THE SHARKS! THEY ARE GOING TO ATTACK HIM!

I MUST SAVE HIM!

ERIK, THE YOUNG VIKING WHO HAD LEFT KARL BEHIND ON ULKA'S ISLAND, BEGAN A FRANTIC RACE TO REACH HIS CHIEFTAIN

QUICK! START ROWING!

A SHARK OPENED ITS JAWS TO SNAP AT KARL'S DRIFTING BODY. BUT, WITH KNIFE IN HAND, ERIK BEGAN TO BATTLE FOR HIS CHIEFTAIN'S LIFE

MORTALLY WOUNDED BY ERIK'S KNIFE SLASH, THE LEADING SHARK SLUNK INTO THE DEPTHS. AND AS THE OTHER SEA KILLERS RUSHED UPON THE TWO MEN —

WE MUST HELP KARL AND ERIK BACK INTO OUR SHIP!

KEEP SHOOTING AT THE SHARKS! DRIVE THEM OFF!

BY THE TIME THE RESCUERS REACHED THEIR COMRADES, ERIK HAD BEEN SAVAGELY WOUNDED BY THE FEARSOME RAZOR TEETH. BUT STILL HE CLUNG TO KARL'S STILL BODY

HURRY! HE... IS ...STILL ALIVE!

THE SHOAL OF SHARKS HAD BEEN KILLED, AND STRONG ARMS LIFTED KARL AND ERIK TO THE SAFETY OF THE LONGSHIP

YOU SAVED KARL'S LIFE, ERIK. THIS WILL ATONE FOR THE WAY YOU DESERTED HIM ON THE ISLAND

NO! IT IS NOT— ENOUGH!

WHEN KARL HAD REGAINED CONSCIOUSNESS, ERIK CONFESSED HIS SHAME.

I TOLD THE OTHERS THAT YOU AND OLEV WERE DEAD — BECAUSE I WANTED TO GET FAR AWAY FROM THAT TERRIBLE ISLAND! BUT I COULDN'T DO IT! I—I HAD TO TELL THEM THAT YOU MIGHT BE STILL ALIVE. I HAD TO MAKE THEM RETURN!

ERIK, I HOLD NO GRUDGE AGAINST YOU! SAY NO MORE ABOUT IT! WE WILL RETURN TO THE ISLAND TO FETCH OLEV — AND THEN WE MUST CONTINUE OUR VOYAGE!

OLEV WAS SAFELY PICKED UP — BUT AS THEY SAILED ON, ERIK BROODED OVER HIS ONE ACT OF COWARDICE.

WE STILL HAVE FAR TO GO! PERHAPS THE GODS WILL GRANT ME AN OPPORTUNITY TO REDEEM MYSELF

TWO LEAGUES AWAY, A CRY DRIFTED DOWN FROM A TALL TOWER — **BUILT OF SOLID GOLD!**

LOOK OUT —STRANGERS ARE COMING!

ERIK'S CHANCE WAS TO COME SOONER THAN HE EXPECTED. FOR, FIVE DAYS LATER, THE VOYAGERS WERE DAZZLED BY A STRANGE LIGHT THAT FLASHED ACROSS THE SEA

WHAT CAN IT BE? IT LOOKS LIKE SOMETHING AFIRE!

IT APPEARS TO BE AN ISLAND! IT IS YELLOW — AND GLOWING — LIKE THE SUN ITSELF!

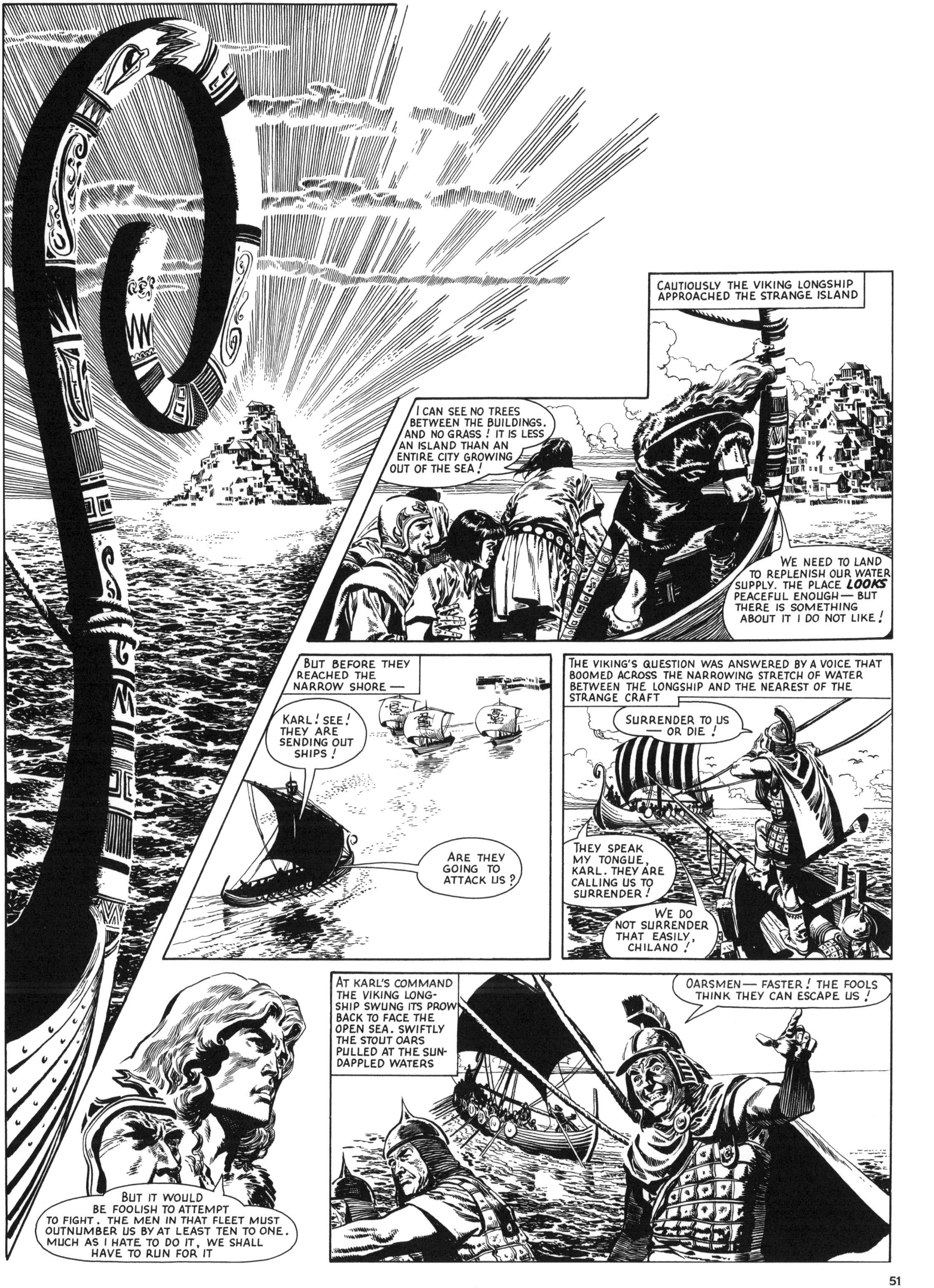

CAUTIOUSLY THE VIKING LONGSHIP APPROACHED THE STRANGE ISLAND
I CAN SEE NO TREES BETWEEN THE BUILDINGS. AND NO GRASS ! IT IS LESS AN ISLAND THAN AN ENTIRE CITY GROWING OUT OF THE SEA !
WE NEED TO LAND TO REPLENISH OUR WATER SUPPLY. THE PLACE LOOKS PEACEFUL ENOUGH — BUT THERE IS SOMETHING ABOUT IT I DO NOT LIKE !
BUT BEFORE THEY REACHED THE NARROW SHORE —
KARL ! SEE ! THEY ARE SENDING OUT SHIPS !
ARE THEY GOING TO ATTACK US ?
THE VIKING'S QUESTION WAS ANSWERED BY A VOICE THAT BOOMED ACROSS THE NARROWING STRETCH OF WATER BETWEEN THE LONGSHIP AND THE NEAREST OF THE STRANGE CRAFT
SURRENDER TO US — OR DIE !
THEY SPEAK MY TONGUE, KARL. THEY ARE CALLING US TO SURRENDER !
WE DO NOT SURRENDER THAT EASILY, CHILANO !
BUT IT WOULD BE FOOLISH TO ATTEMPT TO FIGHT. THE MEN IN THAT FLEET MUST OUTNUMBER US BY AT LEAST TEN TO ONE. MUCH AS I HATE TO DO IT, WE SHALL HAVE TO RUN FOR IT
AT KARL'S COMMAND THE VIKING LONG-SHIP SWUNG ITS PROW BACK TO FACE THE OPEN SEA. SWIFTLY THE STOUT OARS PULLED AT THE SUN-DAPPLED WATERS
OARSMEN — FASTER ! THE FOOLS THINK THEY CAN ESCAPE US !

BUT WITHIN MINUTES KARL SAW THAT FLIGHT WAS USELESS

IT IS NO GOOD! THEIR SHIPS ARE LIGHTER THAN OURS — BUILT FOR SPEED RATHER THAN OCEAN VOYAGING! THEY ARE GAINING ALL THE TIME!

THEN THE ENEMY ARCHERS RELEASED A CLOUD OF WHISTLING ARROWS THAT RAINED DOWN UPON THE VIKINGS

HEAVE TO! LEAVE THE OARS AND TAKE TO YOUR SWORDS! WE WILL FIGHT IT OUT!

BUT THE NORTHMEN WERE FAR OUTNUMBERED. NOT EVEN THEIR FLASHING BLADES AND FEROCIOUS SKILL COULD STEM THE TIDE THAT SURGED OVER THE SIDE OF THE LONGSHIP

WITH A GRINDING CRASH THE PURSUING CRAFT SWUNG ALONGSIDE. BUT THE VIKINGS WERE READY

AT THEM, MY WOLVES! THEIR SHIPS MAY BE FASTER... BUT THEY CANNOT MATCH VIKING STEEL AND VALOUR!

ABOVE THE DIN OF BATTLE CRIES AND THE CLASH OF STEEL AGAINST STEEL, KARL HEARD CHILANO'S PIERCING CRY FOR HELP

KARL! HELP ME!

THE BOY KING IS IN DANGER — AND I GAVE MY WORD TO PROTECT HIM!

SWORD SWINGING, KARL BOUNDED BACK ACROSS THE DECK

TOGETHER, KARL AND CHILANO BROKE DOWN THE ATTACK ON TIHUANA, THE BOY KING. BUT THEN A POWERFUL VOICE ROSE ABOVE THE SOUND OF BATTLE

STOP!

THE OTHER SHIPS HAVE REACHED US NOW!

ROWS OF ARCHERS HAD THEIR STEEL-TIPPED ARROWS LINED UPON THE VIKINGS

RESIST FURTHER, AND YOU WILL SURELY DIE! THROW DOWN YOUR ARMS!

THERE WAS NO NEED FOR CHILANO TO TRANSLATE THE ENEMY OFFICER'S WORDS. DROPPING HIS SWORD TO THE DECK, KARL SPOKE RELUCTANTLY TO HIS MEN

IT IS USELESS TO FIGHT ON. BUT IF WE ALLOW THEM TO TAKE US PRISONER, THERE IS ALWAYS THE CHANCE THAT THE GODS WILL FAVOUR US AGAIN

KARL IS RIGHT! WE CAN DO NO MORE — FOR NOW!

AND SO, WITH ITS CREW NOW BOUND PRISONERS, THE LONGSHIP WAS TOWED TO THE ISLAND CITY OF GOLD

THEY ARE FINE, STRAPPING FELLOWS NOW. BUT AFTER THREE MONTHS HERE THEY WON'T EVEN BE RECOGNISABLE!

TRUE INDEED! I SAW SOME OF THE SLAVES FROM THE INTERIOR WHO WERE BROUGHT OUT FOR EXECUTION BECAUSE THEY WERE NO LONGER OF ANY USE TO US. THEY WERE NOTHING MORE THAN CRAWLING SKELETONS, DRAINED OF EVERY OUNCE OF STRENGTH AND ENERGY. THESE WILL SOON BE THE SAME!

ARMED SENTRIES PULLED OPEN HUGE GATES, AND THE PRISONERS WERE THRUST INTO A CAVE-LIKE TUNNEL IN THE SIDE OF THE MOUNTAIN

WHAT ARE THEY SAYING, CHILANO? YOU UNDERSTAND THEIR LANGUAGE!

THEY ARE CALLING US "SLAVES OF THE INTERIOR" — AND THEY DECLARE THAT WE WILL SOON BE WALKING DEAD MEN!

THEN THE HUGE GATES THUDDED TO BEHIND THEM, LEAVING THEM BLINKING IN THE TORCH-LIGHT, **AND GASPING FOR BREATH IN AN OVEN-LIKE HEAT!**

MOVE ALONG, DOGS! HURRY, OR YOU'LL HAVE THE SKIN FLAYED FROM YOUR BACKS!

THIS HEAT! WHAT IS CAUSING IT?

NEVER HAVE I KNOWN ANY-THING LIKE IT!

FARTHER ALONG THE TUNNEL OTHER GUARDS WERE WAITING WITH ANVILS, HAMMERS — **AND MANACLES!**

WHAT ARE THEY GOING TO DO TO US?

I'D FAR RATHER BE KILLED NOW THAN HAVE TO ENDURE THIS HEAT MUCH LONGER!

WITH THEIR ANKLES CHAINED TOGETHER, THE PRISONERS WERE LED DEEPER INTO THE DARK DEPTHS OF THE MOUNTAIN. THEN THEY SAW AN ASTONISHING SIGHT

BY ODIN! IT IS LIKE A VAST MEADOW — IN THE CENTRE OF THE MOUN-TAIN! AND THE HEAT HERE IS WORSE THAN EVER!

WHIPS LASHED THE AIR ABOVE THE VIKINGS' BACKS, AND A DAY OF BACK-BREAKING TOIL BEGAN

I AM STRONG, KARL. BUT I FEAR I CANNOT STAND MUCH MORE OF THIS. THE HEAT IS SAPPING AWAY MY STRENGTH!

TRY TO HOLD OUT FOR A FEW HOURS LONGER, LIEG. THEY MUST LET US REST SOON!

AT LAST, ALMOST DROPPING WITH EXHAUSTION, THE PRISONERS WERE HERDED INTO A HUGE CELL

REST WELL, CARRION. IT WILL SOON BE YOUR TURN AGAIN TO WATER OUR CROPS!

HURRY OUT, YOU OTHERS! YOU HAVE BEEN FED AND RESTED ... NOW YOU MUST PAY FOR IT WITH MORE WORK IN THE FIELD!

AS THE NORTHMEN GATHERED ABOUT THE OPEN, BARRED WINDOW AND GULPED DOWN THE REVIVING COOL AIR, CHILANO QUESTIONED ANOTHER "SLAVE OF THE INTERIOR"

OLD MAN, TELL ME ABOUT THIS TERRIBLE PLACE

I WILL TELL YOU. BUT DO NOT THINK I AM OLD IN YEARS. IT IS WORKING HERE THAT HAS AGED ME— AFTER BUT TWO MONTHS!

THESE PEOPLE THAT INHABIT THIS CITY OF ATLANTIS ARE EVIL— BUT INGENIOUS. THEY HAVE SOLVED THE SECRET OF TURNING SEA WATER INTO DRINKING WATER. AND FOR THEIR MAIN FOOD THEY EAT THE FRUIT OF THE CROPS WE HAVE TO WATER! IT IS A PLANT THAT CAN THRIVE ONLY IN EXTREME HEAT— AND THE INTERIOR, AS YOU HAVE ALREADY DISCOVERED, HAS PLENTY OF HEAT

BUT WHY DO THEY NOT LIVE ON THE MAINLAND? WHY DO THEY STRUGGLE SO MUCH TO LIVE ON THIS GREENLESS ROCK?

TO THEM, ATLANTIS IS A HOLY CITY, AND THEY BELIEVE THAT THEY ARE THE FAVOURED CHILDREN OF THE SUN GOD. WHEN THEY NEED MEAT OR MORE SLAVES TO WATER THEIR CURSED CROPS, THEY RAID THE MAINLAND. ONLY THEN DO THEY LEAVE THIS ISLAND CITY OF THEIRS!

CHILANO TOLD KARL WHAT HE HAD LEARNT

KARL, CAN IT BE THAT WE ARE DOOMED? THIS OTHER MAN SAID THAT NO PRISONER HAS ESCAPED FROM THE INTERIOR

NEVERTHELESS, CHILANO, SOMEHOW WE SHALL TRY TO ESCAPE! AND IT WILL HAVE TO BE SOON, OR YOUR BOY-KING TIHUANA WILL SOON DIE. THOSE FIENDS MAKE HIM WORK JUST AS IF HE IS A FULL-GROWN MAN!

ALL TOO SOON THE GUARDS WERE BACK — SHOUTING AND SHOVING AT THE NEW BATCH OF PRISONERS

MOVE! HURRY! DAWDLING HERE WILL NOT LESSEN THE HOURS YOU HAVE TO WORK AT THE CROPS! MOVE, YOU DOGS!

A CRUEL WHIP SWUNG HIGH AS THE BOY KING TIHUANA STUMBLED. BUT KARL'S FIGHTING FURY WAS ALREADY AT BURSTING POINT

GET UP! YOU'RE OLD ENOUGH TO WORK LIKE THE OTHERS! TO YOUR FEET, YOU LITTLE CUR!

NO YOU DON'T! LEAVE HIM!

BEFORE THE STARTLED GUARD COULD TURN, KARL WAS UPON HIM— WRENCHING THE SPEAR FROM HIS HANDS

IF WE ARE TO DIE, THEN FAR BETTER WE DIE FIGHTING!

A QUICK, SAVAGE THRUST OF THE SPEAR, AND THE EVIL GUARD FELL WRITHING TO THE GROUND. BUT NOW THE VAST INTERIOR BOOMED TO THE ENRAGED, ECHOING SHOUTS OF OTHER GUARDS

HE HAS KILLED SIRRAGO!

SLAY THE DOG!

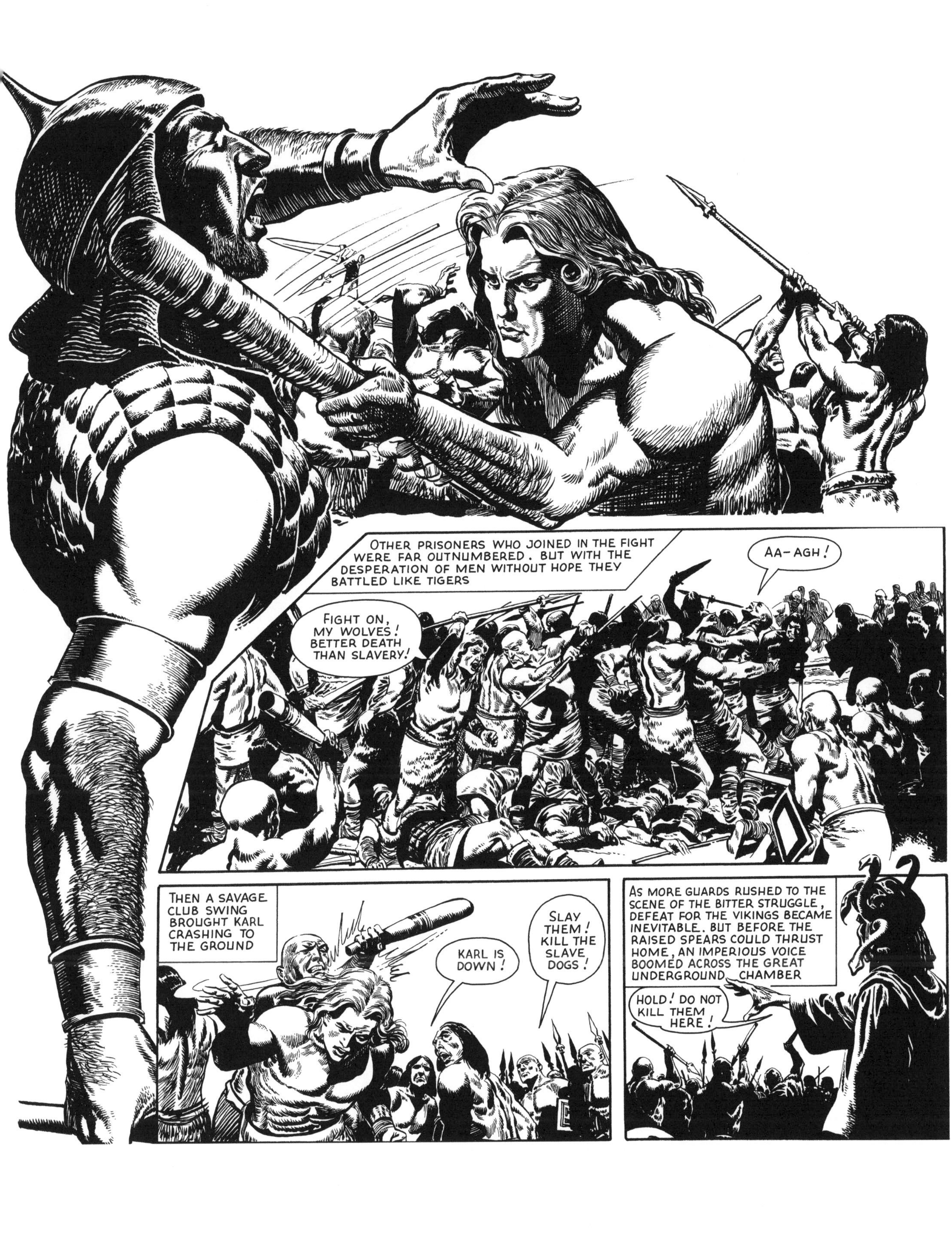

OTHER PRISONERS WHO JOINED IN THE FIGHT WERE FAR OUTNUMBERED. BUT WITH THE DESPERATION OF MEN WITHOUT HOPE THEY BATTLED LIKE TIGERS
AA-AGH!
FIGHT ON, MY WOLVES! BETTER DEATH THAN SLAVERY!
THEN A SAVAGE CLUB SWING BROUGHT KARL CRASHING TO THE GROUND
SLAY THEM! KILL THE SLAVE DOGS!
KARL IS DOWN!
AS MORE GUARDS RUSHED TO THE SCENE OF THE BITTER STRUGGLE, DEFEAT FOR THE VIKINGS BECAME INEVITABLE. BUT BEFORE THE RAISED SPEARS COULD THRUST HOME, AN IMPERIOUS VOICE BOOMED ACROSS THE GREAT UNDERGROUND CHAMBER
HOLD! DO NOT KILL THEM HERE!

COLD, MERCILESS CRUELTY STAMPED THE LEAN, HAUGHTY FEATURES OF THE NEWCOMER

THESE VIKING DOGS HAVE DARED TO SLAY THOSE WHO ARE THE FAVOURED CHILDREN OF THE SUN GOD. TO ATONE THEY MUST DIE *IN SACRIFICE BY FIRE!* DRAG THEM AWAY!

MENACED BY THE GUARDS' SPEARS, THE PRISONERS WERE LED UP A LONG, WINDING STAIRWAY CARVED OUT OF THE ROCK FACE

THEY CAME TO A THICK IRON DOOR WHICH THE GUARDS UNBARRED AND SWUNG OPEN

IN HERE, DOGS!

THAT STENCH — LIKE SOMETHING THAT HAS BEEN SCORCHED BY FIRE! WE WILL SUFFOCATE IN THERE!

THE DOOR CLANGED SHUT BEHIND THEM, LEAVING THE VIKING GROPING IN INKY DARKNESS — AND CHOKING IN THE SULPHUROUS FUMES

I'M ALL RIGHT, NOW. BUT WHAT FURTHER DEVILRY HAVE THEY IN STORE FOR US?

LOOK, KARL. THESE WALLS ARE BLACKENED. IT — IT'S AS IF WE WERE IN AN *OVEN!*

GRADUALLY THEIR EYES BECAME USED TO THE GLOOM. AND IT WAS THEN THAT A VIKING GAVE A CRY OF HORROR

BY ODIN! WHAT IS IT? NEVER HAVE I SEEN SUCH A CRUEL FACE!

IT — IT MUST REPRESENT THEIR SUN GOD!

KARL, HEAR THAT NOISE? IT IS LIKE A GREAT GROWL OF ANGER!

AS THE FEARSOME GROWLING NOISE INCREASED IN VOLUME, THE WALLS AND FLOOR OF THE ROCK CAVE BEGAN TO TREMBLE. THE STENCH OF SULPHUR GREW STRONGER

KARL! CHILANO! WHAT IS IT? I AM FRIGHTENED!

I WISH I KNEW, TIHUANA!

THAT NOISE. I HAVE HEARD IT BEFORE—BUT NOT SO CLOSE AS THIS!

SUDDENLY, FROM THE HIDEOUS, GAPING MOUTH OF THE IDOL, A TONGUE OF FLAME FLASHED ACROSS THE CAVE

AA-AGH! MY ARM....!

DOWN! FLATTEN YOURSELVES TO THE FLOOR!

AGAIN CAME THAT THUNDEROUS GROWL, AND AGAIN THE CAVE SHOOK AS ANOTHER TONGUE OF FLAME SPAT FROM THE IDOL'S MOUTH...

IT IS TRUE WHAT THEY SAID! THEIR GOD IS ANGRY! HE WILL EAT US WITH FIRE!

THE TONGUE OF FLAME SUBSIDED. THEN CHILANO CLUTCHED KARL'S ARM, HIS EYES BULGING WITH TERROR

IT IS NO GOD, KARL—BUT A VOLCANO.. A MOUNTAIN THAT THROWS OUT FIRE! I HAVE SEEN THEM IN MY OWN COUNTRY!

KARL NODDED, HIS EYES GRIMLY FIXED UPON THE SMOKING, CARVED MOUTH

YOU ARE RIGHT, CHILANO. I, TOO, HAVE SEEN THEM! EVERY TIME THE FLAME SHOOTS UP THE CRATER, SOME OF IT SPITS THROUGH THAT HOLE!

BUT THE NOISE, KARL! AND THE WAY THIS WHOLE MOUNTAIN IS SHAKING! SOON IT WILL SURELY SPLIT TO PIECES!

ALMOST AS SOON AS THE WORDS HAD LEFT CHILANO'S LIPS, THERE CAME ANOTHER, DEEPER THUNDEROUS NOISE — AND THE ROOF OF THE ROCK CAVE BEGAN TO CRACK AND CRUMBLE

SEE! THE ROOF! IT IS COLLAPSING! WE WILL BE BURIED ALIVE!

Above the blood-chilling roar of the now-active volcano came the crash of rocks toppling from the bulging, collapsing roof

WE'LL BE CRUSHED —BURIED ALIVE!

Then Karl's eyes blazed with sudden hope as, torn from its hinges, the great iron door of their prison sagged open

COME ON! PERHAPS WE CAN STILL ESCAPE DEATH! I WILL CARRY THE BOY KING TIHUANA— HE IS STILL WEAK FROM BEING FORCED TO SLAVE IN THE FIELDS!

With the sound of rocks crashing behind them, the vikings ran down the long, winding steps

IF ONLY WE COULD FREE OURSELVES FROM THESE CURSED CHAINS WE COULD RUN MORE EASILY

THERE IS NO TIME TO STOP AND DO THAT NOW!

HAVE COURAGE, TIHUANA. WE WILL SOON BE OUTSIDE AGAIN!

As they emerged from the dark mountain into the daylight, they saw before them a nightmare of terror and destruction. The whole city of Atlantis was disintegrating under the terrible wrath of the volcano

THEY BEGAN TO RUN AWKWARDLY THROUGH THE STREETS, STUMBLING OVER THE CHAINS THAT STILL LINKED THEIR ANKLES

MAKE FOR THE HARBOUR! PERHAPS WE CAN GET TO OUR LONGSHIP!

A WALL OF A LOW BUILDING COLLAPSED, AND THROUGH THE PALL OF DUST KARL SAW THE GLEAM OF STEEL

HOLD, MY WOLVES! THAT BUILDING MUST BE AN ARMOURY! LET US TAKE SWORDS AND SPEARS BEFORE WE CONTINUE!

YES, KARL THESE ATLANTIS DEVILS WILL NOT SURRENDER THE BOATS WITHOUT BATTLE!

LOOK! THE SLAVES HAVE ESCAPED! THEY ARE ATTACKING!

BUT, KARL, THE PEOPLE OF THIS CURSED CITY WILL ALSO TRY TO CAST OFF IN THE BOATS!

STOP THEM! KILL THEM, OR WE SHALL LOSE THIS SHIP!

FORCED BY THEIR CHAINS TO BUNCH TOGETHER, THE VIKINGS SMASHED INTO THEIR ENEMIES WITH THE FORCE OF A BATTERING-RAM

AT THE HARBOUR, TERRIFIED MEN WERE SCRAMBLING INTO THE VIKINGS LONGSHIP — WHEN ONE OF THEM LOOKED BACK AND SAW GRIM-FACED NORTHMEN RUSHING UPON THEM

AND IN THE MIDST OF THEM, CHILANO CARRIED HIS BOY KING AND PROTECTED THE LAD'S BODY WITH A SHIELD

AS THEY CUT AND HEWED THEIR WAY TO THE HARBOUR EDGE, THE VIKINGS REMEMBERED THE CRUELTIES THAT HAD BEEN INFLICTED UPON THEM ... AND AGAINST THEIR GRIM, FIGHTING FURY THE SOLDIERS OF ATLANTIS WERE HELPLESS

THIS IS YOUR REWARD FOR CHAINING UP VIKINGS AS IF THEY WERE DOGS!

AAGH!

ONCE AGAIN THE LONGSHIP WAS IN THE HANDS OF ITS TRUE MASTERS

SOME OF YOU MAN THE OARS! LET US LEAVE THIS EVIL PLACE!

KARL FROWNED AT THE ATLANTIS BOATS RIDING AT ANCHOR—AND AT THE CREWS SWIMMING TOWARDS THEM. THEN —

WAIT! WE HAVE FORGOTTEN THOSE POOR WRETCHES OF SLAVES STILL LEFT BEHIND IN THE INTERIOR. WE CANNOT LEAVE WITHOUT TRYING TO SAVE THEM, TOO!

BUT IT IS TOO LATE, KARL! IF WE LEAVE THIS SHIP NOW, THOSE DOGS WILL SEIZE HER AGAIN!

KARL NODDED GRIMLY, AND SPOKE TO A HUGE NORTHMAN WHO GRIPPED A BATTLE-AXE IN HIS MUSCULAR HANDS

I KNOW, AND THEREFORE WILL TRY TO FREE THEM. THE REST OF YOU WILL DEFEND THE SHIP. NOW, SIGUND, STRIKE THIS CHAIN WITH YOUR AXE! HURRY, OR THOSE SLAVES INSIDE THE MOUNTAIN WILL SURELY DIE!

KARL, LET ME GO WITH YOU!

KARL TURNED TO ERIK, WHO, WEEKS BEFORE, HAD LOST HIS COURAGE AND ALMOST CAUSED HIS YOUNG CHIEFTAIN'S DEATH

PLEASE, KARL! YOU KNOW HOW DEARLY I WISH TO WIPE OUT THE SHAME I BROUGHT UPON MYSELF! TAKE ME WITH YOU!

I HAVE TOLD YOU THAT NOT ONE OF US BLAMES YOU FOR YOUR MOMENT OF WEAKNESS. BUT IF YOUR HEART SAYS YOU MUST — THEN COME WITH ME, ERIK!

ONCE SIGUND'S AXE HAD CLEAVED THEM FREE OF THEIR CHAINS, KARL AND ERIK DIVED FROM THE LONGSHIP

WHAT CHANCE WILL TWO BRAVE MEN STAND AGAINST SO MANY?

LITTLE, I FEAR. BUT IT IS OUR CHIEFTAIN'S ORDER THAT WE STAY HERE—AND WE MUST OBEY!

THE WHOLE ISLAND SHOOK WITH THE VIBRATION OF THE VOLCANO. THE CITIZENS OF ATLANTIS WERE TOO TERRIFIED BY THE CRASHING BUILDINGS TO NOTICE THE TWO VIKINGS AMONGST THEM

FASTER, ERIK, OR WE MAY BE TOO LATE TO PREVENT THOSE POOR FOLK FROM BEING BURIED ALIVE IN THE MOUNTAIN!

AT LAST THEY REACHED THE GREAT DOOR GUARDING THE ENTRANCE TO THE UNDERGROUND SLAVE FIELDS

IT—IT WON'T BUDGE! THE WHOLE MOUNTAIN'S SHIFTING ... IT'S JAMMED THE DOOR SOLID!

WE'VE GOT TO GET IT OPEN SOMEHOW! ERIK—THAT PIECE OF TIMBER!

SPURRED ON BY THE EVER-INCREASING THUNDER FROM THE VOLCANIC MOUNTAIN, THE TWO VIKINGS THRUST AGAIN AND AGAIN AT THE GREAT DOOR. THEN—

IT'S GIVING WAY! ANOTHER BLOW WILL DO IT!

THE MOUNTAIN'S SHAKING ITSELF TO PIECES. ANY MOMENT IT WILL COLLAPSE!

WITH AN ECHOING CRASH, THE SPLINTERED DOOR FLEW OPEN— AND A SEA OF HOLLOW, FRIGHTENED FACES SPRANG OUT FROM THE GLOOM

HURRY!

THE BLESSED DAYLIGHT! IF WE MUST DIE, FAR BETTER THAT IT BE OUT THERE THAN BURIED ALIVE IN THE DARKNESS AND THE HEAT!

THE SLAVES OF THE INTERIOR BEGAN TO POUR THROUGH THE SPLINTERED DOORWAY

STEADY! MOVE AS FAST AS YOU CAN — BUT DON'T PANIC!

KARL! THE DOORWAY! IT'S BEGINNING TO COLLAPSE!

AFTER ONE SWIFT GLANCE, KARL SNATCHED UP THE HEAVY PIECE OF TIMBER THEY HAD USED TO BATTER DOWN THE DOOR

I'LL TRY — TO HOLD UP — THIS PART OF THE ROOF. BUT — HURRY! HURRY!

THE BLOOD POUNDED IN KARL'S HEAD. HIS MUSCLES BULGED AND RIPPLED WITH STRAIN AS PART OF THE MOUNTAIN SHIFTED AND SAGGED ON TO THE DOORWAY

I—I CAN'T HOLD IT—ANY LONGER!

JUST A MOMENT LONGER, KARL! THEY ARE NEARLY ALL THROUGH NOW!

THE LAST OF THE SLAVES PASSED INTO THE OPEN — AND WITH A TREMBLING SIGH OF RELIEF, KARL RELEASED HIS HOLD ON THE CRACKING TIMBER AND LEAPT CLEAR

TO THE SHIPS! RUN!

THE FREED SLAVES BEGAN TO FILE ON BOARD, WHILE KARL AND ERIK HELD AT BAY THE EVIL CITIZENS OF ATLANTIS

WHY SHOULD YOU BE SHOWN MERCY — YOU WHO SHOWED NO MERCY TO SO MANY OTHERS?

YOU BUILT THIS EVIL ISLAND CITY! NOW DIE IN IT!

THE VIKINGS SAILED THEIR LADEN LONGSHIP TO WHERE THE ATLANTIS FLEET WAS ANCHORED. THEN A SLAVE SPOKE TO KARL

WE OWE YOU OUR FREEDOM — OUR LIVES! WE WILL NEVER FORGET YOU, NORTHMAN!

FORGET THIS EVIL ISLAND, MY FRIEND. SAIL TO THE MAINLAND IN THESE SHIPS AND REJOIN YOUR FAMILIES!

AS THE SHIPS SEPARATED AND PUT OUT TO SEA, A GREAT PILLAR OF FLAME LEAPT FROM THE TOP OF THE MOUNTAIN

AT THE SAME TIME, SMOKING, WHITE-HOT LAVA BEGAN TO BUBBLE OVER THE EDGE OF THE CRATER

FROM ACROSS THE SEA, THE VIKINGS HEARD THE HIDEOUS GURGLING OF THE STREAMS OF LAVA POURING OVER THE CITY

HURRY, MY WOLVES! PULL AT THOSE OARS! HEAR THAT BUBBLING BENEATH THE WATERS? EVEN NOW, THE GODS HAVE NOT WROUGHT THEIR FULL VENGEANCE UPON THE ISLAND!

THERE CAME A GREAT ROAR, EVEN MORE THUNDEROUS THAN BEFORE. FOR MILES THE SEA WAS CHURNED INTO A HEAVING FROTH AND BEGAN TO ENGULF THE ISLAND CITY

IT IS SINKING BENEATH THE SEA! THE WHOLE ISLAND IS DISAPPEARING!

THE VOLCANO HAS BLOWN AWAY ITS FOUNDATIONS! I HAVE HEARD MEN SPEAK OF SUCH THINGS ...BUT I NEVER BELIEVED IT COULD HAPPEN!

WITHIN SECONDS THE SEA WAS EMPTY — SAVE FOR THE LONGSHIP, THE DISTANT VESSELS CARRYING THE SLAVES TO FREEDOM, AND A GREAT PALL OF STEAM AND SULPHUROUS SMOKE HOVERING ABOVE WATERS WHERE THERE HAD ONCE BEEN ATLANTIS!

IT IS GONE! A CITY BUILT OF GOLD! FOR CENTURIES MEN WILL TALK OF ATLANTIS—THE CITY CLAIMED BY THE SEA!

A FRESH WIND CARRIED THE VIKINGS SPEEDILY SOUTHWARDS —TOWARDS AN ADVENTURE THAT WAS TO PROVE EVEN MORE PERILOUS THAN THE ONE THEY HAD SO NARROWLY SURVIVED. THEN SUDDENLY A LOOK-OUT GAVE AN ALARMED SHOUT

KARL! I CAN SEE SHIPS IN THE DISTANCE — LOTS OF THEM! AND THEY'RE HEADING STRAIGHT FOR US!

Across waters that were stained an unusual muddy colour, the Vikings heard guttural cries of alarm. And the little craft began to scuttle away

THEY'RE RUNNING FROM US! AND LOOK HOW SWIFTLY THEY MOVE!

WE MUST TRY TO STOP THEM! THEY CAN TELL US WHERE WE ARE. — FOR SINCE OUR CHART WAS WASHED AWAY WE DO NOT EVEN KNOW FOR SURE THAT WE ARE SAILING IN THE RIGHT DIRECTION!

The longship gave chase — but even though the Vikings pulled their hardest at the oars, the strange boats continued to draw farther away **TOWARDS A MISTY HAZE THAT OBSCURED THE HORIZON**

IF WE CAN'T CATCH THEM, THEN WE MUST *FOLLOW* THEM! THEY MUST BE MAKING FOR *SOME-WHERE!*

BUT SEE HOW THE SEA WATER GROWS THICKER. IT'S LIKE MUD! AND THAT MIST AHEAD OF US ... WHAT CAN IT BE?

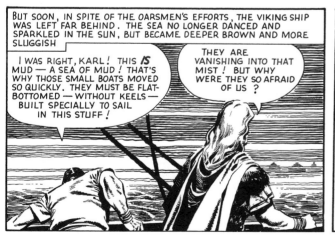

But soon, in spite of the oarsmen's efforts, the Viking ship was left far behind. The sea no longer danced and sparkled in the sun, but became deeper brown and more sluggish

I WAS RIGHT, KARL! THIS *IS* MUD — A SEA OF MUD! THAT'S WHY THOSE SMALL BOATS MOVED SO QUICKLY. THEY MUST BE FLAT-BOTTOMED — WITHOUT KEELS — BUILT SPECIALLY TO SAIL IN THIS STUFF!

THEY ARE VANISHING INTO THAT MIST! BUT WHY WERE THEY SO AFRAID OF US?

The longship gradually came to a stop. No longer could the oarsmen pull against the sticky, reeking mud. Karl called Chilano to his side

THERE *MUST* BE A VILLAGE OUT THERE, CHILANO. THOSE MEN MUST LIVE *SOME-WHERE!* WHAT DO YOU MAKE OF IT?

I AM COMPLETELY AT A LOSS, KARL. I HAVE NEVER HEARD OF LAND IN THIS SEA. I HAVE NEVER KNOWN MUD LIKE THIS IN THE MIDDLE OF AN OCEAN — AND I HAVE NEVER SEEN SUCH STRANGE CRAFT AS THEY USED!

KARL LOOKED AGAIN AT THE GREAT BANK OF MIST — THEN CAME TO A DECISION

IF WE CANNOT TAKE OUR LONGSHIP ANY FARTHER INTO THIS MUD, THEN WE MUST MAKE A RAFT! I WILL SEE WHAT LIES BEYOND THAT MIST — AND TRY TO FIND THOSE MEN WE SAW!

AT KARL'S COMMAND, A RAFT WAS MADE OF OARS LASHED TOGETHER. THEN THE YOUNG VIKING CHIEF AND THREE OTHERS POLED THEIR WAY ACROSS THE SEA OF MUD

I HAVE TO TAKE YOU WITH ME, CHILANO, IN CASE THE PEOPLE WE SEEK SPEAK YOUR LANGUAGE.

I DOUBT THAT THEY WILL, KARL. YOU SAW THEM. THEY SEEMED SHAGGY AND HAIRY — LIKE BEASTS!

THE MUD GREW THICKER AS THEY MOVED CLOSER TO THE MIST... AND THE STENCH GREW WORSE

PHEW! THIS SMELL! IT NEARLY CHOKES ME!

KEEP PULLING AT THOSE OARS. WE ARE INTO THE MIST NOW!

KARL! LOOK!

AHEAD OF THEM, THE DARK SHAPE OF LAND LOOMED VAGUELY THROUGH THE EVIL-SMELLING VAPOUR

LAND! KARL, YOU WERE RIGHT!

TO YOUR OARS AGAIN! WE HAVE FOUND THE ISLAND! NOW WE MUST FIND THE PEOPLE WHO LIVE ON IT!

IT TOOK ANOTHER HOUR OF ROWING AND THRUSTING IN THE STICKY, SUCKING SEA. THEN THEY WERE CLOSE TO THE SHORE!

THERE'S THE VILLAGE! IT APPEARS TO BE A FITTER PLACE FOR CATTLE THAN MEN!

WE SHALL SEE! WE'RE GOING ASHORE!

THESE FISH THAT ARE HANGING UP TO DRY — THEY SMELL WORSE THAN THE MUD OUT THERE! WHAT MANNER OF PEOPLE **ARE** THESE?

AND **WHERE** ARE THEY? THERE'S NOT A SOUND — NOT A SIGN OF LIFE!

BUT, UNSEEN BY KARL —

A KEEN-EYED VIKING CAUGHT THE SUDDEN MOVEMENT IN THE SHADOWS OF ONE OF THE MUD HUTS. DESPERATELY HE YELLED A WARNING — AND PUSHED HIS YOUNG CHIEF ASIDE

KARL! LOOK OUT!

OVER THERE! THEY ARE COMING!

FROM THE FAR END OF THE VILLAGE CAME YELPING CRIES THAT SEEMED SCARCELY HUMAN. AND THEN THE VIKINGS SAW THE SQUAT, WILD-HAIRED ATTACKERS

HAVE YOUR SWORDS IN READINESS, MY WOLVES! WE WISH THESE PEOPLE NO HARM — BUT IT SEEMS THAT WE MUST DEFEND OUR LIVES AGAINST THEM!

FROM BEHIND THE VIKINGS CAME THE PAD OF OTHER RUNNING FEET

WE ARE TRAPPED!

WITH LITTLE HOPE IN THEIR HEARTS, THE VOYAGERS GRIPPED THEIR SWORDS — AND WAITED FOR DEATH!

THERE ARE TOO MANY! ALL WE CAN DO IS SELL OUR LIVES AS DEARLY AS WE CAN!

As the wild men closed in, Karl and his Vikings struck out at the menacing spears and clubs

IF ONLY THEY WOULD REALISE WE MEAN THEM NO HARM!

But even though they fought back with skill and unflinching courage, the Vikings knew that the odds against them were too great!

Death seemed certain. Then, suddenly, the leader of the villagers shouted a guttural command and the wild men drew back

WHY HAS HE CALLED OFF THE FIGHT? WE STAND LITTLE CHANCE AGAINST SUCH NUMBERS. THEY MUST KNOW THAT!

I CAN UNDERSTAND THE LANGUAGE THEY SPEAK! IT IS LIKE MY OWN—YET DIFFERENT IN A HARSH, GRUNTING MANNER!

Eagerly Chilano strained his ears to catch the words of the villagers' leader

HE IS SAYING THAT WE ARE OBVIOUSLY MEN WHO ARE SKILLED AT FIGHTING. HE IS GOING TO BARGAIN WITH US—OUR LIVES IN EXCHANGE FOR HELPING HIS PEOPLE TO DEFEAT THE FORESTMEN!

THE FORESTMEN! I WONDER WHO THEY ARE?

When Chilano called to the chief of the village that he understood his tongue, a strange story was unfolded

ON THIS LAND THERE ARE TWO KINDS OF PEOPLE. WE OF THE FISH TRIBE DWELL IN VILLAGES NEAR THE EDGE OF THE MUD SEA, AND ARE PEACEFUL MEN WHO LIVE BY THE HARVESTS WE GAIN FROM THE LAND AND THE SEA. BUT THE OTHER PEOPLE— THE FORESTMEN—THEY ARE SAVAGES WHO REJOICE IN KILLING. THEY EXIST ON MEAT OR WHAT THEY CAN STEAL FROM US!

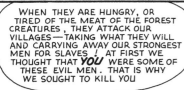

WHEN THEY ARE HUNGRY, OR TIRED OF THE MEAT OF THE FOREST CREATURES, THEY ATTACK OUR VILLAGES—TAKING WHAT THEY WILL AND CARRYING AWAY OUR STRONGEST MEN FOR SLAVES! AT FIRST WE THOUGHT THAT *YOU* WERE SOME OF THESE EVIL MEN. THAT IS WHY WE SOUGHT TO KILL YOU

KARL THOUGHT DEEPLY. THEN—

VERY WELL, WE WILL HELP THEM, CHILANO. THEY WILL GIVE US THE PROVISIONS WE NEED FOR OUR JOURNEY—AND *WE* WILL SEE WHAT WE CAN DO TO PUT A STOP TO THESE RAIDS!

BECKONING HIS MEN TO FOLLOW HIM, KARL STRODE TO THE HUGE STOCKADE THAT GUARDED THE VILLAGE FROM THE DANGERS OF THE DARK FOREST BEYOND

TELL THE CHIEFTAIN THAT IT IS NECESSARY FOR US TO BE ABLE TO JUDGE THE MEN WE ARE TO FIGHT AGAINST. WE MUST GO INTO THE FOREST TO DISCOVER MORE ABOUT THEM—AND TO DO THIS, ONE OF HIS PEOPLE MUST GO WITH US AS GUIDE!

BUT KARL'S REQUEST PRODUCED ONLY A CRY OF HORROR AND A TERRIFIED REFUSAL

NO! NO! NONE OF US HAS EVER GONE INTO THE FOREST, UNLESS DRAGGED THERE BY THE EVIL ONES! IT IS A TERRIBLE PLACE, FULL OF DEMONS AND HIDEOUS MONSTERS! DON'T GO IN THERE ...I BESEECH YOU!

IT IS NO USE, KARL! THEY ARE TOO FRIGHTENED!

THEN WE MUST GO ALONE!

MINUTES LATER, THE VOYAGERS STOOD ON THE OUTER SIDE OF THE GREAT STOCKADE

WITH NO ONE TO GUIDE US, WE MUST MAKE MARKS ON TREES SO THAT WE CAN FIND OUR WAY BACK

TRUE, KARL FOR NEVER HAVE I SEEN A FOREST SO THICK AND DARK. THIS WILL INDEED BE AN EASY PLACE TO LOSE OUR-SELVES IN!

THEY HEADED FOR THE TANGLED GROWTH, WITH THE SHOUTS OF THE VILLAGERS GROWING FAINTER

DON'T GO INTO THERE! IT IS DEATH! YOU DO NOT KNOW THE DANGERS THAT AWAIT YOU!

WHAT CHANCE WILL YOU STAND AGAINST THE MEN OF THE FOREST—LET ALONE AGAINST THE FEARSOME ANIMALS THAT DWELL THERE?

MAKING SURE THAT THEY LEFT A CLEARLY-MARKED TRAIL BEHIND THEM, KARL AND HIS MEN STRUGGLED DEEPER INTO THE FOREST—THROUGH LUSH, MATTED FOLIAGE AND ACROSS TREACHEROUS SWAMPS

THIS IS A BAD PLACE, AND IT GETS WORSE ALL THE TIME. PERHAPS THE VILLAGERS WERE RIGHT. PERHAPS WE SHOULD NEVER HAVE VENTURED BEYOND THEIR STOCKADE

WE *MUST* GO ON! BY ALL ACCOUNTS THE FORESTMEN MUST FEEL VERY SECURE AND SAFE IN HERE. THEIR VILLAGES ARE PROBABLY UNGUARDED!

ALL AT ONCE THERE CAME THE SOUND OF A SINISTER, SLITHERING NOISE ... AND THE SWISH AND CRACK OF VIOLENTLY-DISTURBED UNDERGROWTH

WHAT IS IT, KARL?

I HAVE HEARD NOTHING LIKE THAT BEFORE. BUT WHATEVER IT IS, IT MUST NOT SEE OR HEAR US! *TAKE COVER, AND KEEP STILL AND QUIET!*

BUT AS THE NOISE GREW LOUDER AND LOUDER, ONE OF THE VIKINGS COULD NOT RESIST RAISING HIS HEAD. THEN A SCREAM OF TERROR BURST FROM HIS TREMBLING LIPS

NO! NO! AA—AAGH!

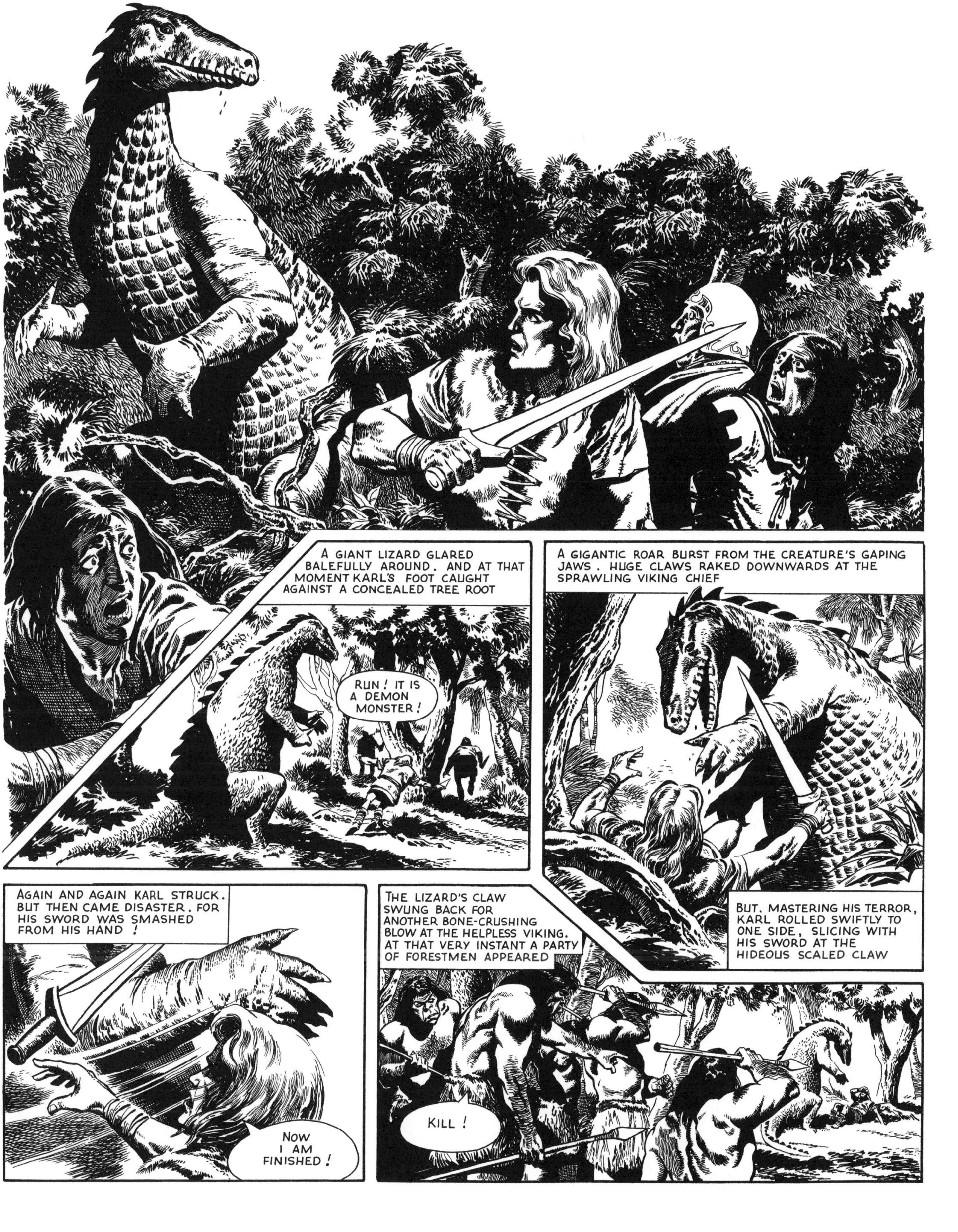

A GIANT LIZARD GLARED BALEFULLY AROUND. AND AT THAT MOMENT KARL'S FOOT CAUGHT AGAINST A CONCEALED TREE ROOT
RUN! IT IS A DEMON MONSTER!
A GIGANTIC ROAR BURST FROM THE CREATURE'S GAPING JAWS. HUGE CLAWS RAKED DOWNWARDS AT THE SPRAWLING VIKING CHIEF
BUT, MASTERING HIS TERROR, KARL ROLLED SWIFTLY TO ONE SIDE, SLICING WITH HIS SWORD AT THE HIDEOUS SCALED CLAW
AGAIN AND AGAIN KARL STRUCK. BUT THEN CAME DISASTER. FOR HIS SWORD WAS SMASHED FROM HIS HAND!
NOW I AM FINISHED!
THE LIZARD'S CLAW SWUNG BACK FOR ANOTHER BONE-CRUSHING BLOW AT THE HELPLESS VIKING. AT THAT VERY INSTANT A PARTY OF FORESTMEN APPEARED
KILL!

THE NIGHTMARE CREATURE'S ROARS CHANGED TO A SCREAM OF RAGE AND PAIN AS THE CRUDE SPEARS THUDDED INTO ITS SCALY HIDE.

THEN ROCKS BEGAN TO SMASH AGAINST ITS BODY, AND THE LIZARD DARTED FOR THE SAFETY OF THE FOREST DARKNESS

THEY MUST BE THE FORESTMEN! YET BY THEIR APPEARANCE THEY ARE MORE APE THAN HUMAN!

GABBLING IN THEIR STRANGE, GROWLING TONGUE, THE FORESTMEN ADVANCED UPON THE LONE VIKING

IT'S NO USE RUNNING, FOR THESE MEN-CREATURES MUST KNOW THIS FOREST LIKE THE BACKS OF THEIR HANDS! BUT THE LONGER I CAN FIGHT THEM OFF, THE LESS LIKELY THEY ARE TO TRACK DOWN MY FRIENDS!

THE MENACING HALF-CIRCLE OF FOREST-MEN STOPPED A FEW FEET AWAY FROM THE YOUNG NORTHMAN. THEN ONE OF THEM SNIFFED LIKE AN ANIMAL AND GAVE A GROWL OF DISGUST

UGH! HE CARRIES WITH HIM THE STENCH OF THE FISH-PEOPLE!

THAT IS TRUE! HE IS NOT ONE OF THEM — BUT HE MUST COME FROM THEIR VILLAGE!

IF ONLY I COULD UNDERSTAND WHAT THEY ARE SAYING

A RED FLUSH OF ANGER MOUNTED THE LEADER'S HAIRY, HEAVY FACE. THEN —

HE DARES TO ENTER THE FOREST-LAND? SEIZE HIM!

DESPERATELY KARL FOUGHT BACK. BUT THE COMBINED WEIGHT OF THE FORESTMEN WAS TOO MUCH. HE SLUMPED TO THE GROUND AS A STONE CRACKED AGAINST HIS SKULL

NO! DO NOT CLUB HIM! THERE IS ANOTHER DEATH FOR HIM—DEATH BY KA-TAK AND HIS HUNTERS!

WHEN KARL RECOVERED CONSCIOUSNESS HE WAS IN THE TREE-VILLAGE OF THE FORESTMEN

FETCH ONE OF THE FISH-PEOPLE SLAVES! HE SHALL SEE WHAT HAPPENS TO THIS BEING WHO DARED TO ENTER OUR DOMAIN!

A BLACK NIGHT FELL, AND KARL WAS TIED TO A STAKE ON THE TOP OF A MOUND OF EARTH

SOON YOU SHALL SEE THE ANGER OF KA-TAK! THEN YOU WILL BE RETURNED TO YOUR REEKING VILLAGE — SO THAT YOU CAN WARN ALL OTHERS OF THE FATE THAT AWAITS THEM ON ENTERING OUR FOREST!

KARL FELT HIS BLOOD RUN COLD AS THE FOREST PEOPLE LIFTED THEIR HEADS TO THE NIGHT SKY AND YAPPED AND BAYED LIKE STARVING WOLVES

KA-TAK, GREATEST OF ALL HUNTERS! HEAR THE CALL OF YOUR CHILDREN! COME FROM THE FOREST, KA-TAK!

FROM DEEP IN THE FOREST CAME AN ANSWERING HOWL — A TERRIFYING SOUND THAT TOLD KARL WHAT HIS FATE WAS TO BE!

I—I'M TO BE EATEN ALIVE!

AWAY, SLAVE! YOU WILL NOT WISH TO BE HERE WHEN KA-TAK AND HIS HUNTERS ARRIVE!

As a shaft of moonlight pierced the darkness of the forest, Karl saw some huge, hideous, wolf-like creatures racing towards him

KA-TAK AND HIS HUNTERS ARE COMING!

WOLVES! ... NO, THEY'RE CREATURES EVEN WORSE THAN WOLVES!

Frantically the young Viking jerked and pulled at the hide thongs that held him to the sacrificial stake

IT'S NO USE ... I ... CAN'T ... GET FREE!

At that instant, a razor-edged knife flashed through the air. It had been thrown by Karl's friend, Chilano!

QUICK! COME THIS WAY!

Reaching out with his bound hands, the young Viking chief sprang towards a hanging creeper

He swung dizzily above the heads of the racing wolves

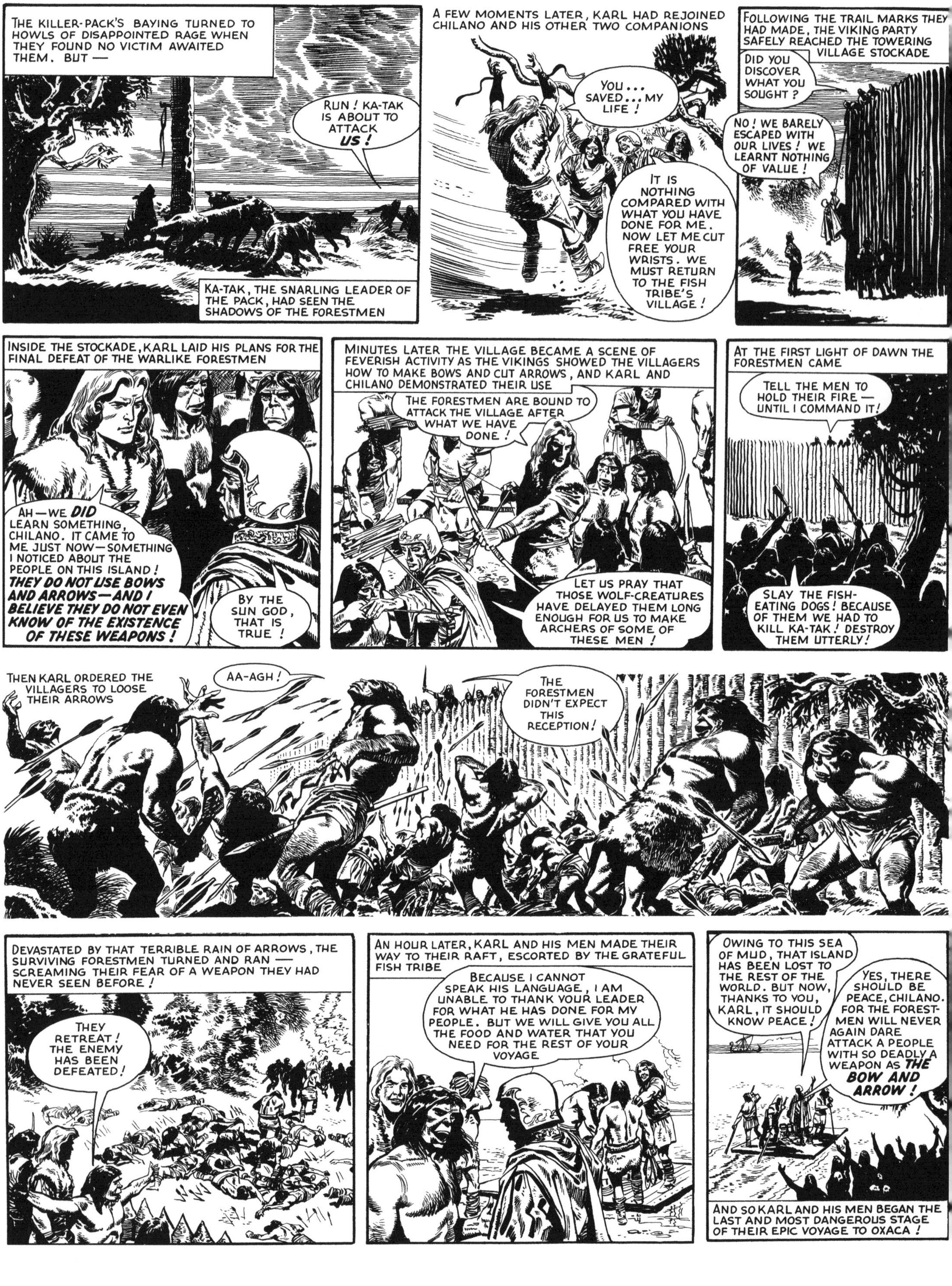

THE KILLER-PACK'S BAYING TURNED TO HOWLS OF DISAPPOINTED RAGE WHEN THEY FOUND NO VICTIM AWAITED THEM. BUT —
RUN! KA-TAK IS ABOUT TO ATTACK US!
KA-TAK, THE SNARLING LEADER OF THE PACK, HAD SEEN THE SHADOWS OF THE FORESTMEN
A FEW MOMENTS LATER, KARL HAD REJOINED CHILANO AND HIS OTHER TWO COMPANIONS
YOU... SAVED... MY LIFE!
IT IS NOTHING COMPARED WITH WHAT YOU HAVE DONE FOR ME. NOW LET ME CUT FREE YOUR WRISTS. WE MUST RETURN TO THE FISH TRIBE'S VILLAGE!
FOLLOWING THE TRAIL MARKS THEY HAD MADE, THE VIKING PARTY SAFELY REACHED THE TOWERING VILLAGE STOCKADE
DID YOU DISCOVER WHAT YOU SOUGHT?
NO! WE BARELY ESCAPED WITH OUR LIVES! WE LEARNT NOTHING OF VALUE!
INSIDE THE STOCKADE, KARL LAID HIS PLANS FOR THE FINAL DEFEAT OF THE WARLIKE FORESTMEN
AH — WE DID LEARN SOMETHING, CHILANO. IT CAME TO ME JUST NOW — SOMETHING I NOTICED ABOUT THE PEOPLE ON THIS ISLAND! THEY DO NOT USE BOWS AND ARROWS — AND I BELIEVE THEY DO NOT EVEN KNOW OF THE EXISTENCE OF THESE WEAPONS!
BY THE SUN GOD, THAT IS TRUE!
MINUTES LATER THE VILLAGE BECAME A SCENE OF FEVERISH ACTIVITY AS THE VIKINGS SHOWED THE VILLAGERS HOW TO MAKE BOWS AND CUT ARROWS, AND KARL AND CHILANO DEMONSTRATED THEIR USE
THE FORESTMEN ARE BOUND TO ATTACK THE VILLAGE AFTER WHAT WE HAVE DONE!
LET US PRAY THAT THOSE WOLF-CREATURES HAVE DELAYED THEM LONG ENOUGH FOR US TO MAKE ARCHERS OF SOME OF THESE MEN!
AT THE FIRST LIGHT OF DAWN THE FORESTMEN CAME
TELL THE MEN TO HOLD THEIR FIRE — UNTIL I COMMAND IT!
SLAY THE FISH-EATING DOGS! BECAUSE OF THEM WE HAD TO KILL KA-TAK! DESTROY THEM UTTERLY!
THEN KARL ORDERED THE VILLAGERS TO LOOSE THEIR ARROWS
AA-AGH!
THE FORESTMEN DIDN'T EXPECT THIS RECEPTION!
DEVASTATED BY THAT TERRIBLE RAIN OF ARROWS, THE SURVIVING FORESTMEN TURNED AND RAN — SCREAMING THEIR FEAR OF A WEAPON THEY HAD NEVER SEEN BEFORE!
THEY RETREAT! THE ENEMY HAS BEEN DEFEATED!
AN HOUR LATER, KARL AND HIS MEN MADE THEIR WAY TO THEIR RAFT, ESCORTED BY THE GRATEFUL FISH TRIBE
BECAUSE I CANNOT SPEAK HIS LANGUAGE, I AM UNABLE TO THANK YOUR LEADER FOR WHAT HE HAS DONE FOR MY PEOPLE. BUT WE WILL GIVE YOU ALL THE FOOD AND WATER THAT YOU NEED FOR THE REST OF YOUR VOYAGE
OWING TO THIS SEA OF MUD, THAT ISLAND HAS BEEN LOST TO THE REST OF THE WORLD. BUT NOW, THANKS TO YOU, KARL, IT SHOULD KNOW PEACE!
YES, THERE SHOULD BE PEACE, CHILANO. FOR THE FOREST-MEN WILL NEVER AGAIN DARE ATTACK A PEOPLE WITH SO DEADLY A WEAPON AS THE BOW AND ARROW!
AND SO KARL AND HIS MEN BEGAN THE LAST AND MOST DANGEROUS STAGE OF THEIR EPIC VOYAGE TO OXACA!

THE FARTHER THEY TRAVELLED SOUTH, SO THE DAYS GREW HOTTER. NO BREATH OF WIND EASED THE TORTUROUS HEAT

THIS CURSED SUN EVEN REACHES THROUGH THE SHADE FROM OUR SAIL. FOR FIVE DAYS WE HAVE ENDURED THIS. HOW MUCH LONGER?

IN THAT REMORSELESS, UNENDING HEAT, NERVES TAUTENED AND TEMPERS STRETCHED TO BREAKING POINT. AS ONE VIKING KNOCKED AGAINST ANOTHER, KARL HEARD A CRY OF ANGER

YOU CLUMSY HOUND, HALGORD!

STOP THEM—BEFORE THEY ATTACK EACH OTHER!

BUT KARL WAS TOO LATE TO PREVENT THE FIRST VICIOUS SWORD-BLOW. IT MISSED ITS TARGET AND CUT DEEP INTO THE WOODEN WATER CASK

YOU FOOL! OUR DRINKING WATER!

FOR A BRIEF MOMENT, THE VIKINGS STOOD AGHAST. AND BY THE TIME KARL HAD SPRUNG FORWARD AND PLUGGED THE GASH IN THE WATER CASK, THE DAMAGE HAD BEEN DONE

IT'S NEARLY ALL GONE. WHAT LITTLE REMAINS WILL NOT LAST US FOR MORE THAN ANOTHER DAY!

KARL, I AM SORRY! THE HEAT MADE ME LOSE MY TEMPER

I SUPPOSE IT IS THIS CLIMATE THAT IS TO BLAME. BUT YOU SHOULD KNOW THE SERIOUSNESS OF OUR PLIGHT. WE HAVE VIRTUALLY NO WATER—AND HAVE NO IDEA WHEN WE WILL STRIKE LAND!

BY MY RECKONING WE SHOULD HAVE COME TO LAND LONG AGO. BUT WE HAVE SEEN NO SIGN OF IT—PERHAPS BECAUSE OF THIS HEAT-MIST THAT FOGS THE SEA!

FOR TWO MORE DAYS THE VIKINGS SAILED ACROSS SUN-STILLED, MIST-SHROUDED WATERS. THEN CAME A MOMENTARY BREAK IN THE FOG.

LOOK! LAND! THE PEAK OF A MOUNTAIN!

I SEE IT, TOO!

BUT ALMOST IMMEDIATELY THE MIST ROLLED BACK ACROSS THAT TANTALISING VISION OF LAND.

I — I AM AFRAID TO BELIEVE WHAT WE SAW, CHILANO. IT COULD HAVE BEEN JUST A TRICK OF CLOUD AND MIST!

TRUE, KARL. YET I HAD THE FEELING THAT I HAD SEEN SUCH A MOUNTAIN PEAK BEFORE!

BUT AS THE DAY WORE ON WITHOUT FURTHER SIGHT OF LAND, ANOTHER OF THE VOYAGERS SPRANG TO HIS FEET. A CRY OF DESPAIR RINGING FROM DRY, SWOLLEN LIPS. IT WAS TIHUANA, THE BOY KING OF OXACA.

I MUST HAVE WATER! I CANNOT STAND IT ANY LONGER! I MUST DRINK — EVEN SEA WATER!

NO, TIHUANA! HOLD HIM BACK!

BUT CRAVING LENT STRENGTH AND AGILITY TO THE BOY-KING. HE THRUST BACK THE RESTRAINING ARMS AND STRETCHED CUPPED HANDS DOWN TO THE SPARKLING SEA...

NO, HIGHNESS! DO NOT DRINK IT! THE SALT WILL MAKE YOU THIRST MORE!

TO DRINK SEA WATER MEANS DEATH... MADNESS!

I MUST DRINK!

BEFORE ANYONE COULD STOP HIM, TIHUANA GULPED GREEDILY AT THE WATER. THEN HE LIFTED ASTONISHED EYES.

KARL! CHILANO! THIS... IS NOT SEA WATER! THERE IS NO TASTE OF SALT!

THIRST HAS TURNED THE BOY'S HEAD! LET ME TASTE IT!

HE IS RIGHT!

IT IS DRINKING WATER!

KARL, THE SEA HAS LOST ITS SALT!

IT WAS UNBELIEVABLE, BUT TRUE! AND AS THE VOYAGERS SLAKED THEIR THIRST, MORE GOOD FORTUNE FOLLOWED...

THE MISTS ARE LIFTING! CHILANO, I THINK I SEE LAND!

WITHIN MINUTES THEY COULD ALL SEE THE GREEN-FORESTED BANK STRETCHING AWAY INTO THE VAST DISTANCE. TIHUANA CLUTCHED KARL'S ARM...

KARL! CHILANO! I KNOW NOW WHERE WE ARE. WE CAME PAST HERE WHEN WE SAILED AWAY FROM OXACA!

THEN WHERE ARE WE, TIHUANA? CAN YOU TELL US?

NOW I KNOW WHY THE WATER DID NOT TASTE OF SALT! IT IS BECAUSE WE HAVE BEEN SAILING UP A RIVER — A VAST RIVER — THE FATHER OF ALL RIVERS! WE CALL IT THE AMAZONA, WHICH MEANS "THE BREAKER OF BOATS"!

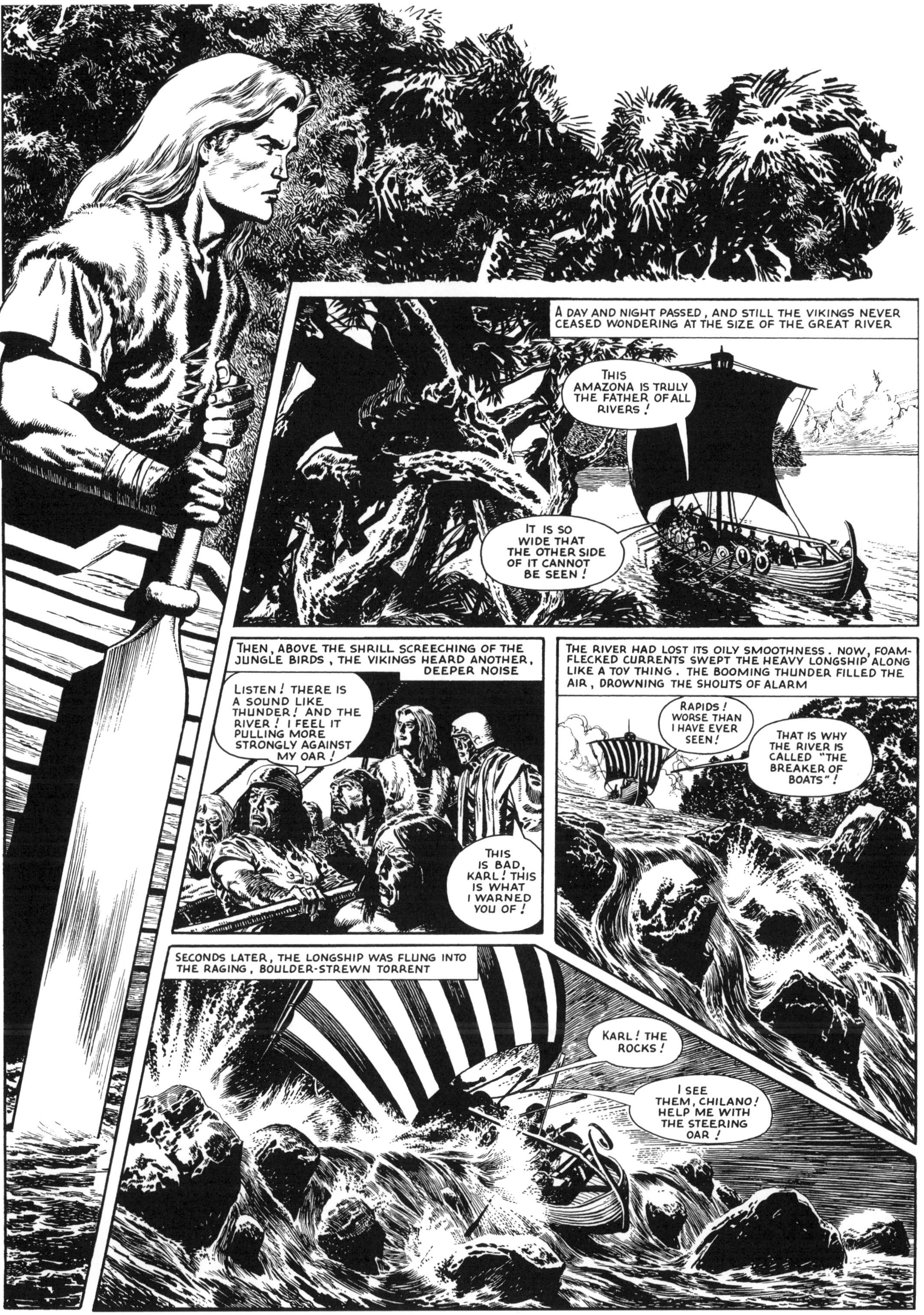

A DAY AND NIGHT PASSED, AND STILL THE VIKINGS NEVER CEASED WONDERING AT THE SIZE OF THE GREAT RIVER
THIS AMAZONA IS TRULY THE FATHER OF ALL RIVERS!
IT IS SO WIDE THAT THE OTHER SIDE OF IT CANNOT BE SEEN!
THEN, ABOVE THE SHRILL SCREECHING OF THE JUNGLE BIRDS, THE VIKINGS HEARD ANOTHER, DEEPER NOISE
LISTEN! THERE IS A SOUND LIKE THUNDER! AND THE RIVER! I FEEL IT PULLING MORE STRONGLY AGAINST MY OAR!
THIS IS BAD, KARL! THIS IS WHAT I WARNED YOU OF!
THE RIVER HAD LOST ITS OILY SMOOTHNESS. NOW, FOAM-FLECKED CURRENTS SWEPT THE HEAVY LONGSHIP ALONG LIKE A TOY THING. THE BOOMING THUNDER FILLED THE AIR, DROWNING THE SHOUTS OF ALARM
RAPIDS! WORSE THAN I HAVE EVER SEEN!
THAT IS WHY THE RIVER IS CALLED "THE BREAKER OF BOATS"!
SECONDS LATER, THE LONGSHIP WAS FLUNG INTO THE RAGING, BOULDER-STREWN TORRENT
KARL! THE ROCKS!
I SEE THEM, CHILANO! HELP ME WITH THE STEERING OAR!

EVEN THE STRENGTH OF TWO POWERFUL MEN WAS INADEQUATE AGAINST THE AWESOME FURY OF THE RIVER

WE—CANNOT HOLD IT, KARL! THE RIVER IS TOO STRONG!

WE NEED MORE HELP! COME, YOU OTHERS!

BUT AT THAT MOMENT THE LONGSHIP WAS SWEPT PAST A JAGGED ROCK—AND THE WOODEN RUDDER SNAPPED LIKE A ROTTEN TWIG!

WE CAN NO LONGER STEER HER, KARL. NOW WE ARE AT THE MERCY OF THE AMAZONA!

BUT LUCK WAS STILL WITH THEM. FOR A SWIRLING CURRENT CAUGHT UP THE SPRAY-LASHED LONGSHIP AND SMASHED IT INTO THE SHORE

DAZEDLY THE CREW PICKED THEMSELVES UP AND STAGGERED ON TO DRY LAND

IT IS A MIRACLE THAT NO ONE HAS BEEN LOST! BUT YOUR FATHER OF ALL RIVERS HAS NEARLY WRECKED OUR LONGSHIP, CHILANO!

AT LEAST THE RAPIDS HAVE DONE ONE THING TO HELP US, KARL...

I HAVE NOW A BETTER IDEA OF WHICH WAY WE SHOULD GO FOR WHEN WE LEFT OXACA WE DIDN'T MEET THIS RAPID!

HOW THEN DID YOU REACH THE OCEAN?

CHILANO POINTED TO A SHADOWY TRIBUTARY

WE MUST HAVE COME DOWN ONE OF THE MANY SMALL RIVERS THAT LEAD INTO THE AMAZONA. IF WE TAKE THIS ONE, IT SHOULD BEAR US EAST, WITH LUCK, TOWARDS A HIGH MOUNTAIN RANGE THAT BORDERS OXACA

I SEE! THEN WE WILL DO AS YOU SUGGEST, CHILANO. BUT FIRST WE MUST TRY TO REPAIR OUR SHIP!

ALL THE REST OF THE DAY, THE VOYAGERS LABOURED. THEN, AS NIGHT FELL, KARL MOPPED HIS STREAMING BROW

THERE, IT IS DONE! I ONLY HOPE THAT THE LONGSHIP WILL BE STRONG ENOUGH. CERTAINLY IT WILL NOT HOLD TOGETHER AGAINST ANY MORE RAPIDS

THERE SHOULD BE NO RAPIDS, KARL. NOW WE HAVE TO FIGHT THE JUNGLE ITSELF — NOT THE RIVER!

USING THEIR OARS AS PUSHING POLES, THE VIKINGS GUIDED THE BOAT INTO THE JUNGLE-LINED TRIBUTARY

UGH! CAN YOU FEEL THE WEEDS ALONG THE BOTTOM OF THIS RIVER?

IN TRUTH, ORLAF, THIS COULD BE AS BAD AS THE RAPIDS. WHAT IF THE WEEDS CHOKE THE RIVER? WE SHOULD BE STUCK FAST IN THIS JUNGLE! STRANDED!

LUCKILY THE RIVER REMAINED DEEP ENOUGH TO ALLOW THE LONGSHIP TO GLIDE OVER THE WEEDS. BUT ALL THE TIME THE JUNGLE PRESSED IN

CAN YOU BE SURE WE HAVE TAKEN THE RIGHT ROUTE, CHILANO? THIS RIVER SEEMS TO BE PETERING OUT!

THERE ARE SO MANY OF THESE SMALL RIVERS, KARL, THAT I—I CANNOT BE SURE! BUT WE HAVE NO CHOICE OTHER THAN TO CONTINUE!

THE OARSMEN STRUGGLED ON, PUSHING AND STRAINING THE LONGSHIP THROUGH THE CLINGING FOLIAGE — INTO EVEN GREATER DANGER. FOR AN INDIAN ARMED WITH A BLOW-PIPE CROUCHED ON A TREE-BRANCH ABOVE THEM!

GLITTERING EYES HAD WATCHED THE APPROACHING STRANGERS

INTENT UPON CARRYING THE NEWS TO HIS DISTANT VILLAGE, THE SWIFTLY-RUNNING JUNGLE DWELLER FAILED TO SEE THE HUGE SHADOW MOVING TOWARDS HIM

THEN THE SHADOW BLOTTED OVER HIM — AND HE HEARD THE SWISH OF MONSTROUS, BEATING WINGS AS A GIANT CONDOR SWOOPED FOR THE KILL!

FRANTICALLY THE INDIAN THREW HIMSELF TO ONE SIDE BUT THE CRUEL TALONS RAKED FOR HIS FLESH. HIS EYES BULGED WITH TERROR, AND FROM HIS LIPS GUSHED A SHRILL, TERRIBLE SCREAM OF MORTAL FEAR

AA-AGH!

ON THE VIKINGS' LONG-SHIP, KARL PEERED INTO THE JUNGLE

DID YOU HEAR, CHILANO? IT WAS A HUMAN VOICE. — THAT OF SOMEONE IN DIRE PERIL!

SOMEONE WHO DESPERATELY NEEDS HELP!

WITH KARL AT THEIR HEAD, A PARTY OF VIKINGS LEAPT FROM THE LONGSHIP AND RACED THROUGH THE JUNGLE

HURRY! I CAN HEAR NO MORE CRIES! PERHAPS EVEN NOW WE ARE TOO LATE!

THE SOUNDS CAME FROM AHEAD OF US, KARL

AT THE EDGE OF THE CLEARING, THEY SAW THE GREAT CONDOR FLUTTERING DOWN TO PICK WITH ITS VICIOUS BEAK AT THE FLESH OF ITS UNCONSCIOUS VICTIM!

BY ODIN, AT FIRST I THOUGHT IT WAS AN EAGLE... BUT THAT IS AN EVEN BIGGER BIRD! AND LOOK AT ITS CLAWS!

IF HE IS NOT DEAD ALREADY, THAT MAN'S ONLY CHANCE LIES IN THE SPEED OF THIS ARROW!

AS KARL'S ARROW BIT HOME, THE CONDOR SCREECHED WITH FURY, ITS GLOWING RED EYES SEEKING THE NEW ENEMY

KARL, IT IS TOO BIG TO BE KILLED BY ONE ARROW! IT IS GOING TO ATTACK US!

ITS GREAT WINGS DRUMMING, THE TERRIFYING BIRD OF PREY RUSHED TOWARDS KARL — WHO, ALONE, FACED ITS ONSLAUGHT CALMLY, PULLING BACK AT THE BOW-STRING TO RELEASE ANOTHER ARROW

INTO THE TREES, KARL. IT IS A DEVIL BIRD!

STILL KARL STOOD HIS GROUND. HE SIGHTED CAREFULLY... BUT A SPLIT SECOND BEFORE HE COULD RELEASE THE ARROW, **THE BOW STRING SNAPPED!**

THEN THE SCREECHING CONDOR WAS UPON HIM

QUICKLY! KARL IS NOW UNARMED! HE WILL BE KILLED!

SOMEHOW KARL MANAGED TO DODGE THE SLASHING TALONS. DESPERATELY HE BEGAN TO BATTER AT THE HUGE FEATHERED BODY WITH HIS FISTS

HELP — ME—MY FRIENDS!

A VIKING SWORD BIT DEEPLY. BUT THE CONDOR HAD WEAPONS OTHER THAN ITS RAZOR-EDGED BEAK AND ITS DAGGER-LIKE TALONS. ITS MASSIVE, HEAVY WING SMASHED INTO THE NORTHMEN, BOWLING THEM OVER AND **KNOCKING KARL SENSELESS**

THEN THE CONDOR FLUTTERED UPWARDS, TAKING THE UNCONSCIOUS VIKING CHIEF WITH IT!

WE FAILED HIM! KARL—OUR CHIEFTAIN— IS DEAD!

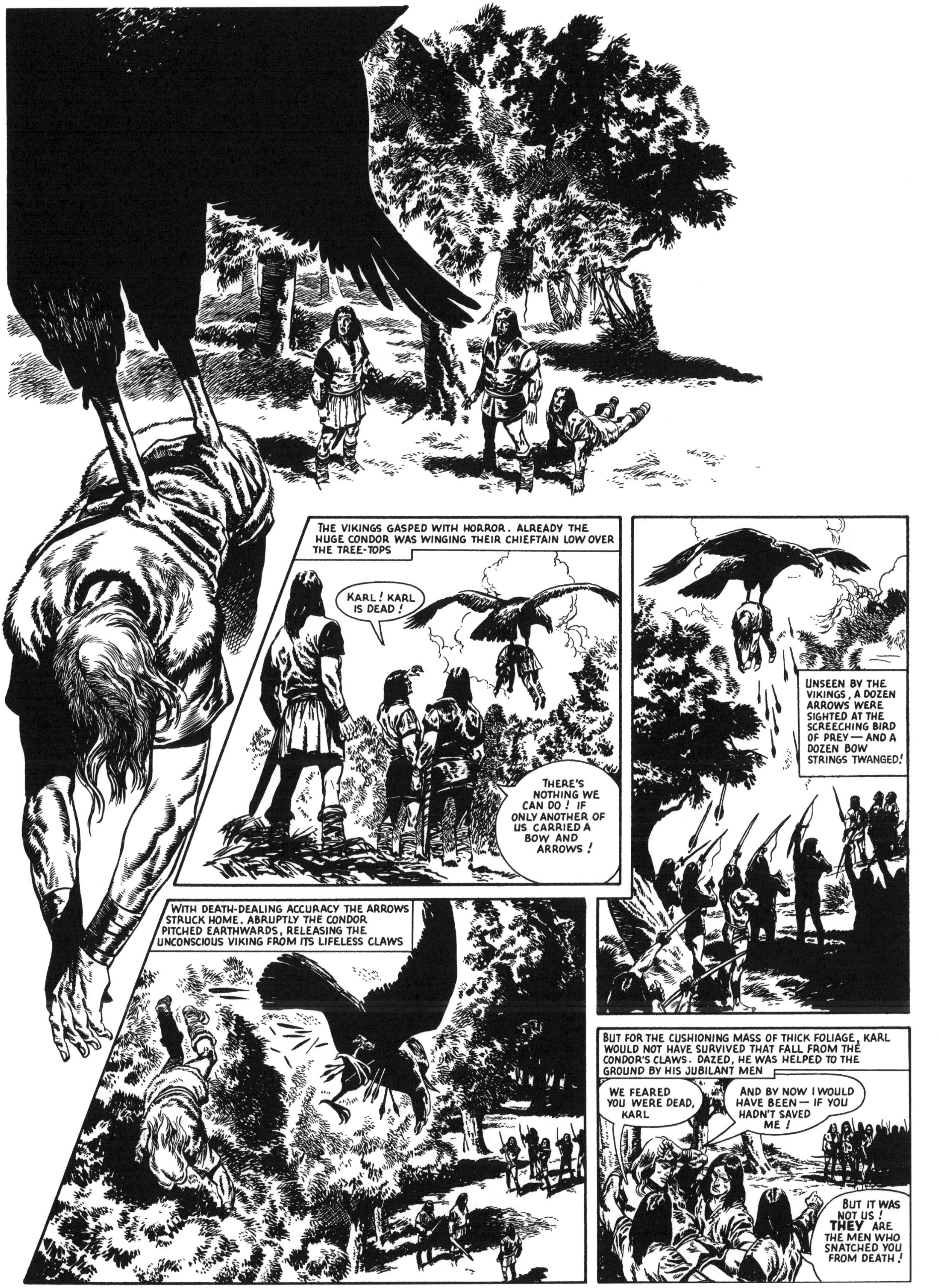
THE VIKINGS GASPED WITH HORROR. ALREADY THE HUGE CONDOR WAS WINGING THEIR CHIEFTAIN LOW OVER THE TREE-TOPS
KARL! KARL IS DEAD!
THERE'S NOTHING WE CAN DO! IF ONLY ANOTHER OF US CARRIED A BOW AND ARROWS!
UNSEEN BY THE VIKINGS, A DOZEN ARROWS WERE SIGHTED AT THE SCREECHING BIRD OF PREY — AND A DOZEN BOW STRINGS TWANGED!
WITH DEATH-DEALING ACCURACY THE ARROWS STRUCK HOME. ABRUPTLY THE CONDOR PITCHED EARTHWARDS, RELEASING THE UNCONSCIOUS VIKING FROM ITS LIFELESS CLAWS
BUT FOR THE CUSHIONING MASS OF THICK FOLIAGE, KARL WOULD NOT HAVE SURVIVED THAT FALL FROM THE CONDOR'S CLAWS. DAZED, HE WAS HELPED TO THE GROUND BY HIS JUBILANT MEN
WE FEARED YOU WERE DEAD, KARL
AND BY NOW I WOULD HAVE BEEN — IF YOU HADN'T SAVED ME!
BUT IT WAS NOT US! THEY ARE THE MEN WHO SNATCHED YOU FROM DEATH!

THE COPPER-SKINNED WARRIORS LISTENED GRAVELY AS CHILANO TRANSLATED KARL'S GRATITUDE. THEN--

THEY SAY THEY ARE GRATEFUL TO **YOU**, KARL! THEY SAW YOU RISK YOUR LIFE TO SAVE THAT OF THE HEADMAN'S SON—AND THEY ASK WHAT THEY CAN DO TO REPAY YOU!

IF THEY CAN TELL US THE ROUTE TO OXACA, THAT WILL BE REWARD INDEED!

AN HOUR LATER THEY WERE STRIKING INLAND, LED BY ONE OF THE JUNGLE-DWELLERS!

THIS IS BETTER THAN WE HAD HOPED, CHILANO. WE WOULD NEVER HAVE FOUND OUR WAY THROUGH THIS TANGLE OF VEGETATION!

BUT IT WILL BE A LONG MARCH, KARL. OUR GUIDE SAYS IT WILL TAKE THREE DAYS TO REACH THE MOUNTAIN RANGE THAT BORDERS MY COUNTRY!

FROM THE TOP OF A HILL THE VIKINGS LOOKED BACK AT THEIR LONGSHIP LYING DESERTED IN THE JUNGLE-CHOKED RIVER

IT WAS A GOOD AND FAITHFUL SHIP. IT BROUGHT US SAFELY THROUGH TERRIBLE SEAS. NOW WE HAVE TO LEAVE IT TO ROT IN THIS DAMP HEAT!

WE SHALL BUILD ANOTHER— PROVIDED ANY OF US RETURN FROM OXACA! THERE WILL BE MUCH FIGHTING THERE I THINK!

DAYS LATER THE DARK, STEAMING JUNGLE ENDED AT THE TOWERING SLOPES OF THE OXACA MOUNTAINS

THE GUIDE'S JOB IS DONE! HE HAS BROUGHT US TO THE BORDERS OF YOUR COUNTRY, TIHUANA. NOW THE REST IS UP TO US ALONE!

THE HIGHER THEY CLIMBED, THE COLDER IT GREW. THERE WAS SNOW ON THE PLATEAU AT THE TOP OF THE MOUNTAIN. **AND ALSO AN UNSEEN WATCHER!**

IT—IT IS TIHUANA, THE BOY KING!

STILL UNSEEN BY KARL AND HIS MEN, THE RIDER TURNED HIS SHAGGY HILL PONY AND RACED TOWARDS THE CITY AT THE FOOT OF THE MOUNTAIN

I MUST TELL SORAC! AT ONCE!

IN THE PALACE, SORAC, TREACHEROUS UNCLE OF THE BOY KING, LISTENED TO HIS CAPTAIN'S EXCITED OUTPOURINGS THEN HIS BRUTAL FEATURES TWISTED IN A SNARL OF FURY

SO, AFTER ALL THIS TIME TIHUANA STILL LIVES! AND IN ANOTHER TEN DAYS I WOULD HAVE BEEN ELIGIBLE TO CLAIM HIS THRONE. NOTHING, NOBODY IS GOING TO STOP ME BECOMING RULER OF OXACA. CAPTAIN, TELL NO ONE OF THIS—BUT TAKE THE PALACE GUARDS AND KILL THE BOY AND THOSE WITH HIM! NOW! BEFORE ANY OF THE PEOPLE SEE THAT THEIR KING IS NOT DEAD!

THE TROOP OF HEAVILY-ARMED SOLDIERS THUNDERED FROM THE CITY

WHERE DO THEY GO IN SUCH A HURRY?

WHEREVER IT IS THEY WILL BRING MISERY AND SUFFERING! THOSE ARE THE TYRANT SORAC'S MEN! I FEAR THE DAY WHEN THAT DEMON BECOMES KING IN PLACE OF TIHUANA! IF ONLY OUR BOY RULER WAS STILL ALIVE!

AN HOUR LATER, THE AMBUSH WAS SET

WAIT UNTIL THEY ARE CROSSING THE BRIDGE! IT WILL MAKE OUR JOB EASIER!

BUT IN SPITE OF THE CAPTAIN'S WORDS, AN ARROW SLIPPED FROM THE TREMBLING FINGERS OF A TENSE BOWMAN AND STRUCK A VIKING

AA-AGH!

BY THE GODS—WE ARE BEING ATTACKED! WE HAVE RUN INTO AN AMBUSH SET BY SORAC!

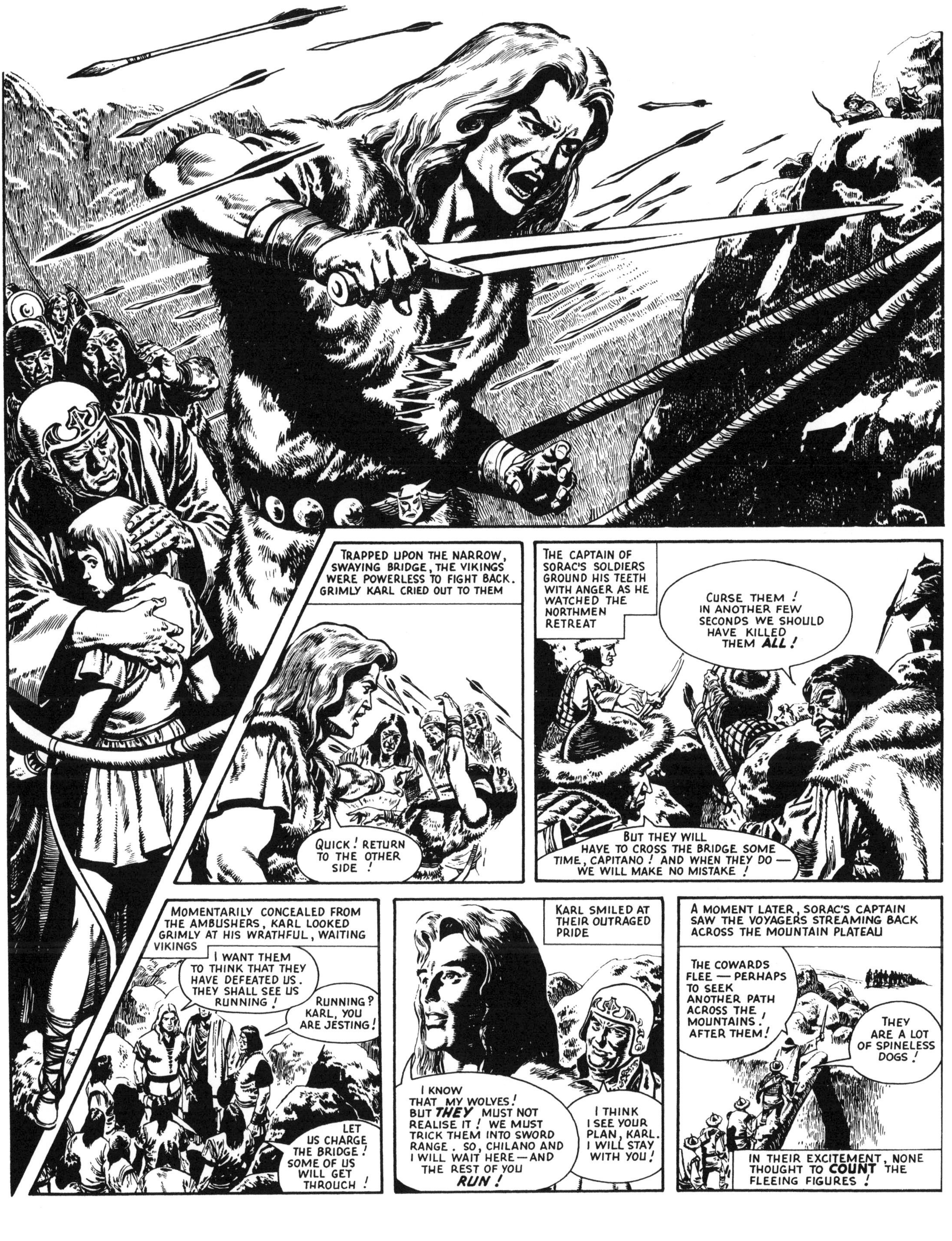

TRAPPED UPON THE NARROW, SWAYING BRIDGE, THE VIKINGS WERE POWERLESS TO FIGHT BACK. GRIMLY KARL CRIED OUT TO THEM
QUICK! RETURN TO THE OTHER SIDE!
THE CAPTAIN OF SORAC'S SOLDIERS GROUND HIS TEETH WITH ANGER AS HE WATCHED THE NORTHMEN RETREAT
CURSE THEM! IN ANOTHER FEW SECONDS WE SHOULD HAVE KILLED THEM ALL!
BUT THEY WILL HAVE TO CROSS THE BRIDGE SOME TIME, CAPITANO! AND WHEN THEY DO — WE WILL MAKE NO MISTAKE!
MOMENTARILY CONCEALED FROM THE AMBUSHERS, KARL LOOKED GRIMLY AT HIS WRATHFUL, WAITING VIKINGS
I WANT THEM TO THINK THAT THEY HAVE DEFEATED US. THEY SHALL SEE US RUNNING!
RUNNING? KARL, YOU ARE JESTING!
LET US CHARGE THE BRIDGE! SOME OF US WILL GET THROUGH!
KARL SMILED AT THEIR OUTRAGED PRIDE
I KNOW THAT MY WOLVES! BUT THEY MUST NOT REALISE IT! WE MUST TRICK THEM INTO SWORD RANGE. SO, CHILANO AND I WILL WAIT HERE — AND THE REST OF YOU RUN!
I THINK I SEE YOUR PLAN, KARL. I WILL STAY WITH YOU!
A MOMENT LATER, SORAC'S CAPTAIN SAW THE VOYAGERS STREAMING BACK ACROSS THE MOUNTAIN PLATEAU
THE COWARDS FLEE — PERHAPS TO SEEK ANOTHER PATH ACROSS THE MOUNTAINS! AFTER THEM!
THEY ARE A LOT OF SPINELESS DOGS!
IN THEIR EXCITEMENT, NONE THOUGHT TO COUNT THE FLEEING FIGURES!

BUT AS SOON AS THE SOLDIERS REACHED THE OTHER SIDE OF THE BRIDGE, KARL AND CHILANO LEAPT FROM AMONG THE BOULDERS

NOW, CHILANO! STRIKE THEM DOWN! THEY ARE TOO CLOSE TO USE THEIR BOWS AND ARROWS!

THE KEEN MOUNTAIN AIR ECHOED TO THE CLASH OF BATTLE AND THE VIKING WAR-CRIES

HEE-AAH! FOR ODIN!

FOR TIHUANA! DIE, ENEMIES OF THE TRUE KING!

THE ODDS WERE HEAVILY AGAINST KARL AND CHILANO, BUT THEIR FIGHTING FURY WAS MORE THAN A MATCH FOR THE TRAITOR GUARDS

FOR THE TWO VIKINGS WERE BOTH EXPERIENCED MEN OF MANY BATTLES — NOT MERELY BULLYING THUGS UNUSED TO OPPOSITION

IN A MATTER OF SECONDS, SORAC'S MEN WERE REDUCED TO A TERRIFIED HANDFUL. DESPERATELY THEIR CAPTAIN STRETCHED HIS BOW

THEY HAVE TRICKED US! YET IF I FAIL SORAC I WILL DIE — HORRIBLY!

ANOTHER INSTANT AND KARL'S FIGHTING HEART WOULD HAVE BEEN PIERCED BY THE CAPTAIN'S ARROW. **BUT ANOTHER MARKSMAN STRUCK FIRST!**

UU-UGH!

INTO THE CHASM HURTLED THE CAPTAIN

AA-AA-AGH!

SOMEONE SAVED MY LIFE! BUT WHO?

THE REST OF THE CURS ARE RUNNING! THEY WILL WARN SORAC OF OUR TRUE STRENGTH!

THE SURVIVORS OF SORAC'S GUARDSMEN, HOWEVER, DID NOT EVEN REACH THE OTHER SIDE OF THE BRIDGE

SOMEONE IS USING A SLING AGAINST THEM—SOMEONE WHO MUST HATE SORAC AS MUCH AS I DO!

AA-AAGH!

THEN —

HOLA! CHILANO, FRIEND OF OXACA'S TRUE KING, WE KNOW YOU!

THEY ARE SHEPHERDS! TO KEEP THE WOLVES AND CONDORS FROM THEIR FLOCKS, SUCH MEN DEVELOP GREAT SKILL WITH THEIR SLINGS!

WHEN CHILANO TOLD THEM THAT THE BOY KING HAD RETURNED, THE SHEPHERDS' FACES LIT WITH JOY

SORAC TOLD THE PEOPLE THAT TIHUANA WAS DEAD! AND KNOWING HIS LUST FOR POWER, WE BELIEVED HIM — THINKING THAT *HE HIMSELF* HAD KILLED THE BOY!

YOU SHALL SEE THAT TIHUANA IS STILL FLESH AND BLOOD!

SEE— HE AND THE OTHERS ARE COMING NOW!

THE SHEPHERDS REVERENTLY GREETED THE YOUNG RULER. THEN THEIR VOICES ROSE IN A CRY OF ALLEGIANCE

LET US FIGHT WITH YOU, MAJESTY! WE WOULD WILLINGLY DIE TO STOP SORAC FROM TAKING THE THRONE! *ALL THE PEOPLE OF SORAC WAIT ONLY FOR A LEADER!*

KARL! IF WHAT THESE MEN SAY IS TRUE, WE HAVE OUR ANSWER. WE WILL RAISE AN ARMY OF SUCH MEN — *AND YOU MUST LEAD THEM INTO BATTLE!*

BY ENLISTING SUCH LOYAL SUBJECTS OF TIHUANA AS THESE MEN, WE WILL BUILD UP THE ARMY WE NEED TO BREAK THE POWER OF SORAC. AND YOU, KARL, MUST BE THE ONE TO LEAD THEM!

I WILL GLADLY LEAD THEM, CHILANO.

CHILANO TURNED TO THE THREE SHEPHERDS

FIND US MEN WHO ARE STRONG AND BRAVE. BUT THEY MUST BE MEN WHO CAN HOLD THEIR TONGUES. FOR SORAC MUST NOT HEAR OF THIS — UNTIL WE ARE READY TO STRIKE!

WE KNOW OF MANY SUCH MEN, CHILANO. BUT DO NOT FORGET THEY WILL ONLY BE SHEPHERDS AND WORKMEN OF THE CITY. NONE OF US ARE SOLDIERS!

THAT I REALISE. SO, FIRST, LEAD US TO A PLACE WHERE WE CAN WAIT IN HIDING. THEN, WE WILL TRAIN YOUR FRIENDS FOR THE DAY WHEN WE WILL REPLACE OUR KING UPON HIS RIGHTFUL THRONE!

AND SO, UNDER COVER OF DARK-NESS, MEN BEGAN TO SLIP UNSEEN INTO THE MOUNTAINS

THERE IS THE VALLEY WHERE OUR KING AND HIS NORTHMEN LIE IN WAIT

NIGHT AFTER NIGHT THEY WERE TRAINED IN THE ART OF THE SWORD, THE SPEAR AND THE FIGHTING AXE

GIVE US ANOTHER FEW WEEKS AND THESE GOOD FELLOWS WILL BE READY FOR BATTLE!

THAT IS RIGHT, MY LOYAL FRIEND. YOU LEARN FAST!

IN HIS PALACE, SORAC UNEASILY PONDERED ON THE DANGER THAT THREATENED HIM

WE HAVE SEARCHED THE MOUNTAINS AND THE FORESTS, HIGHNESS. BUT WE CAN FIND NO TRACE OF THE SUPPORTERS OF TIHUANA

IF ONLY I KNEW THEIR STRENGTH! CONTINUE TO SEARCH... THEY MUST BE *SOMEWHERE!*

FOR DAYS SORAC'S SOLDIERS HUNTED IN VAIN FOR THE ENEMY, NOT REALISING THAT THEY WERE BEING SPIED UPON AT EVERY TURN

IN TWO DAYS THE REGIMENT FROM ATHUJA WILL ARRIVE TO SWELL OUR RANKS. THEN IT WILL TAKE A MIGHTY ARMY INDEED TO DEFEAT US!

AT ONCE THE NEWS WAS CARRIED TO CHILANO IN THE SECRET VALLEY

THE KING OF ATHUJA IS AS CORRUPT AS SORAC HIMSELF — BUT HIS SOLDIERS ARE WELL EQUIPPED AND TRAINED. AND WE ARE NOT NEARLY READY YET. OUR OWN ARMY IS STILL PITIFULLY SMALL!

SMALL, YES! BUT SORAC DOESN'T KNOW *HOW* SMALL!

IF WE WAIT TWO DAYS IT WILL BE TOO LATE! WE MUST START NOW — TONIGHT! BUT WE MUST CHANGE OUR PLAN. *THIS* IS HOW WE SHALL STRIKE AGAINST SORAC...

AT THE FIRST LIGHT OF DAWN THE FOLLOWING DAY, THE FIRST BLOW TO RESCUE THE PEOPLE OF OXACA FROM SORAC'S TYRANNY WAS STRUCK

AA-AGH!

SOUND THE ALARM! TO ARMS! TO ARMS!

SORAC RUSHED TO THE CITY BATTLEMENTS — THEN GAPED AS HE SAW HIS ENEMY FOR THE FIRST TIME

IS—IS THAT ALL THEY NUMBER? THEN THE FIRST REPORT THAT I HAD WAS CORRECT — THEY ARE ONLY A HANDFUL!

I NEED ONLY ONE SQUAD TO PUT PAID TO THEM, HIGHNESS. HAVE I YOUR PERMISSION TO GO AFTER THESE INSOLENT DOGS?

EAGERLY SORAC NODDED. AND MOMENTS LATER A GROUP OF MOUNTED SOLDIERS DASHED THROUGH THE OPENED CITY GATES

ALREADY THEY FLEE! AFTER THEM! KILL THEM ALL!

BUT AS SORAC'S TROOPS PURSUED THE FLEEING NORTHMEN INTO THE BLACK-SHADOWED FOREST —

UU-UUGH!

NOW, MY WOLVES, WE STOP RUNNING!

SILENTLY, GRIMLY, KARL'S VIKINGS POUNCED

FROM THE CITY BATTLEMENTS, SORAC HEARD THE SOUNDS OF BATTLE CEASE. THEN HE GAVE A CRY OF DELIGHT

MY MEN HAVEN'T KILLED THEM! THEY ARE BRINGING THEM IN AS PRISONERS! OPEN THE GATES!

BUT AS SOON AS THE PROCESSION HAD ENTERED THE CITY, THE PRISONERS AND SOLDIERS REVEALED THEMSELVES AS VIKINGS AND SHEPHERDS, AND RENT THE AIR WITH THEIR BLOOD-STIRRING BATTLE CRIES

FOR ODIN! FOR VALHALLA!

NOW! HATERS OF THE TYRANT SORAC — *FIGHT FOR YOUR FREEDOM!*

FROM THE PALACE OF SORAC, MORE OF THE TYRANT'S SOLDIERS RUSHED TO THE BATTLE RAGING AT THE CITY GATES

THERE ARE BUT FEW OF THEM! THEY CANNOT MATCH OUR NUMBERS! HURRY!

BUT IT WAS THEN THAT THE SHEPHERDS OF OXACA REVEALED THEIR LOYALTY TO THE BOY KING TIHUANA. SHEEP WERE DELIBERATELY DRIVEN INTO THE PATH OF THE RUNNING SOLDIERS!

FOOLS! GET THESE CURSED ANIMALS OUT OF THE WAY!

SPURRED BY THE RINGING BATTLE CRIES OF THE FIGHTING VIKINGS, THE SHEPHERDS THEN ATTACKED WITH STICKS AND CUDGELS

DOWN WITH SORAC! FOR TIHUANA, OUR KING!

AA-AGH!

FROM HOUSE WINDOWS, OTHER SHEPHERDS MADE FULL USE OF THEIR AMAZING SKILL WITH SLINGS

CHILANO WAS RIGHT! ALL THESE PEOPLE NEEDED WAS SOMEONE TO LEAD THEM!

UGH!

AND EVEN THE WOMEN OF OXACA RALLIED TO THE SELFLESS COURAGE AND FIGHTING FURY OF THE LIBERATORS FROM THE NORTH

TAKE THAT, TRAITORS!

LOOK OUT! ...AA-AGH!

IN TRUTH, SIGURD, I AM GLAD THAT THESE PEOPLE ARE ON *OUR* SIDE!

KARL'S LUNGING SWORD PITCHED ANOTHER OF THE TYRANT'S THUGS TO THE GROUND. THEN HIS EYES FLASHED TO THE BATTLEMENTS AS CHILANO GAVE A TENSE CRY

KARL! THERE IS SORAC! HE OF ALL THESE TRAITORS MUST DIE!

SHOOT! KILL THE LEADER OF THESE ACCURSED WARRIORS

DESPITE THE FLYING ARROWS, KARL LEAPT FORWARD AT THE HEAD OF HIS MEN

FOLLOW ME, MY WOLVES!

FOOLS, DON'T LET THEM PANIC YOU! AIM TRULY — CAREFULLY — OR ALL IS LOST!

BUT, UNNERVED BY THE FEROCITY OF THE WILD-HAIRED NORTHMAN, SORAC'S ARCHERS FLED... AND THE TRAITOR TYRANT'S DREAM OF POWER VANISHED UNDER THE FLASH OF KARL THE VIKING'S SWORD

SO PERISH ALL ENEMIES OF KING TIHUANA!

WITH THE DEATH OF SORAC, OXACA'S REIGN OF TERROR CAME TO AN END

LOOK AT THE PEOPLE, KARL. THEY ARE HAPPY ONCE MORE — AND IT IS BECAUSE OF YOU!

THE BATTLE OVER, THE BOY KING TIHUANA RETURNED TO HIS CAPITAL CITY — ALONG STREETS LINED WITH CHEERING SUBJECTS

LONG REIGN TIHUANA!

PRAISE TO CHILANO, HIS PROTECTOR — AND THE WARRIORS FROM THE NORTH!

THE FOLLOWING DAY, KARL AND HIS MEN WERE SUMMONED TO THE THRONE ROOM IN THE PALACE OF OXACA

I CAN NEVER THANK YOU ENOUGH, KARL THE VIKING! BUT MY COUNTRY ABOUNDS IN THE YELLOW METAL YOU CALL GOLD. EVEN NOW, MY PEOPLE ARE CARRYING THIS GOLD TO THE SHIP THAT WE HAVE BUILT FOR YOUR JOURNEY BACK TO THE NORTH!

LATER, SAILING ALONG ANOTHER TRIBUTARY OF THE GIANT RIVER THAT WAS CALLED THE AMAZONA, THE VIKINGS BEGAN THE LONG VOYAGE HOME

GOODBYE, KARL. WE WILL NEVER FORGET YOU!

FAREWELL, TIHUANA AND CHILANO! FAREWELL, OXACA!

FOR MANY DAYS THEY SAILED DOWN THE MIGHTY FATHER OF ALL RIVERS. THEN, ONCE MORE, THE VIKINGS FELT THE CHOPPY STIRRING OF THE OCEAN

IN THE PROW OF HIS SHIP, KARL TURNED HIS EYES AWAY FROM THE SUN-MISTED HILLS OF OXACA — AND FACED NORTH

AHEAD, THOUSANDS OF MILES ACROSS THE SEA, ANOTHER ADVENTURE WAS EVEN NOW BEING BORN. A PERIL, FIERCER THAN HE HAD EVER KNOWN, WAS DESCENDING FROM THE CRAGGY, SNOW-CAPPED MOUNTAINS AND MAKING READY TO STRIKE WITH BLOOD-LUSTING CRUELTY AT KARL'S DOMAIN!

V

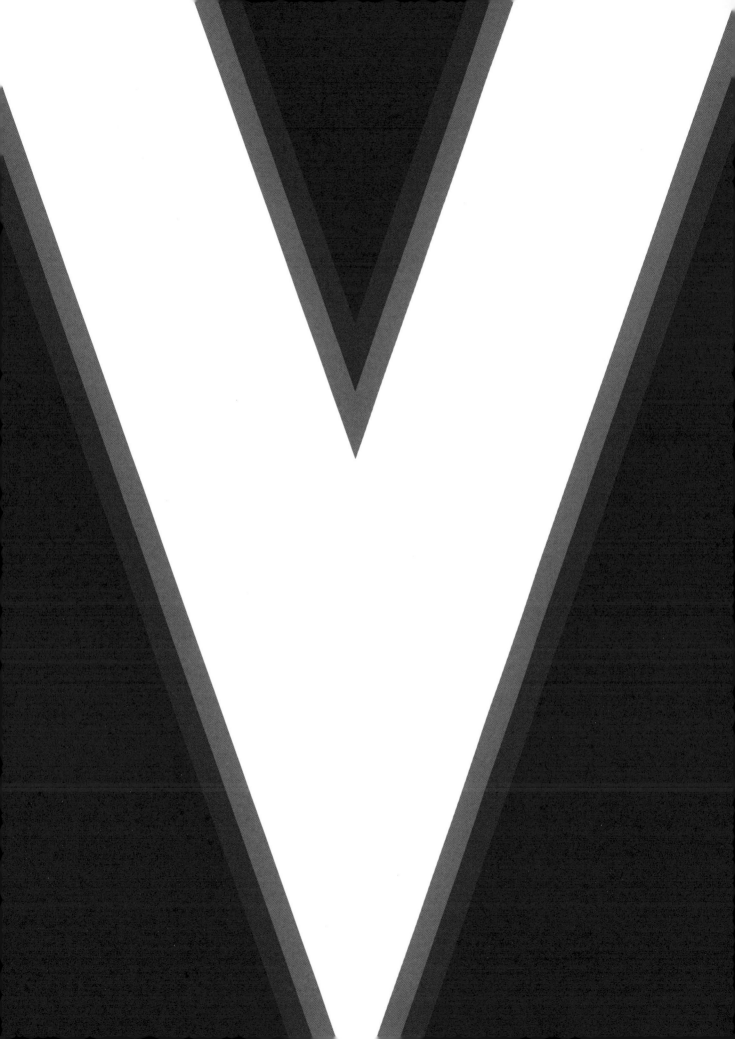

SELGOR THE WOLF

Serialised in **Lion**
29th July – 11th November 1961

Written by
Ted Cowan

Art by
Don Lawrence

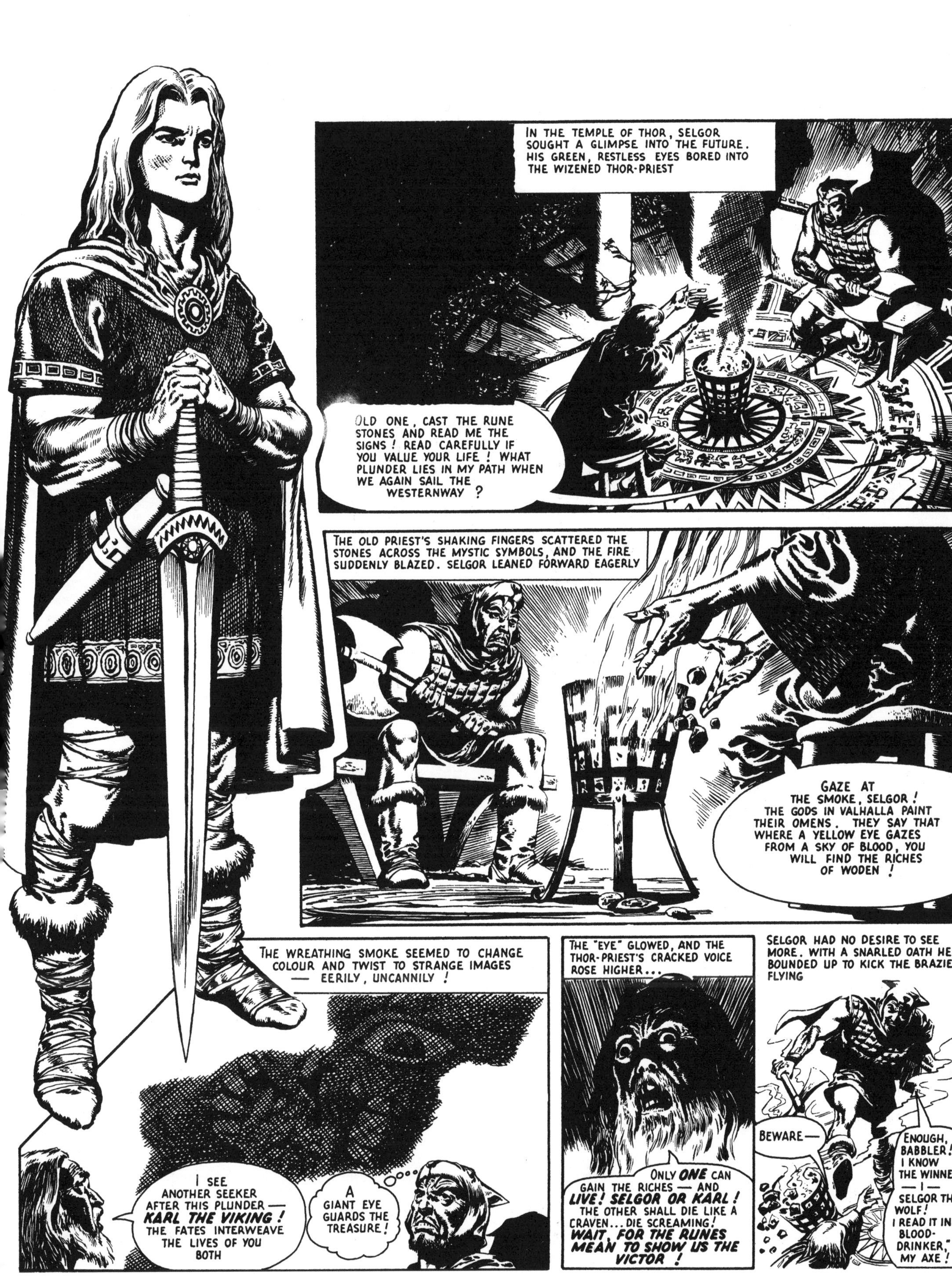
IN THE TEMPLE OF THOR, SELGOR SOUGHT A GLIMPSE INTO THE FUTURE. HIS GREEN, RESTLESS EYES BORED INTO THE WIZENED THOR-PRIEST
OLD ONE, CAST THE RUNE STONES AND READ ME THE SIGNS! READ CAREFULLY IF YOU VALUE YOUR LIFE! WHAT PLUNDER LIES IN MY PATH WHEN WE AGAIN SAIL THE WESTERNWAY?
THE OLD PRIEST'S SHAKING FINGERS SCATTERED THE STONES ACROSS THE MYSTIC SYMBOLS, AND THE FIRE SUDDENLY BLAZED. SELGOR LEANED FORWARD EAGERLY
GAZE AT THE SMOKE, SELGOR! THE GODS IN VALHALLA PAINT THEIR OMENS. THEY SAY THAT WHERE A YELLOW EYE GAZES FROM A SKY OF BLOOD, YOU WILL FIND THE RICHES OF WODEN!
THE WREATHING SMOKE SEEMED TO CHANGE COLOUR AND TWIST TO STRANGE IMAGES — EERILY, UNCANNILY!
I SEE ANOTHER SEEKER AFTER THIS PLUNDER — KARL THE VIKING! THE FATES INTERWEAVE THE LIVES OF YOU BOTH
A GIANT EYE GUARDS THE TREASURE!
THE "EYE" GLOWED, AND THE THOR-PRIEST'S CRACKED VOICE ROSE HIGHER...
ONLY ONE CAN GAIN THE RICHES — AND LIVE! SELGOR OR KARL! THE OTHER SHALL DIE LIKE A CRAVEN... DIE SCREAMING! WAIT, FOR THE RUNES MEAN TO SHOW US THE VICTOR!
SELGOR HAD NO DESIRE TO SEE MORE. WITH A SNARLED OATH HE BOUNDED UP TO KICK THE BRAZIER FLYING
BEWARE—
ENOUGH, BABBLER! I KNOW THE WINNER — I — SELGOR THE WOLF! I READ IT IN BLOOD-DRINKER, MY AXE!

A HAND LIKE A VICE CLASPED THE THOR-PRIEST AND FLUNG HIM AFTER THE BRAZIER

READ YOUR OWN FUTURE, YOU SNIVELLING OLD FOOL. LET ME HELP! I SEE A GLITTERING AXE BLADE!

AS THE GREAT AXE SWUNG BACK, THE THOR-PRIEST'S GAZE MET SELGOR'S FOR THE LAST TIME. THE HATRED IN IT ALMOST MADE SELGOR CHECK

STRIKE, THEN — AND MY CURSE BE ON YOU! SELGOR THE WOLF, WOLF SHALL YOU BE! BY THE TIME THE MOON RISES --

YOU SHALL NOT SEE IT!

A CHOKING SCREAM REACHED THE EARS OF SELGOR'S BERSERKS WHO WAITED OUTSIDE. THEN THE FIGURE OF SELGOR, HANDS CLAPPED TO FACE, PLUNGED FROM THE TEMPLE AND RAN MADLY PAST THEM

BY THE HAMMERER, HE HAS KILLED THE THOR-PRIEST!

WHAT AILS HIM? HE RUNS INTO THE PINES! LEAVE HIM UNTIL HIS TEMPER HAS COOLED!

FILLED WITH A TERROR THEY COULD NOT EXPLAIN, THE BERSERKS KEPT BACK AS SELGOR FELL PANTING IN THE SHADOW OF THE TREES. THE MOON SLOWLY ROSE

THE OLD TRICKSTER LIED! A PITY I COULD NOT HAVE KILLED HIM TWICE FOR THAT CURSE ... AAH, BUT MY FACE BURNS!

HE BREATHES LIKE AN ANIMAL

SUDDENLY THE PAIN LEFT SELGOR. HE ROSE AND LAUGHED — LAUGHED AT THE MOON. THE BAYING OF A WOLF THROBBED THE ECHOES

HE CALLED ME A WOLF! THEN KARL THE VIKING SHALL FEEL THE WOLF'S BITE. ONLY ONE VICTOR CAN WIN THE RICHES OF WODEN!

SELGOR ROSE AND BELLOWED AN ORDER. AND STARK FEAR SPURRED THE BERSERKS TO INSTANT OBEDIENCE OF THEIR TRANSFORMED LEADER

LOOK! HIS FACE HAS CHANGED! HE'S MORE LIKE AN ANIMAL!

PREPARE OUR LONG SERPENT BOAT! WE SAIL WHILE THE MOON IS HIGH. *SELGOR'S WOLF-PACK IS READY TO HUNT!*

THE GREAT SHIP — 100 FEET LONG AND WITH FIFTY WARRIORS APART FROM ITS ROWERS — SPED FOR A FIORD NEAR TO THE VILLAGE WHERE KARL THE VIKING LIVED

PULL! BREAK YOUR BACKS! I HAVE A RIVAL TO DEAL WITH BEFORE WE SEEK THE YELLOW EYE GUARDING THE RICHES OF WODEN. OUR STEEL SHALL NOT GO THIRSTY TODAY

AYE, SELGOR! WE HUNT!

THE MURDEROUS HORDE LANDED STEALTHILY — TO SURPRISE A PARTY OF LUCKLESS HORSE-DEALERS. PARTY AND ESCORT WERE KILLED TO A MAN

SPARE THE HORSES! TODAY, MY WOLVES, WE ARE RIDING!

MERCY — AA-AGH!

A FEW MILES AWAY, KARL WAS SETTING OUT WITH A DIFFERENT KIND OF HUNTING-PARTY. THE DEPLETED VILLAGE HAD NO REASON TO SUSPECT THEIR DANGER

KARL, MAY THE GODS GUIDE THE TUSKED BOARS TOWARDS YOUR SPEARS. TONIGHT WE FEAST!

OUR SPEARS NEED NO GUIDANCE! 'TIS THE BOARS WHICH NEED LUCK!

KARL, VIKING CHIEFTAIN, WAS AS UNTAMED AS THE QUARRY THEY HUNTED

RIDE! WHEN VIKINGS HUNT, THE GROUND TREMBLES! A GOLD SHIELD BOSS FOR THE FIRST MAN TO MAKE A KILL!

BUT THE FIRST KILL—THE SECOND —THE THIRD HAD ALREADY BEEN MADE. SELGOR'S PATH WAS MARKED BY A TRAIL OF HORROR. AND HIS VOICE ROSE MIGHTILY

ON TO THE VILLAGE! BY SUNSET THERE SHALL BE NO KARL, NO VILLAGE, NO VILLAGERS. WHEN A WOLF BITES, IT SINKS ITS FANGS DEEP!

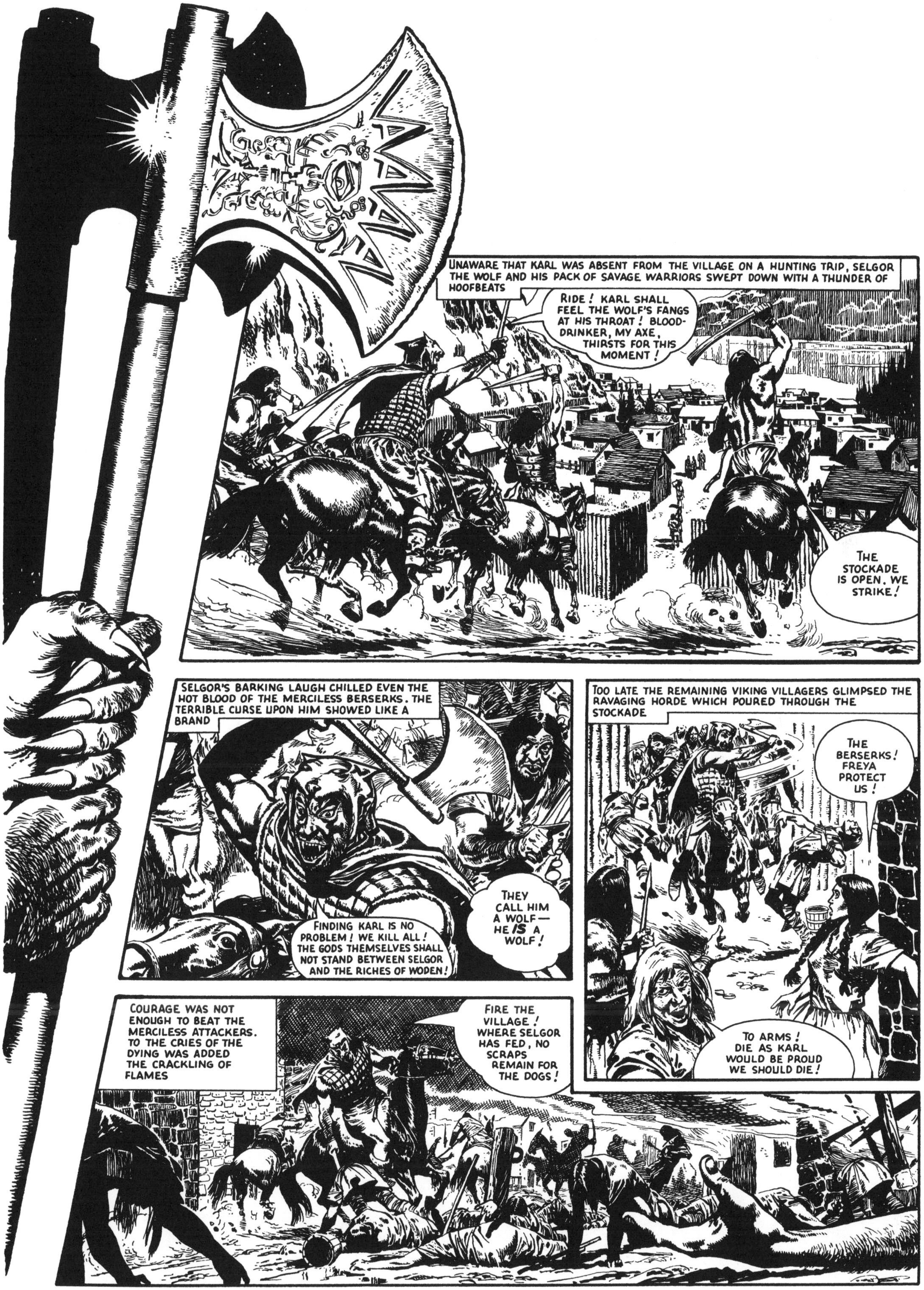
UNAWARE THAT KARL WAS ABSENT FROM THE VILLAGE ON A HUNTING TRIP, SELGOR THE WOLF AND HIS PACK OF SAVAGE WARRIORS SWEPT DOWN WITH A THUNDER OF HOOFBEATS
RIDE! KARL SHALL FEEL THE WOLF'S FANGS AT HIS THROAT! BLOOD-DRINKER, MY AXE, THIRSTS FOR THIS MOMENT!
THE STOCKADE IS OPEN. WE STRIKE!
SELGOR'S BARKING LAUGH CHILLED EVEN THE HOT BLOOD OF THE MERCILESS BERSERKS. THE TERRIBLE CURSE UPON HIM SHOWED LIKE A BRAND
FINDING KARL IS NO PROBLEM! WE KILL ALL! THE GODS THEMSELVES SHALL NOT STAND BETWEEN SELGOR AND THE RICHES OF WODEN!
THEY CALL HIM A WOLF— HE IS A WOLF!
TOO LATE THE REMAINING VIKING VILLAGERS GLIMPSED THE RAVAGING HORDE WHICH POURED THROUGH THE STOCKADE
THE BERSERKS! FREYA PROTECT US!
TO ARMS! DIE AS KARL WOULD BE PROUD WE SHOULD DIE!
COURAGE WAS NOT ENOUGH TO BEAT THE MERCILESS ATTACKERS. TO THE CRIES OF THE DYING WAS ADDED THE CRACKLING OF FLAMES
FIRE THE VILLAGE! WHERE SELGOR HAS FED, NO SCRAPS REMAIN FOR THE DOGS!

KARL'S DYING FRIEND, GELDA, GAZED CONTEMPTUOUSLY AT THE WILD FIGURE WHOSE SHADOW CUT OUT THE LIGHT

WOLF-MAN, YOU CAN THANK YOUR EVIL GODS THAT KARL WAS NOT HERE. A BOAR-HUNT ROBBED US OF HIM AND HIS WARRIORS — OR HIS SWORD WOULD HAVE BROKEN YOUR FANGS!

THE NEWS WAS UNEXPECTED, AND SELGOR'S AXE CHECKED. THEN THE BALEFUL GREEN EYES LIT WITH A DEMONIACAL CUNNING

SO! KARL IS NOT IN MY NET! THEN I MUST CAST IT WIDER. VALGAN, FETCH ME A BOAR FROM THE PEN!

WHAT DOES HE PLAN? BY THOR! I COULD ALMOST PITY THIS KARL!

MEANWHILE, UNAWARE OF THE TRAGEDY AND MASSACRE, KARL AND HIS PARTY HAD CORNERED A WILD BOAR IN THE WOODS. RECKLESSLY KARL DISMOUNTED

WAIT! 'TIS MADNESS TO MEET THAT BRUTE'S CHARGE ON FOOT!

THE BRUTE'S A VIKING BOAR! HIS BLOOD OR MINE! WE MEET ON EQUAL TERMS

THE BOAR, WHOSE RAZOR TUSKS COULD HAVE SEVERED A LEG, CHARGED — BUT KARL WAS STILL FASTER

FROM THE RANSACKED, RAVAGED VILLAGE THE RED FLAMES ROSE HIGHER, AND SMOKE DRIFTED OUT OVER THE WOODS

CAUGHT BY THE WIND, THE SMOKE WREATHED TOWARDS KARL'S HUNTING-PARTY. IT GLOWED RUDDILY AND TOOK ON STRANGE SHAPES

KARL! BY THE BLOOD OF THOR, GAZE AT THE SKY! AN EYE! A GIANT EYE!

SUPERSTITIOUS FEAR GRIPPED THE VIKINGS

A SHRILL, CRACKED VOICE BROKE THE SILENCE THAT FOLLOWED, AND A GREY-HAIRED OLD WOMAN STUMBLED OUT FROM THE TREES

KARL, THE RUNES SPEAK TO YOU! SAIL THE WESTERNWAY AND SEEK THE RICHES OF WODEN. DEATH AND A GIANT YELLOW EYE GUARD THEM! YOUR DESTINY IS WRITTEN THERE IN THE SKY —

WHO ARE YOU, CRONE — A WITCH?

THE SMOKE SHAPES CHANGED, AND THE VOICE OF THE HAG-LIKE WOMAN CACKLED EERILY

HEH! HEH! NAMES MATTER NOT, VIKING — EXCEPT ONE. REMEMBER SELGOR THE WOLF! THE GODS MEAN TO DECIDE WHO IS THE GREATER OF YOU!

WAIT, HAG! TELL ME MORE!

KARL WOULD HAVE CHASED AFTER THE CRONE, BUT A CRASHING FROM THE UNDERGROWTH HALTED HIM

GELDA! MY FRIEND AND BLOOD-BROTHER! HE IS BOUND TO A BOAR!

THE BOAR WAS CAPTURED AND GELDA CUT FREE. WITH HIS DYING BREATH HE THEN GASPED OUT WORDS THAT KARL WOULD NEVER FORGET

I WAS CAUGHT BY — THE — THE WOLF! SELGOR — VILLAGE — MASSACRE AAH — !

THEN GELDA SLUMPED BACK

THE SIGNIFICANCE OF THE FIRE-TINGED SMOKE NOW BECAME CLEAR TO KARL

SPIRIT OF GELDA, YOU SHALL LOOK DOWN FROM VALHALLA TO SEE SELGOR THE WOLF PAY FOR THIS FOUL DEED! IT IS HIS BLOOD OR MINE! KARL THE WOLF-HUNTER WILL SEEK HIS TRAIL TO THE LAND OF SHADES OR BEYOND!

AT THE VILLAGE, SELGOR AND HIS BERSERKS PREPARED AMBUSH. GELDA HAD BEEN THEIR BAIT TO MAKE SURE OF KARL'S STORMING RETURN

KARL WILL COME — TO MEET MY AXE! AND WHEN WE HAVE FOUGHT, NO KARL WILL REMAIN BETWEEN ME AND THE RICHES OF WODEN!

Beneath a sky darkening strangely with storm, Karl and his vikings spurred madly for where crimson smoke marked their village's fiery destruction

REVENGE! GIVE US REVENGE!

RIDE! RIDE! I SWEAR BY MIGHTY THOR THAT MY SWORD SHALL NOT SLEEP TILL SELGOR THE WOLF LIES DEAD BEFORE IT

The distant scene appalled even the hardiest of the battle-scarred vikings — but the danger was greater than they knew! For amidst the grim ruins Selgor and his berserks waited in unseen ambush

As Selgor had guessed, Karl's grief and fury made him forget caution. Blinded by hatred, he urged his mount forward

A BERSERK MASSACRE! SELGOR THE WOLF, I WILL FIND YOU!

KARL, WAIT! THIS IS MADNESS! SEND DOWN SCOUTS FIRST

The storm wind rose — and what followed was to be stamped for ever on the memories of the onlookers. A grey, snarling shape sprang at Karl

A WOLF! KARL, BEWARE!

Karl's javelin sped from his hand towards those mighty jaws, but fear suddenly gripped him

WHAT MANNER OF WOLF WOULD ATTACK WITHOUT ITS PACK? NO NORMAL BRUTE! IT IS AN OMEN!

From the shadows of the ravaged village a throbbing, terrible cry echoed that of the dying wolf. Selgor who had been cursed to resemble a wolf, staggered forward

AAIEE-EE-EE!

HE CRIES LIKE A WOLF IN ITS DEATH THROES!

A STABBING PAIN BURNED THROUGH HIM!

THE DISTURBANCE WARNED KARL AND BROUGHT HIM TO HIS SENSES. VIKING ARCHERS OBEYED HIS COMMANDS

LOOSE YOUR SHAFTS INTO THE SHADOWS! BY THE HAMMERER, LET US SEE IF THE BERSERKS LIE IN AMBUSH!

LIKE FALLING HAIL THE DEADLY SHAFTS RAINED DOWN ON THE SPOT WHERE THE BERSERKS HAD HIDDEN — AND THEIR POSITIONS WERE REVEALED

WOLF-PACK, GATHER! IF KARL WILL NOT RIDE TO SEEK US, I WILL SEEK HIM!

SELGOR UNDERESTIMATED HIS ENEMY. COVERED BY THE FIRE OF THE ARCHERS, KARL AND HIS VIKINGS SWEPT DOWN WITH STEEL BARED

WHILE THE STORM GATHERED ACROSS THE FIORDS, STEEL CLASHED AGAINST STEEL AND BATTLE RAGED IN STARK SAVAGERY. KARL'S SHOUTS WERE ECHOED BY A SUDDEN BARKING LAUGH

KARL, I AM HERE! I'LL KILL ANY BERSERK WHO ROBS ME OF SLAYING YOU!

WOLF-MAN, WHERE ARE YOU? BARE YOUR FANGS TO MEET ME!

DISMOUNTING, KARL PLUNGED THROUGH SMOKE — AND CAME FACE TO FACE WITH SELGOR!

SO YOU ARE KARL! COME, QUENCH THE THIRST OF BLOOD-DRINKER, MY AXE!

HE — IT — ISN'T HUMAN!

KARL WAS FAST — FAST AS SUMMER LIGHTNING AND DEADLY AS AN ADDER'S BITE

DIE, YOU CREATURE OF EVIL!

BUT SELGOR'S GLITTERING AXE FORMED A WALL OF WHISTLING STEEL

YOU SHALL NOT ESCAPE ME, WOLF-MAN!

AGAIN AND AGAIN SWORD SPARKED ON AXE.

GODS OF VALHALLA, HELP ME TO OVERCOME THIS MONSTER. HE DOES NOT TIRE! HIS VERY BREATH IS LIKE THAT OF A WOLF!

KARL'S SENSES BEGAN TO REEL FROM EXHAUSTION. EVIL AND POWER SEEMED TO RADIATE FROM THE GIANT BERSERK, THEN —

KARL CRASHED HEADLONG — EXHAUSTED, DEFENCELESS. AND SELGOR'S PEALING LAUGHTER WAS HORRIBLE TO HEAR

WEAKLING, YOU HAVE NOT FOUND THE RICHES OF WODEN — BUT DEATH! BLOOD-DRINKER SHALL MAKE YOU INTO TWO MEN! TWO HALVES!

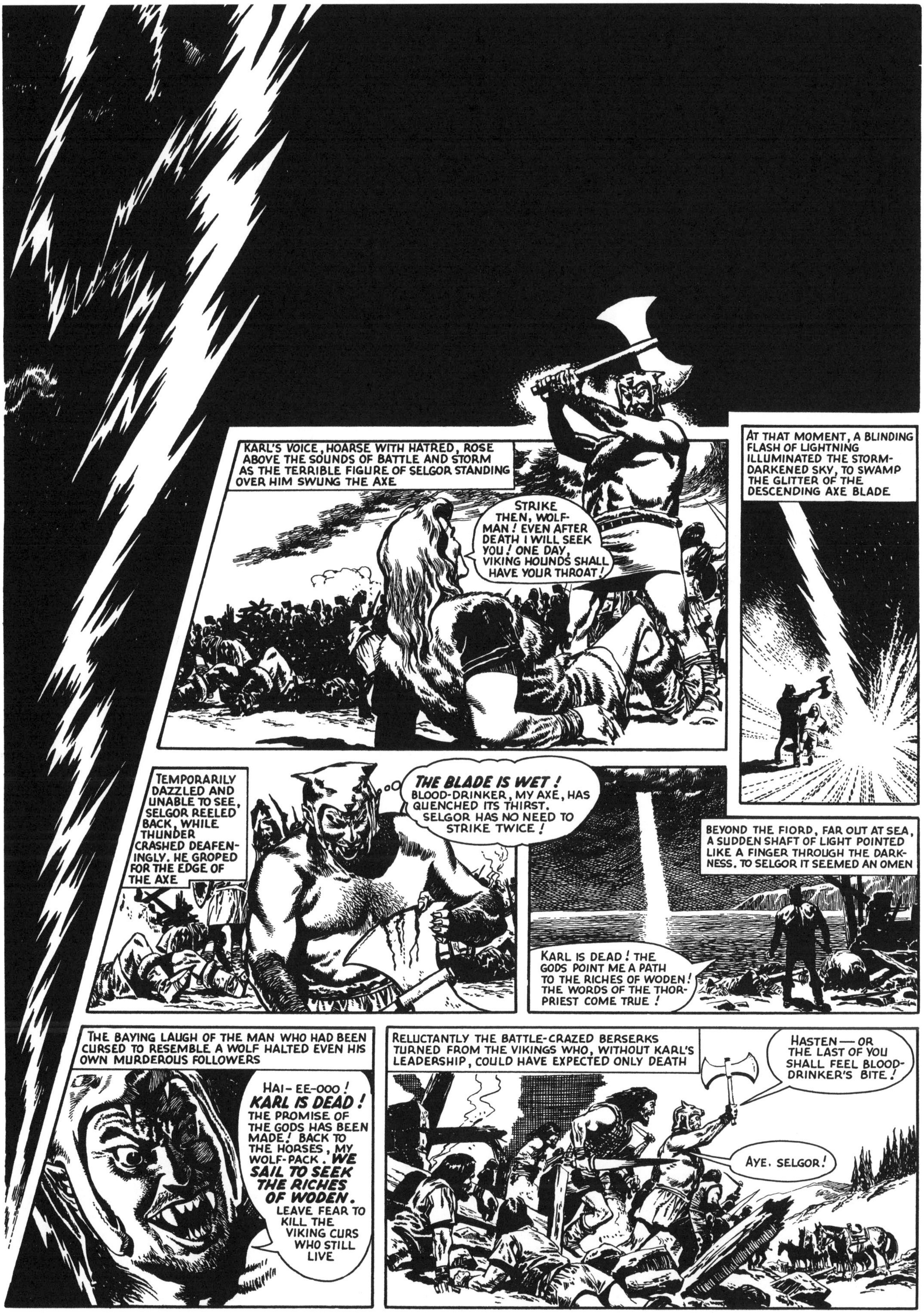

KARL'S VOICE, HOARSE WITH HATRED, ROSE ABOVE THE SOUNDS OF BATTLE AND STORM AS THE TERRIBLE FIGURE OF SELGOR STANDING OVER HIM SWUNG THE AXE
STRIKE THEN, WOLF-MAN! EVEN AFTER DEATH I WILL SEEK YOU! ONE DAY, VIKING HOUNDS SHALL HAVE YOUR THROAT!
AT THAT MOMENT, A BLINDING FLASH OF LIGHTNING ILLUMINATED THE STORM-DARKENED SKY, TO SWAMP THE GLITTER OF THE DESCENDING AXE BLADE
TEMPORARILY DAZZLED AND UNABLE TO SEE, SELGOR REELED BACK, WHILE THUNDER CRASHED DEAFENINGLY. HE GROPED FOR THE EDGE OF THE AXE
THE BLADE IS WET! BLOOD-DRINKER, MY AXE, HAS QUENCHED ITS THIRST. SELGOR HAS NO NEED TO STRIKE TWICE!
BEYOND THE FIORD, FAR OUT AT SEA, A SUDDEN SHAFT OF LIGHT POINTED LIKE A FINGER THROUGH THE DARKNESS. TO SELGOR IT SEEMED AN OMEN
KARL IS DEAD! THE GODS POINT ME A PATH TO THE RICHES OF WODEN! THE WORDS OF THE THOR-PRIEST COME TRUE!
THE BAYING LAUGH OF THE MAN WHO HAD BEEN CURSED TO RESEMBLE A WOLF HALTED EVEN HIS OWN MURDEROUS FOLLOWERS
HAI-EE-OOO! KARL IS DEAD! THE PROMISE OF THE GODS HAS BEEN MADE! BACK TO THE HORSES, MY WOLF-PACK. WE SAIL TO SEEK THE RICHES OF WODEN. LEAVE FEAR TO KILL THE VIKING CURS WHO STILL LIVE
RELUCTANTLY THE BATTLE-CRAZED BERSERKS TURNED FROM THE VIKINGS WHO, WITHOUT KARL'S LEADERSHIP, COULD HAVE EXPECTED ONLY DEATH
HASTEN—OR THE LAST OF YOU SHALL FEEL BLOOD-DRINKER'S BITE!
AYE, SELGOR!

SELGOR SPURRED INTO THE FIORD WHERE KARL'S SHIP WAS MOORED THEN —

GO FREE ON THE WAVES! WHAT SELGOR CANNOT KILL HE DESTROYS!

KEEP BACK! IF YOU ANGER HIM HE WILL SLAY US, TOO!

SELGOR AND HIS BERSERKS RODE FROM THE PLACE OF RUIN...

BACK TO OUR SHIP! THE STORM WIND SHALL FILL OUR SAIL AND LEAD US! THE VERY GODS FEAR ME!

SOON, SELGOR'S WOLF-PACK SET OUT TO FOLLOW THE FADING FINGER OF LIGHT...

WE VOYAGE TO SEEK THE YELLOW EYE WHICH GUARDS THE RICHES OF WODEN. PLUNDER AND WEALTH SHALL BE YOURS, MY WOLVES. PULL HARD, YOU ROWERS!

IN THE SACKED VILLAGE, THE SURVIVORS OF THE SMALL VIKING FORCE SEARCHED FOR THE BODY OF THEIR LEADER. SUDDENLY A PILE OF RUBBLE MOVED, AND —

KARL!

STAY — I AM NO GHOST! THE — THE LIGHTNING SAVED ME. SELGOR'S AXE WAS ROBBED OF ITS PREY. IT ONLY GRAZED ME!

SHOCK FOLLOWED SHOCK! AGAIN THE CRACKED VOICE OF AN OLD WOMAN, WHOM THE VIKINGS HAD SEEN BEFORE, RANG ON THEIR EARS...

HEH! HEH! YOUR HOUR HAD NOT COME, KARL! NOT SO SOON DO THE GODS DECIDE THE VICTOR BETWEEN YOU AND SELGOR. MORE BLOOD WILL FLOW BEFORE YOU MEET HIM FOR THE LAST TIME!

SLOWLY KARL'S GAZE PASSED OVER THE REMAINS OF THE VILLAGE...

THE DEAD CRY OUT FOR VENGEANCE. OLD WOMAN, TELL ME WHERE I MAY FIND SELGOR. HOW MAY I OVERTAKE HIM? SPEAK!

THE HAG'S UNEARTHLY CACKLE BLENDED WITH THE SOUND OF THE WIND...

BRAVE WORDS, VIKING! YET HOW BRAVE ARE YOU? THE TERRORS YOU HAVE TO FACE BEFORE YOU REACH SELGOR MAY DRAIN EVEN A VIKING OF COURAGE!

KARL TOOK A STEP FORWARD. HIS WINTRY EYES GLEAMED...

HAG, I SWEAR BY THE GODS I AM IN NO MOOD FOR MOCKERY. BE CAUTIOUS! I WOULD FACE THE VERY POWERS OF EVIL TO REACH THE WOLF-BEAST!

KARL, BEWARE!

AT THE OLD WOMAN'S LAUGHTER, A GUST OF FLAME SPRANG FROM SMOULDERING EMBERS. HARALD, KARL'S FRIEND, WAS WHITE WITH FEAR AS HE LISTENED....

HEH! HEH! VIKING, YOU SHALL SEE FOR YOUR-SELF! TELL YOUR FRIEND TO BRING ME A VIKING WARRIOR'S SHIELD...!

YOU HEARD, HARALD. DO AS THE CRONE BIDS!

THE SHIELD WAS BROUGHT, AND THE HAG POLISHED ITS BOSS. KARL'S HEART THROBBED WITH A STRANGE SENSATION...

COME, MY BOLD ONE. GAZE INTO THE GOLD BOSS! OR HAS YOUR COURAGE ALREADY STARTED TO FAIL?

I KEEP MY OATH. SHOW ME HOW TO FIND SELGOR!

WHILE THE UNEARTHLY GLARE OF THE FIRE AND LIGHTNING FLICKERED ACROSS THE WHITE FACES OF THE VIKING SURVIVORS, KARL STEELED HIMSELF TO GAZE AT THE GOLDEN BOSS OF THE SHIELD

KARL, YOU ASKED TO SEE SELGOR! **SO YOU SHALL!**

BY THE HAMMERER, THE GOLDEN BOSS GLOWS!

IT IS WITCHCRAFT!

THE STRANGE RADIANCE REACHED A MIGHTY INTENSITY, AND THE LUMINOUS SHADOW OF SELGOR'S SHIP APPEARED TO RISE FROM WITHIN IT

VIKING! BEHOLD YOUR WOLF-MAN ENEMY AND HIS FOLLOWERS OF EVIL!

KARL'S SENSES REELED, FOR IT SEEMED THAT HE COULD HEAR THE CRACK OF SAIL-CLOTH AND THE VOICE OF THE MAN CURSED TO RESEMBLE A WOLF

KARL IS DEAD, AND THE WIND DRIVES US TO SEEK THE RICHES OF WODEN! ON, ON, MY WOLF-PACK! BOOTY AND PLUNDER SHALL BE YOURS!

KARL WAS FILLED WITH HATE OF THE EVIL WOLF-MAN

I AM STILL ALIVE — BUT SELGOR DESERVES TO DIE! CRONE, HOW MAY I OVERTAKE HIM?

I WILL TELL YOU. LISTEN!

SUDDENLY THE FANTASTIC PICTURES IN THE SHIELD BECAME SO TERRIBLE THAT KARL STARTED BACK

AA-AAGH! HAG, WHAT IS IT?

HEH! HEH! YOU SHALL FIND OUT WHEN YOU SAIL. TO OVERTAKE SELGOR, YOU MUST VOYAGE THROUGH THE JAWS OF SULLA AND TO THE MIST LAND BEYOND. FOLLOW THE RED FIN OF THE FISH, KARL! FOLLOW — AND BEWARE!

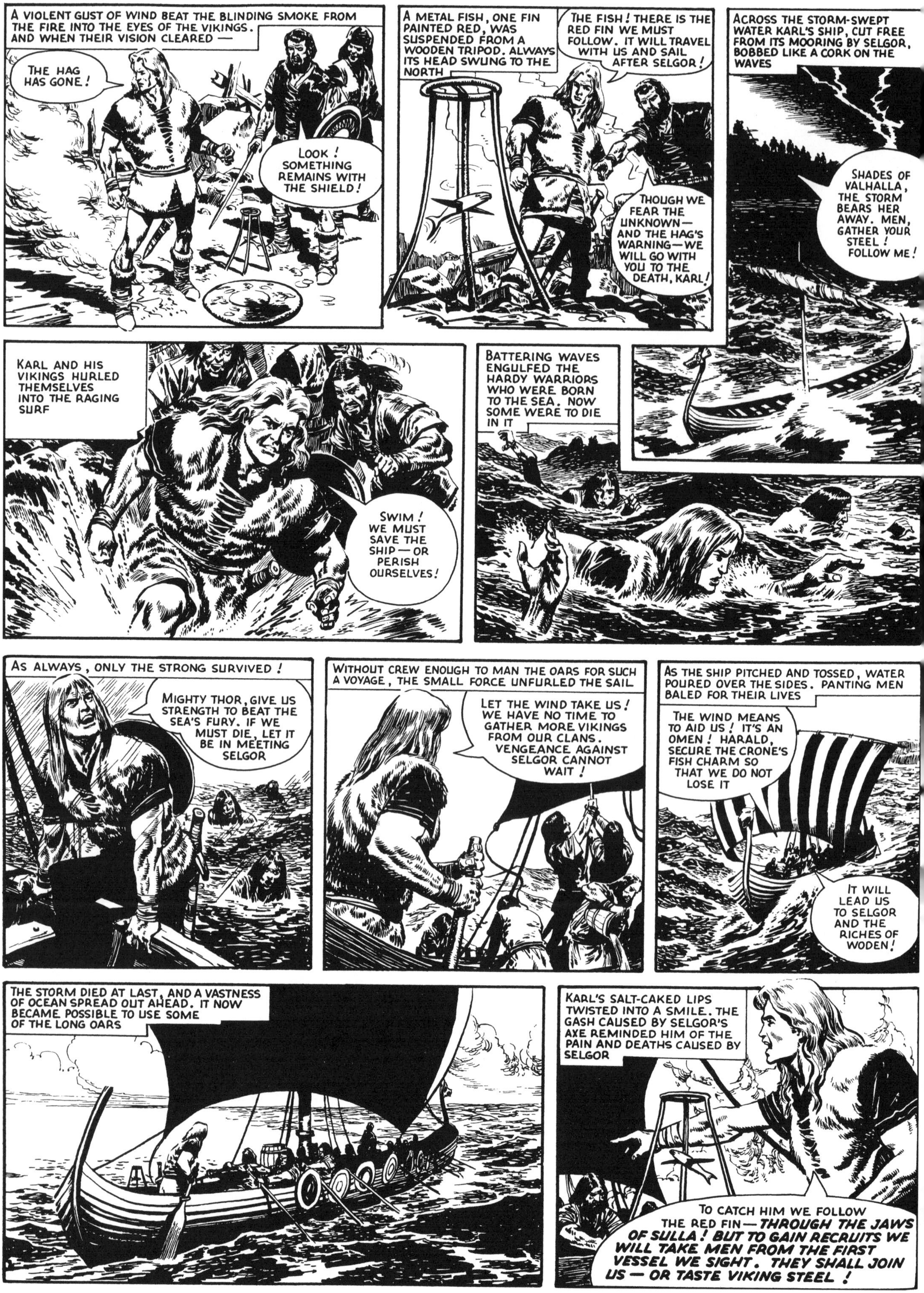

A VIOLENT GUST OF WIND BEAT THE BLINDING SMOKE FROM THE FIRE INTO THE EYES OF THE VIKINGS. AND WHEN THEIR VISION CLEARED —
THE HAG HAS GONE!
LOOK! SOMETHING REMAINS WITH THE SHIELD!
A METAL FISH, ONE FIN PAINTED RED, WAS SUSPENDED FROM A WOODEN TRIPOD. ALWAYS ITS HEAD SWUNG TO THE NORTH
THE FISH! THERE IS THE RED FIN WE MUST FOLLOW. IT WILL TRAVEL WITH US AND SAIL AFTER SELGOR!
THOUGH WE FEAR THE UNKNOWN— AND THE HAG'S WARNING—WE WILL GO WITH YOU TO THE DEATH, KARL!
ACROSS THE STORM-SWEPT WATER KARL'S SHIP, CUT FREE FROM ITS MOORING BY SELGOR, BOBBED LIKE A CORK ON THE WAVES
SHADES OF VALHALLA, THE STORM BEARS HER AWAY. MEN, GATHER YOUR STEEL! FOLLOW ME!
KARL AND HIS VIKINGS HURLED THEMSELVES INTO THE RAGING SURF
SWIM! WE MUST SAVE THE SHIP—OR PERISH OURSELVES!
BATTERING WAVES ENGULFED THE HARDY WARRIORS WHO WERE BORN TO THE SEA. NOW SOME WERE TO DIE IN IT
AS ALWAYS, ONLY THE STRONG SURVIVED!
MIGHTY THOR, GIVE US STRENGTH TO BEAT THE SEA'S FURY. IF WE MUST DIE, LET IT BE IN MEETING SELGOR
WITHOUT CREW ENOUGH TO MAN THE OARS FOR SUCH A VOYAGE, THE SMALL FORCE UNFURLED THE SAIL
LET THE WIND TAKE US! WE HAVE NO TIME TO GATHER MORE VIKINGS FROM OUR CLANS. VENGEANCE AGAINST SELGOR CANNOT WAIT!
AS THE SHIP PITCHED AND TOSSED, WATER POURED OVER THE SIDES. PANTING MEN BALED FOR THEIR LIVES
THE WIND MEANS TO AID US! IT'S AN OMEN! HARALD, SECURE THE CRONE'S FISH CHARM SO THAT WE DO NOT LOSE IT
IT WILL LEAD US TO SELGOR AND THE RICHES OF WODEN!
THE STORM DIED AT LAST, AND A VASTNESS OF OCEAN SPREAD OUT AHEAD. IT NOW BECAME POSSIBLE TO USE SOME OF THE LONG OARS
KARL'S SALT-CAKED LIPS TWISTED INTO A SMILE. THE GASH CAUSED BY SELGOR'S AXE REMINDED HIM OF THE PAIN AND DEATHS CAUSED BY SELGOR
TO CATCH HIM WE FOLLOW THE RED FIN—THROUGH THE JAWS OF SULLA! BUT TO GAIN RECRUITS WE WILL TAKE MEN FROM THE FIRST VESSEL WE SIGHT. THEY SHALL JOIN US — OR TASTE VIKING STEEL!

A STIFF WIND SENT KARL'S SHIP SCUDDING ONWARD. SOON, A STRANGE VAPOUR CLOUDED THE AIR — AND GLOWED LIKE A RAINBOW!

THE OLD HAG DID NOT LIE! WE TRAVEL FAST! THE GODS ARE AIDING US TO OVERTAKE SELGOR

BUT KARL'S EXCITED WORDS FADED AS A STRANGE, DISTANT SCREAM AROSE, AND THE SHIP STARTED TO GATHER UNNATURAL SPEED

KARL —I SENSE EVIL! THE WIND DROPS — YET THE WATERS MOVE FASTER!

THE STEERING OAR SNATCHED AND JUMPED IN KARL'S GRASP, AND THE EERIE RADIANCE MADE HIM RECALL WHAT THE OLD CRONE HAD SAID

THE NOISE COMES FROM *THE JAWS OF SULLA*, THROUGH WHICH THE HAG TOLD US TO SAIL!

FEAR CLAWED AT THE HEARTS OF THE VIKINGS WHO WOULD HAVE DIED GLADLY IN BATTLE, BUT NOW —

AA-EEE-AA-A!

KARL, TURN BACK! THE SCREAM IS OF SPIRITS WHO SEEK TO DEVOUR US!

THE TERRIBLE SOUND MADE EVEN KARL HESITATE

IF WE TURN BACK WE WILL NEVER OVERTAKE SELGOR. BUT IF WE GO ON — WHO KNOWS WHAT TERRIBLE EVIL LIES AHEAD?

THEN KARL REMEMBERED HIS COMRADES WHO HAD BEEN KILLED BY SELGOR. A VIVID PICTURE ROSE IN HIS MIND

KILL! KILL! WHERE SELGOR HAS FED, NO SCRAPS REMAIN FOR THE DOGS!

AGAIN KARL RECALLED HIS DEFEAT BY THE WILD, MERCILESS BERSERK WHO WAS CURSED TO RESEMBLE A WOLF

CRINGE, VIKING WHELP — AND MEET BLOOD-DRINKER, MY AXE!

LOWER THE SAIL! UNSHUTTER THE PORTS AND MAN THE OARS! WE GO ON! *I HAVE SWORN TO SLAY SELGOR. THERE WILL BE NO TURNING BACK!*

KARL'S RINGING TONES QUELLED THE STIRRINGS OF PANIC. BUT HARDLY WERE THE CREW AT THE OARS WHEN THE LOOK-OUT UTTERED A STARTLED SHOUT

KARL! ANOTHER SHIP ENTERS THE JAWS OF SULLA! WE ARE NOT ALONE!

AS THE SPRAY BEAT ON HIS FACE, KARL FELT A SAVAGE TRIUMPH WHICH CONQUERED ALL FEAR

WHERE ANOTHER CRAFT GOES SO CAN WE! PULL, MY VIKINGS! BEAR UP FROM THE WIND! THE FATE OF THE OTHER VESSEL SHALL GUIDE US!

IT MUST BE SELGOR'S SHIP!

BOTH VESSELS THRUST DEEPLY INTO THE CLOUD OF SPRAY, AND THE TERRIBLE WAILING SOUNDED LIKE A SOUL IN TORMENT. KARL FELT THE BLOOD DRAIN FROM HIS FACE

IT'S A MAELSTROM! MIGHTY THOR, GIVE US STRENGTH!

THE SHIP IS NOT SELGOR'S — AND WE ARE ALL DOOMED!

ABOARD THE LEADING SHIP OARS SHATTERED AND THE CREW WERE FLUNG IN ALL DIRECTIONS

AA-AAGH!

AS IF CLUTCHED BY A MIGHTY, IRRESISTIBLE HAND, THE STRICKEN VESSEL CAREERED MADLY IN THE SHRIEKING CIRCLES OF WHITE-FLECKED WATER

ODIN! WE PERISH!

KARL BELLOWED ORDERS WHICH THE SOUND OF THE WIND AND WATER ALMOST CARRIED AWAY

EVERY MAN TO THE STARBOARD OARS! PULL TO TURN THE SHIP FROM THE CURRENT!

DESPITE EVERY EFFORT, KARL'S SHIP BEGAN TO TURN — NOT TO PORT — **BUT INTO THE SPINNING POOL WHICH SPELT DEATH!**

IT — IT IS NO GOOD! WE HAVE LOST! WE'LL BE SUCKED DOWN INTO THE FUNNEL OF THE SEA!

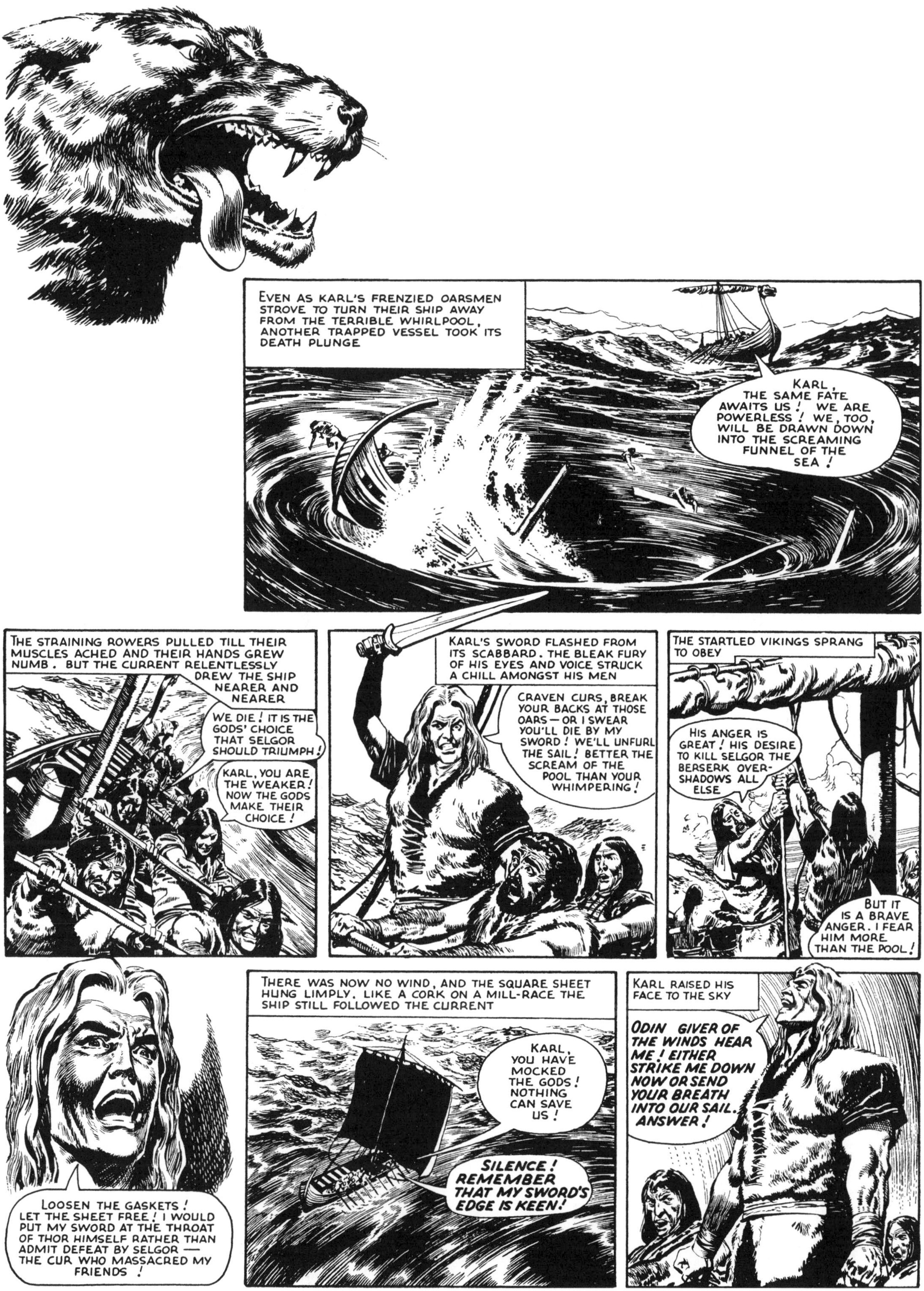

EVEN AS KARL'S FRENZIED OARSMEN STROVE TO TURN THEIR SHIP AWAY FROM THE TERRIBLE WHIRLPOOL, ANOTHER TRAPPED VESSEL TOOK ITS DEATH PLUNGE
KARL, THE SAME FATE AWAITS US! WE ARE POWERLESS! WE, TOO, WILL BE DRAWN DOWN INTO THE SCREAMING FUNNEL OF THE SEA!
THE STRAINING ROWERS PULLED TILL THEIR MUSCLES ACHED AND THEIR HANDS GREW NUMB. BUT THE CURRENT RELENTLESSLY DREW THE SHIP NEARER AND NEARER
WE DIE! IT IS THE GODS' CHOICE THAT SELGOR SHOULD TRIUMPH!
KARL, YOU ARE THE WEAKER! NOW THE GODS MAKE THEIR CHOICE!
KARL'S SWORD FLASHED FROM ITS SCABBARD. THE BLEAK FURY OF HIS EYES AND VOICE STRUCK A CHILL AMONGST HIS MEN
CRAVEN CURS, BREAK YOUR BACKS AT THOSE OARS — OR I SWEAR YOU'LL DIE BY MY SWORD! WE'LL UNFURL THE SAIL! BETTER THE SCREAM OF THE POOL THAN YOUR WHIMPERING!
THE STARTLED VIKINGS SPRANG TO OBEY
HIS ANGER IS GREAT! HIS DESIRE TO KILL SELGOR THE BERSERK OVER-SHADOWS ALL ELSE
BUT IT IS A BRAVE ANGER. I FEAR HIM MORE THAN THE POOL!
LOOSEN THE GASKETS! LET THE SHEET FREE! I WOULD PUT MY SWORD AT THE THROAT OF THOR HIMSELF RATHER THAN ADMIT DEFEAT BY SELGOR — THE CUR WHO MASSACRED MY FRIENDS!
THERE WAS NOW NO WIND, AND THE SQUARE SHEET HUNG LIMPLY. LIKE A CORK ON A MILL-RACE THE SHIP STILL FOLLOWED THE CURRENT
KARL, YOU HAVE MOCKED THE GODS! NOTHING CAN SAVE US!
SILENCE! REMEMBER THAT MY SWORD'S EDGE IS KEEN!
KARL RAISED HIS FACE TO THE SKY
ODIN GIVER OF THE WINDS HEAR ME! EITHER STRIKE ME DOWN NOW OR SEND YOUR BREATH INTO OUR SAIL. ANSWER!

SUDDENLY, ABOVE THE THROBBING SCREAM OF THE WHIRLPOOL, SOMETHING STIRRED — AND THE SAILCLOTH CRACKED VICIOUSLY TO FILL WITH A SALTY GUST!

THE WIND! THE WIND! ODIN ANSWERS!

THE SHIP STARTS TO TURN!

NOW THE SWELLING WIND HAD A GREATER STRENGTH THAN THE CURRENT, AND A SUPERHUMAN FORCE DROVE THE SHIP FROM THE CLUTCH OF THE POOL

KARL, WE RIDE FREE! WE SPEED ON TO OVERTAKE SELGOR!

IT IS GOOD! WE WILL EAT AND DRINK TO GAIN STRENGTH FOR WHAT LIES AHEAD!

ONCE REFRESHED, AND WITH BLOOD RUNNING HOT AGAIN, KARL AND HIS VIKINGS MADE PLANS

TO MEET SELGOR'S WOLF-PACK WE NEED A FULL CREW. OUR STEEL SHALL GAIN US ONE. WE ATTACK THE NEXT SHIP WE SEE!

THAT IS TRUE VIKING TALK. LEAD US, KARL!

IT WAS THE FOLLOWING DAWN WHEN KARL'S LOOK-OUT GAVE THE CRY EVERY VIKING AWAITED

SAIL-HO! A NORSE TRADER— BUT ARMED!

CLOSE IN FROM WINDWARD! SHE'LL FIGHT HARD!

WITH HIS OWN CREW OUTNUMBERED, KARL STAKED HIS HOPES ON THE ELEMENT OF SURPRISE

FIRE-ARROWS WILL CUT DOWN HER SAIL! THEN WE WILL RAM HER AND USE GRAPPLING-IRONS FOR THE BOARDING!

ONE FLAMING SHAFT SPED. THEN ANOTHER. KARL'S HAIL FOLLOWED ON THE WIND

WE NEED THIRTY VOLUNTEERS TO SAIL WITH US AGAINST SELGOR THE WOLF. EITHER YOU SUPPLY THEM — OR FIGHT!

THE ANSWER CAME BACK IN A FORM WHICH SILENCED A BURLY VIKING FOR EVER

WE FIGHT, VIKING! IT'S YOUR DECK THAT WILL RUN WITH BLOOD. YOU'LL FIND OUR FANGS NO LESS SHARP THAN SELGOR'S!

MEANWHILE, ONLY A FEW MILES TO WESTWARD, SELGOR THE WOLF AND HIS BERSERKS TOOK A REST FROM THEIR OARS. IT WAS AS IF SELGOR SENSED THE DISTANT SEA BATTLE ABOUT TO TAKE PLACE

WHAT AILS YOU, SELGOR?

I FEEL THAT KARL LIVES! I HEARD HIM SHOUTING MY NAME!

SELGOR'S FOLLOWERS SHUDDERED AS THE MAN, CURSED TO RESEMBLE A WOLF, THREW BACK HIS HEAD AND LAUGHED BAYINGLY

KARL LIVES! VOICES IN MY MIND TELL ME HOW I MAY FIND HIM! HE HUNTS ME — BUT I SHALL HUNT HIM!

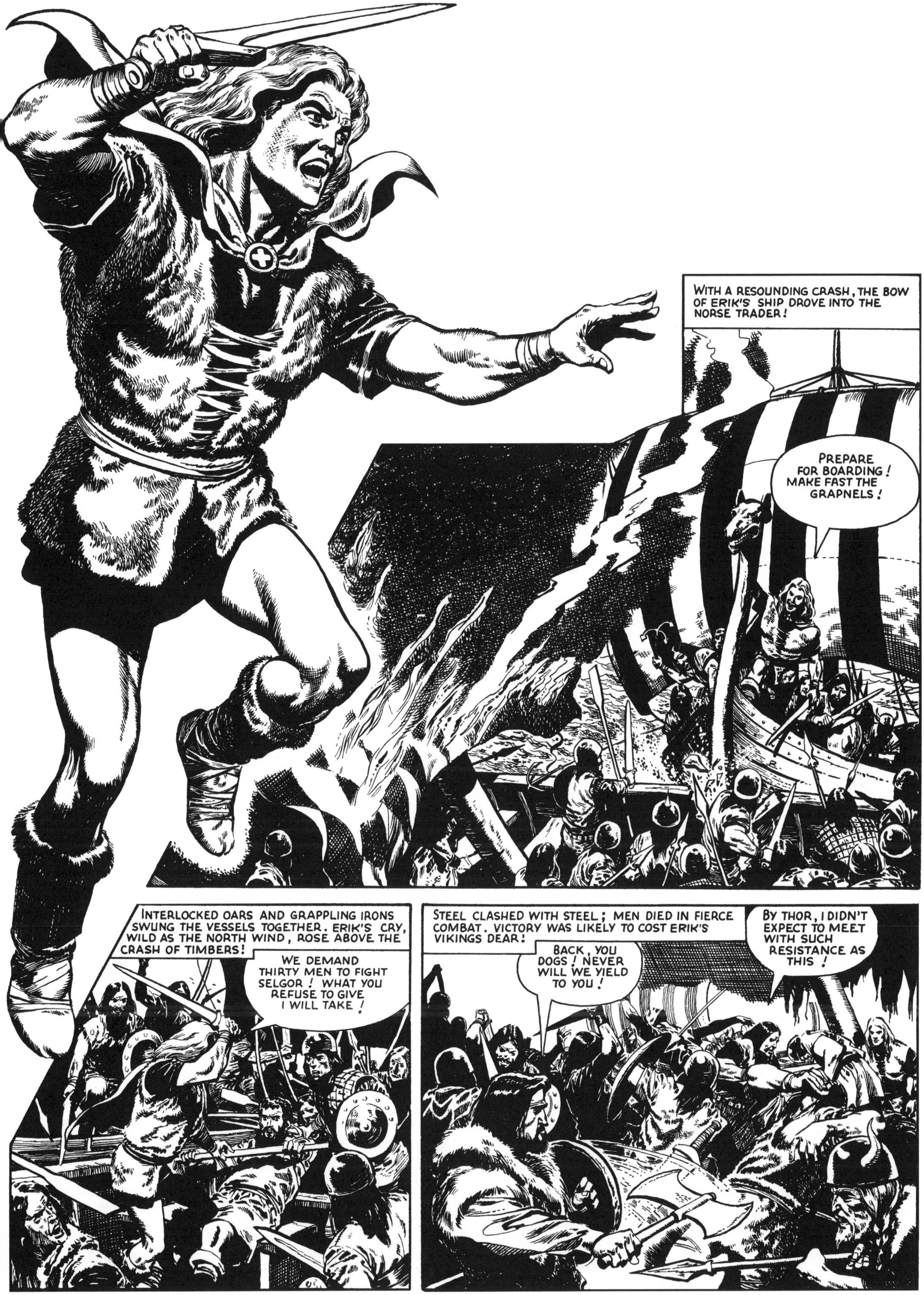
WITH A RESOUNDING CRASH, THE BOW OF ERIK'S SHIP DROVE INTO THE NORSE TRADER!
PREPARE FOR BOARDING! MAKE FAST THE GRAPNELS!
INTERLOCKED OARS AND GRAPPLING IRONS SWUNG THE VESSELS TOGETHER. ERIK'S CRY, WILD AS THE NORTH WIND, ROSE ABOVE THE CRASH OF TIMBERS!
WE DEMAND THIRTY MEN TO FIGHT SELGOR! WHAT YOU REFUSE TO GIVE I WILL TAKE!
STEEL CLASHED WITH STEEL; MEN DIED IN FIERCE COMBAT. VICTORY WAS LIKELY TO COST ERIK'S VIKINGS DEAR!
BACK, YOU DOGS! NEVER WILL WE YIELD TO YOU!
BY THOR, I DIDN'T EXPECT TO MEET WITH SUCH RESISTANCE AS THIS!

KARL REALISED THE DANGER, AND HE QUICKLY SINGLED OUT THE KEY FIGURE AMONG THE DEFENDERS...

HE IS THE MAN FOR ME!

COME, VIKING — I, AJARN, AWAIT YOU!

AS AJARN'S GLITTERING AXE SWUNG, KARL SIDE-STEPPED...

FOOL! I HAVE FACED THE AXE OF SELGOR THE BERSERK — AND STILL LIVE!

KARL'S SWORD CUT ITS WAY RIGHT THROUGH THE HAFT OF THE OTHER'S AXE!

THEN, SWIFT AS LIGHT, ERIK DROVE THE SWORD HILT AGAINST AJARN'S JAW!

HAD YOU BEEN SELGOR, IT WOULD HAVE BEEN THE SWORD'S EDGE AND YOUR THROAT!

AJARN FELL BACK BUT ERIK GRABBED HIM BY ONE ANKLE...

FOLLOWERS OF AJARN, I WANT THIRTY MEN — OR THERE WILL BE NO AJARN TO FOLLOW!

KILL AND HAVE DONE!

BUT AJARN'S CRUSHING AND UNEXPECTED DEFEAT HAD AN IMMEDIATE REACTION ON THE LUSTY SEAFARERS WHO RESPECTED ONLY STRENGTH...

SPARE HIM! YOU HAVE WON YOUR VOLUNTEERS, VIKING!

ONLY THOR THE HAMMERER COULD PUT THAT STRENGTH IN YOUR ARM!

KARL CLAIMED AJARN AND TWENTY-NINE OTHERS, AND AT LAST HIS SHIP COULD SET SAIL WITH FULL CREW...

AJARN, THE RUNES TELL ME THAT THE RICHES OF WODEN ARE PROTECTED BY A YELLOW EYE GAZING DOWN FROM A SKY OF BLOOD. I SEEK THOSE RICHES — AND THE DEATH OF SELGOR, THE BERSERK WHO HAS BECOME A HUMAN WOLF!

FOR MANY HOURS THE SHIP FOLLOWED THE DIRECTION OF THE STRANGE COMPASS GIVEN TO KARL BY AN OLD WOMAN WHO WAS THOUGHT TO BE A WITCH. THE WIND FELL AS THEY ENTERED A DAMP, CLINGING MIST...

WE REACH THE SEA OF SHADES! KARL, THE MIST GLOWS. I SENSE EVIL!

GUARD YOUR WEAK TONGUE. IT IS ONLY THE SUN COLOURING THE MIST!

YET EVIL THERE WAS! ANOTHER VESSEL, ITS OARS MUFFLED, TRACKED IN SILENT PURSUIT OF KARL'S...

THE TERRIBLE FIGURE OF SELGOR IN THE BOW OF THE SILENT PURSUER RAN A RED TONGUE OVER STRANGELY-TWISTED LIPS...

THE DEAD THOR-PRIEST WHO CURSED ME TO RESEMBLE A WOLF DID FAVOUR ME! I SCENTED KARL FROM AFAR. AND STEALTH AIDS A WOLF IN ITS KILL!

SELGOR'S POWERFUL HAND GRIPPED HIS GREAT AXE!

KARL, YOU WILL HEAR NOTHING — UNTIL MY AXE FLASHES SILENTLY ACROSS THE DISTANCE BETWEEN US. AT FIFTY PACES I CAN CUT A SAPLING IN TWO!

NEARER AND NEARER DREW SELGOR'S VESSEL. KARL'S ROWERS FAILED TO DETECT IT — FOR AT THAT MOMENT, THEIR SHIP DREW CLEAR OF THE MIST...

LAND-HO! KARL, I SEE CLIFFS!

THE CRY OF KARL'S LOOK-OUT SWITCHED ABRUPTLY FROM EXCITEMENT TO HOARSE TERROR. FROM HIGH OVER THE ROCK PEAK A STRANGE, GLARING RAY FLASHED!

'TIS THE GREAT YELLOW EYE THAT PROTECTS THE RICHES OF WODEN!

THE FEARSOME RAY FOCUSED ON THE SHIPS DRAWING CLEAR OF THE MIST, AND THE SKY SEEMED TO REDDEN WITH THE UNNATURAL BRILLIANCE

THE WORDS OF THE WITCH COME TRUE! THE YELLOW EYE BLAZES FROM A SKY OF BLOOD TO GUARD THE RICHES OF WODEN!

EVEN SELGOR, WHO WAS IN THE VERY ACT OF AIMING AN AXE AT THE UNSUSPECTING KARL, WAS PUT OFF HIS AIM. YET STILL THE AXE LEFT HIS HAND

THE WHIRLING BLADE, RAZOR-KEEN, SPED OFF COURSE. NOW, FOR THE FIRST TIME, KARL SIGHTED HIS ENEMY!

IT'S *SELGOR*, THE WOLF-MAN!

THE SEARING HEAT FROM THE YELLOW EYE BURNED SO FIERCELY THAT IT SCORCHED THE FEATHERS OF PASSING BIRDS

A PITILESS COMMON DANGER MENACED BOTH BERSERK AND VIKING

SELGOR, THE SAIL SMOKES—AND THE SEA STEAMS!

THE HEAT! IT'S—IT'S TERRIBLE!

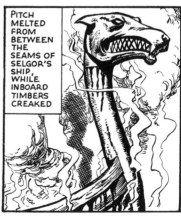

PITCH MELTED FROM BETWEEN THE SEAMS OF SELGOR'S SHIP, WHILE INBOARD TIMBERS CREAKED

DESPERATELY BOTH KARL AND SELGOR RAVED ORDERS

MOVE, YOU DOGS! SOAK THE TIMBERS IN WATER!

FURL THE SAIL! BACK YOUR OARS AND SEEK THE COVER OF THE MIST!

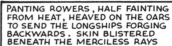

PANTING ROWERS, HALF FAINTING FROM HEAT, HEAVED ON THE OARS TO SEND THE LONGSHIPS FORGING BACKWARDS. SKIN BLISTERED BENEATH THE MERCILESS RAYS

THE EVIL EYE SEEKS TO SEND THE LONGSHIPS FORGING BACKWARDS.

THE EVIL EYE SEEKS TO BOIL OUR BLOOD!

PULL! THE MIST WILL SHIELD US — TURN!

AT LAST THE COOL DEPTHS OF THE SEA MIST BROUGHT SAFETY, AND ROWERS SANK ON THEIR OARS. VAINLY KARL SCANNED THE DRIFTING MIST FOR A GLIMPSE OF SELGOR

WOLF-MAN, ONLY THE MIST SAVES YOU FROM ME! SOME DAY THE LIFE SHALL RUN FROM YOU AT THE POINT OF MY SWORD. WHATEVER THE YELLOW EYE GUARDS SHALL BE MINE!

AN ANSWERING CRY ROSE AND FELL LIKE THAT OF A WOLF

KAA-ARL! THE MIST FAVOURS YOU! YOU SHALL WAIT AND FEAR — UNTIL I HAVE BLINDED THE YELLOW EYE AND LOOTED THE RICHES OF WODEN. THEN WE WILL MEET!

WITH NO CHANCE OF HUNTING HIS ENEMY, KARL CONCENTRATED ON MAKING A LANDING WHICH MIGHT ESCAPE THE TERRIBLE HEAT OF THE "YELLOW EYE". FOR HOURS THE VIKINGS CIRCLED IN THE MIST

WHEN DARKNESS STARTED TO FALL—

SINCE THE YELLOW EYE GLOWS LIKE A SUN, IT SHOULD NOT SHINE AT NIGHT-TIME. AT MOONRISE WE WILL MAKE A LANDING. THE QUEST SET BY THE GODS MUST BE CARRIED OUT!

BENEATH A BRILLIANT MOON THE VIKING SHIP GLIDED FOR AN INLET ON THE STRANGE COAST

KARL, WHAT LIES BEYOND? THERE IS A SILENCE OF DEATH I DO NOT LIKE

SOON WE SHALL SEE!

AS THEY BEACHED THE SHIP, KARL FELT THE SAME UNCANNY FEAR

BY THE GODS, MY OWN BLOOD SEEMS TO BE TURNING TO WATER. AM I A VIKING OR A COWARD? WHAT IS WRONG WITH THIS SHORE?

BUT FOR HIS HATRED OF SELGOR, KARL COULD ALMOST HAVE TURNED BACK. FEAR PLAYED LIKE A WIND ON THEM WHILE THEY CLIMBED

CEASE YOUR WHISPERING AND WHIMPERING! THE GODS BROUGHT US. WHATEVER LIES AHEAD HAS TO BE FACED!

IT IS NOT HUMANS WE FEAR

THEY GAINED THE BROW AND STUMBLED TO SOME WHITE OBJECTS REFLECTED IN THE MOONLIGHT. SUDDENLY KARL GASPED IN HORROR

BONES — HUMAN SKELETONS! WHY ARE THEY UNBURIED? AND WHAT — WHAT SLEW THEM?

ON THE DESOLATE, WIND-SWEPT MOOR AT THE HEAD OF THE CLIFFS, THE SCATTERED COLLECTION OF BONES GLEAMED WHITE IN THE MOONLIGHT

SOME OF THE SKELETONS ARE IN HALF! BY THE RUNES, WHAT DEVIL'S WORK CAUSED THIS?

NO HUMAN SLEW THEM!

KARL'S MEN, WHO FEARED NOTHING IN BATTLE, NOW ADVANCED HESITANTLY. ALL AT ONCE—

SEE! A SILVERY TRAIL! KARL, IT WAS MADE BY SOMETHING WHICH CRAWLED!

HALT!

FROM THE DISTANCE CAME THE SWEET, SICKLY ODOUR OF SWAMPLAND — AND SOMETHING, SEMI-LUMINOUS, WAS RETREATING

THIS AREA IS ACCURSED, KARL. I WOULD RATHER FACE THE LAND OF SHADES THAN GO ON!

STILL YOUR TONGUE, AJARN! OUR TASK IS NOT TO MAKE FOR THE SWAMP!

I HAVE SWORN TO KILL SELGOR AND CAPTURE THE RICHES OF WODEN. ANY VIKING WHO WISHES TO TURN BACK WILL MEET MY SWORD. THE QUEST SET BY THE GODS MUST BE FULFILLED!

THE VIKINGS AVOIDED THE SWAMPS, AND, BY DAWN, AGAIN SIGHTED THE FORTRESS ON THE TOWERING HEADLAND. CLOUDS HID THE SUN

THEN SELGOR WILL NOT BE FAR AWAY!

BEHIND THOSE WALLS LIE THE RICHES OF WODEN! ADVANCE WITH CARE! REMEMBER, SELGOR'S WOLF-PACK SEEKS THE SAME GOAL

SELGOR WAS NEARER THAN MIGHT HAVE BEEN GUESSED, FOR NO "BURNING RAY" NOW GUARDED THE SEA APPROACH TO THE FORTRESS

FOLLOW, MY WOLVES! WE CLIMB TO STORM THE FORTRESS AND TEAR AWAY ITS SECRETS. TODAY BLOOD-DRINKER, MY AXE, SHALL BE FED!

CHAOS FOLLOWED. THE TREACHEROUS SHALLOWS HELD CONCEALED MAN-TRAPS

FORWARD! LET THE TRAPPED FREE THEMSELVES!

AA-AGH! SELGOR — RELEASE ME!

THE TERRIBLE FIGURE, WHO WAS CURSED TO RESEMBLE A WOLF, HAD ALL A WOLF'S SAVAGERY AND LACK OF PITY

FOR EACH MAN I LOSE, THE FORTRESS SHALL LOSE TWENTY!

THE VERY GODS FEAR SELGOR!

FROM THE BATTLEMENTS OF THE FORTRESS A GIANT CATAPULT WENT INTO ACTION

AIM WELL! HURL BACK THE NORSEMEN!

MISSILE AFTER MISSILE RAINED DOWN

AA-AGH!

THERE WAS NO HALTING THE SAVAGE, BATTLE-CRAZED BESIEGERS. DESPERATELY SELGOR DROVE THEM ON

WHEN A WOLF BARES ITS FANGS, THE SHEEP PANIC! SOMEONE HAND ME A BOW!

A BOW-STRING SANG, AND AN ARMOURED FIGURE DIED WITH A WOLF-CRY RINGING IN HIS EARS

AYE —EEH! HE FEELS SELGOR'S BITE!

FROM AFAR, KARL AND HIS FOLLOWERS WATCHED THE SIEGE OF THE FORTRESS

SELGOR STRIKES FIRST! THAT SUITS ME WELL. WHILE HE BLUNTS HIS FANGS WE CAN APPROACH FROM THE REAR

THE DEFENDERS OF THE FORTRESS WERE TOO OCCUPIED BY THE BERSERKS TO GUARD THE REAR RAMPARTS — AND KARL'S VIKINGS, CAMOUFLAGED WITH CUT BRACKEN, MOVED ON

SUDDENLY AN EXCITED CRY BURST FROM AJARN, ONE OF KARL'S MEN

BY THE THUNDERER — A TUNNEL! LUCK FAVOURS US! IT CAN LEAD NOWHERE BUT INTO THE FORTRESS!

KARL'S EVERY NERVE SCREAMED AN INSTINCTIVE WARNING OF DANGER, BUT THE LURE OF A SECRET ENTRY INTO THE FORTRESS PROVED TOO GREAT. HE MADE A FATEFUL DECISION...

BRING FLINT AND STEEL! MAKE TORCHES! WE WILL ADVANCE— TO ROB SELGOR OF HIS PREY!

TORCHES FLICKERED EERILY
IN THE DAMP, CHILL AIR WHICH
DRIFTED FROM THE FORBIDDING
DEPTHS OF THE TUNNEL. GRIMLY
KARL ADVANCED...

FORWARD! LET
US CONQUER THE
FORTRESS FROM WITHIN
AND THEN TAKE SELGOR'S MEN
BY SURPRISE. VIKING STEEL
SHALL HURL THEM BACK FROM
THE RAMPARTS

A BEATING OF HUGE WINGS MADE AJARN
START BACK WITH A CRY OF ALARM...

AA-AGH!
BY THE
HAMMERRER

WHAT AILS
YOU? SHALL VIKINGS
LOSE THEIR COURAGE
BECAUSE OF TWITTERING
BATS?

THEN KARL HIMSELF HALTED IN AMAZE-
MENT. FOR THE FLOOR OF THE TUNNEL
REVEALED A STRANGE, SILVERY TRAIL!

WHAT CAN IT MEAN? SEE
— IT GLOWS! WHAT
COULD HAVE PASSED
ALONG HERE?

WYRD, WEAVER
OF DESTINY,
PROTECT US!

THE TRAIL LED PAST OTHER
GRISLY REMAINS—AND KARL
GRIPPED HIS SWORD UNTIL THE
HILT BIT DEEP INTO HIS PALM

BONES—HUMAN
BONES! WE
SAW SOME
THAT NIGHT
WHEN
SOMETHING
MYSTERIOUS
VANISHED
INTO THE
MARCHES

THE VIKINGS REMEMBERED THE PULSING,
MOVING SHAPE THAT HAD BAFFLED THEM
EARLIER...

WHAT HAD IT BEEN?

ON — TO
SLAY SELGOR
AND WIN THE
RICHES OF
WODEN! IF
THE WOLF-MAN
COULD SEE US
NOW, HOW HE
WOULD MOCK
US! WE
TREMBLE
BEFORE
MARKS IN
THE GROUND!

THE LASHING WORDS STUNG KARL'S PARTY INTO
ACTION. THEY PRESSED ON — UNTIL ONE OF THEM
SUDDENLY STEPPED INTO SPACE!

WH-WHAT HAS
HAPPENED?

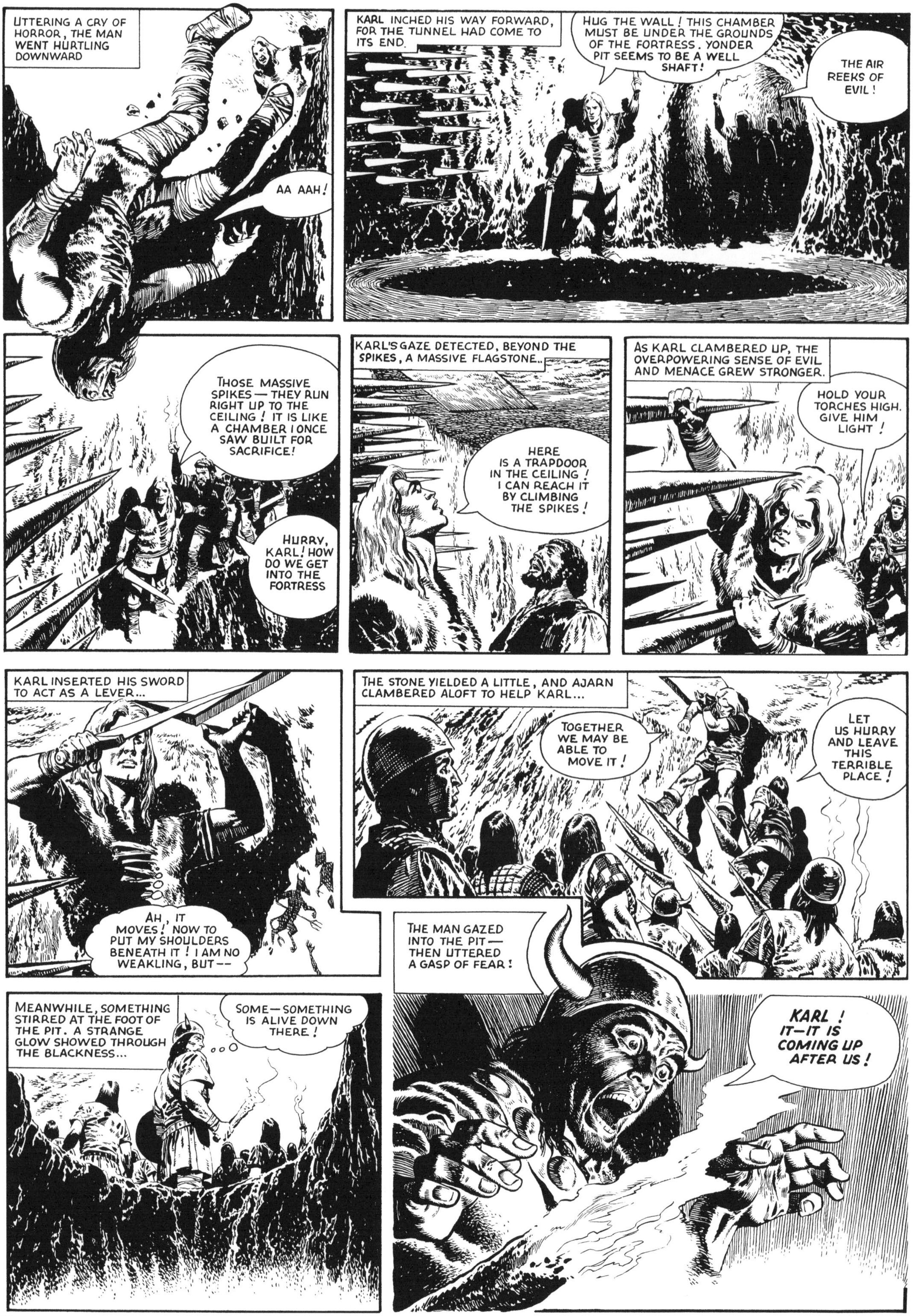

UTTERING A CRY OF HORROR, THE MAN WENT HURTLING DOWNWARD
AA AAH!
KARL INCHED HIS WAY FORWARD, FOR THE TUNNEL HAD COME TO ITS END.
HUG THE WALL! THIS CHAMBER MUST BE UNDER THE GROUNDS OF THE FORTRESS. YONDER PIT SEEMS TO BE A WELL SHAFT!
THE AIR REEKS OF EVIL!
THOSE MASSIVE SPIKES — THEY RUN RIGHT UP TO THE CEILING! IT IS LIKE A CHAMBER I ONCE SAW BUILT FOR SACRIFICE!
HURRY, KARL! HOW DO WE GET INTO THE FORTRESS
KARL'S GAZE DETECTED, BEYOND THE SPIKES, A MASSIVE FLAGSTONE..
HERE IS A TRAPDOOR IN THE CEILING! I CAN REACH IT BY CLIMBING THE SPIKES!
AS KARL CLAMBERED UP, THE OVERPOWERING SENSE OF EVIL AND MENACE GREW STRONGER.
HOLD YOUR TORCHES HIGH. GIVE HIM LIGHT!
KARL INSERTED HIS SWORD TO ACT AS A LEVER...
AH, IT MOVES! NOW TO PUT MY SHOULDERS BENEATH IT! I AM NO WEAKLING, BUT--
THE STONE YIELDED A LITTLE, AND AJARN CLAMBERED ALOFT TO HELP KARL...
TOGETHER WE MAY BE ABLE TO MOVE IT!
LET US HURRY AND LEAVE THIS TERRIBLE PLACE!
MEANWHILE, SOMETHING STIRRED AT THE FOOT OF THE PIT. A STRANGE GLOW SHOWED THROUGH THE BLACKNESS...
SOME—SOMETHING IS ALIVE DOWN THERE!
THE MAN GAZED INTO THE PIT— THEN UTTERED A GASP OF FEAR!
KARL! IT—IT IS COMING UP AFTER US!

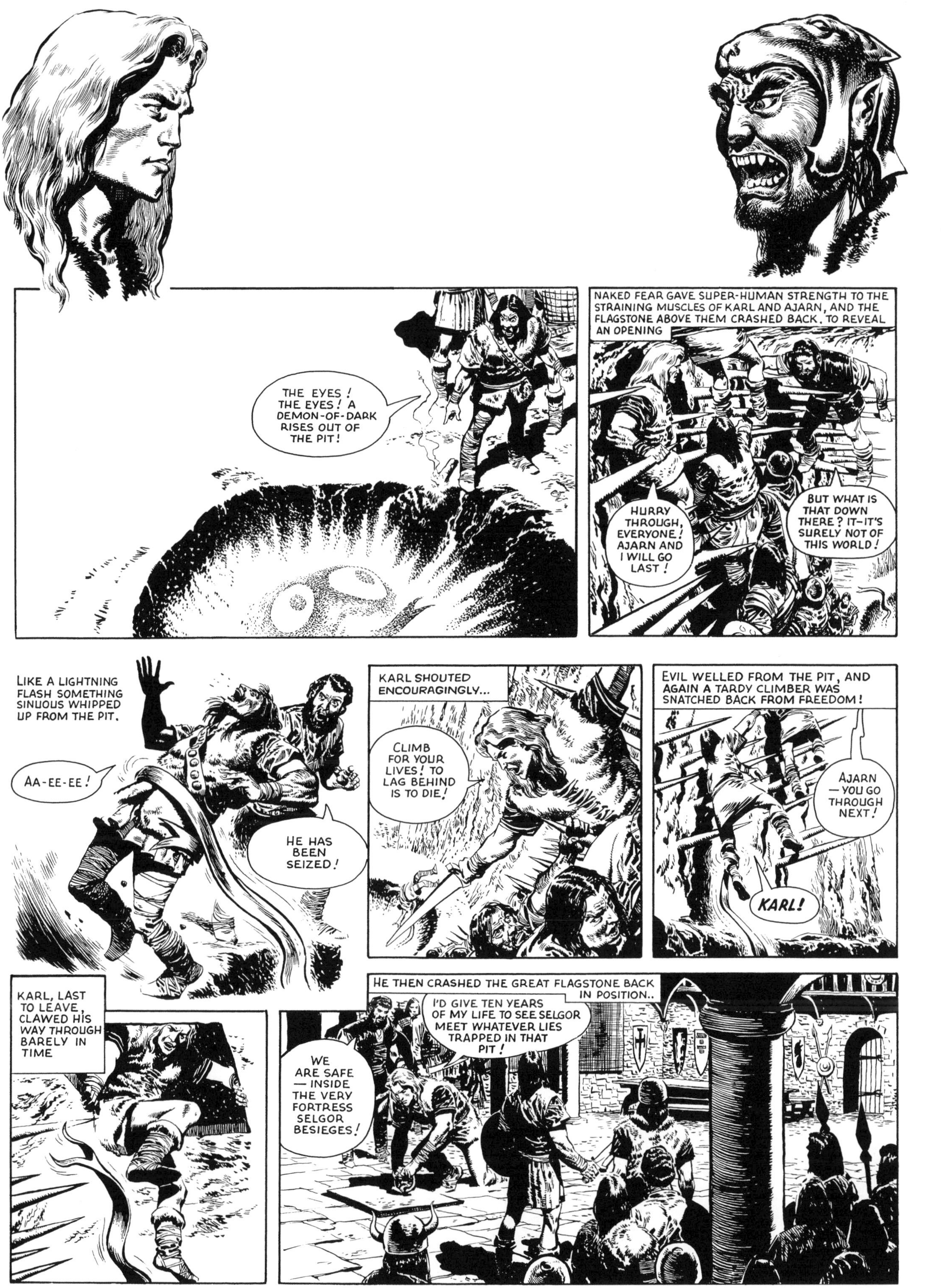

THE EYES! THE EYES! A DEMON-OF-DARK RISES OUT OF THE PIT!
NAKED FEAR GAVE SUPER-HUMAN STRENGTH TO THE STRAINING MUSCLES OF KARL AND AJARN, AND THE FLAGSTONE ABOVE THEM CRASHED BACK, TO REVEAL AN OPENING
HURRY THROUGH, EVERYONE! AJARN AND I WILL GO LAST!
BUT WHAT IS THAT DOWN THERE? IT-IT'S SURELY NOT OF THIS WORLD!
LIKE A LIGHTNING FLASH SOMETHING SINUOUS WHIPPED UP FROM THE PIT.
AA-EE-EE!
HE HAS BEEN SEIZED!
KARL SHOUTED ENCOURAGINGLY...
CLIMB FOR YOUR LIVES! TO LAG BEHIND IS TO DIE!
EVIL WELLED FROM THE PIT, AND AGAIN A TARDY CLIMBER WAS SNATCHED BACK FROM FREEDOM!
AJARN — YOU GO THROUGH NEXT!
KARL!
KARL, LAST TO LEAVE, CLAWED HIS WAY THROUGH BARELY IN TIME
HE THEN CRASHED THE GREAT FLAGSTONE BACK IN POSITION..
WE ARE SAFE — INSIDE THE VERY FORTRESS SELGOR BESIEGES!
I'D GIVE TEN YEARS OF MY LIFE TO SEE SELGOR MEET WHATEVER LIES TRAPPED IN THAT PIT!

WITH STEEL BARED AND READY, KARL'S VIKINGS PREPARED TO MAKE THE MOST OF THEIR SECRET ENTRY INTO THE FORTRESS...

WE'LL SURPRISE THE DEFENDERS, WIN THE FORTRESS, AND THEN HURL SELGOR'S WOLVES BACK FROM THE RAMPARTS. THE RICHES OF WODEN SHALL BE OURS — PAID FOR IN BERSERK BLOOD. SELGOR SHALL BE THE ONE TO DIE !

ARMOURED DEFENDERS WHEELED IN HORROR TO MEET THE WILD, STEEL-SWINGING RAIDERS WHO HAD COME FROM THE SEA !

BEWARE ! THE VIKINGS !

BY THE GODS, YOU KNOW US ! SO NOW LEARN THAT THE FURY OF TH NORSEMEN IS NO LIE !

QUARTER WAS NEITHER GIVEN NOR EXPECTED ; DEFENDERS AND ATTACKERS DIED GALLANTLY. THE FURY OF THE BATTLE TOOK ITS GRIM TOLL

SELGOR TROD A PATH ACROSS THE FALLEN — AND LAUGHED!

OUTSIDE THE FORTRESS, THE BESIEGING BERSERKS WERE PUZZLED BY A VISIBLE SLACKENING OF THE DEFENCE THE GREAT CATAPULTS NO LONGER RAINED

SELGOR, THE COWARDS WEAKEN. ORDER US TO BREACH THE WALLS AND TAKE THEM BY STORM !

THEY MAY AL BE DEAD !

THOR, LET SOME OF THEM LIVE FOR ME TO KILL ! WE WILL FASHION BATTERING-RAMS—AND SMASH OUR WAY IN !

THE SUN WAS SETTING BY THE TIME THE BATTERING-RAMS WERE MADE READY. AGAIN AND AGAIN STOUT TIMBERS RESISTED A MERCILESS ASSAULT.

THE TORTURED DOOR SPLINTERED AT LAST, BRINGING A CRY OF TRIUMPH FROM THE MAN CURSED TO RESEMBLE A WOLF —

THE FORTRESS IS MINE—AND WHATEVER IT HOLDS ! NOW SHALL THE FATES GUIDE ME TO THE RICHES OF WODEN—AND KARL ! MY QUEST SET BY THE GODS NEARS ITS END.

SELGOR KNEW NOTHING OF THE BATTLE WITHIN THE FORTRESS—NOR OF ITS TOLL. VICTORY HAD COST KARL'S VIKINGS DEAR, FOR THEY WERE WHITTLED DOWN TO A SMALL HANDFUL OF MEN

AJARN, GAZE FROM THE WINDOW ! I HEARD SELGOR'S VOICE ! HOW MANY MEN DOES HE HAVE ? OUR LOSSES HAVE ALL BUT BLED US TO DEATH

THE LAND OF GHOSTS AWAITS US ALL ! WE ARE OUTNUMBERED BEYOND POSSIBLE HOPE !

SELGOR'S FOLLOWERS CHECKED AS THEY GAZED AT THE DEAD WITHIN THE GROUNDS OF THE FORTRESS. THEY DIDN'T KNOW THAT KARL HAD ALREADY CAPTURED THE STRONGHOLD — AND SUPERSTITIOUS FEAR GRIPPED THEM

WAIT, SELGOR EVIL BREATHES FROM THE WALLS! OUR STEEL NEVER CUT DOWN THESE DEFENDERS. WHO — OR WHAT — SLEW THEM

SELGOR SPUN ON HIS HEEL, AND HIS TERRIBLE AXE HISSED IN A SWIFT, GLITTERING ARC

DEATH SLEW THEM! PERHAPS FEAR OF SELGOR DOES ANYONE ELSE SHARE THIS CRAVEN'S DOUBTS?

No!

UNSEEN, HIGH ABOVE, KARL AND THE HANDFUL OF VIKING SURVIVORS WATCHED THE SENSELESS KILLING... WATCHED STONILY — WITHOUT FEAR, WITHOUT HOPE!

KARL, VIKING COURAGE IS OF LITTLE USE AGAINST SUCH NUMBERS. THE TIME NEARS FOR US TO JOIN THE LAND OF GHOSTS

YONDER WOLF-PACK WILL SOON BE AT OUR THROATS. WE ARE DOOMED!

HATRED OF ALL SELGOR STOOD FOR CONSUMED KARL. YET EVEN HE FELT A TREMOR AT THE IMMENSITY OF WHAT SUDDENLY ENTERED HIS MIND

ALONE WE HAVE NO CHANCE AGAINST THE WOLF-MAN. BUT — WE ARE *NOT* ALONE! THE FORTRESS HOLDS A TERROR GREATER THAN HE — *THE DEMON-OF-DARK WHICH LURKS IN THE PIT!*

KARL — ARE YOU MAD?

AS KARL OUTLINED THE PLAN, HIS LISTENERS REMEMBERED THE UNKNOWN MENACE WHICH HAD RISEN FROM THE PIT TO SNATCH ITS PREY!

NEXT MOMENT, WITH A STRANGELY WHITE-FACED AJARN BEHIND HIM, KARL LEFT THE OTHER SURVIVORS. CHILLINGLY HIS FINAL INSTRUCTIONS RANG BACK

YOU KNOW YOUR PARTS — ACT! WHAT AJARN AND I HAVE TO DO MUST BE DONE!

I WOULD RATHER FACE SELGOR!

THEN BOWSTRINGS SANG! KARL'S ARCHERS LOOSED THEIR SHAFTS TOWARDS THE ADVANCING BERSERKS!

SELGOR — KARL STILL AWAITS YOU!

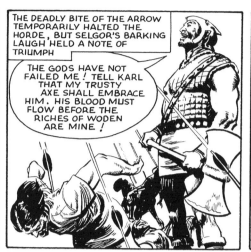

THE DEADLY BITE OF THE ARROW TEMPORARILY HALTED THE HORDE, BUT SELGOR'S BARKING LAUGH HELD A NOTE OF TRIUMPH.

THE GODS HAVE NOT FAILED ME! TELL KARL THAT MY TRUSTY AXE SHALL EMBRACE HIM. HIS BLOOD MUST FLOW BEFORE THE RICHES OF WODEN ARE MINE!

MEANWHILE, THE FLEEING FOOT-FALLS OF KARL AND AJARN ECHOED THROUGH A STONE-FLAGGED HALL HUNG WITH TAPESTRIES...

KARL, IT IS STILL NOT TOO LATE TO TURN BACK. FORGET THIS PLAN! BETTER TO FIGHT SELGOR AND DIE!

IF YOUR COURAGE FAILS YOU, I WILL GO ON ALONE!

IN THE FLOOR WAS THE STONE TRAP-DOOR WHICH LED DOWN TO THE PIT. AJARN CHOKING BACK THE HORROR WHICH GRIPPED HIM SPED TO AID KARL...

I AM NO COWARD!

I NEVER THOUGHT SO COME — LIFT!

INCH BY INCH, PRISED BY STRAINING MUSCLES, THE STONE WAS DRAWN OPEN. A WAVE OF DANK, EVIL-SMELLING AIR AROSE..

UGH!

SAVE YOUR BREATH. WE HAVE TO WORK FAST!

IN THE DEPTHS OF THE PIT SOMETHING RUSTLED AND STIRRED...

THE TWO VIKINGS HEARD THE OMINOUS SOUNDS AND WERE SPURRED ON TO DESPERATE SPEED...

THE THING MOVES! QUICK — GATHER THESE WOVEN DECORATIONS WE'LL LOWER THEM TO COVER THE IRON SPIKES WHICH MUST BE MEANT TO KEEP THE—THE THING FROM ESCAPING!

THE HEAVY TAPESTRIES WERE LOWERED — LENGTH AFTER LENGTH THE SPIKES PIERCED THEM BUT WERE FINALLY COVERED

NOW IT — WHATEVER IT IS — CAN CLIMB OUT!

HARDLY WAS THE TASK COMPLETED THAN A LUMINOUS MIST BLOSSOMED UP FROM THE PIT OPENING. THEN —

RUN, AJARN — RUN FOR YOUR LIFE!

SELGOR'S BERSERKS HOWLED WOLFISHLY AS THE CRIES AND THE SOUND OF RUNNING FEET REACHED THEM. NO LONGER DID THE ARROWS DELAY THEM, AND AXE-BLADES BIT THROUGH THE DOOR INTO THE TOWER..

ODIN — SPARE US!

THEY CRY IN TERROR. VICTORY SHALL BE OURS!

SELGOR AND HIS BERSERKS SHALL FACE IT!

FASTER, KARL! FASTER! I WOULD RATHER DIE THAN FACE THAT CREATURE OF EVIL!

TIMBERS SHATTERED BENEATH THE AXES OF THE BESIEGING BERSERKS. SELGOR, WHO HAD BEEN CURSED TO RESEMBLE A WOLF, BAYED HIS BLOOD-CHILLING TRIUMPH!

HAI-EE-OOO! THE FORTRESS AND ALL IT HOLDS IS MINE! FORWARD, MY WOLVES! LEAVE NO-ONE LIVING, BUT SAVE KARL FOR ME!

THE SOUNDS GUIDED THE PULSING, GLOWING MENACE WHICH HAD CRAWLED FROM THE PIT. A SILVERY, LUMINOUS TRAIL WAS THE SIGN OF ITS PASSING

A STRANGE SILENCE GREETED THE SHRIEKING BERSERKS WHO ENTERED THE FORTRESS. BUT FEAR OF SELGOR DROVE THEM

THERE IS NO-ONE HERE — ONLY THE HUSH OF THE GRAVE!

THERE'LL BE GRAVES ENOUGH FOR KARL'S VIKINGS! SEEK FOR SURVIVORS!

A SUDDEN CRY RANG OUT! FROM THE SHADOWS OF THE HALL, AN EERIE WHITE FORM MOVED LIKE A WHIPLASH AND ENCIRCLED TWO BERSERKS

AAAA—AAGH!

THE VICTIMS VANISHED! TWO MORE WERE PLUCKED FROM THE MERCILESS INVADERS WHO NOW STOOD FROZEN, PARALYSED BY SENSE-SAPPING FEAR!

SHADES OF VALHALLA! SPARE US

MEANWHILE, KARL AND AJARN REJOINED THEIR HANDFUL OF VIKING SURVIVORS. INSTANTLY KARL PUT THE REST OF HIS PLAN INTO ACTION...

CLIMB FOR YOUR LIVES! REACH THE GROUND AND SEEK SAFETY! THE BERSERKS HAVE MET AN ENEMY WHO'LL WHITTLE DOWN THEIR NUMBERS. THEN WE'LL BE ABLE TO ATTACK THEM!

MAN AFTER MAN SOUGHT REFUGE FROM THE FORTRESS AND THE TERRORS IT HELD

PREPARE AN AMBUSH FOR THOSE BERSERKS WHO ESCAPE. LET GOOD VIKING STEEL FINISH THE TASK STARTED BY THAT CREATURE!

THE HUMAN WOLVES SHALL PAY FOR THE MANY VIKINGS THEY HAVE SLAIN!

THEN KARL SPOKE TO AJARN...

YOU FOLLOW THE OTHERS. MY FATE MUST BE DECIDED HERE WITH SELGOR, AS THE WITCH-WOMAN WARNED ME. THE WOLF-MAN AND I SHALL FIGHT TO THE DEATH FOR THE RICHES OF WODEN

SO BE IT!

HARDLY HAD AJARN REACHED THE VIKING SURVIVORS OUTSIDE THE WALLS THAN THE REMNANTS OF SELGOR'S TERROR-STRICKEN RAIDERS BURST FROM THE FORTRESS!

THEY OUTNUMBER US STILL, BUT THE ODDS ARE LESS HEAVY. BY THOR, THEY'LL RECEIVE A GREETING THEY LITTLE EXPECT!

STEEL FLASHED AS AJARN AND HIS COMRADES HURLED THEMSELVES ON THE CRUEL SLAYERS WHO HAD WIPED OUT KARL'S VILLAGE

DEATH TO THE BERSERKS!

THE VIKINGS TRIUMPHED, AND A FULL MOON ROSE OVER THE SCENE...

SELGOR THE WOLF IS NOT NUMBERED WITH THEIR DEAD. IF HE HAS SURVIVED THE MONSTER, HE IS IN THE FORTRESS WITH KARL!

FOLLOWING KARL'S ORDERS, THE GRIM-FACED MEN WAITED — WAITED AND WATCHED UNTIL THE MORNING SUN ROSE...

THERE IS NO SIGN OF KARL! NOTHING MOVES ON THE BATTLE-MENTS

WHAT DOES IT MEAN? WHAT HAS HAPPENED? HOW LONG MUST WE REMAIN HERE?

SUDDENLY FROM ABOVE ONE GREAT TOWER A BLAZING LIGHT SHONE LIKE A GIANT YELLOW EYE. IT INCREASED WITH THE POWER OF THE SUN!

IT IS THE GIANT EYE WHICH GUARDS THE RICHES OF WODEN!

EVERY ONLOOKER FELT HIS NERVES TIGHTEN...

IT'S THE SIGN FROM THE GODS! KARL AND SELGOR ARE AT THE END OF THEIR QUEST. ONE SHALL LIVE, AND ONE DIE LIKE A COWARD! BUT WHICH?

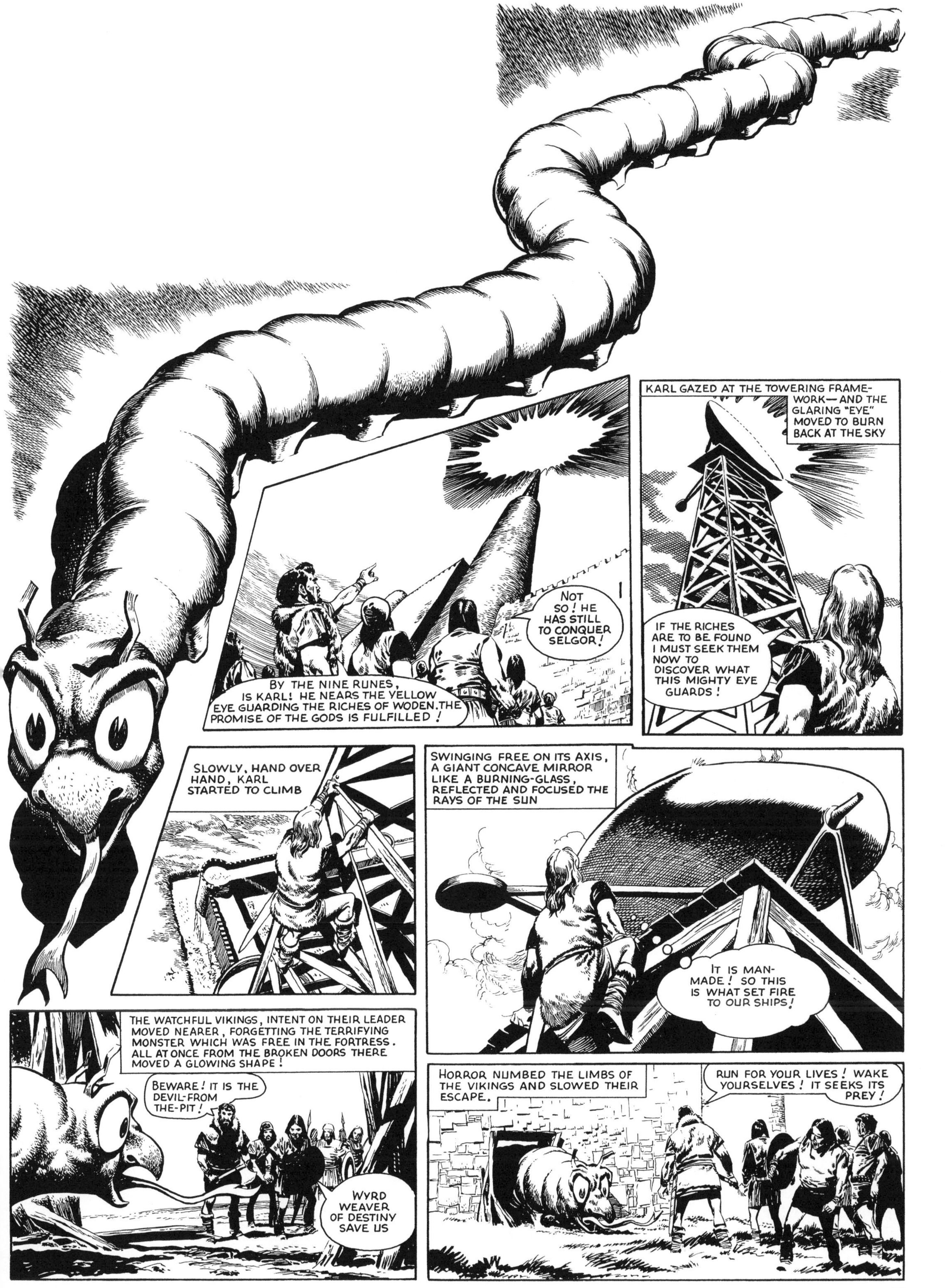
KARL GAZED AT THE TOWERING FRAME-WORK— AND THE GLARING "EYE" MOVED TO BURN BACK AT THE SKY
BY THE NINE RUNES, IS KARL! HE NEARS THE YELLOW EYE GUARDING THE RICHES OF WODEN. THE PROMISE OF THE GODS IS FULFILLED!
NOT SO! HE HAS STILL TO CONQUER SELGOR!
IF THE RICHES ARE TO BE FOUND I MUST SEEK THEM NOW TO DISCOVER WHAT THIS MIGHTY EYE GUARDS!
SLOWLY, HAND OVER HAND, KARL STARTED TO CLIMB
SWINGING FREE ON ITS AXIS, A GIANT CONCAVE MIRROR LIKE A BURNING-GLASS, REFLECTED AND FOCUSED THE RAYS OF THE SUN
IT IS MAN-MADE! SO THIS IS WHAT SET FIRE TO OUR SHIPS!
THE WATCHFUL VIKINGS, INTENT ON THEIR LEADER MOVED NEARER, FORGETTING THE TERRIFYING MONSTER WHICH WAS FREE IN THE FORTRESS. ALL AT ONCE FROM THE BROKEN DOORS THERE MOVED A GLOWING SHAPE!
BEWARE! IT IS THE DEVIL-FROM THE-PIT!
WYRD WEAVER OF DESTINY SAVE US
HORROR NUMBED THE LIMBS OF THE VIKINGS AND SLOWED THEIR ESCAPE.
RUN FOR YOUR LIVES! WAKE YOURSELVES! IT SEEKS ITS PREY!

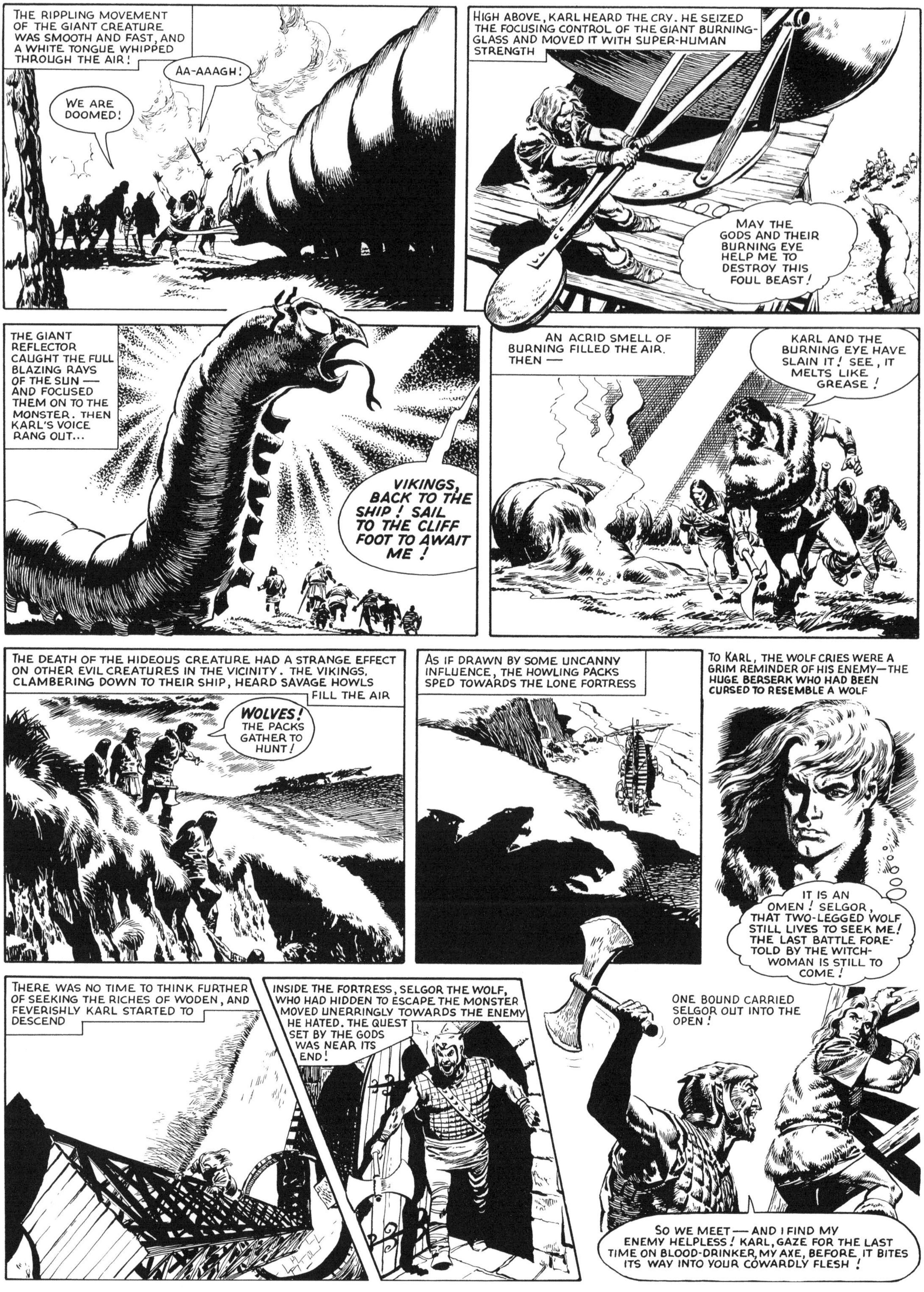

THE RIPPLING MOVEMENT OF THE GIANT CREATURE WAS SMOOTH AND FAST, AND A WHITE TONGUE WHIPPED THROUGH THE AIR!
AA-AAAGH!
WE ARE DOOMED!
HIGH ABOVE, KARL HEARD THE CRY. HE SEIZED THE FOCUSING CONTROL OF THE GIANT BURNING-GLASS AND MOVED IT WITH SUPER-HUMAN STRENGTH
MAY THE GODS AND THEIR BURNING EYE HELP ME TO DESTROY THIS FOUL BEAST!
THE GIANT REFLECTOR CAUGHT THE FULL BLAZING RAYS OF THE SUN — AND FOCUSED THEM ON TO THE MONSTER. THEN KARL'S VOICE RANG OUT...
VIKINGS, BACK TO THE SHIP! SAIL TO THE CLIFF FOOT TO AWAIT ME!
AN ACRID SMELL OF BURNING FILLED THE AIR. THEN —
KARL AND THE BURNING EYE HAVE SLAIN IT! SEE, IT MELTS LIKE GREASE!
THE DEATH OF THE HIDEOUS CREATURE HAD A STRANGE EFFECT ON OTHER EVIL CREATURES IN THE VICINITY. THE VIKINGS, CLAMBERING DOWN TO THEIR SHIP, HEARD SAVAGE HOWLS FILL THE AIR
WOLVES! THE PACKS GATHER TO HUNT!
AS IF DRAWN BY SOME UNCANNY INFLUENCE, THE HOWLING PACKS SPED TOWARDS THE LONE FORTRESS
TO KARL, THE WOLF CRIES WERE A GRIM REMINDER OF HIS ENEMY—THE HUGE BERSERK WHO HAD BEEN CURSED TO RESEMBLE A WOLF
IT IS AN OMEN! SELGOR, THAT TWO-LEGGED WOLF STILL LIVES TO SEEK ME! THE LAST BATTLE FORETOLD BY THE WITCH-WOMAN IS STILL TO COME!
THERE WAS NO TIME TO THINK FURTHER OF SEEKING THE RICHES OF WODEN, AND FEVERISHLY KARL STARTED TO DESCEND
INSIDE THE FORTRESS, SELGOR THE WOLF, WHO HAD HIDDEN TO ESCAPE THE MONSTER MOVED UNERRINGLY TOWARDS THE ENEMY HE HATED. THE QUEST SET BY THE GODS WAS NEAR ITS END!
ONE BOUND CARRIED SELGOR OUT INTO THE OPEN!
SO WE MEET — AND I FIND MY ENEMY HELPLESS! KARL, GAZE FOR THE LAST TIME ON BLOOD-DRINKER, MY AXE, BEFORE IT BITES ITS WAY INTO YOUR COWARDLY FLESH!

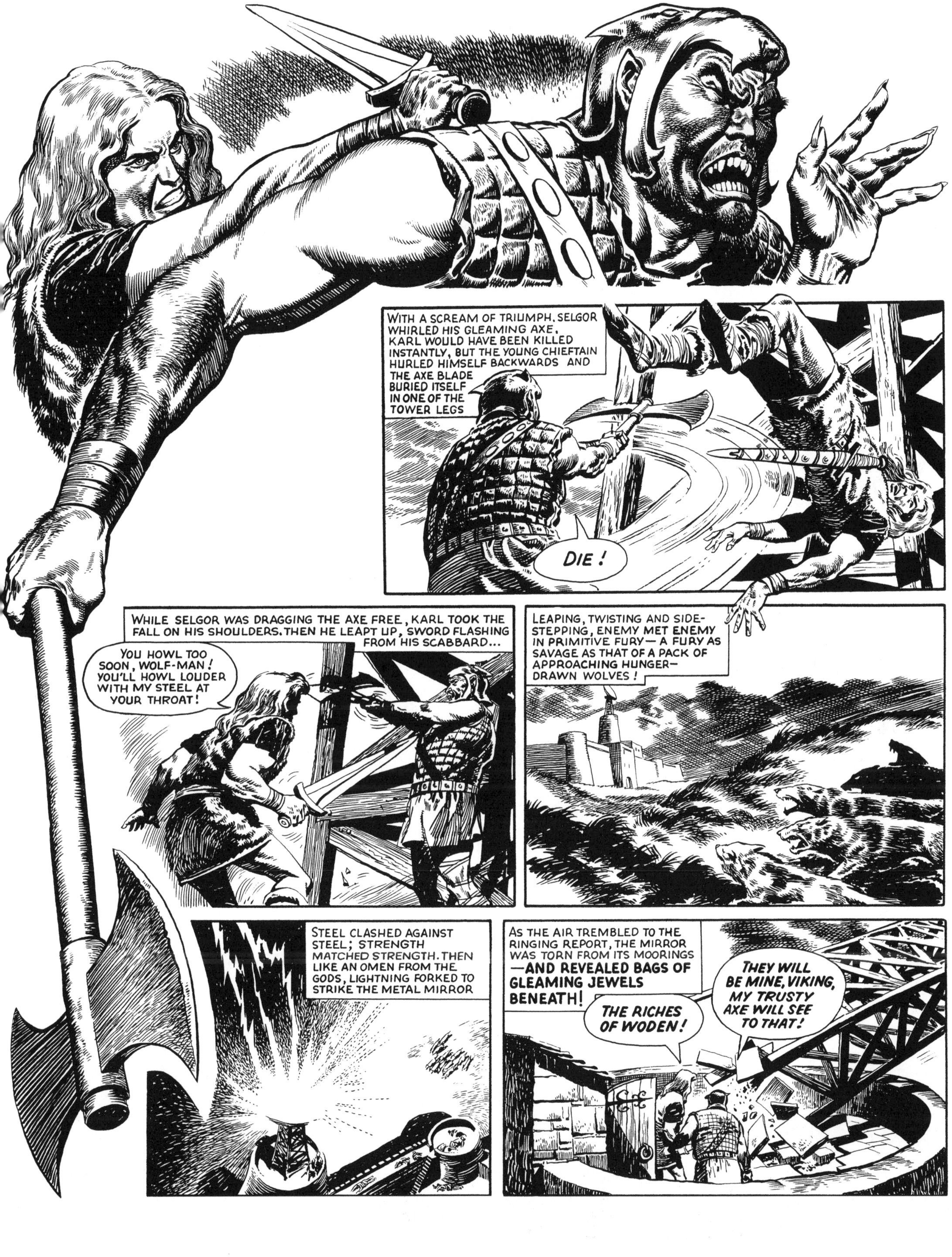

WITH A SCREAM OF TRIUMPH, SELGOR WHIRLED HIS GLEAMING AXE. KARL WOULD HAVE BEEN KILLED INSTANTLY, BUT THE YOUNG CHIEFTAIN HURLED HIMSELF BACKWARDS AND THE AXE BLADE BURIED ITSELF IN ONE OF THE TOWER LEGS
DIE!
WHILE SELGOR WAS DRAGGING THE AXE FREE, KARL TOOK THE FALL ON HIS SHOULDERS. THEN HE LEAPT UP, SWORD FLASHING FROM HIS SCABBARD...
YOU HOWL TOO SOON, WOLF-MAN! YOU'LL HOWL LOUDER WITH MY STEEL AT YOUR THROAT!
LEAPING, TWISTING AND SIDE-STEPPING, ENEMY MET ENEMY IN PRIMITIVE FURY— A FURY AS SAVAGE AS THAT OF A PACK OF APPROACHING HUNGER-DRAWN WOLVES!
STEEL CLASHED AGAINST STEEL; STRENGTH MATCHED STRENGTH. THEN LIKE AN OMEN FROM THE GODS, LIGHTNING FORKED TO STRIKE THE METAL MIRROR
AS THE AIR TREMBLED TO THE RINGING REPORT, THE MIRROR WAS TORN FROM ITS MOORINGS —AND REVEALED BAGS OF GLEAMING JEWELS BENEATH!
THE RICHES OF WODEN!
THEY WILL BE MINE, VIKING, MY TRUSTY AXE WILL SEE TO THAT!

THE FIGHT RAGED THROUGH THE TURRET DOORWAY, KARL BEING DRIVEN SLOWLY BACK...

MAD WITH HUNGER, THE WOLF-PACKS SWEPT THROUGH THE FORTRESS, AND GAUNT, HOWLING SHAPES SIGHTED THEIR PREY AT THE TOP OF THE STAIRS.

TAKE ANOTHER STEP BACK. WOLF-FANGS ARE AHEAD OF YOU — *AND* BEHIND!

AGAIN SELGOR'S AXE CARVED A GLITTERING PATH — BUT KARL WAS FASTER!

YOU MISS, SELGOR! NOW —

AS SELGOR LURCHED FORWARD OFF BALANCE, KARL CLUBBED THE *SWORD* HILT INTO HIS NECK!

ONE TERRIFIED CRY SNAPPED AWAY INTO SPACE, AND SELGOR'S TWISTING BODY SPUN OVER AND OVER...

AA—AA—AAGH!

SNARLING FORMS ENGULFED THE MAN WHO HAD BEEN CURSED TO RESEMBLE A WOLF!

HE DIED SCREAMING, AS THE WITCH-WOMAN SAID! IT IS OVER!

KARL RETREATED SLAMMING THE TURRET DOOR AFTER HIM...

THE QUEST SET BY THE GODS IS ENDED, AND MY DEAD COMRADES AVENGED. I, KARL, PROVED THE STRONGER — THE RICHES OF WODEN ARE MINE!

AT THE FOOT OF THE CLIFFS KARL'S VIKING SURVIVORS STILL WAITED. THEN THEY SAW HIM DESCENDING THE TOWER...

IT IS KARL! HE HAS TRIUMPHED!

SO SELGOR IS DEAD!

JOINING HIS COMRADES KARL EMPTIED THE SKIN BAG WHICH HE HAD FOUND

THE RICHES OF WODEN WE WILL SHARE THEM AMONG US! THEY HAVE COST US THE LIVES OF MANY OF OUR COMRADES. MAY THEIR SPIRITS GAIN REST IN VALHALLA

TO THE SOUND OF HOWLING WOLVES OUTSIDE THE FORTRESS, KARL AND HIS VIKINGS BOARDED THEIR SHIP AND PREPARED FOR ITS RETURN VOYAGE TO SCANDINAVIA — AND WHAT THE FUTURE MIGHT HOLD

GREAT IS KARL!

GREATER EVEN THAN WYRD, THE WEAVER OF DESTINY!

KARL, LOOKING BACK, SUDDENLY SHIVERED. A STRANGE CLOUD, PIERCED BY THE SUN, FILLED HIM WITH UNEASY FOREBODING...

WYRD, THE WEAVER OF DESTINY, IS ALREADY PLANNING OUR FUTURE. WHAT IS IN STORE FOR US? ONLY TIME WILL TELL!

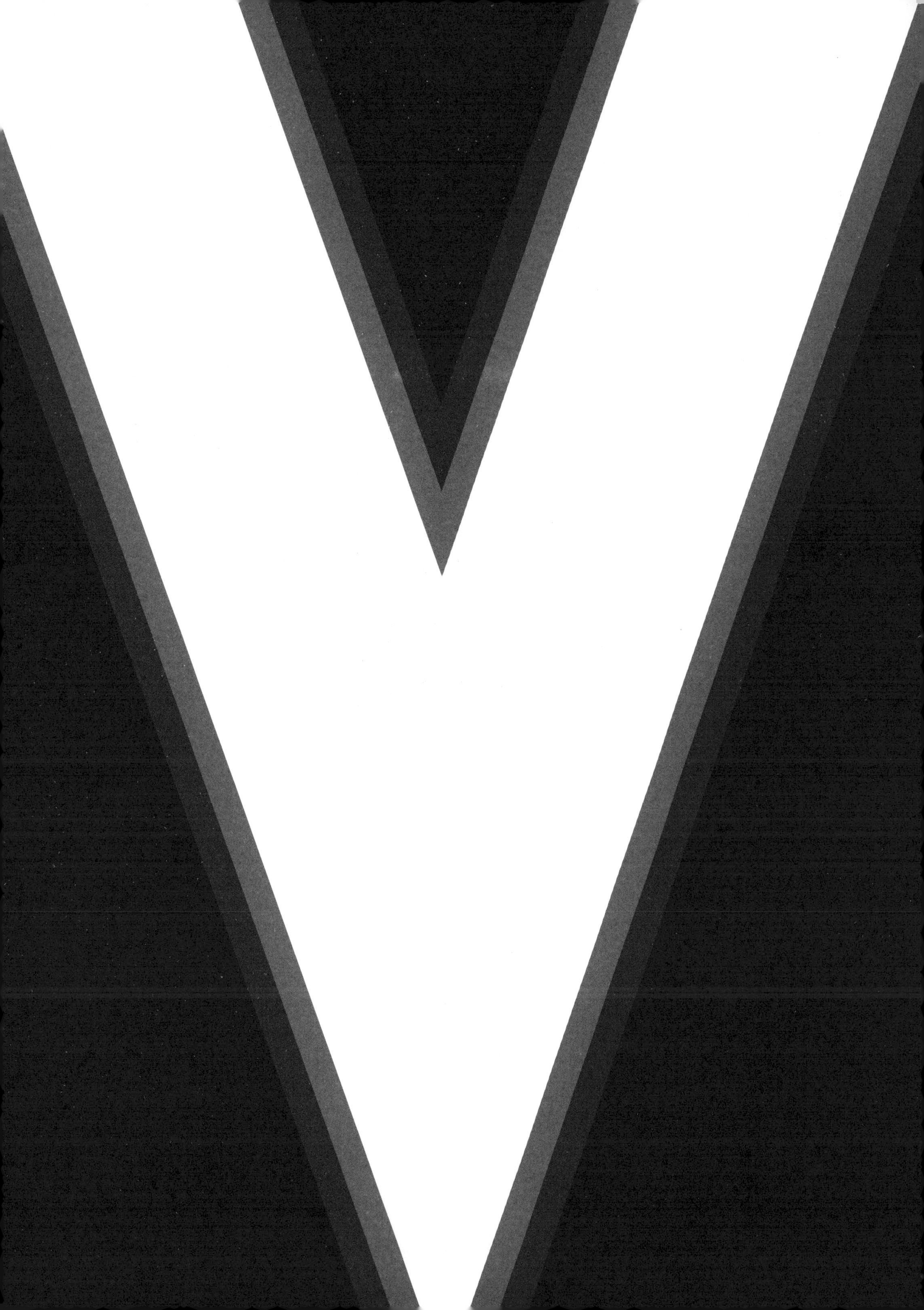
V

THE FALSE GOD

Serialised in **Lion**
18th November 1961 – 24th March 1962

Written by
Ted Cowan

Art by
Don Lawrence

YET EVIL WAS STIRRING! FROM ACROSS LIMPID WATERS A STRANGE, EERIE CRY REACHED THE STARTLED EARS OF TWO FISHERMEN WHO WERE REPAIRING THEIR NETS...

LARS, THAT SOUND! BY ODIN, IT IS THE HOWL OF A WOLF!

FROM THE SEA? YOU ARE MAD, OLAF!

KARL WAS A YOUNG VIKING CHIEFTAIN WHO HAD SUCCEEDED IN WINNING A LONG BATTLE AGAINST HIS TREACHEROUS ENEMY, SELGOR THE WOLF. SELGOR HAD EVENTUALLY BECOME THE VICTIM OF A SAVAGE ATTACK BY A PACK OF WOLVES. NOW, MONTHS LATER, ALL SEEMED PEACEFUL AMONG THE NORWEGIAN FIORDS...

SEIZING THEIR FISHING SPEARS, THE AMAZED VIKINGS BEGAN TO WADE OUT AS THE STRANGE WRECK DRIFTED CLOSER.

COME, WE'LL SALVAGE THE SHIP AND SEARCH HER FOR CARGO. A LUCKY FIND COULD MAKE US RICH MEN!

BE CAREFUL! I SENSE EVIL! HOW DID THE WOLVES GET ABOARD?

THE SOUND RE-ECHOED ABOVE THE IDLE LAPPING OF THE WATER. AT THE BOW OF A WEED-COVERED, DRIFTING HULK, TWO HALF-STARVED SHAPES FORMED A GAUNT, LIVING FIGURE-HEAD...

MAD, AM I? GAZE YONDER!

ON THAT WRECK? THUNDER—YOU WERE RIGHT! THERE ARE TWO WOLVES!

THE WOLVES, YELLOW FANGS BARED, SEEMED LIKE WATCH-DOGS. SUDDENLY—

LOOK OUT! THEY SPRING!

THE SWIFT SPEARS DID THEIR WORK, AND THE FISHERMEN—THRILLED YET UNEASY—CLAMBERED ABOARD...

THE WEEDS WRITHE LIKE SNAKES. LARS, LET US TURN BACK.

THAT IS COWARD'S TALK! LET US SEE IF THERE IS ANYTHING OF VALUE HIDDEN AWAY.

A MOUND OF SEAWEED, STRANGELY FORMED, DREW LARS'S ATTENTION. HE BEGAN TO PROBE IT ASIDE WITH HIS SPEAR.

SOMETHING LIES UNDER HERE!

BEWARE—THE MOUND BREATHES!

THE MOUND HEAVED — AND A GREAT HAND TORE THE SPEAR FROM LARS'S GRASP...

DRAPED IN A MANTLE OF ROTTING SEAWEED, A TERRIFYING SHAPE SPRANG TO ENGULF THE LUCKLESS VIKING...

IT—IT WILL KILL HIM!

AA-AAH!

LARS'S BODY CRASHED TO THE BOARDS, AND THE SLAYER TURNED. TWO HANDS LIFTED BACK THE WEED WHICH COVERED THE UNKNOWN'S HEAD. OLAF UTTERED A GASP OF HORROR...

BY ODIN! CAN—CAN THAT BE HIS FACE?

OVERCOME WITH SUPERSTITIOUS FEAR, OLAF SPRANG OFF THE WRECK AND INTO THE SHALLOW WATER. FRANTICALLY HE SPED TOWARDS THE SHORE...

THE LONE OCCUPANT OF THE SHIP CUT A MASK FROM THE DEAD LARS'S CLOTHING. WATCHED ONLY BY THE GULLS, HE STRODE UP THE BEACH...

THE SUN WAS SETTING UPON THE TEMPLE OF THOR WHEN A HUGE SHADOW CROSSED THE THRESHOLD AND MADE THE THOR-PRIEST GLANCE UP...

GREETINGS, STRANGER! WHAT GIFT DO YOU BRING TO THE SHRINE OF MIGHTY THOR?

I COME TO TAKE, NOT TO GIVE! I AM THOR! I CLAIM WHAT IS MY OWN!

LEAVING THE PRIEST AND HIS ATTENDANT UNCONSCIOUS, THE NEWCOMER ADVANCED SAVAGELY...

THE GOLD HELMET AND HAMMER OF THOR! I NEED THEM. AS THOR THE THUNDERER, I SHALL HOLD MORE POWER THAN ANY VIKING EVER DREAMED OF!

AT THAT MOMENT, MILES AWAY, ONE VIKING — TIRED AFTER HUNTING — **WAS** DREAMING. THAT VIKING WAS KARL, WATCHED BY AJARN, HIS FRIEND. HE STIRRED IN UNEASY SLEEP...

KARL, AWAKE! WHAT AILS YOU? YOU SHOUT AND CRY OUT!

IT SEEMED TO KARL THAT CLAWED HANDS WERE GRIPPING HIS THROAT. HE AWOKE CHOKING — WITH A CRY THAT SHOCKED AJARN..

SELGOR THE WOLF! HE HAS RETURNED FROM THE DEAD!

AJARN, KARL'S FRIEND, SHOUTED IN AMAZEMENT AS KARL BOUNDED UP AND MOUNTED ONE OF THE HORSES...

THIS IS MADNESS! WHAT AILS YOU? SELGOR THE WOLF IS DEAD! YOU YOURSELF SAW HIM DRAGGED DOWN BY WOLVES!

MY DREAM WARNS ME. I HAVE TO MAKE SURE!

AGAIN KARL REMEMBERED THAT LAST BATTLE MANY MONTHS BEFORE — AND HOW SELGOR HAD FALLEN INTO THE ATTACKING WOLF-PACK..

COULD SELGOR HAVE COME BACK FROM THE DEAD?

NOW KARL RODE MADLY, FOLLOWING A ROUTE HE HAD SEEN IN HIS DREAM. AND AJARN WENT WITH HIM...

I DREAMT THAT SELGOR RAIDED THE THOR TEMPLE AT HELGAPOINT! WE GO THERE! BE HE MAN OR DEMON, IT IS THE WILL OF THE GODS THAT I DESTROY HIM!

IT IS STRANGE THAT KARL SHOULD START A THREE-DAY JOURNEY — AS THE RESULT OF A DREAM!

MEANWHILE, IN THE TEMPLE AT HELGAPOINT, SELGOR WAS CLIMBING UP TO THE EFFIGY OF THOR. THE PRIEST WHOM HE HAD PREVIOUSLY ATTACKED WATCHED FEARFULLY...

KARL'S DREAM HAD NOT LIED! SELGOR, HIS FACE STILL MASKED REMOVED THOR'S GOLDEN HELMET AND HAMMER.

WEARING THE HELMET, HE FIERCELY GRASPED THE HAMMER

THE HELMET AND HAMMER OF THOR MAKE ME AS THOR! NOW ALL NORSEMEN WILL OBEY ME.— AS A GOD. THE TIME HAS COME FOR ME TO SEIZE POWER!

SELGOR LEFT THE LOOTED TEMPLE AND PREPARED FOR THE FIRST PART OF HIS PLAN...

FOR A START I WILL SEEK MEN AND SHIPS TO SERVE ME!

BEFORE LONG HE APPROACHED A NORSE SETTLEMENT AT SKILD...

A STRANGER APPROACHES! I AM NO COWARD — YET I FEAR TO CHALLENGE HIM. SEE THAT HELMET AND HAMMER!

ROUSE YOUR COURAGE! OUR ORDERS ARE TO KEEP ALL STRANGERS BACK!

THE GUARD, WHO WAS RECKLESS ENOUGH TO ISSUE A CHALLENGE, DIED WITHOUT HEARING THE ANSWER!

FOOL! WOULD YOU CHALLENGE A GOD?

CONTEMPTUOUSLY SELGOR STRODE ON TO THE GREAT HALL WHERE A BANQUET WAS IN PROGRESS. CHIEFS AND WARRIORS SPRANG TO THEIR FEET...

YOU THERE! WHO ARE YOU?

YOU SHALL LEARN LITTLE CHIEF!

THE MASSIVE GOLD HAMMER SWUNG IN A GLITTERING ARC — TO SMASH THE BANQUET TABLE INTO PIECES!

THOR THE HAMMERER SEEKS YOU! CHOOSE, DOGS! YOU CAN SERVE ME OR DIE!

BRAVE BUT SUPERSTITIOUS MEN TREMBLED WITH FEAR...

THOR, WE SERVE YOU!

MIGHTY ONE, WHY ARE YOU MASKED?

NO VIKING CAN GAZE ON THE FACE OF A GOD AND STILL LIVE. THOR'S LIGHTNING BOLTS WOULD DESTROY YOU. BUT I NEED A MASK MADE OF GOLD!

SELGOR TOSSED THE GOLDEN HAMMER TO THE TREMBLING ONLOOKERS...

TAKE THAT AND HAVE MADE FROM IT A GOLDEN MASK AND DECORATIONS FOR ARMOUR. FIND AN EXPERT SMITH — AND ALSO GET HIM TO FORGE A HAMMER OF IRON!

IT SHALL BE

AT A SMITHY NEARBY, THE IRON HAMMER AND GOLDEN MASK WERE EXPERTLY FORGED...

THE THREE DAYS HAD ENDED WHEN KARL REACHED THE THOR TEMPLE OF HIS DREAM. THERE —

SEE THE BODY, AJARN! 'TIS OF A THOR PRIEST! *SO SELGOR DOES LIVE!* MY DREAM DID NOT LIE!

THE DYING MAN RAISED HIMSELF AS KARL AND AJARN SPRANG DOWN FROM THEIR HORSES. SOME SUPERHUMAN POWER SEEMED TO GIVE HIS VOICE STRENGTH...

YOU—YOU ARE KARL, I KNEW YOU WOULD COME. MIGHTY THOR HAS HELPED ME TO HOLD AT BAY THE SHADOWS OF DEATH TILL OUR MEETING

WHILE THE EYES IN THE THOR-PRIEST'S ASHEN FACE BURNED FEVERISHLY, ERIK OFFERED HIM HIS DRINKING-FLASK

TAKE A SIP OF THIS, OLD FELLOW!

I—I HAVE NO TIME LEFT. RAISE ME! TAKE ME INTO THE TEMPLE! YOUR TASK BEGINS WHERE MINE ENDS!

IN THE LOOTED TEMPLE THE PRIEST TOLD OF THE RUTHLESS SLAYER WHOSE FACE HAD BEEN MASKED

.. HE KILLED FIRST, THEN ROBBED THE SHRINE OF THOR. THOR'S GOLDEN HAMMER AND HELMET WERE TAKEN. THE ROBBER WAS MORE DEMON THAN MAN!

SELGOR! IT COULD ONLY HAVE BEEN SELGOR!

KARL, THE GOLDEN HAMMER AND HELMET MUST BE RESTORED! IF NOT, DISASTER WILL OVERCOME OUR PROUD PEOPLE! EVIL WILL FLOURISH UNTIL THOR RECOVERS WHAT IS HIS OWN!

AS IF TO BEAR OUT THESE WORDS THERE CAME A MIGHTY CLAP OF THUNDER AND LIGHTNING FLASHED BLINDINGLY. THE SUPPORTED FIGURE WENT LIMP!

THE THOR-PRIEST IS DEAD, AJARN! HE LIVED ONLY TO PASS ON HIS MESSAGE!

KARL'S LIPS WERE WHITE WITH A TERRIBLE ANGER WHEN HE AND AJARN HURRIED OUT INTO THE STORM-LADEN AIR

THOR, GOD OF THUNDER AND STORM, I SWEAR TO RECOVER WHAT HAS BEEN STOLEN. THE DEVIL WHO ROBBED YOU IS SELGOR! *THIS TIME I WILL MAKE SURE HE DIES!*

SELGOR THE WOLF IS DEAD! IF HE LIVED, SURELY THOR WOULD GIVE US A SIGN!

AJARN'S WORDS ENDED IN A SHARPLY-DRAWN BREATH. LIGHTNING WREATHED THE HILLS TO DRIVE OUT GREY SHAPES FROM THE TREES

THOR GIVES YOU YOUR ANSWER. SELGOR, WOLF-MAN AND DEVIL, IS THE ONE WE MUST SEEK!

WOLVES!

A MINUTE LATER —

THE BRUTES ATTACK! BY THE RUNES, NOW I BELIEVE YOU!

HOWLING FORMS WERE HACKED ASIDE BY THE TWO COMRADES, BUT THE GREY SHAPES STILL CAME ON

THE HORSES TIRE! WE SHALL BE TORN DOWN AND SLAIN!

RIDE FOR YON POINT!

THE VIKINGS GAINED THE ROCK WALL, DISMOUNTED, AND THEN TURNED AT BAY. FANGED FURY LAUNCHED ITSELF AT THEM

KARL'S STRENGTH WAS BEGINNING TO FAIL HIM WHEN HIS BLADE GLANCED A ROCK. SPARKS SHOWERED AS THE POINT BROKE TO SPLINTERS

AAA-AGH!

THE DISASTER WAS ALSO A MIRACLE. SPARKS FIRED THE TINDER-DRY GRASS, AND A WIND FANNED THE FLAMES INTO THE ATTACKERS

THE BEASTS RUN! FIRE IS THE ENEMY OF ALL WOLVES!

WYRD THE WEAVER OF DESTINY PROTECTS US!

WHILE THE PANICKED WOLVES RETREATED, KARL GAZED AT HIS SWORD BLADE

BEFORE I SEEK SELGOR FURTHER, I SHALL NEED A GOOD SMITH TO REPAIR THIS

THERE IS A SMITHY NOT FAR FROM THE SETTLEMENT AT SKILD. LET US GO TO HIM

IT DIDN'T TAKE THEM LONG TO REACH THE SMITHY IN THE HILLS

REPAIR THE BLADE WELL! I NEED THE EDGE KEEN TO HUNT DOWN A MASKED GIANT WHO HAS STOLEN THE GOLDEN HELMET AND HAMMER OF THOR

THERE WAS A STRAINED, TERRIBLE SILENCE. THEN THE SMITH SPOKE

ARE YOU MAD? THE MAN YOU SEEK IS THOR! WE SERVE HIM! FROM THE HAMMER I FORGED HIM A GOLD MASK AND BREAST-PLATE!

BEFORE KARL COULD RECOVER FROM THE SHOCK OF THIS DISCOVERY, THE OTHER SMITH WITHDREW A RED-HOT SWORD-BLADE FROM THE FORGE. THEN —

THESE ARE THOR'S ENEMIES—SO THEY ARE OUR ENEMIES, TOO! WE WILL SLAY THEM!

KARL HURLED HIMSELF ASIDE AS AJARN SHOUTED A WARNING. A CRAZY, FANATICAL FURY SEEMED TO DRIVE THE SMITHS ON...

DEATH TO ALL ENEMIES OF THOR!

BEWARE, KARL! THESE FOOLS THINK SELGOR THE WOLF IS THE THOR GOD!

ALTHOUGH ARMED WITH AN AXE, AJARN WAS CAUGHT OFF GUARD BY HIS ATTACKER'S SHEER SAVAGERY!

KARL, UNARMED, FACED THE SEARING MENACE OF RED-HOT STEEL WITHDRAWN FROM THE FORGE...

JACKAL, YOU ARE A FOOL TO MOCK THOR! HIS LIGHTNING BOLTS CAN BLIND MEN — LIKE THIS SWORD!

KARL'S SKIN BECAME SCORCHED WITH THE HEAT OF THE SWORD, BUT HIS MOVEMENT WAS AS FAST AS THAT OF A STRIKING ADDER!

SERVANT OF THOR, SUCH MADNESS NEEDS TO BE QUENCHED!

HE SPRANG, AND HIS VICE-LIKE GRIP ENCIRCLED HIS OPPONENT'S SWORD WRIST. THE SMITH WAS THRUST BACK TOWARDS THE HEAT OF THE FORGE

AAA-AGH!

DROP THE SWORD — OR MEET THE FLAMES OF YOUR FURNACE!

MEANWHILE, AJARN HAD RECOVERED HIS OLD SKILL. THE HAFT OF HIS AXE CRASHED HOME AS THE OTHER'S SWORD FELL...

LEAPING BACK, KARL SEIZED HIS CHANCE TO SELECT A SWORD FROM THE RACKS. THEN—

SERVANT OF THOR, WHERE IS THIS GIANT FOR WHOM YOU MADE THE GOLD MASK? SPEAK—OR, BY ODIN, I'LL LOOSEN YOUR TONGUE!

THE MAN HESITATED, BUT KARL'S EYES WERE MERCILESS!

I'LL NOT ASK AGAIN!

SEEK HIM AT THE VILLAGE OF SKILD! BUT YOU'LL BE DOOMED IF YOU FIND HIM!

MOMENTS LATER, THE SOUND OF GALLOPING HOOVES RANG TOWARDS THE NORSE SETTLEMENT AT SKILD. KARL AND AJARN HAD WASTED NO TIME!

BE CAREFUL! THE PEOPLE OF SKILD MAY ALSO THINK SELGOR A GOD!

IT MATTERS NOT! SELGOR, THAT DEMON OF EVIL, MUST BE SLAIN, AND THE STOLEN GOLD RETURNED TO THOR'S TEMPLE!

MEANWHILE, IN THE GREAT HALL AT SKILD, SOME GRIM ENTERTAINMENT WAS FOLLOWING A FEAST. IT WAS WATCHED BY A MASKED FIGURE WHOM ALL THOUGHT TO BE THOR, BUT WHO WAS REALLY SELGOR!

THOR WATCHES! STRIKE AND SLAY!

WITH A CONTEMPTUOUS LAUGH, THE MASKED FIGURE LEANT FORWARD— AND HIS DAGGER UNERRINGLY SEVERED THE ROPE!

ENOUGH! I HAVE SEEN WOLF CUBS FIGHT BETTER. TO SERVE THOR MEANS SHEDDING BLOOD FAST!

SUDDENLY SELGOR TENSED, AND HIS SHADOW TOOK ON A STRANGE SHAPE. HE SEEMED TO BE SCENTING THE AIR...

SERVANTS OF THOR, ENEMIES APPROACH! BY THE GHOSTS OF VALHALLA, IT IS THE SIGN I AWAIT. NOW LISTEN CLOSELY TO MY WORDS—

AHEAD OF KARL AND AJARN, THE SETTLEMENT LAY STRANGELY SILENT...

NOTHING MOVES. THERE IS NO SIGN OF LIFE!

WE RIDE ON! IF SKILD IS DESERTED I WISH TO KNOW WHY!

IN THE FIORD, ROWS OF MANY NEW SHIPS BOBBED AT THEIR MOORINGS!

SKILD SEEMS TO HAVE GATHERED A FLEET. WHY, AJARN? WHY?

IT MIGHT BE WISER NOT TO SEEK THE ANSWER TO THAT QUESTION!

NO SENTRIES HALTED THEM. THE SILENCE WAS DEATHLY YET OPPRESSIVE WITH MENACE.

SIX HUNDRED MEN LIVE AT SKILD. WHERE ARE THEY?

AJARN'S VOICE, HARSH WITH SHOCK, CAME LIKE A THUNDER-CLAP!

LOOK! THE DEVIL YOU SEEK HAS SOUGHT YOU!

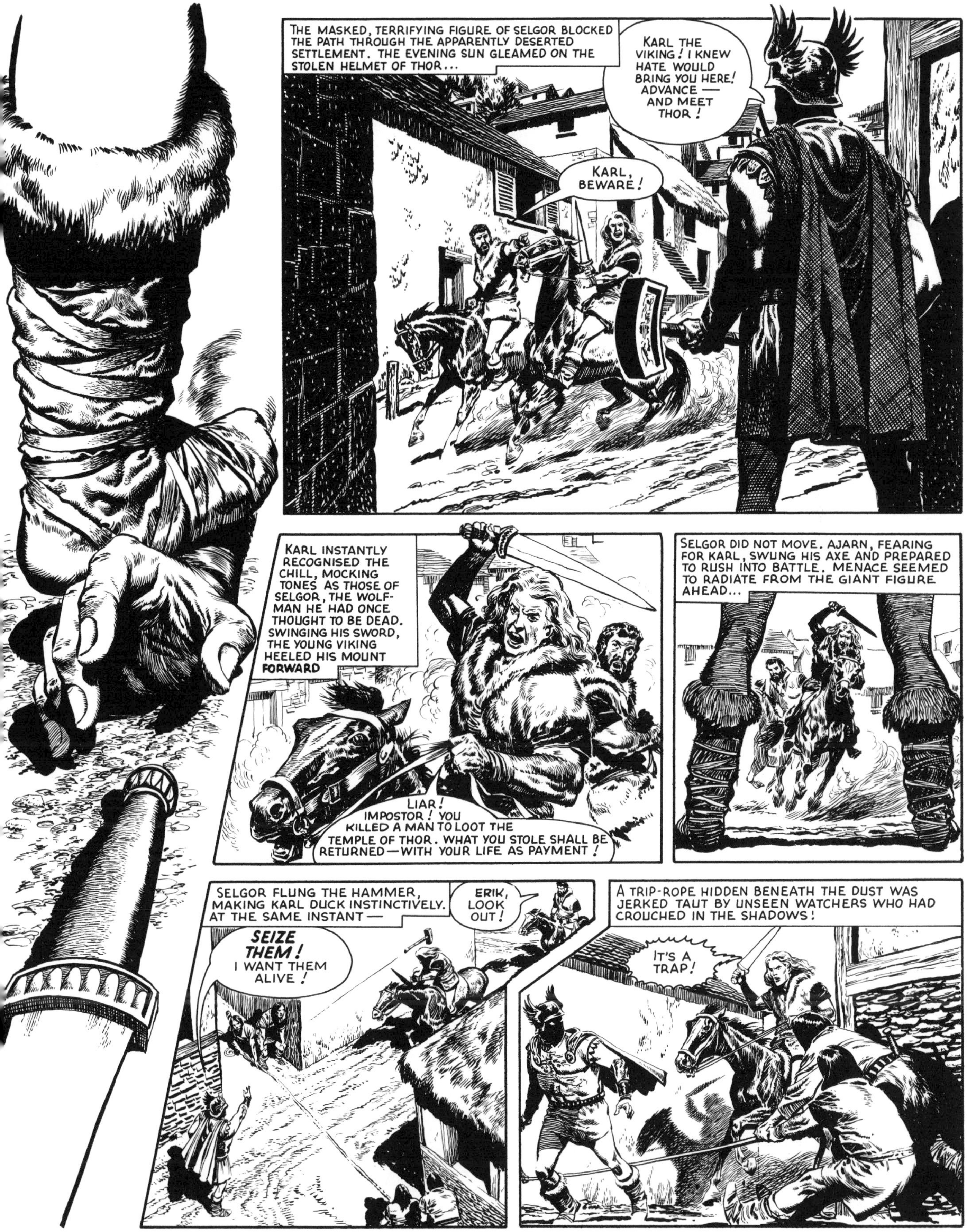

THE MASKED, TERRIFYING FIGURE OF SELGOR BLOCKED THE PATH THROUGH THE APPARENTLY DESERTED SETTLEMENT. THE EVENING SUN GLEAMED ON THE STOLEN HELMET OF THOR...
KARL THE VIKING! I KNEW HATE WOULD BRING YOU HERE! ADVANCE — AND MEET THOR!
KARL, BEWARE!
KARL INSTANTLY RECOGNISED THE CHILL, MOCKING TONES AS THOSE OF SELGOR, THE WOLF-MAN HE HAD ONCE THOUGHT TO BE DEAD. SWINGING HIS SWORD, THE YOUNG VIKING HEELED HIS MOUNT FORWARD
LIAR! IMPOSTOR! YOU KILLED A MAN TO LOOT THE TEMPLE OF THOR. WHAT YOU STOLE SHALL BE RETURNED — WITH YOUR LIFE AS PAYMENT!
SELGOR DID NOT MOVE. AJARN, FEARING FOR KARL, SWUNG HIS AXE AND PREPARED TO RUSH INTO BATTLE. MENACE SEEMED TO RADIATE FROM THE GIANT FIGURE AHEAD...
SELGOR FLUNG THE HAMMER, MAKING KARL DUCK INSTINCTIVELY. AT THE SAME INSTANT —
ERIK, LOOK OUT!
SEIZE THEM! I WANT THEM ALIVE!
A TRIP-ROPE HIDDEN BENEATH THE DUST WAS JERKED TAUT BY UNSEEN WATCHERS WHO HAD CROUCHED IN THE SHADOWS!
IT'S A TRAP!

THE TAUT ROPE SANG AS IT CAUGHT THE FORELEGS OF KARL'S MOUNT!

WHILE KARL, AND HIS HORSE CRASHED HEADLONG, LEAPING WARRIORS CLOSED UPON AJARN!

THE GODS OF VALHALLA HAVE SENT THESE CURS AS A SIGN! THOUGH YOU SPILL YOUR OWN BLOOD, TAKE THEM ALIVE!

USE THE NETS!

A FISHING NET WAS EXPERTLY CAST OVER AJARN!

KARL, DAZED AND BLEEDING, MADE A SUPERHUMAN EFFORT TO REACH HIS SWORD, BUT SELGOR STAMPED DOWN VICIOUSLY!

DO NOT TEMPT ME TO END YOUR LIFE... SUCH SWIFT DEATH IS NOT FOR YOU! VIKING, I NEED YOU FOR SACRIFICE!

PINIONED AND OVERPOWERED, KARL AND AJARN AWAITED WHAT WAS TO COME...

TAKE THEM TO THE POOL WHERE THE FUTURE IS MIRRORED! I HAVE WORK FOR ILGANA, THE SORCERESS!

LO, THE WITCH-WOMAN, IS HERE!

THE MOON WAS RISING WHEN A TORCH-LIGHT PROCESSION MOVED BETWEEN PINES TOWARDS THE "POOL OF WISDOM"...

WHAT DEVILRY DOES SELGOR PLAN FOR US, KARL?

IT IS WELL NOT TO THINK OF IT, AJARN. THE ONLY CHANCE I SEEK IS TO KILL HIM BEFORE WE ARE SLAIN!

THE PRISONERS WERE DRAGGED TO THE EDGE OF THE POOL. THEN SELGOR SPOKE...

SERVANTS OF THOR, I PROMISE YOU POWER AND RICHES BEYOND HUMAN DREAMS. ILGANA WILL USE THE POOL TO SHOW YOU OUR FUTURE—AND HOW ALL WHO TURN AGAINST THOR SHALL DIE!

A STRANGE POWER SEEMED TO GRIP KARL AS THE SORCERESS SEIZED THE BLAZING BRAND AND SPOKE IN A CRACKED, SHRILLY VOICE.

HEH! HEH! GAZE WELL, VIKINGS, AND WATCH THE RIPPLES. WHEN THE TORCH FALLS, THE POOL WILL ANSWER!

MY STRENGTH GOES. I CANNOT RAISE MY EYES FROM THE POOL!

THE TORCH WAS HURLED. STEAM HISSED, AND THE PECULIAR RIPPLES SPREAD QUICKLY...

WHAT WOULD THE WATCHERS SEE? WHAT SACRIFICIAL DEATH LAY IN STORE? KARL'S BREATH CAME FAST...

THE RIPPLES SPREAD WIDER AND FASTER! THE WATER COMES ALIVE! OUR REFLECTIONS BREAK AND CHANGE!

IN THE LIGHT OF THE MOON AND THE TORCHES, THE SHIMMERING POOL BEGAN TO SHOW A NEW IMAGE!

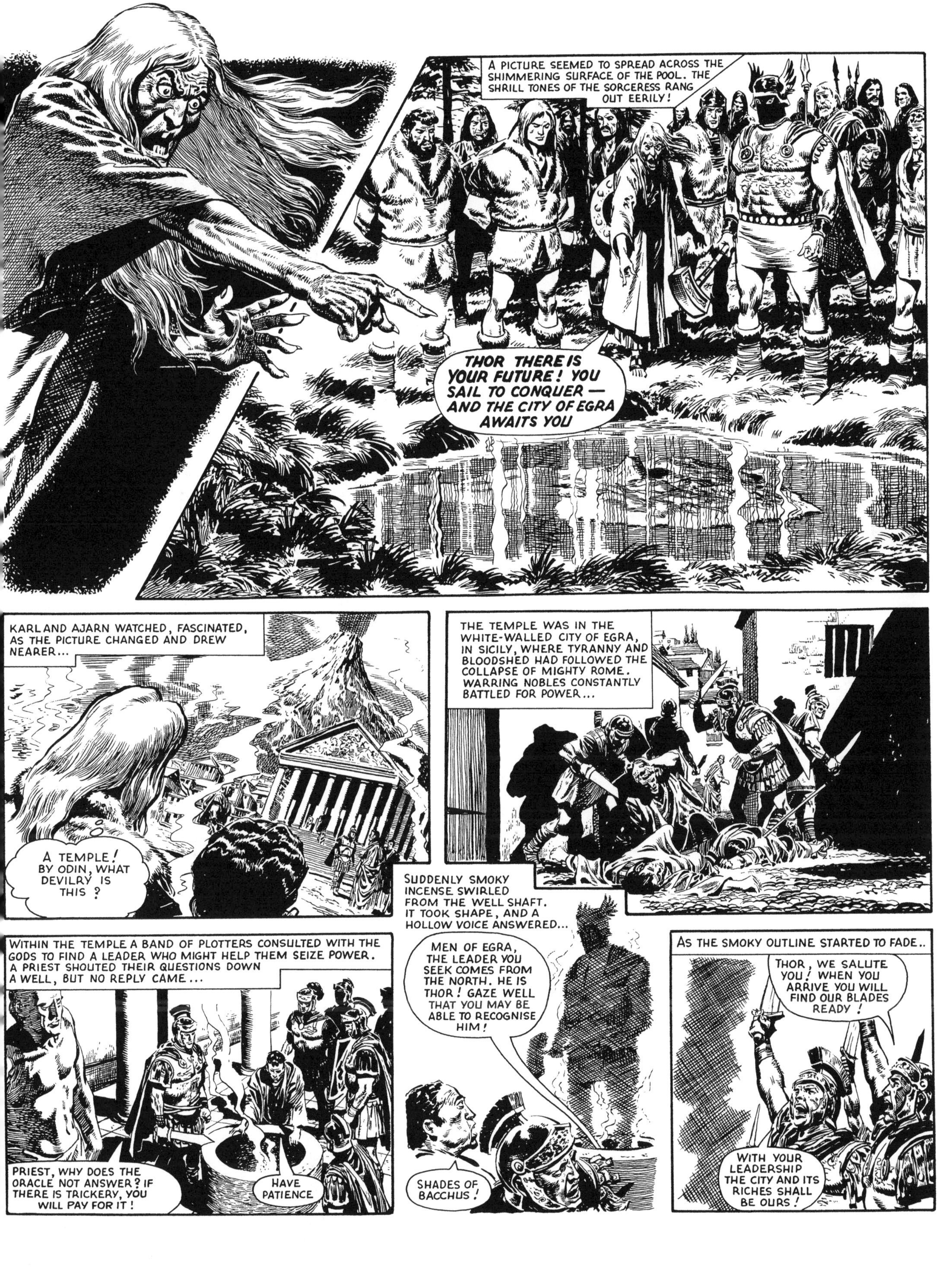
A PICTURE SEEMED TO SPREAD ACROSS THE SHIMMERING SURFACE OF THE POOL. THE SHRILL TONES OF THE SORCERESS RANG OUT EERILY!
THOR THERE IS YOUR FUTURE! YOU SAIL TO CONQUER — AND THE CITY OF EGRA AWAITS YOU
KARL AND AJARN WATCHED, FASCINATED, AS THE PICTURE CHANGED AND DREW NEARER...
A TEMPLE! BY ODIN, WHAT DEVILRY IS THIS?
THE TEMPLE WAS IN THE WHITE-WALLED CITY OF EGRA, IN SICILY, WHERE TYRANNY AND BLOODSHED HAD FOLLOWED THE COLLAPSE OF MIGHTY ROME. WARRING NOBLES CONSTANTLY BATTLED FOR POWER...
WITHIN THE TEMPLE A BAND OF PLOTTERS CONSULTED WITH THE GODS TO FIND A LEADER WHO MIGHT HELP THEM SEIZE POWER. A PRIEST SHOUTED THEIR QUESTIONS DOWN A WELL, BUT NO REPLY CAME...
PRIEST, WHY DOES THE ORACLE NOT ANSWER? IF THERE IS TRICKERY, YOU WILL PAY FOR IT!
HAVE PATIENCE
SUDDENLY SMOKY INCENSE SWIRLED FROM THE WELL SHAFT. IT TOOK SHAPE, AND A HOLLOW VOICE ANSWERED...
MEN OF EGRA, THE LEADER YOU SEEK COMES FROM THE NORTH. HE IS THOR! GAZE WELL THAT YOU MAY BE ABLE TO RECOGNISE HIM!
SHADES OF BACCHUS!
AS THE SMOKY OUTLINE STARTED TO FADE..
THOR, WE SALUTE YOU! WHEN YOU ARRIVE YOU WILL FIND OUR BLADES READY!
WITH YOUR LEADERSHIP THE CITY AND ITS RICHES SHALL BE OURS!

FAR AWAY IN SCANDINAVIA, A CRY OF TRIUMPH BURST FROM SELGOR. THE POOL, HAVING MIRRORED THE FUTURE, CLOUDED OVER...

NORSEMEN, YOU HAVE SEEN AND HEARD! WE SAIL TO EGRA TO CONQUER, PLUNDER AND LAY WASTE. MEN AFTER OUR OWN HEARTS AWAIT US! *I AM THOR!*

WE SAIL! WE SAIL!

KARL AND AJARN WAITED GRIMLY, FOR THEY KNEW WORSE WAS TO COME!

NOW THE POOL IS TO SHOW HOW WE ARE TO BE SACRIFICED!

KEEP YOUR COURAGE HIGH! UNTIL WE ARE DEAD THERE IS HOPE!

AGAIN THE WATERS BRIGHTENED, AND A FURTHER PICTURE FLICKERED OVER THE SURFACE...

THE VOICE OF ILGANA, THE SORCERESS, SHRILLED...

THOR, TAKE YOUR ENEMIES TO THE GULLY OF WYRD! THERE THE DREADED UNKNOWN SHALL CLAIM THEM — THE DEMON WHICH LURKS 'UNDER THE GROUND!

EVEN SELGOR'S DUPED FOLLOWERS SHUDDERED AS THE PRISONERS WERE ROUGHLY THRUST FORWARD TO FOLLOW A PATH THROUGH THE DARK FORESTLAND..

KARL, THE GULLY OF WYRD AWAITS YOU! I HAVE HEARD THE DEVIL SCREAM FROM ITS DEPTHS. THOSE WHO FALL INTO IT NEVER RETURN!

ONE DAY, *YOU* SHALL SCREAM, MONSTER!

THE GULLY, WHICH WAS BELIEVED TO BE BOTTOMLESS, HAD A REPUTATION OF MENACE AND EVIL...

EE-EE-AA-AA-EE-EE!

THE DEMON CRIES OUT! IT SMELLS SACRIFICE!

SUDDENLY THE SORCERESS TURNED ON SELGOR...

THOR, HURL INTO THE GULLY A TORCH, AN AXE AND A SWORD. WHEN THE PRISONERS ARE THROWN DOWN, THEIR HANDS MUST BE FREE. PUNISHMENT WILL COME MORE SLOWLY THAT WAY!

IT IS GOOD I DO NOT WISH THEM TO BE DEVOURED BY THE DEMONS TOO SWIFTLY

THE ORDER WAS OBEYED, AND THE TERRIBLE MOANING SOUND FROM THE DEPTHS SEEMED TO GROW LOUDER!

THE PRISONERS' BONDS WERE CUT...

DESPITE THEIR DESPERATE STRUGGLE KARL AND AJARN WERE HURLED FORWARD

IN WITH THEM!

FOLLOWED BY THE TERRIBLE, WOLFISH LAUGHTER OF SELGOR, KARL AND AJARN SPUN DOWN INTO THE DARKNESS OF THE GULLY OF WYRD!

YOU SHALL BE DEVOURED BY THE SCREAMING DEVIL-OF-DARK WHICH LURKS IN THE DEPTHS

SELGOR, WEARING HIS GOLDEN MASK, WATCHED GLOATINGLY...

NOW THE ONLY ENEMIES WHO KNOW MY SECRET ARE GONE! AS THOR, I HAVE POWER OVER ALL VIKINGS. PLUNDER AND POWER AWAIT MY CONQUEST OF THE CITY OF EGRA!

EVEN THE HUNGRY FOREST WOLVES KEPT BACK AS SELGOR, WHO HAD UNCANNY POWERS, TURNED TO THE SORCERESS WHO HAD REVEALED THE FUTURE...

ILGANA, YOU SHALL SHOW ME THE ROUTE ACROSS THE GREAT OCEANS. THOR WILL LEAD HIS SUBJECTS TO EGRA — AND CONQUER!

GREAT IS THOR! OUR SWORDS ARE READY TO SERVE YOU!

THE ANGLE OF THE GULLY WALLS AND THE SOFT EARTH SAVED KARL AND AJARN FROM DEATH. THEY SPRAWLED NEAR THE TORCH AND WEAPONS WHICH HAD BEEN FLUNG DOWN AHEAD OF THEM

WE LIVE! FOR THE MOMENT, THAT IS ENOUGH!

IMPOSSIBLE, AND FROM SOMEWHERE CAME THE STRANGE SCREAMING WHICH THEY HAD HEARD BEFORE ...

OO-OO-AA-AA.

THOUGH I AM A NORSEMAN, MY HEART QUAILS AT THAT SOUND. WHAT SHALL WE DO KARL?

WE WILL MAKE OUR WAY ALONG THE BOTTOM OF THIS GULLY. KEEP YOUR STEEL READY!

KARL'S FACE SET WITH GRIM DETERMINATION.

I WOULD FACE ALL MANNER OF SPIRIT TO SLAY SELGOR AND RECOVER WHAT HE STOLE FROM THE TEMPLE! IF HE SAILS FOR EGRA, I SHALL FOLLOW. MY QUEST WILL END WITH HIS DEATH — OR MINE!

SUDDENLY KARL'S FOOT SLIPPED AND HE DROPPED HIS SWORD. NEXT MOMENT, AJARN UTTERED A GASP...

KARL! THE STRANGE SCREAM COMES FROM THE WATERS!

AS THE TWO COMRADES PRESSED ON, ANOTHER SURPRISE AWAITED THEM!

HUMAN BONES. THERE IS GREATER EVIL HERE THAN JUST THE CURRENT!

BEWARE! SOMETHING APPROACHES FROM THE DARKNESS!

A MASSIVE SHAPE WITH GLEAMING EYES WAS ADVANCING TOWARDS THEM!

QUICK! PASS ME THE AXE! WE MEET THE DEMON-OF-DARK!

DESPITE ITS BULK, THE UNGAINLY ATTACKER MOVED AT STARTLING SPEED!

HURRY— THE AXE!

THERE CAME A FEARSOME SNARL. KARL STRUCK BUT THE AXE WAS SWEPT ASIDE!

WHILE THE AXE HURTLED TO THE WATERS BENEATH, KARL JAMMED THE FLAMING BRAND TOWARDS THE GREAT BEAR!

BACK, YOU BRUTE!

ONLY KARL'S LIGHTNING AGILITY PREVENTED HIS SKULL FROM BEING CRUSHED BY THE ANIMAL'S PAW!

THE BEAR WILL SURELY KILL HIM!

DESPERATELY AJARN CLUTCHED AT HIS COMRADE TO SAVE HIM FROM FALLING OVER THE EDGE OF THE TWENTY-FOOT DROP!

BUT THE ROOT GRASPED BY AJARN GAVE WAY, AND —

NEXT INSTANT, WITH THE HISSING TORCH EXTINGUISHED, THE TWO VIKINGS WERE SWEPT ALONG IN THE MERCILESS GRIP OF THE UNDERGROUND CURRENT!

A DISTANT ROARING SOUND BEAT ON THEIR EARS AS KARL AND AJARN WERE BATTERED ALONG IN THE GRIP OF THE MERCILESS CURRENT...

THE WATER DEMONS CRY OUT IN TRIUMPH. THEY THINK WE ARE THEIR PREY!

BUT WE WILL DEFEAT THEM YET! THERE IS DAYLIGHT AHEAD!

KARL, HOWEVER, KNEW THAT IT WOULD TAKE ALL THEIR STRENGTH TO KEEP AFLOAT. THEN HE SAW SOMETHING TO HELP THEM...

AJARN, CLING TO THIS LOG! IT WILL SAVE US FROM BEING HURLED AGAINST THE ROCKS!

WITH THE FURY OF DESPERATION KARL DRAGGED HIS EXHAUSTED COMPANION ON TO THE LOG. THEN THEY SWEPT ONWARDS.

SEE— WE CAN USE IT AS A BOAT!

GREAT SPLINTERS FLEW FROM THE LOG

COURAGE, AJARN! HOLD ON, AS YOU VALUE YOUR LIFE!

ON AND ON THE TWO COMRADES WERE CARRIED WITH THE NOISE OF THE WATER ECHOING LIKE THUNDER

HARDLY AWARE OF WHAT WAS HAPPENING TO THEM, THEY WERE AT LAST WASHED ASHORE...

AS STRENGTH RETURNED TO THEIR BATTERED BODIES THEY WERE ABLE TO STAGGER UPRIGHT...

WE LIVE! AGAIN SELGOR'S BID TO SLAY US HAS FAILED!

IT IS AN OMEN! MAY THE FATES AID US TO REACH SELGOR BEFORE HE SETS SAIL WITH THE FOOLS WHO BELIEVE HIM TO BE THOR. HE MUST BE UNMASKED, KILLED, AND HIS TREACHERY EXPOSED!

KARL AND AJARN MADE THEIR WAY TO THE EDGE OF A CLIFF. AND SUDDENLY, DOWN BELOW, THEY SAW WHAT THEY NEEDED TO TAKE THEM TO THE SETTLEMENT AT SKILD...

TWO HORSES! FOLLOW ME — QUICK!

BY ODIN—

BATTLE AND PLUNDER WERE IN THE BLOOD OF EVERY TRUE VIKING— AND KARL'S NEED WAS DESPERATE!

OUR FISTS WILL EXPLAIN OUR HURRY BETTER THAN WORDS!

WITHIN A FEW MINUTES THE TWO HORSEMEN HAD BEEN OVERCOME!

NOW TO TURN OUR ATTENTION TO SELGOR!

THAT EVIL MOCKER OF THOR WILL THINK WE RETURN FROM THE DEAD!

THE HORSES WERE LATHERED WITH SWEAT BY THE TIME KARL AND AJARN SIGHTED THE NORSE SETTLEMENT. THEN—

WE ARE TOO LATE! ONLY WOMEN AND CHILDREN REMAIN!

THE FLEET OF LONG SHIPS HAS GONE. SELGOR HAS SAILED!

THERE THEY GO! AND THE STOLEN GOLD OF THOR GOES WITH THEM!

ON BOARD ONE OF THE SHIPS, SELGOR, WEARING HIS MASK, TURNED TO ILGANA, THE SORCERESS...

YOU WILL GUIDE US TO THE WARM OCEAN AND THE ISLAND WHICH HOLDS THE CITY OF EGRA. I, THOR, WILL CRUSH EGRA AND MAKE ITS POWER MINE!

THE SORCERESS LAUGHED EVILLY...

YOUR ENEMY KARL, WHO MIGHT HAVE STOPPED YOU, IS DEAD. HEH! HEH! HAVE NO FEAR, THOR, YOUR HAMMER AND LIGHTNING BOLTS WILL TAKE EGRA!

KARL THE VIKING WASTED NO TIME IN WATCHING THE FLEET...

WHERE SELGOR GOES, I FOLLOW! UNTIL HE IS SLAIN AND THE LOOT RESTORED TO THE TEMPLE, THE WRATH OF THE TRUE THOR LIES OVER US. RIDE! WE WILL RAISE SHIPS AND MEN!

AJARN WAS A BRAVE MAN, YET A STRANGE CHILLNESS MADE HIM SHUDDER UNEASILY...

THREE MAGPIES RISE FROM THAT TREE... THEY BODE ILL! I FEEL THAT POWERS OF EVIL ARE ABOUT TO AID SELGOR!

WHILE KARL AND HIS FRIEND, AJARN, WERE JOURNEYING TO THE NEAREST NORSE SETTLEMENT, A GREAT PACK OF WOLVES, APPARENTLY MAD WITH HUNGER, FORCED THEIR WAY THROUGH THE STOCKADE GATES..

BY ODIN, EVIL SPIRITS MUST POSSESS THEM!

BEAT THEM BACK! KILL THEM — BEFORE THEY KILL US!

THE ATTACK WAS COMPLETELY UNEXPECTED. CASUALTIES WERE HEAVY...

KARL AND AJARN, ARRIVING LATER, WERE SHOCKED — AND DISAPPOINTED!

A WOLF RAID! NOTHING ON EARTH WILL PERSUADE THESE VIKINGS TO SAIL WITH US AND LEAVE THEIR FAMILIES UNPROTECTED!

I WARNED YOU THAT SELGOR IS AIDED BY POWERS OF EVIL. NOT FOR NOTHING IS HE MORE WOLF THAN MAN!

THE PAIR STAYED ONLY LONG ENOUGH TO CHANGE HORSES, THEN—

WE'LL TRAVEL WEST TO THE CLANS AT KATTRA! NOT EVERY SETTLEMENT CAN HAVE BEEN LAID WASTE BY WOLVES!

BE CAREFUL, KARL, OR YOUR DETERMINATION MAY LEAD YOU TO YOUR DEATH!

THE CLANS OF TWO SETTLEMENTS HAD ALREADY SAILED WITH SELGOR, BELIEVING HIM TO BE THOR. BUT AT KATTRA —

FELLOW VIKINGS! A CURSE LIES ON US UNTIL THOR'S GOLDEN HELMET IS RECOVERED FROM SELGOR AND RESTORED TO THE TEMPLE. SELGOR HAS SAILED TO EGRA. TO CAPTURE THIS JACKAL WE NEED SHIPS AND MEN!

A DEATHLY SILENCE WARNED OF THE DISBELIEF OF THE LISTENERS. BERL, CHIEF OF THE CLAN, DROPPED HIS HAND TO HIS SWORD..

YOU LIE! THE ONE YOU CALL SELGOR IS THOR! TRAITORS LIKE YOU CARRY THE CURSE!

LOOK OUT, KARL — BEHIND YOU!

EVEN AS AJARN YELLED THE WARNING HE HIMSELF WAS STRUCK DOWN!

YOU TREACHEROUS DOGS! YOU'LL PAY FOR THAT!

THE DEADLY SPEED OF KARL'S BLADE ACCOUNTED FOR TWO ATTACKERS, AND FOR A MOMENT THE CLANSMEN HELD BACK...

TO EVERYONE'S ASTONISHMENT, KARL THEN DROVE HIS SWORD INTO THE EARTH, AND HIS VOICE RANG OUT TO THE SKY...

ODIN ALLFATHER — GOD OF THE WINDS AND SEA — GIVE ME A SIGN TO PROVE TO THESE CURS THAT I SPEAK THE TRUTH — THAT SELGOR IS NO GOD!

FROM HIGH OVER-HEAD, A WILD FALCON SUDDENLY DROPPED LIKE A STONE...

LOOK!

STRAIGHT DOWN TO THE SWORD HILT SWEPT THE FIERCE, GLITTERING-EYED BIRD

KARL POINTED TO THE FALCON IN TRIUMPH!

ODIN HAS ANSWERED! NOW WILL YOU SAIL WITH ME AFTER THE DEVIL-OF-DARK WHO CALLS HIMSELF THOR AND WEARS THE GOLDEN HELMET?

WITH A SWIFT MOVEMENT, BERL DREW HIS SWORD AND STRUCK WITH IT AT KARL'S!

I KNOW NOT! LET THE GODS DECIDE!

EVERY EYE TURNED TO BERL, CHIEF OF THE CLAN...

SHALL WE FOLLOW HIM, O BERL?

DOES HE SPEAK THE TRUTH AFTER ALL?

AT AN ORDER FROM BERL, AJARN WAS DRAGGED CLEAR — AND KARL STOOD ALONE. THE GIANT CLAN CHIEF RAN A TONGUE OVER THIN LIPS

DRAW YOUR DAGGER! IF YOU SPEAK THE TRUTH, THE GODS WILL GUARD YOU AGAINST THE BITE OF MY SWORD. FIGHT, KARL! FIGHT WITH YOUR DAGGER AGAINST MY SWORD!

WITHOUT A SECOND'S HESITATION, KARL ACCEPTED THE CHALLENGE. DOWN CAME BERL'S SWORD IN A MIGHTY BLOW, AND —

MY SHIELD! WITHOUT IT I AM LOST!

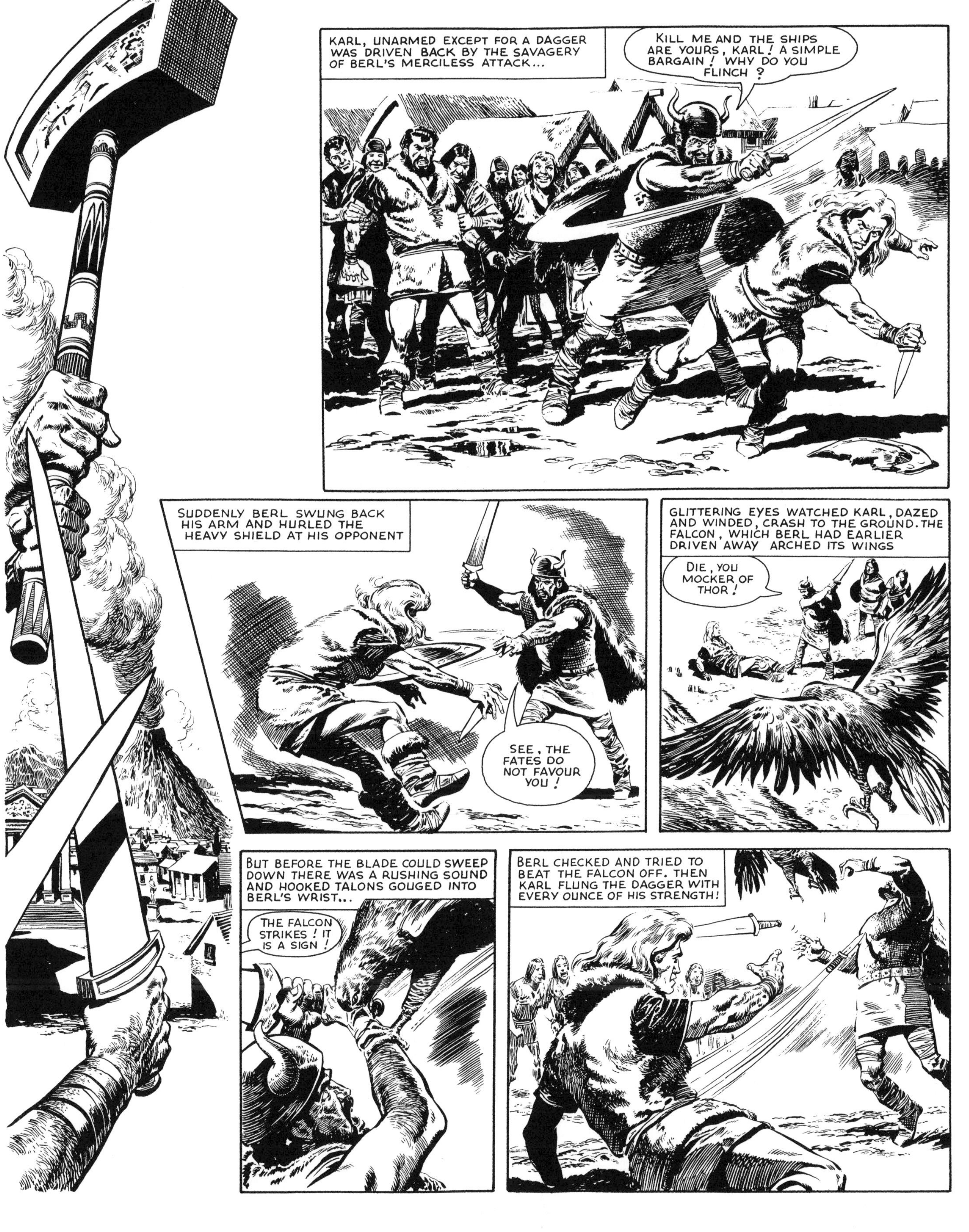
KARL, UNARMED EXCEPT FOR A DAGGER WAS DRIVEN BACK BY THE SAVAGERY OF BERL'S MERCILESS ATTACK...
KILL ME AND THE SHIPS ARE YOURS, KARL! A SIMPLE BARGAIN! WHY DO YOU FLINCH?
SUDDENLY BERL SWUNG BACK HIS ARM AND HURLED THE HEAVY SHIELD AT HIS OPPONENT
SEE, THE FATES DO NOT FAVOUR YOU!
GLITTERING EYES WATCHED KARL, DAZED AND WINDED, CRASH TO THE GROUND. THE FALCON, WHICH BERL HAD EARLIER DRIVEN AWAY ARCHED ITS WINGS
DIE, YOU MOCKER OF THOR!
BUT BEFORE THE BLADE COULD SWEEP DOWN THERE WAS A RUSHING SOUND AND HOOKED TALONS GOUGED INTO BERL'S WRIST...
THE FALCON STRIKES! IT IS A SIGN!
BERL CHECKED AND TRIED TO BEAT THE FALCON OFF. THEN KARL FLUNG THE DAGGER WITH EVERY OUNCE OF HIS STRENGTH!

WHILE AWED VIKINGS GAZED AT THE LIFELESS BODY OF THEIR LEADER, KARL DRAGGED HIMSELF TO HIS FEET...

Now do you believe me when I tell you that the man who sails to conquer Egra is not the god Thor—but Selgor the Wolf? Who joins me in my quest to track him down and destroy him

WE SAIL WITH YOU, KARL!

THE GOLD HELMET OF THOR SHALL BE RECOVERED!

KARL AND HIS FRIEND, AJARN, HAD WON THE SUPPORT THEY SO DESPERATELY NEEDED. WITHOUT DELAY LONG-SHIPS WERE LOADED FOR THE VOYAGE...

WE SAIL TONIGHT! I HAVE A PILOT WHO HAS ALREADY BEEN ONCE TO THE WARM SEAS!

MEANWHILE, SELGOR THE WOLF WHOM HIS FOLLOWERS THOUGHT TO BE THE SCANDINAVIAN WAR GOD, NEARED THE CITY OF EGRA HIS FACE WAS HIDDEN BY A GOLD MASK MADE FROM THE STOLEN HAMMER OF THOR...

Mighty Thor, yonder lies the island which my spell revealed to you. Follow the river inland—and Egra is yours!

SORCERESS YOUR WITCHCRAFT HAD BETTER SUCCEED, OR THIS HAMMER WILL MAKE YOU ITS FIRST VICTIM!

AT THE DOCKS OUTSIDE THE WALLED CITY, CERTAIN CORRUPT NOBLES AWAITED THE ARRIVAL OF SELGOR. THEY, TOO, THOUGHT HE WAS THOR, AND THAT HE WOULD HELP THEM TO SEIZE POWER!

THE ORACLE COMES TRUE! WITH THOR'S HELP, WE SHALL RULE EGRA!

AN EXCITED PARTY GREETED THE INVADERS

GREETINGS, THOR! FOR LONG WE HAVE AWAITED YOUR COMING!

THE CORRUPT NOBLES — PLOTTERS AGAINST THEIR OWN CITY — MOVED FORWARD...

O NORTHERN WAR GOD, I SPEAK YOUR TONGUE! I AND OTHER LEADERS HAVE A PLAN WHICH WILL ENABLE YOU TO SEIZE EGRA AND—

THE SPOKESMAN'S WORDS WERE NEVER COMPLETED

FOOL! SILENCE YOUR TONGUE! THOR ALONE MAKES THE PLANS!

SELGOR THEN LED HIS MEN IN A VICIOUS ATTACK ON THE NOBLES...

DEATH TO ALL WHO WILL NOT SERVE ME AS SLAVES!

BODY AFTER BODY CRASHED DOWN TO THE WATERS...

THE WATCHING TROOPS, HIRED BY THE NOBLES, HAD NO WISH TO OPPOSE THE MERCILESS INVADERS. SELGOR GRINNED WITH TRIUMPH...

SEE, THE HIRED RABBLE IS READY TO MARCH WITH US! I TAKE EGRA — BUT ON MY OWN TERMS! *THOSE WHO OPPOSE US SHALL DIE!*

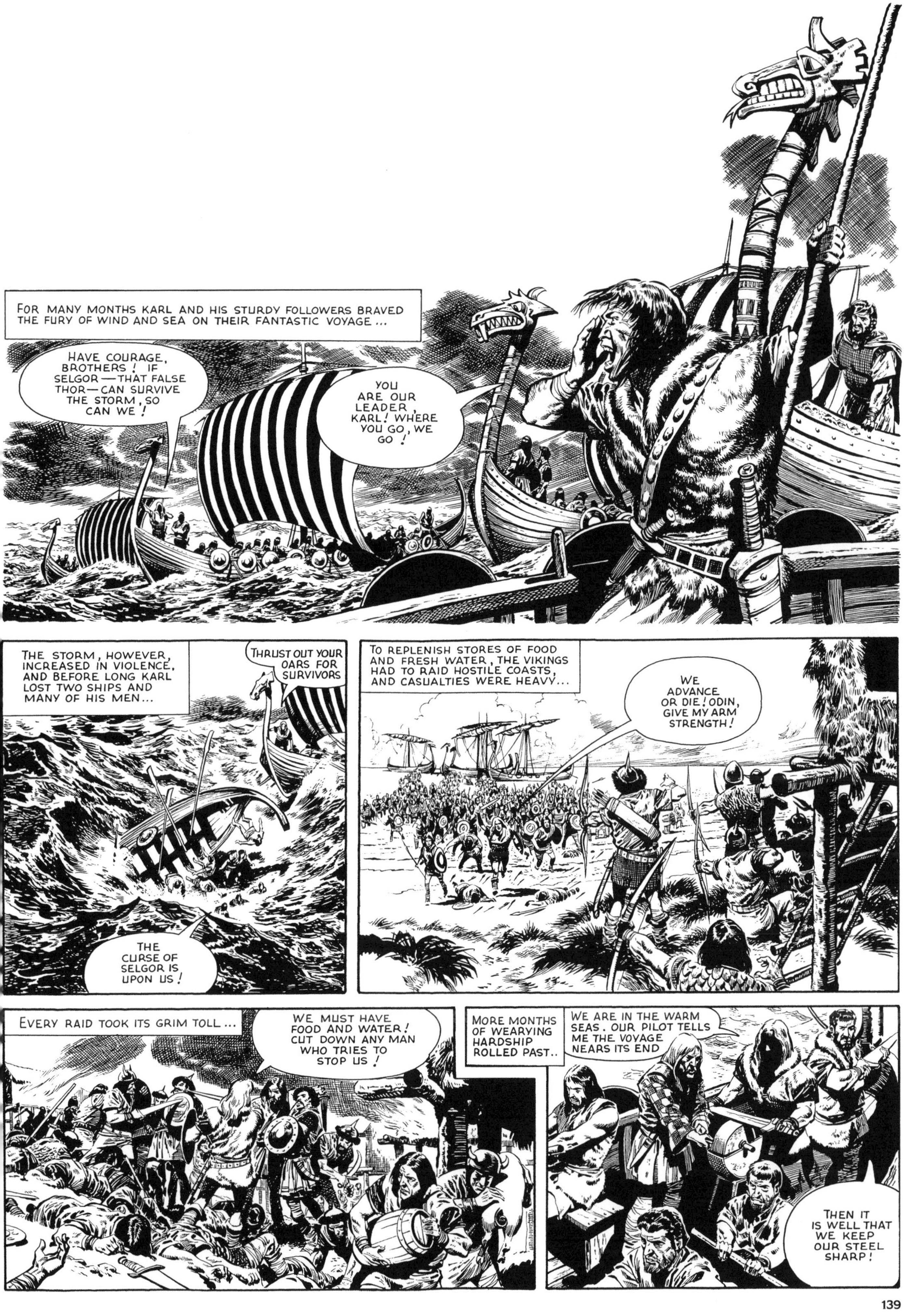
FOR MANY MONTHS KARL AND HIS STURDY FOLLOWERS BRAVED THE FURY OF WIND AND SEA ON THEIR FANTASTIC VOYAGE ...
HAVE COURAGE, BROTHERS! IF SELGOR—THAT FALSE THOR—CAN SURVIVE THE STORM, SO CAN WE!
YOU ARE OUR LEADER, KARL! WHERE YOU GO, WE GO!
THE STORM, HOWEVER, INCREASED IN VIOLENCE, AND BEFORE LONG KARL LOST TWO SHIPS AND MANY OF HIS MEN...
THRUST OUT YOUR OARS FOR SURVIVORS
THE CURSE OF SELGOR IS UPON US!
TO REPLENISH STORES OF FOOD AND FRESH WATER, THE VIKINGS HAD TO RAID HOSTILE COASTS, AND CASUALTIES WERE HEAVY...
WE ADVANCE OR DIE! ODIN, GIVE MY ARM STRENGTH!
EVERY RAID TOOK ITS GRIM TOLL ...
WE MUST HAVE FOOD AND WATER! CUT DOWN ANY MAN WHO TRIES TO STOP US!
MORE MONTHS OF WEARYING HARDSHIP ROLLED PAST..
WE ARE IN THE WARM SEAS. OUR PILOT TELLS ME THE VOYAGE NEARS ITS END
THEN IT IS WELL THAT WE KEEP OUR STEEL SHARP!

AT LAST, BEYOND A BLUE, SHINING SEA AND ROCKY BAYS, THE GOAL WHICH ERIK SOUGHT CAME INTO SIGHT. IN THE SHADE OF THE TOWERING VOLCANO NESTLED THE CITY OF EGRA...

WE WILL SAIL UP THE RIVER AND THEN LAND! THIS IS AS I SAW IT IN THE WITCH-WOMAN'S SPELL!

KARL, GO WARILY! MAY THE GODS GRANT THAT SELGOR THE WOLF HAS NOT ALREADY SEIZED POWER

KARL'S EYES NARROWED, BUT FANATICAL DETERMINATION STIRRED HIS BLOOD...

THE FATES WILL LEAD ME TO SELGOR—TO SLAY HIM! OVER HIS DEAD BODY WILL I RETURN THE GOLDEN HELMET TO THE TEMPLE OF THOR!

BUT THE CITY OF EGRA WAS ALREADY WITHIN SELGOR'S GRIP. HE HAD BEGUN A REIGN OF TERROR UNEQUALLED SINCE THAT OF THE WORST ROMAN TYRANTS. HIS ENEMIES WERE FORCED TO FIGHT TO THE DEATH IN THE ARENA...

SELGOR'S LACK OF MERCY FRIGHTENED EVEN HIS OWN WAR-HARDENED VIKINGS..

THE CURS RUN! KILL THEM! KILL THEM ALL!

I FEAR THOR. HE WILL DESTROY US ALL!

SHRINES AND TEMPLES WERE RANSACKED...

SPARE NO-ONE! THOR'S NAME MUST STRIKE FEAR!

STILL SELGOR THE WOLF WAS NOT SATISFIED, AND FRESH PLANS WERE MADE...

FOLLOWERS OF THOR, WE SHALL NOT PAUSE UNTIL THE WHOLE ISLAND IS UNDER MY HEEL. FROM EGRA WE WILL SWEEP LIKE A TIDAL WAVE OF STEEL TO LOOT EVERY VILLAGE AND TOWN!

THEN, ONE DAY, A STRANGE IMPULSE MADE SELGOR DRIVE TO THE OUTSKIRTS OF THE CITY...

STAND ASIDE! MAKE WAY FOR THOR!

THE CHARIOT CAREERED ON TO THE TOP OF THE GREAT WALL...

AN ENEMY COMES FROM THE SEA! I SENSE HIS COMING!

FROM THE TOP OF THE WALL, TWO APPROACHING LONG-SHIPS WERE CLEARLY VISIBLE...

IT IS KARL! HE LIVES! THIS COMPLETES MY TRIUMPH. I'LL PREPARE A WELCOME FOR HIM SUCH AS WILL MAKE EVEN HIS BLOOD RUN COLD!

A STRANGE SILENCE HUNG OVER THE UNGUARDED DOCKS OUTSIDE THE CITY OF EGRA AS KARL'S SHIPS DREW NEAR TO THE RIVER BANK...

YONDER VESSELS ARE VIKING CRAFT! SELGOR AND HIS RAIDERS MUST ALREADY BE IN THE CITY!

WE WILL LAND AND SEEK HIM OUT!

UNOPPOSED AND APPARENTLY UNSEEN, THE VIKINGS SCRAMBLED ASHORE

THIS LANDING GOES TOO EASILY KARL. WHY IS THERE NO-ONE ABOUT?

I KNOW NOT. WE MUST BE PREPARED, AJARN. HAVE GOOD STEEL READY!

STEALTHILY THE DARING INVADERS HEADED FOR THE WHITE-WALLED, SILENT CITY..

KEEP UNDER COVER UNTIL WE COME TO THE GATES AND GET READY TO DEAL WITH THE SENTRIES!

I SEE NO SENTRIES. CAN IT BE THAT THE CITY IS DESERTED?

THE MASSIVE, IRON-STUDDED GATES WHICH LED INTO EGRA WERE TEMPTINGLY OPEN...

KARL, I AM NO COWARD —BUT LET US TURN BACK. IT IS LIKE A CITY OF THE DEAD. NOT A MERCHANT OR A MULE TRAIN TREADS THE ROAD!

GRASP YOUR AXE TIGHTER. WE ADVANCE! THERE WILL BE NO TURNING BACK!

A SHORT, SAVAGE RUSH CARRIED THE INVADERS BEYOND THE GATES AND INTO THE CITY. THE SILENCE BEGAN TO TEAR EVEN AT KARL'S NERVES.

THIS IS MADNESS! SURELY EGRA CANNOT BE EMPTY! BY ODIN! IF ONLY I COULD SEE ONE PERSON!

IF I KNOW SELGOR YOU'LL SEE MORE THAN YOU BARGAIN FOR!

SUDDENLY, A FIGURE DARTED FROM THE SHADOWS!

LO! ONE OF SELGOR'S CRAZED JACKALS!

HE SHALL NOT ESCAPE FAR!

SELGOR'S FOLLOWER WHIRLED TO MEET THE HUMAN TIGER WHO SPRANG AT HIM. STEEL SPARKED ON STEEL, THEN—

YOU ARE LUCKY. I NEED YOU ALIVE!

KARL DRAGGED HIS OPPONENT FROM THE FULLER'S VAT

YOU FELT THE FLAT OF MY BLADE. WHERE IS THE MAN WHO CALLS HIMSELF THOR? SPEAK, OR YOU'LL TASTE THE EDGE!

THOR WAITS BEYOND THE GATE TO HIS TEMPLE! THE MIGHTY HAMMERER SPEAKS WITH THE REST OF THE GODS. GO—AND BE DESTROYED!

NEXT MOMENT—

UNCONSCIOUSNESS WILL TAKE CARE YOU DON'T WARN HIM. SELGOR SHALL SPEAK WITH ME!

ALONG A DESERTED AVENUE KARL AND HIS VIKINGS FOLLOWED THE DIRECTIONS THEY HAD BEEN GIVEN...

YONDER MUST BE THE TEMPLE. WE WILL DIVIDE OUR MEN HERE, AND I SHALL LEAD ONE PARTY INSIDE!

HAVE A CARE, KARL! THE JACKAL GAVE THE INFORMATION TOO READILY!

CATO

THE INVADERS DIVIDED, AND ONE PARTY WAITED. KARL AND AJARN LED THE REST OF THE VIKINGS INSIDE...

BY THE RUNES, IT IS A STRANGE KIND OF TEMPLE! SOMETHING IS WRONG! RETREAT!

KARL SENSED DANGER TOO LATE! THE HUGE GATE, OPERATED BY A CONCEALED MECHANISM, SLAMMED SHUT!

WE ARE TRAPPED!

A GIANT, GOLDEN-MASKED FIGURE ROSE FROM THE LOFTY TIERS OF SEATS WITH OTHER FOLLOWERS, AND A VOICE FILLED WITH MOCKERY RANG OUT...

KARL! MY FELLOW GODS ANSWERED ME! YOU HAVE COME! YOU ARE THE SACRIFICE WHICH MY TEMPLE AWAITS!

IT IS SELGOR!

THE CITY WAS SILENT NO LONGER! TRUMPETS BLARED AND PEOPLE RUSHED INTO THE STREETS URGED ON BY SOLDIERS.

OUT, YOU DOGS! GET TO THE AMPHITHEATRE! MIGHTY THOR PROVIDES ENTERTAINMENT!

EGRA'S CITIZENS, ALREADY COWED BY SELGOR'S REIGN OF TERROR, SURGED TOWARDS THE HUGE AMPHITHEATRE...

MAY THE FATES HAVE PITY ON THOR'S LUCKLESS ENEMIES!

THERE WILL BE NO PITY. DEATH TAKES STRANGE AND TERRIBLE FORMS FOR THOSE WHO THOR HATES!

KARL, THERE IS NO WAY OUT! SELGOR'S JACKALS HAVE CUT OFF EVERY MEANS OF ESCAPE!

GUARDS ARE DRIVING THE CITIZENS IN TO WATCH US DIE!

SELGOR'S ARCHERS STOOD READY TO PREVENT THE TRAPPED VICTIMS FROM GETTING AWAY. HIS WORD WAS LAW, FOR THE PEOPLE THOUGHT HIM TO BE THE THOR GOD

SELGOR, THAT DEMON-OF-DARKNESS, TAKES NO CHANCES! ONLY BY KILLING HIM COULD I GAIN CONTROL OF THOSE SOLDIERS!

SELGOR, HIS FACE HIDDEN BY A GOLD MASK, ADDRESSED THE PRISONERS IN THE ARENA...

ENEMIES OF THOR, PREPARE TO BE SACRIFICED! KARL, YOU ONCE SAW ME DRAGGED DOWN BY WOLVES. FOR YOU I HAVE FOUND EVEN MORE SAVAGE BEASTS!

THE WORDS ENDED IN A WOLF-HOWL OF TRIUMPH!

OPEN THE GRATINGS! KARL, I AM LETTING LOOSE THOSE WHO HUNGER TO MEET YOU!

GRATINGS CLATTERED OPEN, AND STARVING, TAWNY SHAPES BOUNDED FROM TUNNELS LEADING INTO THE ARENA...

HAVE SPEARS AND SHIELDS READY, MY BROTHERS!

CLOSE RANKS! FORM A SQUARE! LET THE LIONS MEET FOUR WALLS OF STEEL!

KARL'S COMMAND OVERCAME THE FIRST FEELINGS OF PANIC, AND A HOLLOW SQUARE OF VIKINGS FORMED UP

BY THE RUNES, WE'LL SELL OUR LIVES DEARLY! QUICK—GIVE ME YOUR SPEAR! SELGOR'S LAUGH MAY YET END IN A DEATH-CRY!

KARL FLUNG THE HEAVY SPEAR WITH ALL THE STRENGTH HE POSSESSED!

THOR, BEWARE!

SELGOR'S SPEED SAVED HIM FROM DEATH, BUT THE SPEAR SCORED HIS SHOULDER!

AA—AAGH!

KARL'S SHOUT RANG OUT TRIUMPHANTLY.

SUPPORTERS OF THOR, YOUR GOD CAN BE HURT AN ORDINARY MAN! SEE, HE IS NOT IMMORTAL!

THE FALSE THOR HAD TO THINK SWIFTLY. CONCEALING THE WOUND, HE GAVE A FURTHER COMMAND.

HASTEN THE SPORT! RELEASE AGRILLA, THE MONSTER FROM THE HOT LANDS! LET HIM BREAK THE SQUARE OF VIKINGS AND HELP THE LIONS WITH THEIR PREY

ANOTHER GRATING SWUNG OPEN.

KARL, WHAT IS IT?

ODIN, GIVE US STRENGTH! BRACE YOURSELVES!

THREE TONS OF JUNGLE FURY PLOUGHED A PATH THROUGH THE HOLLOW SQUARE OF DESPERATE MEN..

DIE! NOW THE WARY LIONS CAN CLOSE IN!

A LION LAUNCHED ITSELF AT KARL'S FRIEND, AJARN!

AJARN'S DEADLY AXE BEAT OFF THE SAVAGE ATTACKER, BUT TWO MORE VIKINGS DIED!

KARL, WE ARE DOOMED! WE WILL MEET AGAIN ONLY AFTER DEATH!

KARL SWERVED AWAY FROM THE CHARGING RHINO — AND STRUCK! THE ONLY EFFECT WAS TO INCREASE THE BEAST'S FURY...

ITS HIDE IS LIKE IRON!

THE END COULD NOT BE FAR OFF FOR THE VIKING SURVIVORS, YET ITS VERY NEARNESS GAVE KARL AN IDEA...

THE FIERCE HATRED OF THE GIANT MONSTER IS CENTRED ON ME ALONE! *PERHAPS I CAN USE THAT FURY TO SAVE THE LIVES OF THE OTHERS*

KARL KNEW HIS TRAPPED VIKINGS WERE DOOMED UNLESS THEY COULD ESCAPE FROM THE ARENA. HIS MIND WORKED SWIFTLY AS THE ENRAGED RHINOCEROS AGAIN CHARGED TOWARDS HIM

THE MASSIVE BULK OF THE MONSTER GATHERS SPEED. BY ODIN, I'LL TRY TO USE ITS STRENGTH AND WEIGHT TO OUR ADVANTAGE.!

KARL APPEARED TO BACK FEARFULLY TOWARDS THE GREAT GATES, AND SELGOR— THE FALSE THOR— LAUGHED IN MOCKERY!

SEE! THE COWARD RETREATS! KARL CRINGES—BUT HIS FEAR WILL NOT SAVE HIS NECK!

THE LAUGHTER WAS DROWNED BY THE POUNDING THUNDER OF FEET. SUDDENLY, WHEN THE BRUTE WAS ALMOST ON HIM, KARL TWISTED ASIDE ...

THE HURTLING ANIMAL CRASHED HEADLONG INTO THE GATES, CAUSING THE HINGES TO GIVE WAY...

MY PLAN WORKED! THERE IS A PATH TO FREEDOM!

WHILE THE DAZED RHINOCEROS LUMBERED ON BLINDLY INTO THE STREETS, KARL'S RALLYING SHOUT PUT NEW HEART INTO THE SURVIVING VIKINGS!

FIGHT YOUR WAY FROM THE ARENA! FORWARD, MY BROTHERS IF WE DIE, WE'LL DIE AS FREE MEN!

SELGOR'S COMMAND RANG ABOVE THE NOISY CONFUSION, AND HIS SOLDIERS TOOK AIM AT THE VIKINGS BELOW..

ARCHERS, KILL! KILL! LET NO-ONE ESCAPE!

ACCURATE AIM WAS IMPOSSIBLE. BUT ONE ARCHER MADE A FATAL MISTAKE. HIS ARROW WOUNDED A LION IN FRONT OF AJARN, KARL'S FRIEND

THE BEAST TURNS FROM ME! IT SEEKS ITS ATTACKER!

THE LION, ROARING WITH RAGE, LAUNCHED ITSELF TOWARDS THE HORRIFIED BOWMAN OTHERS FOLLOWED ITS EXAMPLE...

AAA-AGH!

MEANWHILE, OUTSIDE THE GREAT AMPHITHEATRE, A SECOND PARTY OF KARL'S VIKINGS HAD SOUGHT COVER. THEY, TOO, HEARD HIS RALLYING SHOUT, AND NOW PLUNGED FROM CONCEALMENT

FORWARD TO AID KARL! CUT DOWN SELGOR'S GUARDS!

OUR STEEL SHALL SPEAK FOR US!

THE TERROR UNLEASHED BY THE ESCAPE OF THE STARVING, CRAZED LIONS DISORGANISED SELGOR'S MEN. KARL FOUGHT HIS WAY THROUGH THE EXIT...

OUR COMRADES ARE WAITING FOR US! NOTHING SHALL PREVENT US FROM JOINING THEM!

THE SWORDS AND AXES OF KARL AND HIS MEN SCYTHED A PATH THROUGH THOSE WHO STROVE TO HALT THEM...

SEIZE THE CHARIOTS! TO DEFEAT SELGOR WE MUST LEAVE THE CITY AND RAISE A FORCE TO REBEL AGAINST THE TYRANT!

THEN KARL GLIMPSED AHEAD THE CHARIOTS LEFT OUTSIDE THE AMPHITHEATRE BY THE WEALTHIER CITIZENS OF EGRA

AYE, WE ARE ONLY A HANDFUL AGAINST HIS MURDEROUS HORDE!

DESPERATELY THE VIKINGS MANNED THE CHARIOTS AND WHIPPED UP THE HORSES...

MAKE FOR THE CITY GATES! SHOULD WE BE CUT OFF, SELGOR WILL LEAVE NO-ONE ALIVE!

BUT THE CONFUSION AT THE AMPHITHEATRE HAD ALREADY ENDED. AT SELGOR'S COMMAND, TRUMPETERS SIGNALLED AN ALARM WHICH WOULD ALERT GARRISONS AT EVERY GATE LEADING OUT OF EGRA...

KARL SHALL NOT GET FAR! THE CITY WILL BECOME AN IRON BAND TO ENCIRCLE HIM. IT SHALL BE AN OPEN GRAVE FOR HIM AND HIS CURS!

MASSIVE GATES SLAMMED SHUT IN RESPONSE TO THE TRUMPET CALLS. EVERY EXIT WAS SEALED OFF AND HEAVILY DEFENDED.

SELGOR AND HIS CAVALRY SAVAGELY SET OUT IN PURSUIT OF THE CHARIOTS MANNED BY KARL'S OUTNUMBERED VIKINGS...

SPUR YOUR MOUNTS TILL THEY DROP! DEATH WILL SOON COME TO THE ENEMIES OF THOR!

IN THE LEADING CHARIOT, KARL AND HIS FRIEND, AJARN, HEADED AT FANTASTIC SPEED FOR THE CITY'S GATES!

FASTER! WE MUST ESCAPE AND RAISE A FORCE STRONG ENOUGH TO DEFEAT SELGOR!

BUT ALREADY THE MASSIVE GATES OF EGRA WERE CLOSED, AND WATCHFUL ARCHERS CROUCHED IN POSITION. A SHOWER OF DEADLY ARROWS GREETED THE VIKINGS

LET NOT ONE OF THE DOGS GET PAST!

WE'RE TRAPPED

AA-ARGH!

THE ACCURSED CITY IS SEALED OFF!

TURNING HIS CHARIOT, KARL SHOUTED INSTRUCTIONS TO HIS FOLLOWERS

HAVE COURAGE, BROTHERS! YOU ARE VIKINGS — NOT CORNERED RATS FOLLOW ME!

AS THE CHARIOTS CLATTERED AWAY DOWN A SIDE-STREET, THERE WAS A CRY OF TRIUMPH FROM THE SPURRING PURSUERS!

THE WITLESS FOOLS MEAN TO DRIVE THEIR CHARIOTS ON TO THE TOP OF THE WALL. CLOSE IN BEHIND THEM SO THAT THEY CANNOT RETREAT!

SELGOR'S GUESS WAS WRONG! AT THE FOOT OF THE RAMP THE VIKINGS ALIGHTED AND CUT THE TEAMS FREE

STAMPEDE THE HORSES INTO SELGOR'S CAVALRY! USE THE CHARIOTS TO FORM A BARRICADE!

INSTANTLY THE CAVALRY REALISED THEIR DANGER.

LOOK OUT! TURN BACK!

NEXT MOMENT

SEE KARL— THEY GO DOWN LIKE FLIES!

EAGERLY KARL LED THE WAY UP THE RAMP...

WE MAY YET FIND A WAY OF ESCAPE. SELGOR'S JACKALS SHALL LEARN THAT TO CORNER US IS DANGEROUS!

GUARDS WHO RUSHED FROM THE WALL'S WATCH-TOWERS WERE MERCILESSLY CUT DOWN!

YET AJARN'S HEART SANK AS HE GAZED FROM THE TOP OF THE WALL. HE TURNED TO KARL WITH A WORRIED FROWN..

KARL, IT IS IMPOSSIBLE TO REACH THE OPEN COUNTRY BEYOND! EVEN IF WE MANAGED TO CLIMB DOWN, OUR SMALL FORCE WOULD BE WIPED OUT BY TROOPS FROM THE CITY!

I'LL NOT ADMIT DEFEAT UNTIL OUR VERY LAST DROP OF BLOOD HAS BEEN SHED!

IN THE STREET BELOW, SELGOR RECEIVED A REPORT FROM ONE OF HIS MEN..

THOR, WE HAVE LOST FIFTY DEAD! SEE, THE CURS HAVE WON THEIR WAY ON TO THE WALL. THOUGH THEY CANNOT ESCAPE, IT WILL PROVE COSTLY TO REACH THEM

FOOL! EVEN IF A THOUSAND OF YOU DIE I WANT MY ENEMIES SLAUGHTERED! FETCH SCALING LADDERS. CLIMB THE WALL!

AT THAT MOMENT, ILGANA THE SORCERESS FORCED HER WAY THROUGH THE CROWD...

MIGHTY THOR — WAIT! BE WARNED! THE CITY IS NO LONGER SAFE FOR YOU. THE SKY DARKENS, AND THERE IS EVIL ABROAD!

ABOVE THE TOWERING HEIGHT OF THE VOLCANO, MOUNT ETNA, STEAM AND FUMES FORMED AN OMINOUS SHAPE ...AN OMEN OF TERROR TO COME!

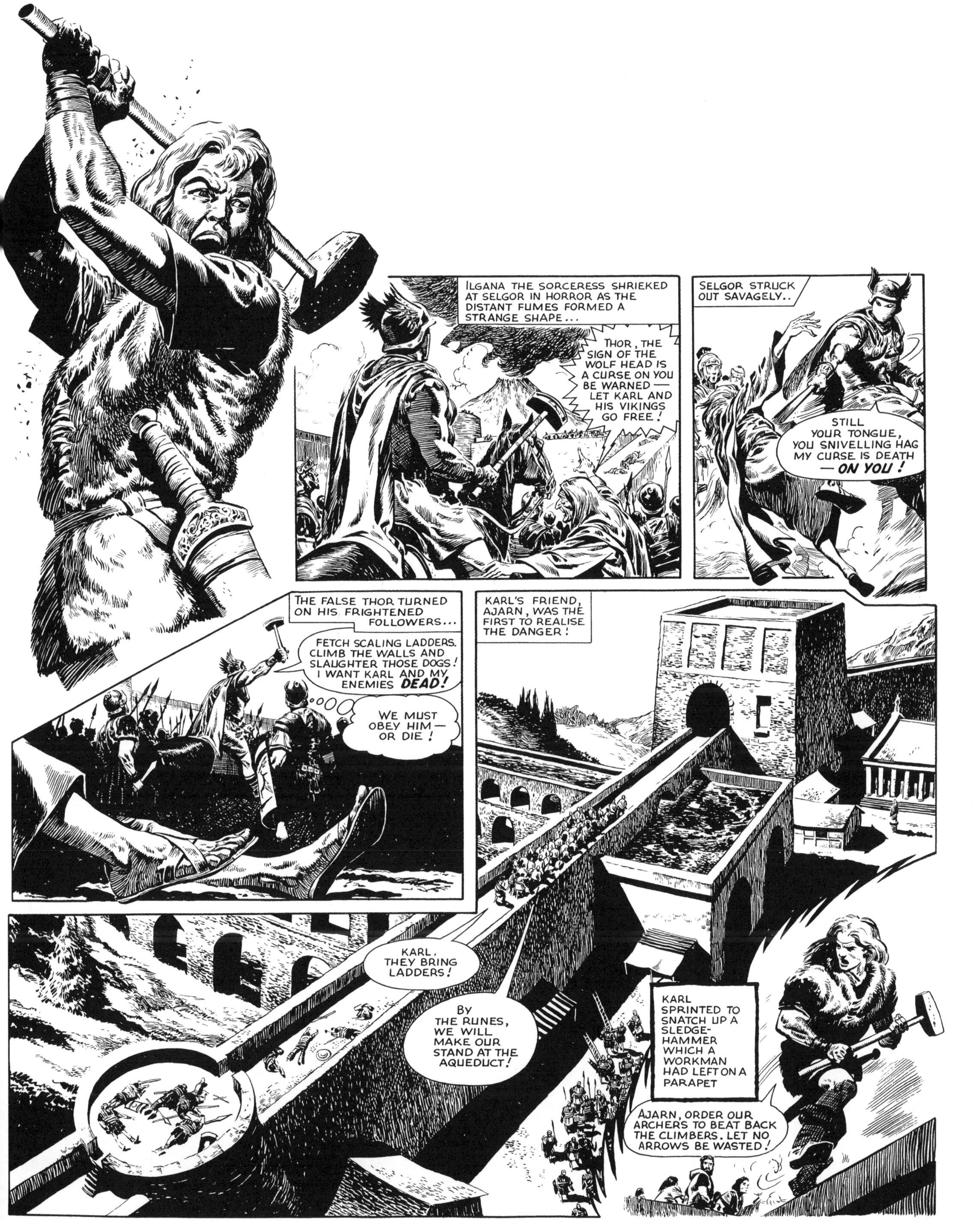

ILGANA THE SORCERESS SHRIEKED AT SELGOR IN HORROR AS THE DISTANT FUMES FORMED A STRANGE SHAPE...
THOR, THE SIGN OF THE WOLF HEAD IS A CURSE ON YOU BE WARNED — LET KARL AND HIS VIKINGS GO FREE!
SELGOR STRUCK OUT SAVAGELY..
STILL YOUR TONGUE, YOU SNIVELLING HAG MY CURSE IS DEATH — ON YOU!
THE FALSE THOR TURNED ON HIS FRIGHTENED FOLLOWERS...
FETCH SCALING LADDERS. CLIMB THE WALLS AND SLAUGHTER THOSE DOGS! I WANT KARL AND MY ENEMIES DEAD!
WE MUST OBEY HIM — OR DIE!
KARL'S FRIEND, AJARN, WAS THE FIRST TO REALISE THE DANGER!
KARL, THEY BRING LADDERS!
BY THE RUNES, WE WILL MAKE OUR STAND AT THE AQUEDUCT!
KARL SPRINTED TO SNATCH UP A SLEDGE-HAMMER WHICH A WORKMAN HAD LEFT ON A PARAPET
AJARN, ORDER OUR ARCHERS TO BEAT BACK THE CLIMBERS. LET NO ARROWS BE WASTED!

THE SOUND OF HEAVY BLOWS SPLINTERING STONE DREW SELGOR'S ATTENTION...

QUICK, YOU FOOLS — *HE'LL HAMMER A BREAK IN THE RESERVOIR!* BRING HIM DOWN BEFORE HE RELEASES A FLOOD!

BUT THE MARKSMEN COMMANDED BY AJARN LOOSED THEIR ARROWS FIRST, AND THE ARCHERS BELOW CRUMPLED IN AGONY

AA-AGH!

GIVE KARL COVER! OUR ARROWS ARE HIS ONLY SHIELD!

MEANWHILE, KARL SWUNG THE HAMMER WITH ALL HIS STRENGTH!

SUDDENLY THE WEAKENED PARAPET CRACKED

PENT-UP WATERS BURST FREE!

KARL BARELY HAD TIME TO LEAP BACK TO SAFETY

FLOOD-WATERS SHALL CLEAR THE STREETS OF SELGOR'S RABBLE!

SCALING-LADDERS AND CURSING MEN CRASHED TO THE GROUND

YET THE VIKINGS REALISED THEY HAD ONLY WON A TEMPORARY ADVANTAGE..

THE WATERS DISPERSE. NOW WILL COME SELGOR'S REVENGE!

SELGOR — MAD WITH RAGE — URGED HIS MEN TO NEW ENDEAVOURS..

REACH THE WALL BY CLIMBING OUT THROUGH THE BUILDINGS! DESTROY MY ENEMIES. I'LL KILL ANY MAN WHO TURNS BACK!

MORE OF SELGOR'S SUPPORTERS BROKE THROUGH THE BARRICADE WHICH KARL HAD EARLIER ERECTED...

THE SMALL PARTY OF VIKINGS WAS TRAPPED BETWEEN TWO ADVANCING FORCES..

WE ARE DOOMED WITHOUT HOPE! NOW NOTHING CAN SAVE US FROM SELGOR'S FURY

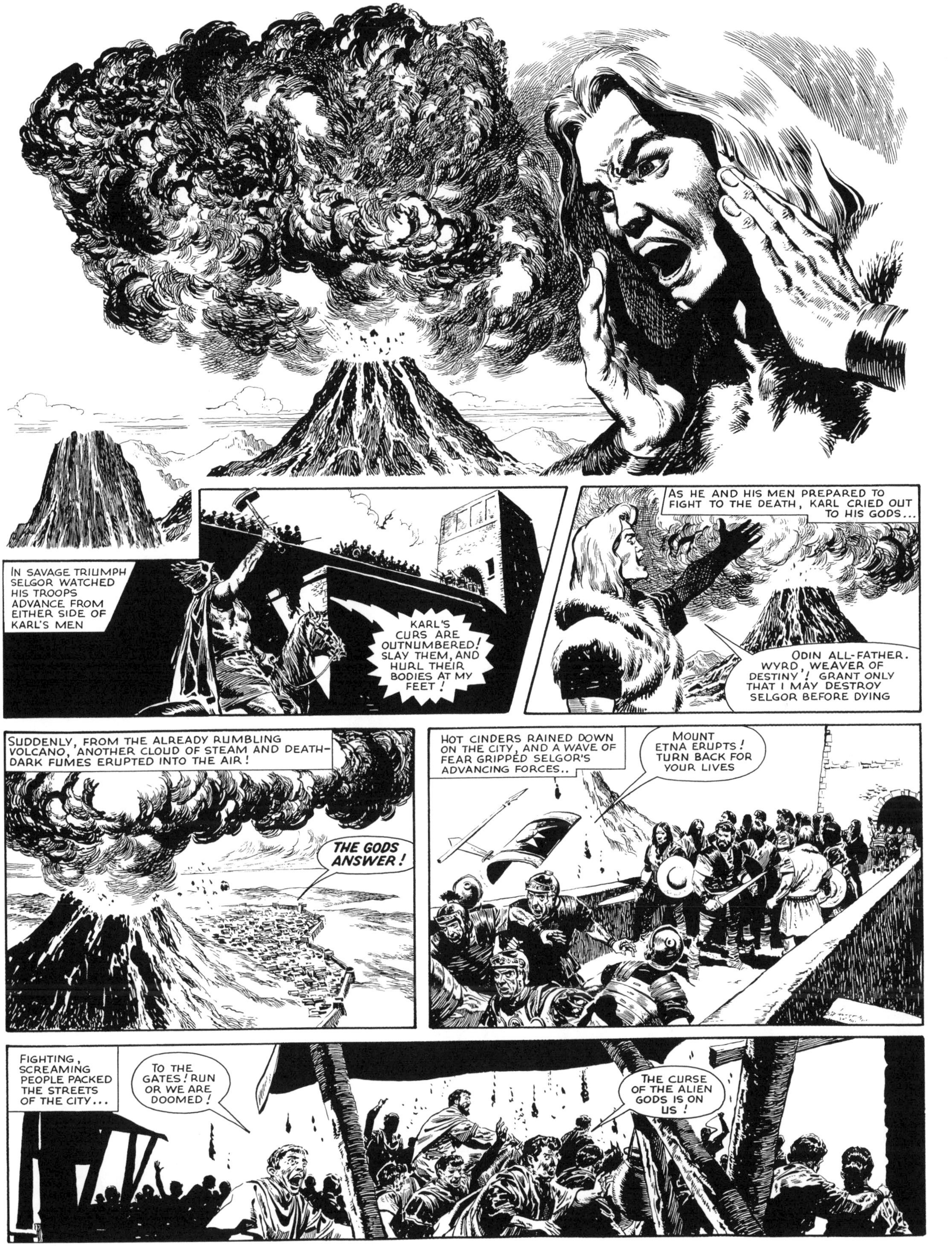

IN SAVAGE TRIUMPH SELGOR WATCHED HIS TROOPS ADVANCE FROM EITHER SIDE OF KARL'S MEN
KARL'S CURS ARE OUTNUMBERED! SLAY THEM, AND HURL THEIR BODIES AT MY FEET!
AS HE AND HIS MEN PREPARED TO FIGHT TO THE DEATH, KARL CRIED OUT TO HIS GODS...
ODIN ALL-FATHER. WYRD, WEAVER OF DESTINY! GRANT ONLY THAT I MAY DESTROY SELGOR BEFORE DYING
SUDDENLY, FROM THE ALREADY RUMBLING VOLCANO, ANOTHER CLOUD OF STEAM AND DEATH-DARK FUMES ERUPTED INTO THE AIR!
THE GODS ANSWER!
HOT CINDERS RAINED DOWN ON THE CITY, AND A WAVE OF FEAR GRIPPED SELGOR'S ADVANCING FORCES..
MOUNT ETNA ERUPTS! TURN BACK FOR YOUR LIVES
FIGHTING, SCREAMING PEOPLE PACKED THE STREETS OF THE CITY...
TO THE GATES! RUN OR WE ARE DOOMED!
THE CURSE OF THE ALIEN GODS IS ON US!

NOT EVEN THE MAD FURY OF SELGOR COULD HALT THE CRAZED FLOOD...

STOP! STOP! I, THOR, COMMAND THAT YOU STAY!

KARL AND HIS VIKINGS PLUNGED TOWARDS A BUILDING FROM WHICH THEY COULD DESCEND TO THE STREETS...

WE MUST SEIZE THIS CHANCE TO ESCAPE! THE CITY MAY BE WIPED OUT WITHIN THE HOUR

FIND HORSES AND CHARIOTS! FLEE FROM THE CITY AND RETURN TO OUR SHIPS. ONLY I, KARL, MUST STAY!

I SEEK SELGOR! AFTER I HAVE SLAIN HIM, AJARN, AND RECOVERED WHAT HE STOLE FROM THOR'S TEMPLE, I WILL JOIN YOU. SAIL WITHOUT ME, SHOULD MY TASK TAKE TOO LONG!

AJARN, HOWEVER, INSISTED UPON ACCOMPANYING KARL!

KARL, I REMAIN WITH YOU! WE LIVE OR DIE TOGETHER IN SEEKING SELGOR!

SO BE IT!

MEANWHILE, TERROR WITHIN THE THREATENED CITY INCREASED. HOT VOLCANIC CINDERS HAD FALLEN INTO A HAY-CART...

FIRE!

FANNED BY THE WIND, THE BLAZE SPREAD WITH FANTASTIC SPEED!

IN THE CONFUSION KARL BECAME SEPARATED FROM AJARN

THE FATES HAVE DECIDED THAT I MUST HUNT SELGOR ALONE. SOMEWHERE THE FALSE THOR AWAITS ME. DEVIL THOUGH HE IS, HE WILL NOT HAVE FLED

SUDDENLY A RIDER APPEARED THROUGH THE SMOKE. KARL, RECOGNISING HIM, SPRANG LIKE A TIGER!

IT IS ONE OF SELGOR'S BODY-GUARD!

KARL HURLED HIM FROM THE SADDLE

WHERE IS THOR? SPEAK, OR YOU'LL REMAIN SILENT FOR EVER!

HE AWAITS YOU IN THE TEMPLE OF MITHRAS! THOR SENT ME TO FIND YOU. GO TO HIM IF YOU DARE!

DETERMINED TO GET TO GRIPS WITH SELGOR, KARL WENT DASHING ALONG THE ROAD WHICH LED TO THE TEMPLE!

YOU GO TO YOUR DEATH! NO MAN IS STRONG ENOUGH TO OVERCOME THOR!

LIKE A BEAST OF PREY SELGOR WATCHED KARL DRAW NEARER...

AT LAST! THIS JAVELIN SHALL REMOVE HIM FROM MY PATH!

SELGOR'S HIDING-PLACE WAS REVEALED BY A SUDDEN GOUT OF FLAME WHICH WAS REFLECTED FROM HIS GOLDEN HELMET. IN THE NICK OF TIME KARL DODGED TO ONE SIDE AND MISSED DEATH BY AN INCH

AH — I DRAW FIRST BLOOD!

ALTHOUGH KARL WAS WOUNDED, THE FURY OF THE FOLLOWING DUEL WAS AS FIERCE AS THE SEARING HEAT OF THE FLAMES

KARL WAS WEAKENING. NOT EVEN HIS STAUNCH COURAGE COULD WARD OFF FOR EVER SELGOR'S SAVAGE HAMMER BLOWS!

STUNNED, KARL CRASHED BACKWARDS, CRYING OUT IN DESPAIR TO HIS GODS!

ODIN! WYRD! IF DIE I MUST, LET ME TAKE THIS FIEND WITH ME!

SELGOR PAUSED, THEN TORE OFF HIS MASK...

GAZE WELL, KARL, ON MY SCARRED FACE— HOW IT WAS MADE UGLY BY A WOLF WHICH ONCE CAME TO YOUR RESCUE! FOR THAT YOU WILL DIE!

KARL CLUTCHED AT THE BURNING CURTAINS...

HE HURLED THEM TO ENGULF HIS ADVANCING ENEMY!

IN ONE MOVEMENT KARL REACHED HIS SWORD...

GRASPING IT IN BOTH HANDS, HE BOUNDED UPWARD AND LEAPT AT THE KILLER WHO HAD THWARTED HIM FOR SO LONG

DIE, WOLF-MAN

KARL STRIPPED FROM HIS DEAD ENEMY THE GOLDEN HELMET AND BREASTPLATE. THEN, AS HE REELED FROM THE TEMPLE, THE ROOF CRASHED TO THE GROUND!

KARL'S FRIEND, AJARN, HAD STAYED BEHIND IN THE DOOMED CITY OF EGRA. IN SEEKING FOR KARL HE HAD FOUND THE LAST CHARIOT.

KARL! I AM HERE

NEXT MOMENT—

THE GODS WERE WITH ME AJARN! WHAT SELGOR STOLE FROM THE THOR TEMPLE IS RECOVERED THE WOLF-MAN IS DEAD!

IT IS JUSTICE, KARL, BUT WE ARE STILL IN GRAVE DANGER—WE HAVE TO ESCAPE FROM THIS CITY OF FIRE!

KARL KNEW HIS VIKINGS AND THEIR SHIPS WOULD BE WAITING ON THE RIVER BEYOND THE CITY. BUT THE JOURNEY TO THE CITY'S GATES WAS A RACE AGAINST THE FLAMES...

FASTER! FASTER! VOLCANIC TREMORS SHAKE THE EARTH!

AGAIN THE GROUND SHUDDERED, AND STONE PILLARS GAVE WAY!

THE ARCH FALLS! WE'LL BE RUSHED!

As Ajarn stared in horror at the devastation, Karl snatched the reins from him...

I'LL TAKE YOUR PLACE AND DRIVE SLOWING DOWN WILL NOT SAVE US!

Whip and shouts urged the horses forward in a mad crescendo of speed!

A rumble like doom drowned the noise of the chariot wheels...

DEATH IS UPON US!

Only inches prevented disaster! The ground shook, and mortar dust clouded the air. Then —

BY THE WEAVER OF DESTINY, WE ARE THROUGH!

Karl spared no time to look back. Pursued by the fury of fire and descending gases from the volcano, he headed out of the city...

MY MEN AWAIT US AT THE SHIPS! ODIN ALL-FATHER, LEND US SPEED!

SUPER-HEATED STEAM DESTROYED ANY REMAINING LIFE IN THE CITY WHERE SELGOR LAY BURIED IN THE RUBBLE

SELGOR'S TYRANNY LAY AS DEAD AS HIMSELF AND THE CITY. THE HUNDREDS OF ESCAPING SICILIAN SURVIVORS FELT ONLY JOY AND RELIEF...

THE CITY HAS GONE—AND EVIL WITH IT. THE FAIR-HAIRED ONE, KARL, SAVED US ALL!

HE SERVED STRANGE GODS, BUT THEIR POWER WAS WITH HIM

MEANWHILE, KARL'S VIKINGS WAITED AT THE DOCKS...

WE DARE NOT DELAY MUCH LONGER KARL AND AJARN MUST HAVE PERISHED!

WAIT! A CHARIOT APPROACHES

KARL SLASHED THE TRACES SO THAT THE HORSES COULD RUN FREE. JOYFULLY AJARN SHOUTED TO THE MEN IN THE BOATS

SELGOR—THE FALSE THOR—IS SLAIN! SEE, KARL HAS RECOVERED THE GOLD STOLEN FROM THE TEMPLE!

WITH KARL AND AJARN AT LAST SAFELY ABOARD, THE LONG-SHIPS SET SAIL

WE RETURN TO OUR HOMELAND IN TRIUMPH! WHAT WAS STOLEN FROM THOR MUST BE RETURNED!

IT WAS MANY MONTHS LATER THAT THE SHIPS REACHED SCANDINAVIA...

SEND FOR THE FINEST GOLDSMITH WE KNOW! SELGOR'S GOLDEN MASK AND BREASTPLATE SHALL BE MELTED DOWN TO AGAIN FORM THE GOLDEN HAMMER OF THOR!

IN THE TEMPLE OF THOR THE HELMET AND HAMMER WERE REPLACED ON THE STATUE

A SHAFT OF SUNLIGHT SUDDENLY BLAZED THROUGH A WINDOW...

IT IS AN OMEN! MIGHTY THOR SHOWS HIS PLEASURE! WE HAVE NO FURTHER TERRORS TO FEAR!

WE HAVE NO FURTHER TERRORS TO FEAR. THE DARK CLOUD HAS BEEN LIFTED!

BUT KARL WAS WRONG! MANY MILES AWAY, ON A MIST-SHROUDED ISLAND, SEEDS OF A NEW EVIL WERE GROWING. EACH POD, LIGHT AS THISTLE-DOWN, STIRRED IN THE WIND

WHEN THE WIND STRENGTHENED, THE LIGHT PODS WERE CARRIED AWAY

EVIL TRAVELLED IN THEM—EVIL WHICH WOULD ONE DAY GROW AND FLOURISH IN KARL'S HOMELAND!

V

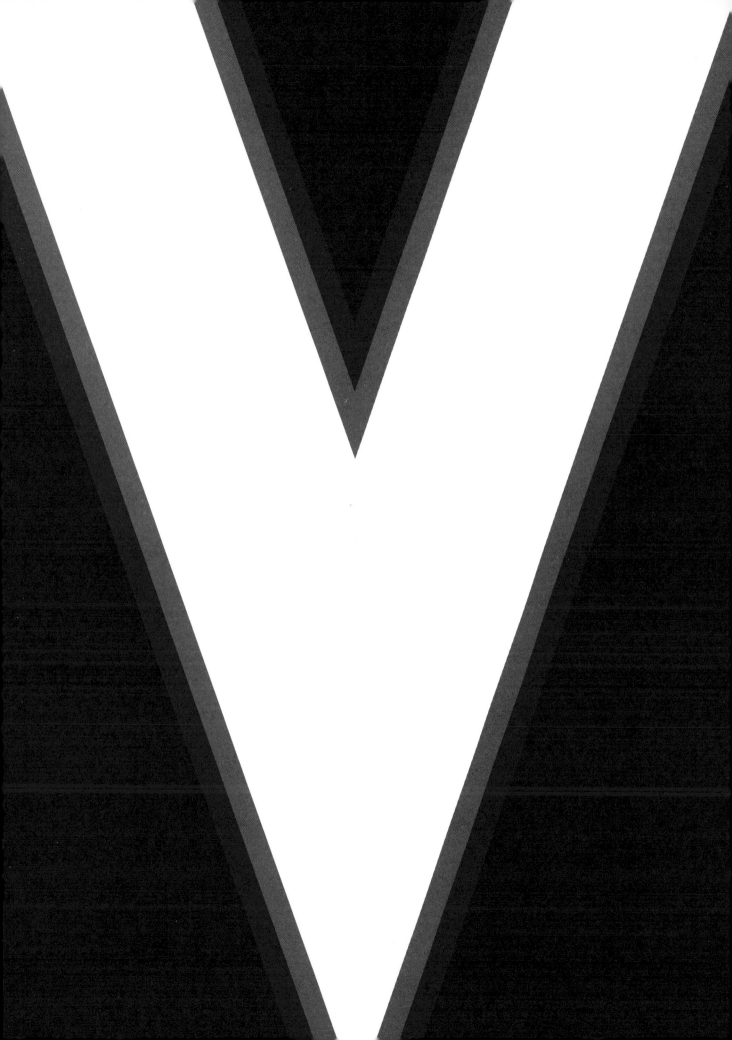

THE POWERS OF HELVUD

Serialised in **Lion**
31st March – 28th July 1962

Written by
Ted Cowan

Art by
Don Lawrence

After a victorious expedition to Sicily, Karl the Viking returned to Scandinavia. For a time all was peaceful. Then war broke out between rival Norse clans. The result was terrible devastation

Crops, ships and food stocks were destroyed in the merciless fighting.

Madness drives the men on! Winter will bring hunger to those who survive

Winter was severe, and starving wolves scattered the herds of red deer. Famine was everywhere.

The Vikings at Karl's settlement fared no better than the rest. Even with the coming of spring, the position was desperate.

Feed the horses! We need them for hunting farther afield

Aye, with Karl's leadership we have a chance to beat death

When Karl's hunting party set off, he shouted to the man who was left in charge

Veldi, guard my dogs well. Use your hunting skill in fields near the settlement!

Our word shall be law. I'll see that everyone obeys

Karl was not to know that Veldi was dangerously ambitious!

One day MY word shall be law. Karl's death could be very convenient. When the right opportunity arrives — I shall act swiftly!

THAT OPPORTUNITY WAS COMING! CARRIED BY WIND AND SEA FROM AFAR, STRANGE SEED-PODS FELL ON THE RUGGED COAST

WHERE THE SEEDS LANDED, THEY GREW ...GREW WITH ALL THE MYSTERIOUS SPEED OF A FUNGUS... GREW IN THE SHAPE OF GNARLED HANDS!

VELDI AND A HUNTING-COMPANION WERE THE FIRST TO SET EYES ON THEM

FOOD, VELDI! FOOD! SURELY THOSE THINGS YONDER ARE MUSHROOMS?

BUT WITH A STARTLED OATH, THE MAN STOPPED SHORT

BY ODIN, THEY LOOK TOO MUCH LIKE HUMAN HANDS!

LOOKS MEAN NOTHING, FOOL! ALL THAT MATTERS IS WHETHER OR NOT THEY ARE SAFE TO EAT!

THREE OF KARL'S PRIZED HOUNDS DECIDED THE ANSWER!

THE FUNGUS ATTRACTS THEM! THE DOGS EAT WITH RELISH! THEY FIND IT WHOLESOME, SO WILL WE!

IF YOU ARE RIGHT, WE NEED GO HUNGRY NO LONGER TODAY!

WHAT FOLLOWED WAS AMAZING. THE HOUNDS, HAVING EATEN, SUDDENLY SNIFFED THE AIR — THEN WENT RUSHING MADLY AWAY!

COME BACK! TO HEEL, YOU BRUTES! TO HEEL! — THEY REFUSE TO OBEY!

WHAT DOES IT MATTER? THEY HAVE PROBABLY SCENTED A HARE

VELDI'S EYES BURNED MENACINGLY AS HE SPOKE

I ORDER YOU TO GATHER THE FUNGUS. COOKED, IT WILL FEED THE SETTLEMENT. OR WOULD YOU CARE TO ARGUE WITH THIS SWORD?

I—I OBEY!

A LITTLE LATER, WHEN KARL AND HIS PARTY WERE RETURNING, A VIKING NAMED AJAR SIGHTED ONE OF THE HOUND

KARL, THERE IS BARE FANG! HE COMES TO GREET YOU!

LAUGHINGLY KARL CALLED TO HIS FAVOURITE HOUND

HERE, BARE FANG!

YOU ARE HONOURED. TO SEEK YOU HE HAS EVEN LEFT VELDI.

BARE FANG UTTERED NO JOYOUS BARK. INSTEAD, THE GREAT JOWLS WRINKLED BACK IN A SNARL...

WHAT AILS THE BRUTE? BY ODIN — IT IS GOING TO ATTACK KARL — KARL, ITS BELOVED MASTER!

LOOK OUT! THE BRUTE'S MAD!

KARL PROTECTED HIMSELF WITH HIS SHIELD JUST IN TIME!

ITS BREATH REEKS OF EVIL! AND NEVER HAVE I SEEN SUCH HATRED IN AN ANIMAL'S EYES

THUDDING TO EARTH, THE HOUND TURNED AND BOLTED CRAZILY AWAY. IT SEEMED ALMOST TO BE FOLLOWING A SCENT...

COME, MEN, WE WILL FOLLOW IT! THERE MUST BE SOME SPECIAL REASON FOR ITS STRANGE BEHAVIOUR

SEE — ITS BODY GLOWS!

THE CHASE WAS SHORT. FOR THE HOUND SUDDENLY REACHED A DEEP GULLY — AND FAILED TO STOP!

THE BEAST JUMPS DELIBERATELY TO ITS DEATH!

WHEN THE PARTY GAZED INTO THE DEPTH THEY COULD SEE THREE STILL FORMS AT THE BOTTOM.

THE OTHER TWO DOGS ARE ALSO THERE. THEY TOO, HAVE DESTROYED THEMSELVES!

THE DOGS WERE LEFT IN VELDI'S CARE. *SOMETHING IS WRONG!* THIS IS AN OMEN! COME, WE RIDE BACK TO THE SETTLEMENT

MEANWHILE, VELDI RETURNED TO THE VILLAGE WITH THE PECULIAR FUNGUS WHICH HE AND A COMRADE HAD GATHERED

THE GODS HAVE SENT FOOD FOR US! KARL IS STILL HUNTING — BUT I HAVE HAD GREATER SUCCESS

DESPITE THEIR HUNGER THE OTHER VIKINGS HELD BACK

THOUGH THE FUNGUS SMELLS GOOD, IT LOOKS EVIL

I ORDER YOU TO COOK AND EAT IT!

IT HAS THE APPEARANCE OF HANDS!

THE FUNGUS WAS BEING PREPARED WHEN KARL'S PARTY ARRIVED ON THE SCENE

AH, YOU BRING MEAT IN TIME, KARL! I HAVE SUPPLIED A PLANT TO GO WITH IT. IT GROWS IN PLENTY—A GIFT FROM THE GODS!

HEED NOT THE UNUSUAL APPEARANCE OF THE FUNGUS. IT IS SAFE TO EAT — THE DOGS FED ON IT BEFORE RUNNING AWAY

WHA-AT!

AS HORROR FILLED KARL, HE HAD A STRANGE VISION

THE STEAM TAKES SHAPE! I SEE A HUGE HAND!

THE SWIRLING STEAM APPEARED TO TAKE ON AN EVEN MORE TERRIBLE SHAPE

WHAT — WHAT CAN IT MEAN?

THERE IS ONLY STEAM! YOU ARE TIRED!

THE VISION PASSED, AND KARL SENT THE COOKING-POT FLYING

FOOLS, THE FUNGUS IS ACCURSED! IT HAS BEEN SENT BY A DEMON-OF-DARKNESS

HE TRAMPLED THE FUNGUS UNDERFOOT

THE DOGS ARE DEAD — THIS FOUL GROWTH MUST HAVE ROBBED THEM OF THEIR REASON!

YOU'RE LOSING YOUR WITS, KARL! I TELL YOU, THE FUNGUS IS SAFE! WATCH—AND I'LL PROVE IT. I'M NEITHER LIAR NOR COWARD!

VELDI'S EYES BLAZED WITH SMOULDERING RESENTMENT

BEFORE KARL COULD STOP HIM, VELDI SNATCHED UP A PIECE OF THE FUNGUS AND THRUST IT INTO HIS MOUTH

WAIT!

WOULD VELDI SUFFER THE SAME FATE AS THE DOGS?

KARL HELD HIS BREATH WHILE VELDI GULPED DOWN THE FUNGUS

LOOK, I EAT—YET SUFFER NO HARM! FOOLS, DID YOU EXPECT ME TO WITHER AND DIE?

SUDDENLY VELDI STIFFENED, AND A SHOCKED CRY BURST FROM KARL.

LOOK, AJARN—HE GLOWS! AM I MAD, OR DO YOU ALSO SEE IT?

WHAT FOLLOWED MADE THE OTHER VIKINGS RECOIL WITH TERROR!

BY ODIN—I SEE A HAND CLOSING UPON HIM—A HAND LIKE THE FUNGUS!

THE SHADOWY FINGERS CLASPED VELDI, AND THEN SEEMED TO DISSOLVE INTO HIM

HE GROWS LARGER! SOME TERRIBLE POWER CONTROLS HIM!

VELDI CALLED OUT TO SOMEONE—OR SOMETHING—UNSEEN...

HELVUD, I HEAR YOU AND OBEY! LET MY MIND AND SPIRIT BE YOURS!

VELDI WHIPPED OUT HIS SWORD

DIE, KARL! HELVUD COMMANDS IT!

THE VILLAGERS WERE STUNNED BY THE FEROCITY, OF THE SUDDEN ATTACK—

VELDI FIGHTS LIKE A BERSERK

HE IS NO LONGER A MAN, BUT A DEMON-OF-DARKNESS!

KARL, AN EXPERT AND DEADLY SWORDSMAN, WAS HARD PRESSED

VELDI MOVED WITH MURDEROUS AND UNCANNY SPEED...

FIRST YOUR SWORD, NEXT YOUR THROAT!

AS KARL CRASHED DOWN, HIS GROPING HANDS FOUND A STRAP.

KARL'S DOOMED IT'S TOO LATE TO SAVE HIM!

Ooo....

BUT KARL ROLLED OVER AND—

AA-AGH!

PANTING, KARL ROSE TO HIS FEET, WHILE VELDI SLUMPED UNCONSCIOUS

BRING ROPES AND BIND HIM! I NEED HIM ALIVE IF I'M TO DISCOVER WHAT KIND OF DEVIL HAS POISONED HIS MIND..

THE CHANGE IN HIM WAS CAUSED BY THE FUNGUS!

CARRY HIM INSIDE AND GUARD HIM WITH YOUR LIVES. AJARN, BURN THE REST OF THIS FUNGUS LET NOT A FRAGMENT REMAIN. NOW WE MUST RIDE TO DESTROY IT WHEREVER IT GROWS

ONE FRIGHTENED VIKING KNEW WHERE THE FUNGUS HAD BEEN FOUND

I CAN LEAD YOU. I WAS FIRST TO SEE THE FOUL PLANT!

THEN MOUNT UP! WE HAVE NO TIME TO LOSE!

FEAR AND A TERRIBLE URGENCY DROVE KARL ON

THE FUNGUS HAS A POWER WHICH ALREADY CONTROLS VELDI. THOSE WHO EAT IT BECOME SLAVES OF EVIL. *WE MUST DESTROY IT BEFORE IT CONQUERS US ALL!*

MEANWHILE, MILES AWAY, NEAR ANOTHER SETTLEMENT, THE FUNGUS WAS ALSO SPROUTING

MANY MORE OF THE MYSTERIOUS PLANTS WERE READY TO SPREAD THEIR EVIL!

KARL AND HIS MEN RODE WITH ALL SPEED UNTIL SUDDENLY THE GUIDE POINTED AHEAD

KARL, THERE IT IS! YONDER GROWS THE ACCURSED FUNGUS WHICH HOLDS SUCH EVIL POWER!

KARL URGED HIS HORSE ON EVEN FASTER, AND HIS VOICE RANG OUT WITH A GRIM COMMAND

RIDE THE PLANTS DOWN! POUND THEM INTO THE EARTH, SO THAT THEIR EVIL DIES WITH THEM!

WHAT FOLLOWED WAS FRIGHTENINGLY, UNBELIEVABLY SINISTER. FROM THE NEARBY SEA A THICKENING HAZE ROSE. WITHIN SECONDS IT COVERED THE WHOLE AREA

BY THE RUNES, IT IS MAGIC! IT HIDES THE FUNGUS FROM SIGHT!

IT RISES TO PROTECT THEM!

PANIC GRIPPED THREE VIKINGS, CAUSING THEM TO TURN BACK

THEY ARE COWARDS! THEIR BLOOD IS LIKE WATER!

PERHAPS THEY ARE WISE. JUDGE NOT TOO HARSHLY!

ODIN — GREATEST OF MY GODS — GIVE ME COURAGE! IF YOU WOULD HELP ME AGAINST EVIL, SHOW ME A SIGN!

AS IF IN REPLY, A SHAFT OF SUNLIGHT BURNED DOWN THROUGH THE BLANKET OF MIST

Then, while the mist dispersed—

ODIN ANSWERED! NO LONGER IS THE FUNGUS HIDDEN!

DESTROY IT! THE POWER WHICH SNATCHED VELDI'S MIND SHALL ROB NO ONE ELSE!

Back at the settlement, the vikings who were guarding Veldi stirred uneasily...

SEE— HE REGAINS CONSCIOUSNESS! SOMETHING IS HAPPENING TO HIM!

THE GLOW AROUND HIM BURNS BRIGHTER!

Veldi gave a terrible cry as if suddenly hurt!

AA-AAH! THE FUNGUS DIES! KARL HAS FOUND IT!

VELDI HAS SECOND SIGHT!

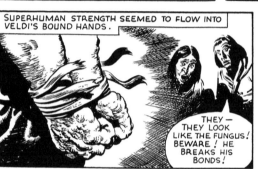

Superhuman strength seemed to flow into Veldi's bound hands.

THEY— THEY LOOK LIKE THE FUNGUS! BEWARE! HE BREAKS HIS BONDS!

The bound viking tore away the stout ropes as if they were made of cotton

SLAY HIM! HE IS POSSESSED BY A DEMON!

The half fearful guards were too late! Veldi knocked both senseless.

The third man had no chance against Veldi's speed

DIE!

Snatching up a sword, Veldi cried to some unseen power

HELVUD SPIRIT OF THE ISLAND—I HEAR YOU AND OBEY. I NOW GO FORTH TO GAIN MORE FOLLOWERS, AND TOGETHER WE WILL DO ALL THAT YOU DESIRE!

He hurled the door wide and plunged outside. Instantly a shout of alarm arose...

VELDI ESCAPES! HE IS FREE!

It was at that very moment that Karl and his friend, Ajarn, had crushed the last fungus growth. The next second, Ajarn was staggered to see Karl reel drunkenly

KARL, WHAT AILS YOU?

A SUDDEN AGONISING PAIN IN HIS HEAD MADE KARL REEL DIZZILY—AND HE KNEW IT FOR AN OMEN OF DISASTER

TO THE HORSES! WE MUST RETURN WITH ALL SPEED TO THE SETTLEMENT! WE ARE NEEDED THERE!

BY THE HAMMERER, YOU ARE WHITE AS DEATH!

KARL'S PREMONITION WAS CORRECT. FOR BACK AT THE SETTLEMENT —

IT IS VELDI! HE HAS ESCAPED!

SLAY HIM! HE HAS MURDERED THE GUARDS!

VELDI TURNED AT BAY...

I HAVE A SWORD THIRSTING FOR BLOOD! HELVUD IS THE SPIRIT WHO RULES ME. HE GIVES ME MY ORDERS. I HAVE POWER BESTOWED UPON ME BY HIM!

TERROR GRIPPED EVEN THE HARDIEST ATTACKER, FOR VELDI'S WHISTLING BLADE WAS WIELDED WITH A SINISTER, UNNATURAL STRENGTH

LOOK AT HIS HANDS! THEY — THEY GLOW AND ARE LIKE THE FOUL FUNGUS PLANTS!

HE IS NO MAN — BUT A FIEND!

FEAR ROBBED KARL'S VIKINGS OF COURAGE. VELDI, TAKING HIS BOW AND A HORSE, HEWED A PATH TO FREEDOM

FOOLS, KARL DESTROYED THE FOOD OF POWER SENT BY HELVUD I LEAVE TO SEEK WORTHIER SUBJECTS. THEY SHALL EAT — AND CONQUER THE WORLD!

AS VELDI RODE HE HEARD A STRANGE VOICE IN HIS MIND.

VELDI, I WILL LEAD YOU TO WHERE MORE FUNGUS GROWS. YOU DO WELL! SPUR TO THE SETTLEMENT AT KARFIN!

BEFORE HE HAD GONE FAR HE WAS SEEN BY KARL AND AJARN

THERE IS VELDI!

HE MUST DIE! EVIL HAS MADE HIM ITS SLAVE!

THE COMRADES SWEAT-LATHERED MOUNTS WERE URGED DOWN THE PERILOUS SLOPE

VELDI, WAIT! YOU AND I MUST SETTLE THIS NOW!

VELDI DREW REIN AND UNSHOULDERED HIS BOW

KARL, YOUR BLOOD SHALL SPILL FIRST!

BEWARE OF HIM AJARN!

KARL DUCKED — BUT THE DEADLY SHAFT STILL FOUND A TARGET

AGH!

AJARN!

AS AJARN'S HORSE BOLTED KARL GALLOPED IN PURSUIT.

HIS FOOT IS TRAPPED IN THE STIRRUP!

VELDI HAD VANISHED BY THE TIME KARL COMPLETED THE RESCUE.

IF AJARN IS TO LIVE, SKILLED HELP IS NEEDED. ONLY THE NEAREST THOR-PRIEST HAS SUCH SKILL!

STAUNCHING HIS COMRADE'S WOUND AS BEST HE COULD, KARL MADE HIS WAY TO THE TEMPLE OF THOR

HOURS LATER, INSIDE THE TEMPLE, AJAR AT LAST STIRRED...

YOUR FRIEND WILL LIVE. ONE OF HIS STRENGTH DOES NOT DIE SO EASILY. THAT IS NOT ALL YOU WISH TO KNOW?

KARL'S EYES BURNED WITH A GREAT ANGER

YOU READ MY THOUGHTS WELL! THOR-PRIEST, I SEEK A MAN — WHO'S NOT A MAN. CAST THE RUNE STONES AND READ THE FUTURE. FIND VELDI FOR ME!

SHADOWS SEEMED TO CLOSE IN AS THE PRIEST CROSSED TO THE BRAZIER AND GATHERED THE RUNE STONES. THEN SUDDENLY HE SHIVERED

KARL, I BEG YOU. DO NOT ASK ME THIS THING! POWERS OF EVIL ARE GATHERING—

ENOUGH! FIND VELDI! CAST THE STONES!

RELUCTANTLY THE THOR-PRIEST CAST THE RUNE STONES, AND THE SMOULDERING BRAZIER SUDDENLY LIT UP.

GAZE WELL AT THE SMOKE, KARL! I WILL REVEAL VELDI TO YOU, AS YOU COMMAND!

SO BE IT!

KARL AND THE PRIEST RECOILED AS THE FUMES GLOWED BRILLIANTLY AND BEGAN TO TAKE SHAPE.

BY ODIN, A—A GIANT HAND! ONE SHAPED LIKE THE FUNGUS!

IT IS THE EVIL I WARNED YOU OF!

THEN, LIKE A MIRROR, THE PALM OF THE HUGE HAND SILVERED OVER. IN ITS DEPTHS KARL WAS ABLE TO SEE VELDI — AND HEAR HIS VOICE...

THE FUNGUS! I HAVE FOUND IT!

DISMOUNTING, VELDI CRIED ALOUD TO THE TERRIBLE MASTER HE SERVED.

HELVUD, I HEAR YOU! I WILL FORCE THE VIKINGS AT KARFIN TO EAT YOUR FUNGUS AND BECOME YOUR SLAVES. IN YOUR NAME I WILL LEAD THEM TO CONQUER THE WORLD!

NEXT MOMENT THERE WAS A SOUND OF THUNDER. THE GIANT HAND SCATTERED THE BRAZIER AND FADED AWAY.

THE VISION HAS FINISHED I HAVE SEEN— AND STILL LIVE!

VELDI RIDES TO THE VIKING SETTLEMENT AT KARFIN! I MUST GO THERE TO PREVENT THE PEOPLE EATING THE FUNGUS. I SWEAR BY THE GODS TO OUTWIT VELDI AND DESTROY THE FOUL PLANTS.

KARL'S FRIEND, AJARN, WHOM VELDI HAD EARLIER WOUNDED, FOUND THE STRENGTH TO STAGGER BACK TO HIS FEET

KARL! I, TOO, SAW THESE EVIL THINGS. I RIDE WITH YOU TO KARFIN. YOU SHALL NOT GO ALONE!

THEN REST LONGER AND BUILD UP YOUR STRENGTH. WE'LL LEAVE AT DAWN

NEXT MORNING, AS DAWN STREAKED THE SKIES —

RIDE AS FAST AS YOUR WOUND WILL ALLOW! IF WE DESTROY THE FUNGUS AND VELDI WE MAY SMASH THE POWER OF THE EVIL SPIRIT CALLED HELVUD.

I'D RISK MORE THAN PAIN TO DO THAT!

THEY RODE HARD UNTIL, AT LAST, A HEAVY MIST CAUSED THEM TO SLOW DOWN.

IT IS STRANGE THAT THE WIND DOES NOT CLEAR THE MIST!

GUIDE YOUR MOUNT WARILY. SINISTER POWERS COULD BE WORKING AGAINST US.

THE DANK WHITENESS SWIRLED ABOUT THEM, SEPARATING THE RIDERS.

AJARN! AJARN! WHERE ARE YOU?

THERE WAS NO REPLY EXCEPT THE WAIL OF THE WIND. FEAR FOR HIS FRIEND GRIPPED KARL

THE MIST IS NOT NATURAL! IT IS LIKE A WALL, YET A GALE WIND CANNOT BREAK IT. I FEAR AJARN IS IN GRAVE DANGER!

AJARN HEARD NOTHING. FEVER CAUSED BY HIS WOUND MADE HIM LIGHT-HEADED AND DIZZY.

I BURN WITH THIRST! IF I GO ANY FARTHER I'LL FALL FROM THE SADDLE. I MUST DRINK — DRINK!

WITH SHAKING HANDS HE RAISED HIS LEATHER FLASK. BUT A GUST OF WIND LASHED A BRANCH AGAINST IT...

AAH!

THE VITAL WATER DRAINED AWAY INTO THE SOIL.

WHERE THE WATER HAD RUN A STRANGE, SINISTER GROWTH BEGAN TO RISE.

THE WATER IS GONE! MY MOUTH AND THROAT ARE ON FIRE! I—I MUST HAVE WATER!

THE WET, GLISTENING FUNGUS GROWTH DREW AJARN TOWARDS IT. HE FLUNG HIMSELF FLAT, AND TRIED VAINLY TO MOISTEN HIS MOUTH AGAINST THE DAMP SOIL. *THEN HE REACHED FOR THE NEAREST FUNGUS AND BIT OFF A PIECE!*

Yet that was not all! In Ajarn's grasp was something which filled Karl with incredulous horror. Something he recognised only too well!

BY THE GODS! HE RAISES THE EVIL PLANT TO HIS LIPS! HE MEANS TO EAT THE DEVIL FUNGUS!

Karl flung himself from the saddle, bounded forward, and kicked the fungus from his friend's hands

STOP! HAVE THE FATES ROBBED YOU OF YOUR WITS

The young chieftain stamped the terrible plant into the ground. Fear and concern for his friend overwhelmed him

AJARN, DID YOU EAT OF THE FUNGUS? CLEAR YOUR BRAIN — AND TELL ME

THE FEVER CAUSED BY AN EARLIER WOUND BEGAN TO LEAVE AJARN

I—I CAN'T REMEMBER. I HAD A BURNING THIRST — THEN I REACHED FOR THE FUNGUS. I—I MUST HAVE BEEN OUT OF MY MIND!

BUT I AM ALL RIGHT NOW. I AM READY TO RIDE AGAIN

THEN MOUNT UP! MY ENEMY VELDI MEANS TO LURE THE VIKINGS AT KARFIN INTO EATING THE FUNGUS. WE MUST GET THERE AHEAD OF HIM, AND PREVENT THE SPREAD OF THIS EVIL!

TOGETHER THEY RACED FOR THE MENACED SETTLEMENT...

WE MUSTN'T LOSE A SINGLE MINUTE. OUR BROTHERS WON'T BE SAFE UNTIL MY SWORD CUTS DOWN VELDI, AND THE LAST FUNGUS PLANT IS DESTROYED!

BUT KARL DID NOT KNOW THAT AJARN HAD ALREADY SWALLOWED A MOUTHFUL OF THE TERRIBLE FUNGUS. MILES AWAY, ACROSS THE SEA, HELVUD—WHO CONTROLLED THE MINDS OF THOSE WHO HAD EATEN THE PLANT—CALLED TO KARL'S FRIEND

AJARN! AJA—ARN!

A VOICE— AN IMPULSE HE WAS UNABLE TO FIGHT— FILLED AJARN'S MIND...

AJARN! HELVUD COMMANDS YOU UNSLING YOUR AXE. SLAY KARL! I DESIRE IT!

AJARN'S FACE CONTORTED, AND HE MOVED WITH SWIFT STEALTH

O HELVUD — I OBEY!

AT THAT INSTANT, A WILD BOAR PLUNGED FROM THE UNDER-GROWTH

THE BOAR, HATE-CRAZED BY A WOUND FROM SOME HUNTER, ATTACKED, MAKING AJARN'S HORSE REAR...

KARL TURNED, BUT MISUNDERSTOOD WHAT HE SAW. HE LITTLE THOUGHT THE AXE HAD BEEN INTENDED FOR HIM

QUICK, AJARN— STEADY YOUR MOUNT! LEAVE THE TUSKED BRUTE TO ME!

THE MURDER BLOW WAS FATED NOT TO BE STRUCK!

THEN, WHILE AJARN'S PANICKED MOUNT BOLTED, KARL ACCOUNTED FOR THE BOAR

KARL LOOKED UP AS THE DEAD BOAR ROLLED OVER

AJARN HAS LOST ALL CONTROL OF HIS HORSE. IT TAKES HIM LIKE THE WIND!

KARL GALLOPED MADLY IN PURSUIT

THE HORSE BOLTS TOWARDS THE SMOKING WELL WHICH SPELLS DEATH. AJARN WILL NEVER HALT THE ANIMAL IN TIME!

172

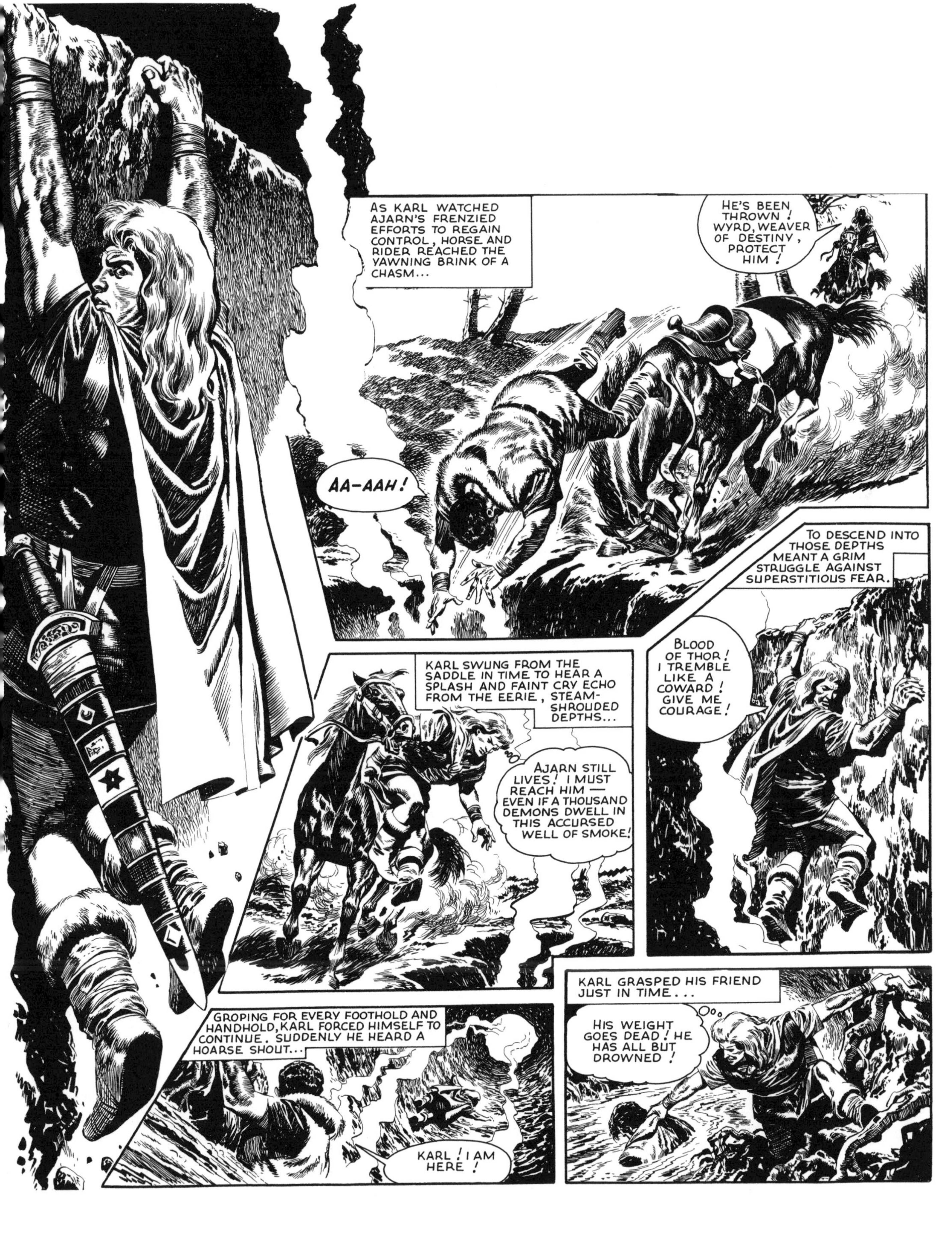

AS KARL WATCHED AJARN'S FRENZIED EFFORTS TO REGAIN CONTROL, HORSE AND RIDER REACHED THE YAWNING BRINK OF A CHASM...
HE'S BEEN THROWN! WYRD, WEAVER OF DESTINY, PROTECT HIM!
AA-AAH!
TO DESCEND INTO THOSE DEPTHS MEANT A GRIM STRUGGLE AGAINST SUPERSTITIOUS FEAR.
KARL SWUNG FROM THE SADDLE IN TIME TO HEAR A SPLASH AND FAINT CRY ECHO FROM THE EERIE, STEAM-SHROUDED DEPTHS...
AJARN STILL LIVES! I MUST REACH HIM — EVEN IF A THOUSAND DEMONS DWELL IN THIS ACCURSED WELL OF SMOKE!
BLOOD OF THOR! I TREMBLE LIKE A COWARD! GIVE ME COURAGE!
GROPING FOR EVERY FOOTHOLD AND HANDHOLD, KARL FORCED HIMSELF TO CONTINUE. SUDDENLY HE HEARD A HOARSE SHOUT...
KARL! I AM HERE!
KARL GRASPED HIS FRIEND JUST IN TIME...
HIS WEIGHT GOES DEAD! HE HAS ALL BUT DROWNED!

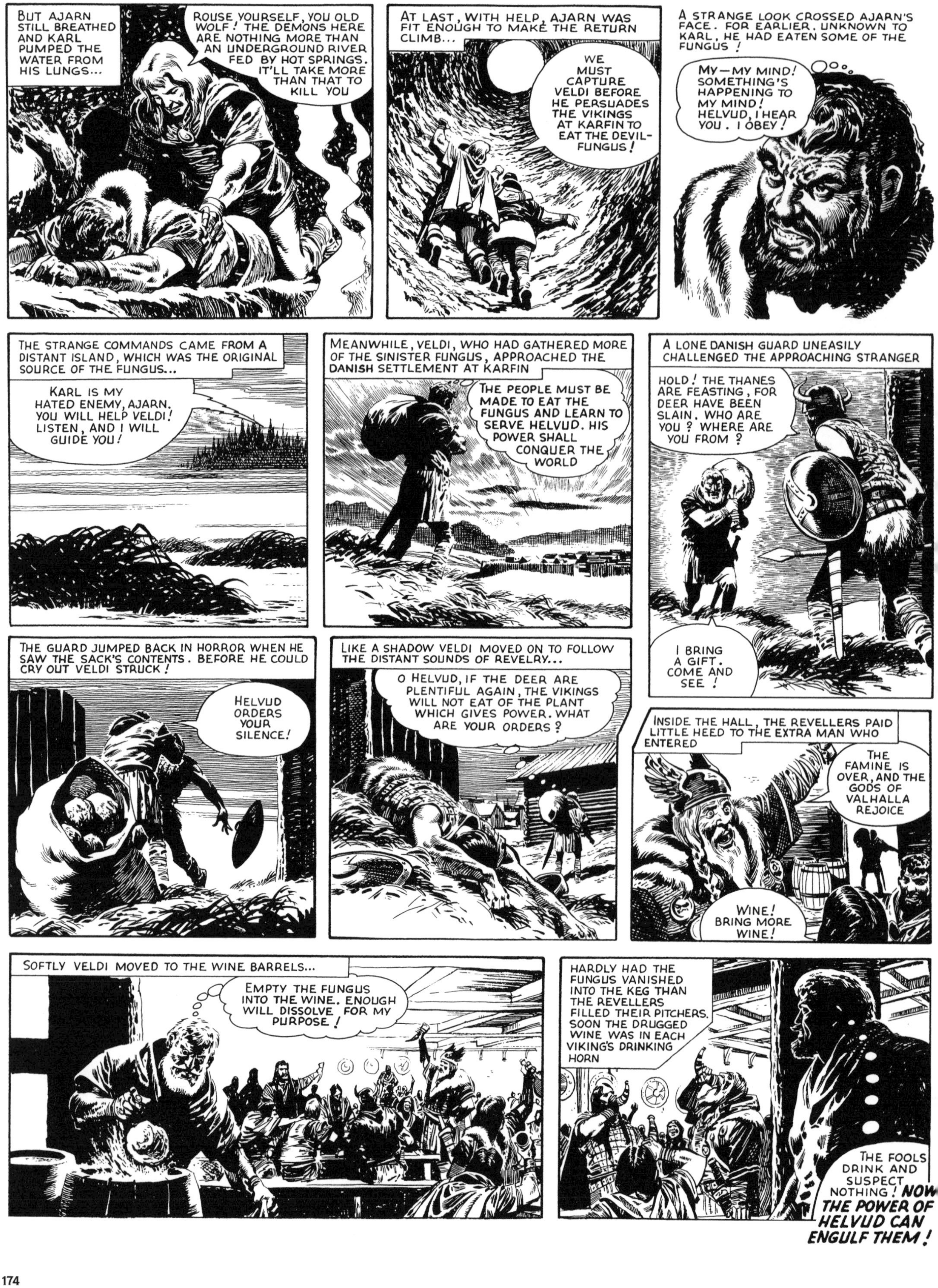

BUT AJARN STILL BREATHED AND KARL PUMPED THE WATER FROM HIS LUNGS...
ROUSE YOURSELF, YOU OLD WOLF! THE DEMONS HERE ARE NOTHING MORE THAN AN UNDERGROUND RIVER FED BY HOT SPRINGS. IT'LL TAKE MORE THAN THAT TO KILL YOU
AT LAST, WITH HELP, AJARN WAS FIT ENOUGH TO MAKE THE RETURN CLIMB...
WE MUST CAPTURE VELDI BEFORE HE PERSUADES THE VIKINGS AT KARFIN TO EAT THE DEVIL-FUNGUS!
A STRANGE LOOK CROSSED AJARN'S FACE. FOR EARLIER, UNKNOWN TO KARL, HE HAD EATEN SOME OF THE FUNGUS!
MY—MY MIND! SOMETHING'S HAPPENING TO MY MIND! HELVUD, I HEAR YOU. I OBEY!
THE STRANGE COMMANDS CAME FROM A DISTANT ISLAND, WHICH WAS THE ORIGINAL SOURCE OF THE FUNGUS...
KARL IS MY HATED ENEMY, AJARN. YOU WILL HELP VELDI! LISTEN, AND I WILL GUIDE YOU!
MEANWHILE, VELDI, WHO HAD GATHERED MORE OF THE SINISTER FUNGUS, APPROACHED THE DANISH SETTLEMENT AT KARFIN
THE PEOPLE MUST BE MADE TO EAT THE FUNGUS AND LEARN TO SERVE HELVUD. HIS POWER SHALL CONQUER THE WORLD
A LONE DANISH GUARD UNEASILY CHALLENGED THE APPROACHING STRANGER
HOLD! THE THANES ARE FEASTING, FOR DEER HAVE BEEN SLAIN. WHO ARE YOU? WHERE ARE YOU FROM?
I BRING A GIFT. COME AND SEE!
THE GUARD JUMPED BACK IN HORROR WHEN HE SAW THE SACK'S CONTENTS. BEFORE HE COULD CRY OUT VELDI STRUCK!
HELVUD ORDERS YOUR SILENCE!
LIKE A SHADOW VELDI MOVED ON TO FOLLOW THE DISTANT SOUNDS OF REVELRY...
O HELVUD, IF THE DEER ARE PLENTIFUL AGAIN, THE VIKINGS WILL NOT EAT OF THE PLANT WHICH GIVES POWER. WHAT ARE YOUR ORDERS?
INSIDE THE HALL, THE REVELLERS PAID LITTLE HEED TO THE EXTRA MAN WHO ENTERED
THE FAMINE IS OVER, AND THE GODS OF VALHALLA REJOICE
WINE! BRING MORE WINE!
SOFTLY VELDI MOVED TO THE WINE BARRELS...
EMPTY THE FUNGUS INTO THE WINE. ENOUGH WILL DISSOLVE FOR MY PURPOSE!
HARDLY HAD THE FUNGUS VANISHED INTO THE KEG THAN THE REVELLERS FILLED THEIR PITCHERS. SOON THE DRUGGED WINE WAS IN EACH VIKING'S DRINKING HORN
THE FOOLS DRINK AND SUSPECT NOTHING! NOW THE POWER OF HELVUD CAN ENGULF THEM!

THE JUICES OF THE FUNGUS, DISSOLVED IN THE WINE, TOOK STARTLING AND IMMEDIATE EFFECT ON THE VIKINGS

HAMMER OF THOR! WHAT AILS US? SOMETHING HAPPENS TO MY MIND!

THE WINE IS CURSED!

VELDI GLOATED AS HE WATCHED

I HAVE COMPLETED MY TASK. NOW THEY, TOO, ARE THE SERVANTS OF HELVUD, MY MASTER!

THEN FROM THE EERIE, DISTANT ISLAND, WHICH HAD FIRST SPREAD THE HIDEOUS FUNGUS, CAME HELVUD'S COMMANDS. VELDI HEARD THEM, FOR EACH ARRIVED LIKE A THOUGHT

NO, VELDI. YOUR TASK IS *BEGINNING!* TO YOU I HAVE GIVEN POWER SECOND ONLY TO MINE. LISTEN WELL —

VELDI STRODE INTO THE CENTRE OF THE HALL

MEN OF KARFIN, I AM VELDI — YOUR LEADER! IN HELVUD'S NAME WE SHALL CONQUER THE WORLD!

UNDER THE INFLUENCE OF THE STRANGE FUNGUS, THE VIKINGS ANSWERED WITH WILD CHEERS

VELDI! VELDI!

LEAD US TO CONQUER!

ALL THROUGH THE NIGHT, PREPARATIONS FOR WAR AND RAIDING WERE MADE.

TO-MORROW WE UN-LOOSE A STORM OF STEEL! OTHERS SHALL SERVE HELVUD—OR DIE! WE'LL CARRY THE FUNGUS OF POWER TO EVERY SETTLE-MENT!

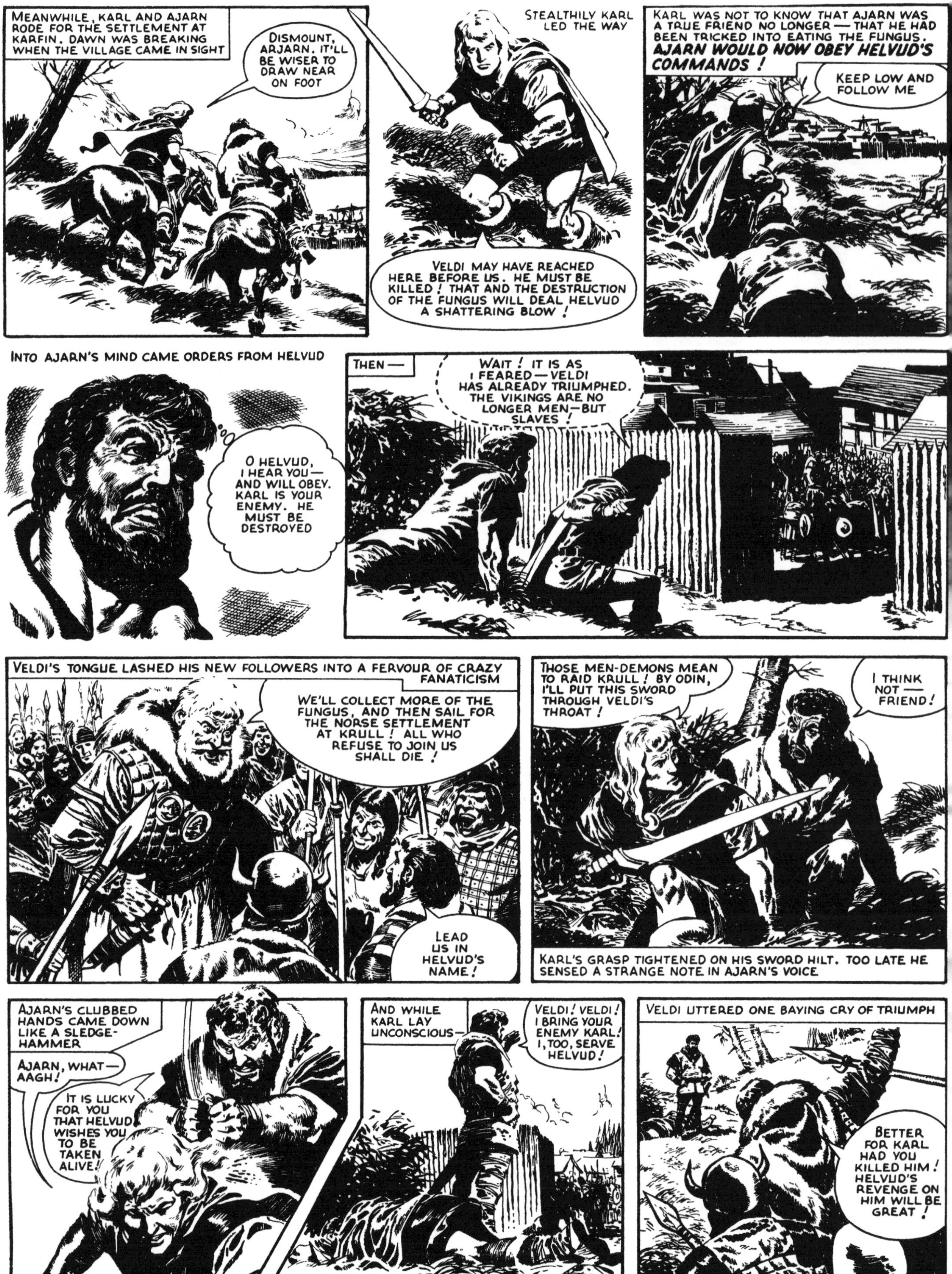
MEANWHILE, KARL AND AJARN RODE FOR THE SETTLEMENT AT KARFIN. DAWN WAS BREAKING WHEN THE VILLAGE CAME IN SIGHT
DISMOUNT, ARJARN. IT'LL BE WISER TO DRAW NEAR ON FOOT
STEALTHILY KARL LED THE WAY
VELDI MAY HAVE REACHED HERE BEFORE US. HE MUST BE KILLED! THAT AND THE DESTRUCTION OF THE FUNGUS WILL DEAL HELVUD A SHATTERING BLOW!
KARL WAS NOT TO KNOW THAT AJARN WAS A TRUE FRIEND NO LONGER — THAT HE HAD BEEN TRICKED INTO EATING THE FUNGUS. AJARN WOULD NOW OBEY HELVUD'S COMMANDS!
KEEP LOW AND FOLLOW ME
INTO AJARN'S MIND CAME ORDERS FROM HELVUD
O HELVUD, I HEAR YOU — AND WILL OBEY. KARL IS YOUR ENEMY. HE MUST BE DESTROYED
THEN —
WAIT! IT IS AS I FEARED — VELDI HAS ALREADY TRIUMPHED. THE VIKINGS ARE NO LONGER MEN — BUT SLAVES!
VELDI'S TONGUE LASHED HIS NEW FOLLOWERS INTO A FERVOUR OF CRAZY FANATICISM
WE'LL COLLECT MORE OF THE FUNGUS, AND THEN SAIL FOR THE NORSE SETTLEMENT AT KRULL! ALL WHO REFUSE TO JOIN US SHALL DIE!
LEAD US IN HELVUD'S NAME!
THOSE MEN-DEMONS MEAN TO RAID KRULL! BY ODIN, I'LL PUT THIS SWORD THROUGH VELDI'S THROAT!
I THINK NOT — FRIEND!
KARL'S GRASP TIGHTENED ON HIS SWORD HILT. TOO LATE HE SENSED A STRANGE NOTE IN AJARN'S VOICE
AJARN'S CLUBBED HANDS CAME DOWN LIKE A SLEDGE-HAMMER
AJARN, WHAT — AAGH!
IT IS LUCKY FOR YOU THAT HELVUD WISHES YOU TO BE TAKEN ALIVE!
AND WHILE KARL LAY UNCONSCIOUS —
VELDI! VELDI! I BRING YOUR ENEMY KARL! I, TOO, SERVE HELVUD!
VELDI UTTERED ONE BAYING CRY OF TRIUMPH
BETTER FOR KARL HAD YOU KILLED HIM! HELVUD'S REVENGE ON HIM WILL BE GREAT!

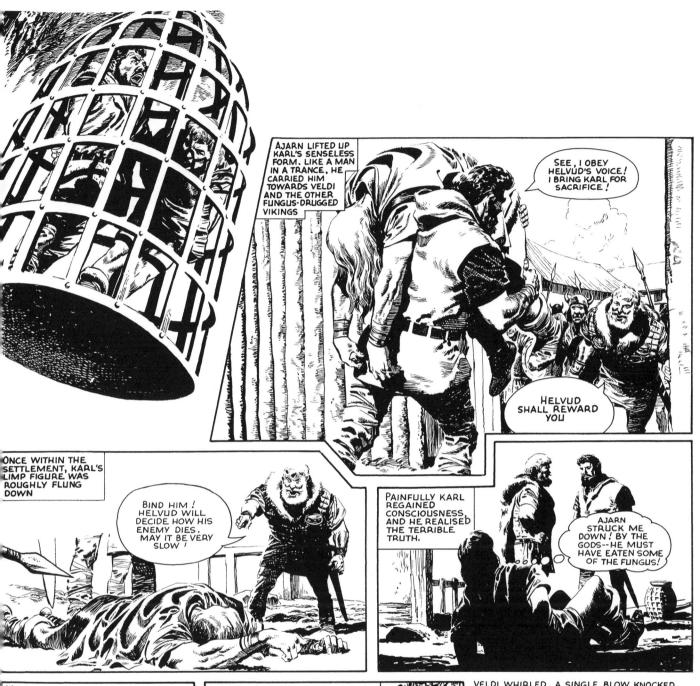

AJARN LIFTED UP KARL'S SENSELESS FORM. LIKE A MAN IN A TRANCE, HE CARRIED HIM TOWARDS VELDI AND THE OTHER FUNGUS-DRUGGED VIKINGS

SEE, I OBEY HELVUD'S VOICE! I BRING KARL FOR SACRIFICE!

HELVUD SHALL REWARD YOU

ONCE WITHIN THE SETTLEMENT, KARL'S LIMP FIGURE WAS ROUGHLY FLUNG DOWN

BIND HIM! HELVUD WILL DECIDE HOW HIS ENEMY DIES. MAY IT BE VERY SLOW!

PAINFULLY KARL REGAINED CONSCIOUSNESS, AND HE REALISED THE TERRIBLE TRUTH.

AJARN STRUCK ME DOWN! BY THE GODS--HE MUST HAVE EATEN SOME OF THE FUNGUS!

VELDI, WHOSE SINISTER POWERS WERE SECOND ONLY TO HELVUD'S, SHOUTED ALOUD

HEAR ME, O HELVUD! I HAVE KARL, YOUR HATED ENEMY, WHO SEEKS TO DESTROY YOU! TAKE YOUR REVENGE BY ORDERING HOW HE SHALL DIE!

MILES AWAY, ON THE MISTY ISLAND FROM WHICH THE TERRIBLE FUNGUS SPORES HAD FIRST SPREAD, HELVUD ANSWERED. THE REPLY WAS LIKE A THOUGHT IN VELDI'S OWN MIND

USE THE IRON CAGE! BUT LISTEN WELL — AJARN IS NOT TO BE TRUSTED. I CAN FEEL THAT MY POWER OVER HIM FADES

VELDI WHIRLED. A SINGLE BLOW KNOCKED AJARN UNCONSCIOUS...

HE HAS SERVED HIS PURPOSE — AND MUST PERISH WITH KARL. BRING THE CAGE!

SOON AJARN ALSO LAY BOUND HAND AND FOOT. THE HOUR HAD COME FOR HELVUD'S REVENGE...

THRUST BOTH OF THEM INSIDE! DEATH WILL BE AT ITS SLOWEST

WAIT! I CLAIM THE DEATH OF A VIKING! IT IS MY RIGHT TO BE GIVEN A SWORD

KARL AND AJARN WERE THRUST INTO THE CAGE...

HERE, HAVE YOUR SWORD! YOU SHALL DIE WITH IT NEAR YOU — BUT OUT OF REACH!

YOU CARRION!

THE BOUND AND HELPLESS PRISONERS WERE CARRIED TO A STEEP SIDE OF THE FJORD.

LOWER THE CAGE BENEATH THE HIGH-WATER MARK. THEY CAN WATCH THE TIDE RISE TILL IT ENGULFS THEM

THE FREE END OF THE ROPE WAS LASHED TO A TREE...

FAREWELL, ENEMY OF HELVUD! WE LEAVE NOW TO SAIL FOR KRULL, THE NEXT SETTLEMENT. THE VIKINGS THERE SHALL EAT THE FUNGUS WE BRING THEM — OR DIE!

VELDI'S SAVAGE HORDE DELAYED ONLY LONG ENOUGH TO GATHER THE LAST OF THE FUNGUS

HASTEN!

A SHORT WHILE LATER—

WE SAIL FOR KRULL! TRAVELLING BY WATER WILL ENABLE US TO TAKE THEM BY SURPRISE. WE NEED THEIR SHIPS!

MEANWHILE, AJARN RECOVERED

MY—MY HEAD! KARL WHAT HAVE I DONE? THE STRANGE MADNESS LEAVES ME. I BETRAYED YOU—

YOU WERE DRUGGED, BUT NOT STRONGLY ENOUGH!

TIME AND AGAIN KARL STRUGGLED VAINLY TO TRY TO REACH THE SWORD.

IT IS USELESS! VELDI KNEW THAT WELL ENOUGH. WITHIN AN HOUR THE WATER WILL BE OVER THE CAGE

IN DESPAIR AND FURY, KARL CALLED TO HIS GODS'...

THOR, GOD OF THUNDER SAVE US LONG ENOUGH TO SLAY VELDI! ODIN, GOD OF BATTLES, RIDE ON YOUR EIGHT-HOOVED HORSE AND GRANT US LIFE UNTIL THE EVIL OF THE FUNGUS HAS BEEN CRUSHED!

THE WIND ROSE, WHIPPING THE WATERS. ABOVE THE SOUND ROSE THE RINGING SCREAM OF GATHERING BIRDS OF PREY.

THEY ARE BUZZARDS! THEY KNOW WE ARE HELPLESS — AND THEY MEAN TO TEAR US APART!

BUZZARDS — FIERCE-EYED BIRDS OF PREY — WHICH HAD GATHERED OVERHEAD, SWOOPED SUDDENLY FOR THE CAGE AND ITS PRISONERS

KARL, THEY ATTACK! IT WOULD HAVE BEEN BETTER TO HAVE DROWNED! THE GODS HAVE TURNED DEAF EARS TO YOUR CRIES

THE SLASHING BEAKS, HOWEVER, DID NOT STRIKE AT KARL AND AJARN — BUT AT THE COMRADES' BONDS!

KARL'S ROPES WERE SHREDDED APART, AND HE TORE HIS CRAMPED WRISTS FREE

THOR AND ODIN HAVE ANSWERED ME! THEY HAVE SENT THESE CREATURES TO SET US FREE, AJARN! MY ENEMY SHALL LIVE TO REGRET THAT HE MOCKED ME BY CASTING MY SWORD INTO THE CAGE

REACHING DOWN, KARL CLASPED THE SWORD THAT VELDI HAD LEFT BEHIND

AFTER CUTTING THE ROPES THAT BOUND THEIR ANKLES, KARL FORCED OPEN THE DOOR OF THE CAGE. THE BUZZARDS ROSE, SCREAMING AS IF IN WILD TRIUMPH

CLIMB THE ROPE TO THE TOP OF THE FIORD, AJARN! ODIN ALL-FATHER, WE THANK YOU!

THE CAGE VANISHES UNDER THE WATER. VELDI HAS BEEN ROBBED OF THE FATE HE PLANNED FOR US!

SOON THEY WERE HURRYING FOR THE SETTLEMENT FROM WHICH VELDI'S RAIDERS HAD ONLY RECENTLY DEPARTED

WE NEED HORSES — AND YOU AN AXE! HERE'S WHERE WE FIND THEM! THEN HARD RIDING CAN GET US TO KRULL AHEAD OF VELDI!

AJARN CREPT UP ON ONE OF THE SENTRIES LEFT POSTED BY VELDI

AUGH!

HERE COME THE OTHER GUARDS! CUT A WAY THROUGH THEM TO THE HORSES!

THE GUARDS WERE DRUGGED BY THE FUNGUS AND POSSESSED TWICE NORMAL STRENGTH

DEATH TO THE ENEMIES OF HELVUD!

ODIN! GUIDE OUR STEEL!

THE SKILL OF KARL AND AJARN COULD NOT BE MATCHED

A MOMENT LATER EACH HAD OBTAINED A HORSE

HEEL YOUR MOUNT! VELDI'S BID TO SPREAD THE POWER OF THE FUNGUS MUST BE CRUSHED

THE TWO DESPERATE RIDERS URGED THEIR SWEAT-LATHERED BEASTS EVER FASTER ACROSS THE SHORTER LAND ROUTE TO KRULL

ON! ON! UNLESS WE WARN THE VIKINGS AT KRULL, THEY TOO WILL BE DOOMED TO BECOME SLAVES OF HELVUD

MEANWHILE, A FIERCE AND BATTERING WIND SLOWED THE PROGRESS OF VELDI'S SHIPS

THE ACCURSED WIND DEFIES US! LOWER SAILS AND ROW!

VELDI RAISED HIS HANDS DRAMATICALLY

O HELVUD, THE VIKINGS AT KRULL SHALL BE FORCED TO EAT THE FUNGUS AND SERVE YOU. TO REFUSE WILL MEAN DEATH!

AT LAST THE FIORD AT KRULL CAME INTO SIGHT

SOUND THE GREETING HORN WHEN I GIVE THE WORD. LOOK-OUTS ARE BOUND TO HAVE SEEN US. WE MUST SEEM TO COME AS FRIENDS — THEN TAKE THEM BY SURPRISE.

THE HORN WAS SOUNDED — AND AN ANSWERING SIGNAL, ONE OF FRIENDSHIP — CAME BACK TO VELDI FROM THE SETTLEMENT

WE ARE WELCOMED — THEY BID US TO LAND! CARRY OUT THE BASKETS OF FUNGUS AS IF THEY ARE GIFTS. KRULL SHALL SOON BE OURS!

OPENLY CARRYING THE BASKETS OF MUSHROOM-LIKE FUNGUS, VELDI'S RAIDERS LEFT THEIR SHIPS AND APPROACHED THE VIKING SETTLEMENT AT KRULL

THE FOOLS THINK WE ARE BRINGING GIFTS TO THEM. BUT THEY WILL DO OUR BIDDING. ANY MAN WHO REFUSES TO EAT THE FUNGUS MUST DIE!

THEN, FROM A MIST-SHROUDED ISLAND, MANY MILES AWAY, THE VOICE OF HELVUD SEEMED TO RING IN VELDI'S EARS...

VELDI, BEWARE! KARL, MY HATED ENEMY, LIVES—AND SEEKS TO DESTROY YOU. *HE TOO HAS REACHED KRULL!*

VELDI SHOUTED A WARNING TO HIS MEN

MAKE FOR COVER! KARL HAS SURVIVED! WE WALK INTO A TRAP!

IT WAS TRUE! KARL AND HIS FRIEND, AJARN, HAD ARRIVED FIRST TO PREPARE THE VIKINGS AT KRULL FOR ATTACK...

ARCHERS — FLIGHT YOUR SHAFTS! KILL! TO BE DEFEATED WILL BRING A GREATER EVIL THAN DEATH!

BOW STRINGS SANG AND ARROWS SOARED HIGH

THEN DEATH RAINED FROM THE SKY ON TO VELDI'S RAIDERS

THE MAIN FORCE OF ATTACKERS SAFELY GAINED COVER HOWEVER, AND BEGAN TO HIT BACK.

I SWEAR TO HELVUD WE'LL NOT LEAVE UNTIL KRULL IS DESTROYED! NEITHER MAN NOR BEAST SHALL ESCAPE! KARL SHALL PAY DEARLY FOR OPPOSING US!

FOR HOUR AFTER HOUR AND FAR INTO THE NIGHT THE SETTLEMENT WAS BESIEGED.

GRIMLY THE CHIEFTAIN OF KRULL TURNED TO KARL

VELDI'S MEN FIGHT LIKE FIENDS. IT IS ONLY A QUESTION OF TIME BEFORE WE ARE OVERRUN AND SLAUGHTERED LIKE CATTLE

HE'S RIGHT, KARL. IT'S IMPOSSIBLE FOR US TO SURVIVE MUCH LONGER

SUDDENLY, HIGH ABOVE IN THE MOONLIGHT, A GIANT WHITE BIRD APPEARED AND CIRCLED ROUND

KARL, LOOK! THE GANNET WHEELS AS IF TO DRAW OUR ATTENTION.

BY THE RUNES, IT COULD BE AN OMEN

LIGHTNING FLASHED, AND A RUMBLE OF THUNDER SEEMED TO PUT WORDS INTO KARL'S MIND

IT IS AN OMEN! THOR SPEAKS!

THOR ORDERS THAT WE FOLLOW THE GANNET! IT WILL LEAD US ACROSS THE SEA TO WHERE WE CAN FIND AND DESTROY HELVUD. ONLY HELVUD'S DESTRUCTION CAN BREAK THE POWER OF THE FUNGUS AND FREE THE MINDS OF HIS SLAVES!

WITH EYES ABLAZE, KARL SUMMONED A PARTY OF THE DEFENDERS

TWENTY OF US MUST BREAK OUT BY STEALTH AND REACH ONE OF THE SHIPS. IF WE SAIL, VELDI WILL FOLLOW. THOSE REMAINING WILL BE SAFE.

TO ESCAPE FROM THE BESIEGED SETTLEMENT REQUIRED A DESPERATE PLAN

ARCHERS, USE THE MOLTEN PITCH TO MAKE FIRE-ARROWS! WE MUST DISTRACT THE RAIDERS' ATTENTION!

AGAIN VELDI'S RAIDERS PREPARED FOR AN ONSLAUGHT

FORWARD! STORM THE STOCKADE!

NEXT MOMENT, KARL'S ARCHERS LET LOOSE THEIR BLAZING ARROWS...

AIM FOR VELDI'S DRAGON SHIPS! SET THEM ALL ON FIRE!

KARL KNEW THAT HIS PLAN HAD TO SUCCEED IF HE AND HIS MEN WERE TO STAND ANY CHANCE OF SURVIVING!

UNERRINGLY THE BLAZING, PITCH-COATED ARROWS THUDDED DOWN INTO THE TIMBERS OF VELDI'S SHIP

AGAIN, MY COMRADES! LAUNCH THE NEXT VOLLEY!

GUTTERING FLAMES REFLECTED FROM THE WATERS OF THE FIORD, AND VELDI CHECKED IN HIS TRACKS...

BACK TO THE SHIPS! WE MUST SAVE THEM BEFORE THE FIRES SPREAD! BY HELVUD, WE WILL HAVE OUR REVENGE ON KARL FOR THIS!

THE RAIDERS BROKE OFF THEIR ATTACK AND DASHED THROUGH THE WATER...

SOAK THE TIMBERS! BEAT OUT THE FLAMES! SOON KARL SHALL FEEL THE FURY OF HELVUD'S HATE!

SWIFTLY KARL ADDRESSED A BAND OF SPECIALLY SELECTED DEFENDERS...

NOW'S OUR CHANCE TO REACH ONE OF YOUR SHIPS. VELDI WILL NOT RENEW THE ATTACK ON YOU ONCE HE KNOWS I'M ESCAPING!

HIGH OVERHEAD CIRCLED A GANNET — AN OMEN OF THOR, THE GOD OF THUNDER AND WAR..

THE GANNET WILL LEAD US TO WHERE WE MAY FIND AND DESTROY HELVUD! ONLY HELVUD'S DESTRUCTION CAN BREAK THE EVIL POWER OF THE FUNGUS AND FREE THE MINDS OF ITS SLAVES!

ONE SHIP RODE AT ANCHOR SOME DISTANCE FROM THE OTHERS

SWIM OUT TO HER! FAILURE MEANS DEATH FOR EVERYONE. MAKE NO SOUND!

THE NOISY CONFUSION AMONGST VELDI'S RAIDERS SWAMPED THE SPLASHING AND GASPING OF KARL'S DESPERATE MEN

ONCE ABOARD, KARL ISSUED FURTHER URGENT ORDERS

MAN THE OARS! AJARN, STEER FOR THE SHADOWS! WE WILL TRY TO PASS VELDI AND MAKE FOR THE OPEN SEA

VELDI'S FOLLOWERS HAD DOUSED THE FLAMES ON THEIR SHIPS WHEN ONE OF THE VIKINGS GAVE A YELL OF ALARM

VELDI! SOME OF THE CURS ARE ESCAPING!

WHILE VELDI HESITATED UNCERTAINLY, FROM THE DISTANT ISLAND WHICH HELVUD INHABITED CAME A WARNING—A COMMAND!

VELDI, KARL AND HIS CREW SEEK TO DESTROY ME! PURSUE THEM!

VELDI'S REACTION WAS IMMEDIATE

THEY SAIL AGAINST HELVUD THE ALL-POWERFUL! OVERTAKE THEM—DESTROY THEM!

IN A MOMENT THE FATE OF THE SETTLEMENT AT KRULL WAS FORGOTTEN BY VELDI

PULL! PULL LIKE MAD! GET WITHIN BOW-SHOT!

AJARN, KARL'S FRIEND, LOOKED BACK AND GAVE A GASP

KARL, THEY GAIN ON US! THEY ROW WITH THE CRAZED STRENGTH OF GIANTS!

KARL CHECKED ON THE DIRECTION OF WIND, THEN—

UNFURL THE SAIL! IT WILL ADD MIGHTILY TO OUR SPEED!

SAIL-CLOTH CRACKED IN THE WIND, AND THE SHIP PLOUGHED GAMELY THROUGH THE WAVES. BUT ALL AT ONCE—

THE WIND CHANGES!

KARL'S SHIP SLOWED DOWN, WHILE THE DEADLY PURSUERS DREW STEADILY NEARER

KARL! THOSE KILLERS WILL SOON BE ON US! WE ARE OUT-NUMBERED—AND DOOM AWAITS US!

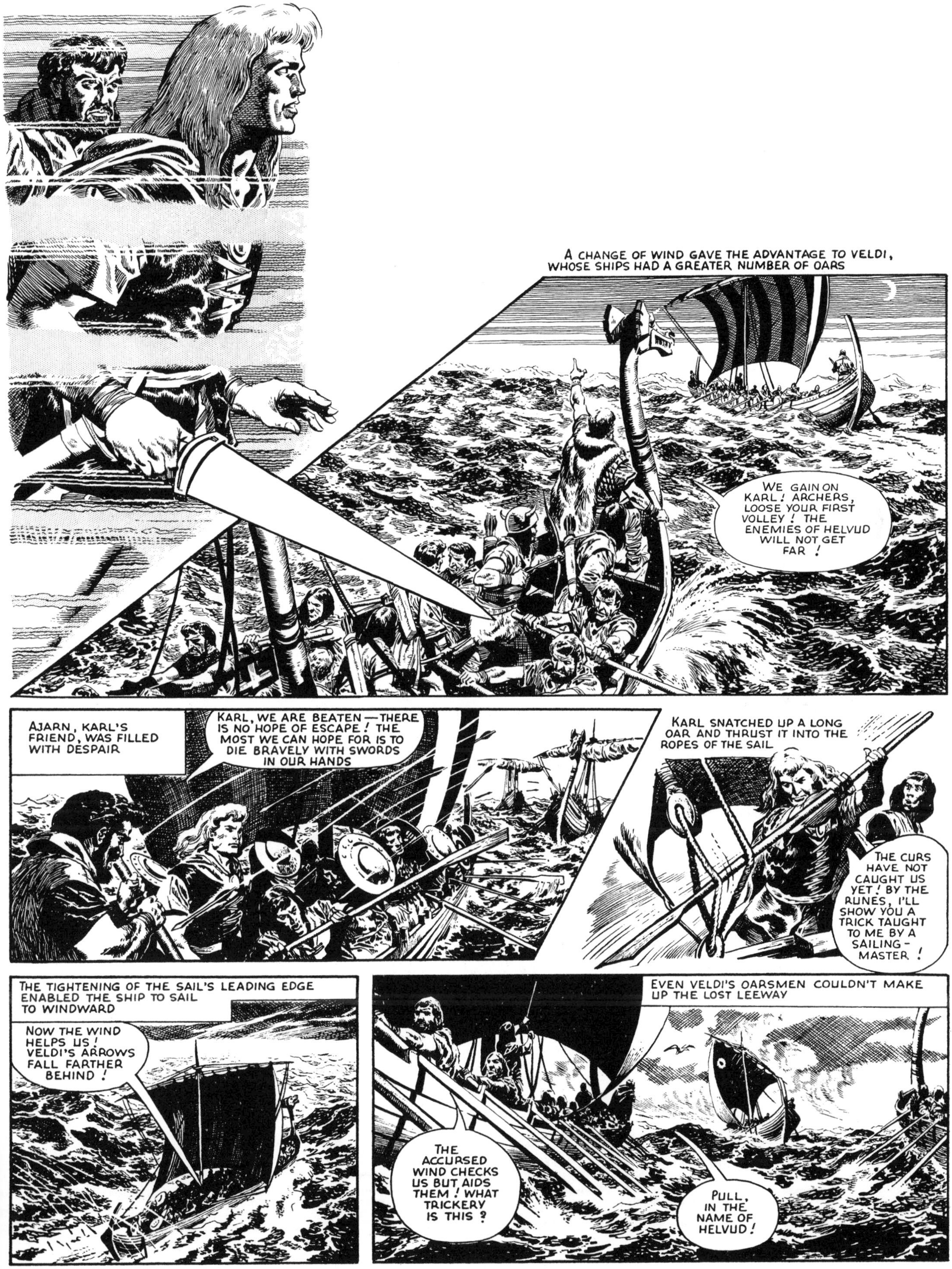

A CHANGE OF WIND GAVE THE ADVANTAGE TO VELDI, WHOSE SHIPS HAD A GREATER NUMBER OF OARS
WE GAIN ON KARL! ARCHERS, LOOSE YOUR FIRST VOLLEY! THE ENEMIES OF HELVUD WILL NOT GET FAR!
AJARN, KARL'S FRIEND, WAS FILLED WITH DESPAIR
KARL, WE ARE BEATEN — THERE IS NO HOPE OF ESCAPE! THE MOST WE CAN HOPE FOR IS TO DIE BRAVELY WITH SWORDS IN OUR HANDS
KARL SNATCHED UP A LONG OAR AND THRUST IT INTO THE ROPES OF THE SAIL
THE CURS HAVE NOT CAUGHT US YET! BY THE RUNES, I'LL SHOW YOU A TRICK TAUGHT TO ME BY A SAILING-MASTER!
THE TIGHTENING OF THE SAIL'S LEADING EDGE ENABLED THE SHIP TO SAIL TO WINDWARD
NOW THE WIND HELPS US! VELDI'S ARROWS FALL FARTHER BEHIND!
EVEN VELDI'S OARSMEN COULDN'T MAKE UP THE LOST LEEWAY
THE ACCURSED WIND CHECKS US BUT AIDS THEM! WHAT TRICKERY IS THIS?
PULL, IN THE NAME OF HELVUD!

FOR MILE AFTER MILE KARL'S PARTY DREW FARTHER AHEAD, FOLLOWING THE GANNET WHICH THEY THOUGHT WAS A MESSENGER FROM THOR, THE SCANDINAVIAN GOD

YONDER BIRD WILL LEAD US TO WHERE WE MAY FIND AND DESTROY HELVUD. ONCE HELVUD IS CRUSHED, THE POWER OF THE EVIL FUNGUS WILL BE NO MORE!

FROM THE SINISTER ISLAND WHICH FORMED HELVUD'S HOME HIS COMMANDS REACHED OUT TO THE MINDS OF THE PURSUERS

FASTER! KARL MUST BE KILLED! THE GODS SIDE WITH HIM AGAINST ME

FOR THREE DAYS KARL'S MEN OUTDISTANCED THEIR ENEMIES, THEN —

AN ISLAND — SHROUDED IN MIST! SEE, THE BIRD MAKES FOR IT! WE MUST BE NEAR HELVUD'S LAIR!

UNEASILY, EACH GRIPPED BY A FEAR HE WAS UNWILLING TO SHOW, THE VIKINGS LANDED

RIDE DOWN THE SAIL! PREPARE TO LAND! HAVE YOUR STEEL READY, FOR WE ADVANCE INTO THE UNKNOWN

THE AIR REEKS OF EVIL. THIS IS A PLACE OF DEMONS. *AND WHO—OR WHAT—IS HELVUD?*

AS IF WAITING FOR THEM, THE GANNET CIRCLED AND THEN MOVED ON

MOVE SLOWLY THROUGH THE MIST AND FEEL FOR EACH STEP. BY ODIN, I WOULD RATHER FACE HUMAN ENEMIES

I FEEL THE VERY ISLAND HATES US

ONE OF THE VIKINGS SUDDENLY STEPPED FROM THE NARROW PATH

AGH! THE GROUND SINKS!

IT IS MARSH! QUICK, DRAG HIM FREE!

THE TERRIBLE MIRE WAS ONLY JUST ROBBED OF ITS PREY

THE MUD SEEMS TO BREATHE, AND THE REEDS LOOK ALIVE

WE ACT LIKE COWARDS! FORWARD — AFTER THE GANNET!

THERE WAS A RUSTLING SOUND, THEN A LIGHTNING MOVEMENT

FLYING ON AHEAD, THE GREAT SEA BIRD SWEPT LOWER OVER SOME TREES

AJARN WAS FIRST TO NOTICE THAT THEIR BIRD GUIDE WAS MISSING

THOR'S MESSENGER HAS VANISHED!

HE FLEW DOWN INTO YONDER WOODS. THAT MUST BE THE WAY TO FIND HELVUD. WE WILL TAKE THE SAME PATH!

KARL LITTLE REALISED THAT THEY WERE HEADING FOR THE VERY PLACE WHERE THE GANNET HAD PERISHED!

SLOWLY KARL AND HIS VIKINGS APPROACHED THE WOODS INTO WHICH A GANNET—A LARGE SEA-BIRD—HAD VANISHED

KARL, THE REEDS AND GRASSES WRITHE LIKE SNAKES! THIS PLACE IS DEMON-CURSED. MUST WE GO FORWARD?

THERE IS NO OTHER WAY. THOR PROMISED THE BIRD WOULD LEAD US TO HELVUD!

SUDDENLY A SHOCKED CRY BURST FROM AJARN, KARL'S FRIEND...

BY THE RUNES! THE GANNET LIES DEAD! KARL, BE WARNED!

KARL FLUNG ASIDE AJARN'S RESTRAINING ARM...

ANY MAN WHOSE STOMACH IS TOO WEAK TO FOLLOW ME CAN STAND BACK!

DESPITE HIS SUPERSTITIOUS FEARS KARL WENT LUNGING FORWARD...

THE TREES SEEM ALIVE. THERE IS SOMETHING EVIL ABOUT THE WAY THE BOUGHS RUSTLE AND SWING

THE GNARLED TREE-TRUNKS APPEARED TO BEAR SINISTER FACES.

NO LONGER WERE THE MOVEMENTS OF THE BOUGHS IDLE—THEY NOW HAD A TERRIBLE PURPOSE

WYRD WEAVER OF DESTINY, PROTECT ME!

NEXT MOMENT —

AJARN! THE TREES ARE TRYING TO CRUSH ME!

HOLD ON, KARL! I AM WITH YOU!

THE DEADLY AXE-BLADE, WIELDED WITH ALL AJARN'S MUSCLE, SHEARED INTO WOOD...

I WILL CUT THEM TO PIECES RATHER THAN LET THEM HARM YOU!

AT LAST THE SINISTER TREES WERE FORCED TO RELINQUISH THEIR VICTIM.

THE TREE-DEMONS GUARD THE PATH LEADING TO HELVUD. THERE IS NO WAY PAST THEM!

THOUGH IT COSTS MY LIFE, I'LL FIND A WAY. ONLY BY HELVUD'S DESTRUCTION CAN WE CONQUER THE FUNGUS WHICH ROBS MEN OF THEIR MINDS

BUT TIME WAS AGAINST KARL, FOR VELDI'S SHIPS WERE IN SIGHT OF THE ISLAND...

PULL ON YOUR OARS! KARL CANNOT BE FAR AHEAD OF US. HELVUD NEEDS OUR AID!

INTO VELDI'S MIND — LIKE HIS OWN THOUGHTS — CAME HELVUD'S INSTRUCTIONS...

I HOLD KARL TRAPPED — HE CANNOT APPROACH. WITH MY HELP, VELDI, YOU WILL CRUSH HIM AND HIS MEN!

VELDI WAS GUIDED TO A LANDING PLACE.

HURRY! MIGHTY HELVUD HAS PLANS FOR US — AND FOR KARL'S DEATH!

SWIFTLY THE FUNGUS-DRUGGED FANATICS FOLLOWED THE MAN TO WHOM HELVUD HAD GIVEN SPECIAL POWERS...

THEIR STEALTHY APPROACH DID NOT PASS UNNOTICED. ONE OF KARL'S VIKINGS SWIFTLY GAVE THE ALARM...

VELDI HAS CUT OFF ANY WAY OF RETREAT. WE ARE TRAPPED BETWEEN HIS MEN AND THE WOODS!

FROM THE HEART OF THE SINISTER WOODLAND A WHISPERING LAUGH SEEMED TO BE BORNE ON THE BREEZE

YOU SHALL DIE, KARL — AND EVERYONE WITH YOU

AJARN, KARL'S FRIEND, VOICED THE VIKINGS' DESPAIR

WE ARE DOOMED — TRAPPED BETWEEN THE WOOD OF DEMONS AND THE HORDE OF VELDI'S MEN! WHAT DEATH DO WE CHOOSE, KARL?

VELDI AND HIS DRUGGED WARRIORS NO LONGER MADE ANY ATTEMPT TO CONCEAL THEMSELVES

O MIGHTY HELVUD, WITNESS THE DEATH OF YOUR ENEMIES!

SUDDENLY KARL'S CRY RANG TO THE SKIES...

ODIN, GOD OF THE WINDS, GOD OF WAR, WE ARE UNDER YOUR SHIELD! GRANT THAT I MAY CRUSH HELVUD BEFORE DYING. GIVE US A SIGN!

ODIN'S ANSWER APPEARED TO COME AT ONCE...

THE WIND RISES TO GALE FORCE! WE SHALL TRIUMPH!

IT WILL TAKE MORE THAN WIND TO DRIVE VELDI BACK, KARL!

SUDDENLY A SHAFT OF SUNLIGHT REFLECTED BLAZINGLY FROM KARL'S SWORD.

THAT MEANS FIRE! WIND AND FIRE SHALL BE OUR DEFENCE AGAINST VELDI'S HORDE. THE GRASS AND REEDS WILL BURN LIKE DRY TINDER!

USING FLINT AND STEEL, KARL SPARKED OFF A FLAME.

ROARING HUNGRILY, FANNED BY THE WIND, THE FIRE SPREAD AT STARTLING SPEED.

VELDI, MEET THE HOT BREATH OF MY ALLY!

A SEA OF FLAME SPEEDS TO GREET THEM!

VELDI'S WARRIORS CHECKED IN HORROR...

RETREAT! BY THE RUNES, WE'LL BE ROASTED ALIVE!

WAIT, YOU CURS!

VELDI WAS FURIOUS AT THE WAY PANIC GRIPPED HIS RETREATING FANATICS.

YOU SHALL PAY, KARL! HELVUD'S VENGEANCE WILL OVERTAKE YOU. THE LAST RECKONING IS STILL TO COME!

THE HEAT AND LIGHT OF THE BLAZE HAD A STRANGE EFFECT ON THE SINISTER TREES WHICH HAD BARRED KARL'S WAY

SEE, EVEN THEY FEAR FIRE! THEY RECOIL BEFORE IT! ODIN SHOWS ME A WAY TO REACH HELVUD

MAKE TORCHES! IF WE CARRY FIRE WE CAN FORCE A PATH THROUGH THE WOODS. FLAMING BRANDS SHALL BE OUR PROTECTION

NO LONGER DID THE GROPING, EVIL BRANCHES, CAPABLE OF CRUSHING A MAN, REACH OUT FOR VICTIMS

IT WORKS! THE TREES GUARDING HELVUD TWIST AND WRITHE TO LET US PASS

DESPERATE MEN PRESSED ON THROUGH THE NIGHTMARISH WOOD

IF OUR TORCHES BURN OUT WE SHALL PERISH!

THE TORCHES HAD TO BE CONTINUALLY REPLACED

SUDDENLY THE TREES THINNED OUT —

A CLEARING! BUT I — I CANNOT SEE PROPERLY. THE LIGHT ALMOST BLINDS ME!

IT WAS A MOMENT BEFORE THE VIKINGS' EYES BECAME ACCUSTOMED TO THE EERIE NEW BRILLIANCE. THEN KARL UTTERED A HORROR-FILLED CRY!

AJARN, LOOK! IT — IT IS HELVUD!

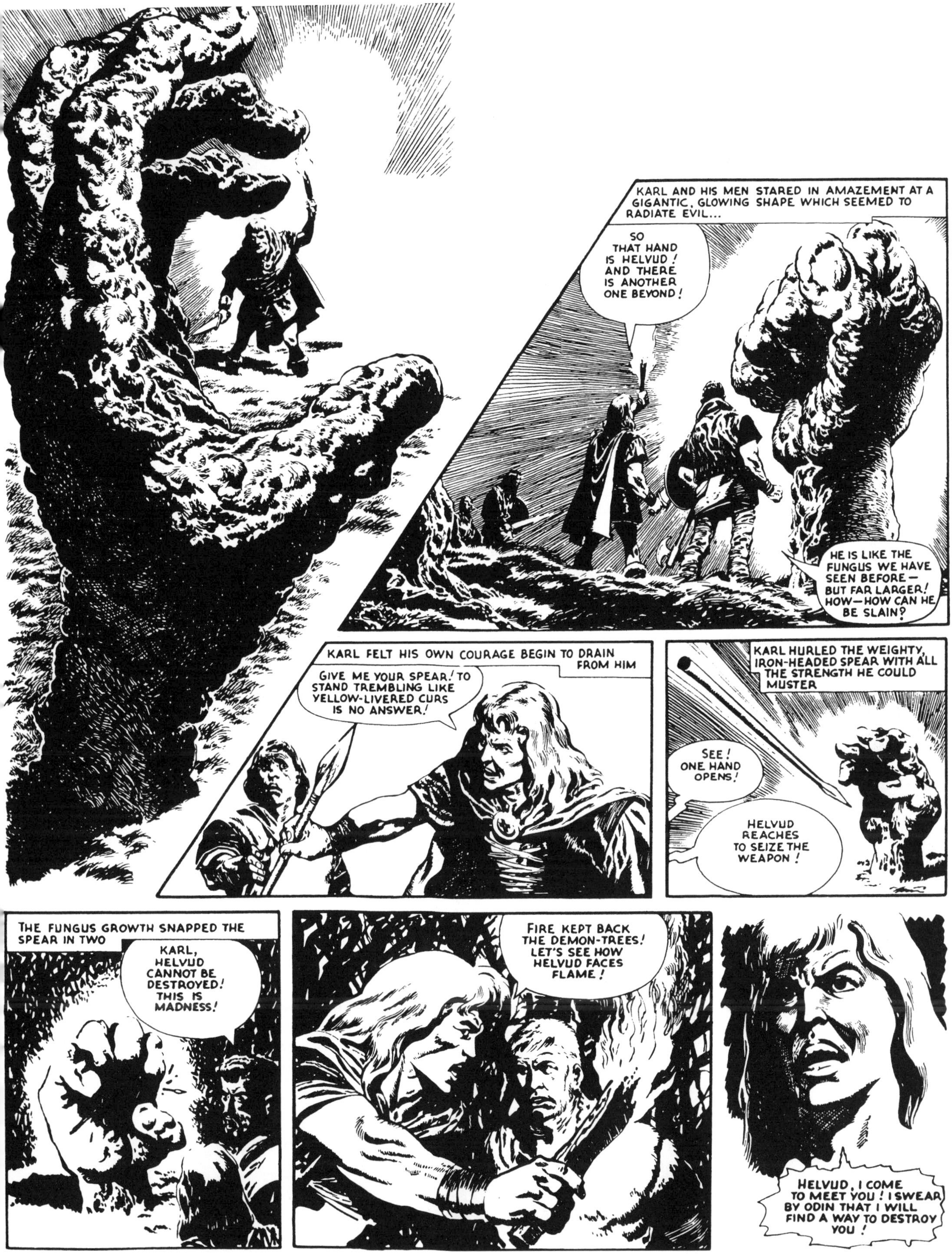

KARL AND HIS MEN STARED IN AMAZEMENT AT A GIGANTIC, GLOWING SHAPE WHICH SEEMED TO RADIATE EVIL...
SO THAT HAND IS HELVUD! AND THERE IS ANOTHER ONE BEYOND!
HE IS LIKE THE FUNGUS WE HAVE SEEN BEFORE— BUT FAR LARGER! HOW—HOW CAN HE BE SLAIN?
KARL FELT HIS OWN COURAGE BEGIN TO DRAIN FROM HIM
GIVE ME YOUR SPEAR! TO STAND TREMBLING LIKE YELLOW-LIVERED CURS IS NO ANSWER!
KARL HURLED THE WEIGHTY, IRON-HEADED SPEAR WITH ALL THE STRENGTH HE COULD MUSTER
SEE! ONE HAND OPENS!
HELVUD REACHES TO SEIZE THE WEAPON!
THE FUNGUS GROWTH SNAPPED THE SPEAR IN TWO
KARL, HELVUD CANNOT BE DESTROYED! THIS IS MADNESS!
FIRE KEPT BACK THE DEMON-TREES! LET'S SEE HOW HELVUD FACES FLAME!
HELVUD, I COME TO MEET YOU! I SWEAR BY ODIN THAT I WILL FIND A WAY TO DESTROY YOU!

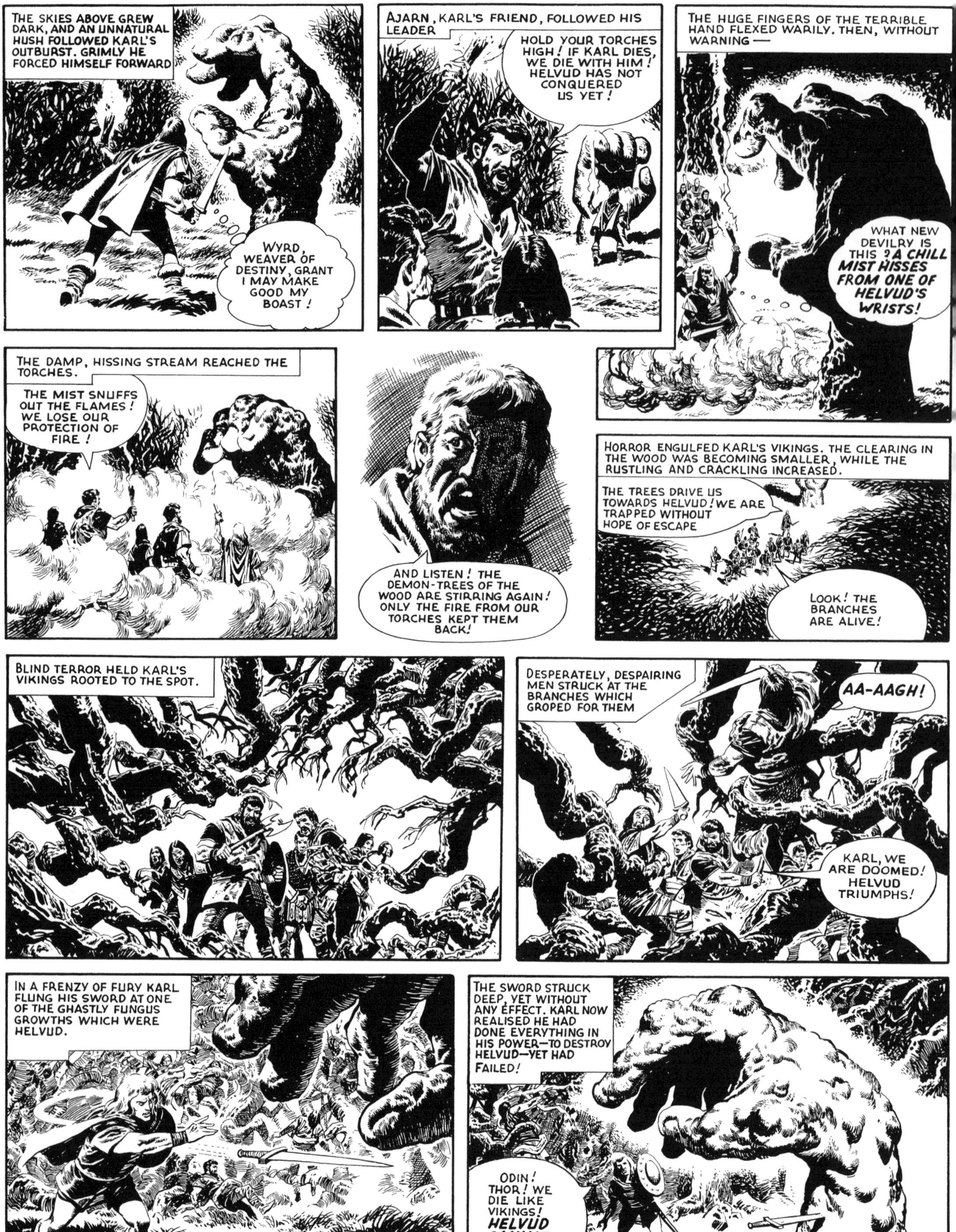
THE SKIES ABOVE GREW DARK, AND AN UNNATURAL HUSH FOLLOWED KARL'S OUTBURST. GRIMLY HE FORCED HIMSELF FORWARD
WYRD, WEAVER OF DESTINY, GRANT I MAY MAKE GOOD MY BOAST!
AJARN, KARL'S FRIEND, FOLLOWED HIS LEADER
HOLD YOUR TORCHES HIGH! IF KARL DIES, WE DIE WITH HIM! HELVUD HAS NOT CONQUERED US YET!
THE HUGE FINGERS OF THE TERRIBLE HAND FLEXED WARILY. THEN, WITHOUT WARNING —
WHAT NEW DEVILRY IS THIS? A CHILL MIST HISSES FROM ONE OF HELVUD'S WRISTS!
THE DAMP, HISSING STREAM REACHED THE TORCHES.
THE MIST SNUFFS OUT THE FLAMES! WE LOSE OUR PROTECTION OF FIRE!
AND LISTEN! THE DEMON-TREES OF THE WOOD ARE STIRRING AGAIN! ONLY THE FIRE FROM OUR TORCHES KEPT THEM BACK!
HORROR ENGULFED KARL'S VIKINGS. THE CLEARING IN THE WOOD WAS BECOMING SMALLER, WHILE THE RUSTLING AND CRACKLING INCREASED.
THE TREES DRIVE US TOWARDS HELVUD! WE ARE TRAPPED WITHOUT HOPE OF ESCAPE
LOOK! THE BRANCHES ARE ALIVE!
BLIND TERROR HELD KARL'S VIKINGS ROOTED TO THE SPOT.
DESPERATELY, DESPAIRING MEN STRUCK AT THE BRANCHES WHICH GROPED FOR THEM
AA-AAGH!
KARL, WE ARE DOOMED! HELVUD TRIUMPHS!
IN A FRENZY OF FURY KARL FLUNG HIS SWORD AT ONE OF THE GHASTLY FUNGUS GROWTHS WHICH WERE HELVUD.
THE SWORD STRUCK DEEP, YET WITHOUT ANY EFFECT. KARL NOW REALISED HE HAD DONE EVERYTHING IN HIS POWER—TO DESTROY HELVUD—YET HAD FAILED!
ODIN! THOR! WE DIE LIKE VIKINGS! HELVUD CANNOT BE KILLED!

FROM THE STORM-DARKENED SKY A BLINDING FLASH SEEMED TO ANSWER KARL'S CRY. HE REELED BACK FROM THE TERRIBLE FUNGUS GROWTH WHICH WAS REACHING OUT FOR HIM

THOR HAS HEARD! HE HURLS HIS LIGHTNING BOLT TO SAVE US!

KARL'S SWORD, ALREADY BURIED IN THE GIANT FUNGUS, ACTED AS A LIGHTNING-CONDUCTOR...

AARGH!

AS HE PICKED HIMSELF UP, HE REALISED THAT THE FLASH OF LIGHTNING HAD CAUSED BOTH FUNGUS HANDS TO MELT AWAY.

HELVUD IS DESTROYED! MY SWORD AND THOR'S THUNDER-BOLT SLEW THE DEMON WHO DARED DEFY THE GODS!

WITH THE DESTRUCTION OF HELVUD THERE DIED THE SPIRIT OF EVIL WHICH GOVERNED THE ISLAND. THE STRANGE TREES GRIPPING THE VIKINGS BEGAN TO CHANGE

THE — THE TREES LOSE THEIR FACES! THEIR BRANCHES ARE NO LONGER LIKE HANDS

THE TRAPPED VIKINGS, THOUGH WHITE AND SHAKEN, WERE NOW ABLE TO CUT THEMSELVES FREE.

WE ARE SAFE! KARL, WILD BIRDS APPROACH. ODIN SENDS A SIGN THAT THE POWER OF HELVUD IS CRUSHED!

THE ISLAND SEEMED SUDDENLY FRIENDLY, AND AJARN, KARL'S FRIEND, SMILED HIS RELIEF...

YOU HAVE TRIUMPHED! WE HAVE NOTHING MORE TO FEAR!

WAIT! YOU FORGET VELDI AND THE OTHER VIKINGS WHO SERVED HELVUD. THEY ARE STILL ON THE ISLAND. HAVE THEY ALSO CHANGED?

BUT THE FUNGUS-DRUGGED VIKINGS WHO WERE LED BY KARL'S ENEMY, VELDI, WERE NO LONGER UNDER HELVUD'S CONTROL

WHAT— WHAT IS HAPPENING ? IT IS AS IF A VEIL HAS LIFTED FROM MY MIND!

WE WERE HUNTING KARL. BUT WHY ?

VELDI RETURNED TO NORMAL, YET HIS HATRED REMAIN

YOU CRAVEN CURS, I ALONE AM LOYAL TO HELVUD! KARL HAS SMASHED THE POWER WHICH MIGHT HAVE MADE ME A CONQUEROR. FOR THAT HE SHALL DIE !

YOU ARE MAD!

BREAKING AWAY FROM HIS MEN, VELDI SOUGHT KARL

BLOOD CRIES OUT FOR BLOOD KARL ! MEET ME, YOU ACCURSED DESTROYER OF HELVUD

THERE IS NO OTHER WAY TO SETTLE THIS. MY STEEL IS READY !

NEXT MOMENT THE TWO WERE FIGHTING SAVAGELY

SWORD SPARKED AGAINST SWORD —

KARL WAITED FOR HIS OPENING, THEN THRUST FORWARD.

UUUAGH !

VELDI'S LIFELESS BODY PITCHED BACKWARDS AND SANK DOWN IN THE MARSH

WELL, HE DIED TRUE TO WHAT HE BELIEVED. DEATH BRINGS NO SHAME

LATER, THE COMPLETE FORCE OF VIKINGS AGAIN SET SAIL FROM THE ISLAND WHICH HAD ONCE HELD ONLY FEAR.

NO LONGER WILL THE FUNGUS GROW IN OUR HOMELAND. THE MENACE IS OVER. THERE SHALL BE FEASTING AND JOY ON OUR RETURN

KARL WAS RIGHT ! THE FUNGUS PLANTS GROWING IN SCANDINAVIA HAD ROTTED AWAY AT THE DESTRUCTION OF HELVUD

THE FUNGUS IS DEAD. THEN KARL AND OUR MENFOLK ARE SAFE ! THE GODS HAVE BEEN GOOD

YET THE REMOVAL OF ONE MENACE WAS TO MAKE WAY FOR ANOTHER DANGER. FROM THE VALLEYS OF THE NILE AND THE EUPHRATES — AND BEYOND—CAME A FORCE MORE SAVAGE THAN THE VIKINGS THEMSELVES

V

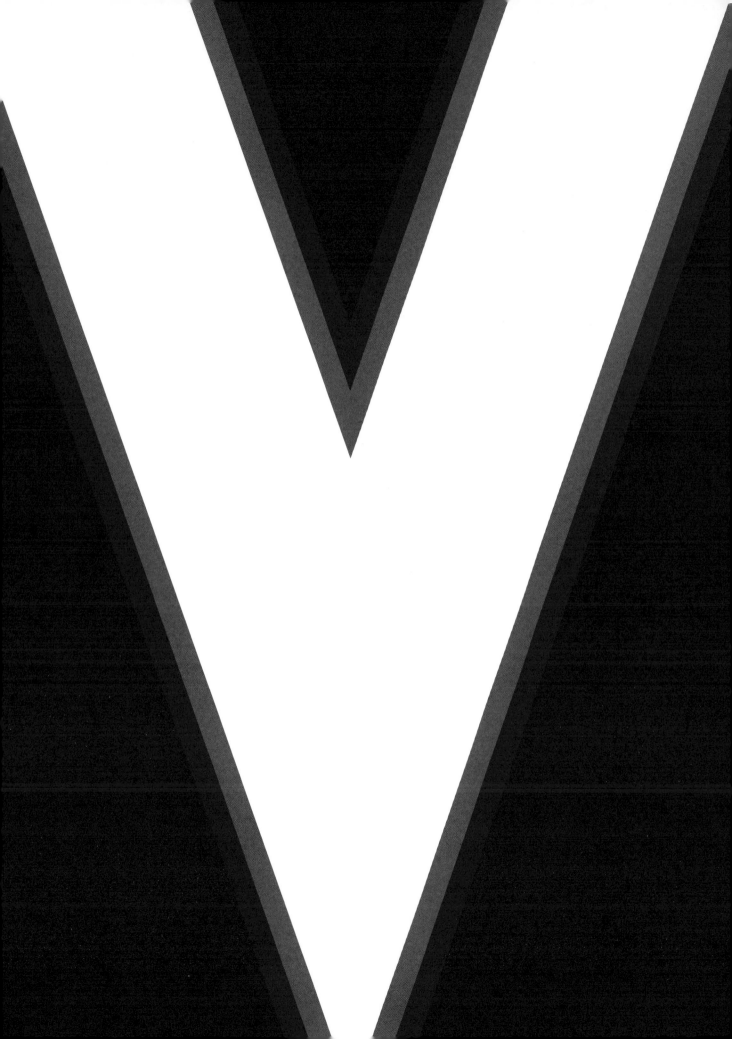

EL SARID THE MERCILESS

Serialised in **Lion**
4th August – 1st December 1962

Written by
Ted Cowan

Art by
Don Lawrence

KARL WAS A YOUNG VIKING CHIEFTAIN. ACCOMPANIED BY AJARN, HIS CLOSE FRIEND, HE SET OUT TO HUNT DEER — AND IT WASN'T LONG BEFORE THEY LOCATED A SMALL HERD. SIDE BY SIDE THEY GALLOPED IN PURSUIT...

BOTH VIKINGS WERE IN HIGH SPIRITS...

BY ODIN, I'LL WAGER MY SPEAR BRINGS DOWN THE HERD-LEADER, AJARN! HE'S MINE!

I DOUBT IT, KARL. YON STAG HAS GOT A FINE TURN OF SPEED!

IN A SPIRIT OF FIERCE COMPETITION THEY SPURRED THEIR MOUNTS HARDER. THEN AJARN'S HORSE HAPPENED TO STUMBLE AGAINST KARL'S...

AJARN — YOU CLUMSY OAF!

THE YOUNG CHIEF CRASHED INTO A MUDDY STREAM!

AJARN UTTERED A ROAR OF LAUGHTER!

HA, HA, HA! TOO BAD, KARL! WYRD, THE WEAVER OF DESTINY, HAS QUENCHED YOUR THIRST IN THE BROOK AND LOST YOU THE WAGER!

KARL'S BITTER DISAPPOINTMENT AT LOSING THE STAG MADE HIM ANSWER IMPULSIVELY — AND ANGRILY.

YOU MOCK ME! DEMON-OF-DARK TAKE YOU! YOU MADE ME FALL ON PURPOSE! NO TRUE FRIEND OF MINE WOULD DO THIS TO ME!

NEXT MOMENT KARL HAD HIS REVENGE!

NOW YOU FEEL WHAT IT IS LIKE TO BE UNSEATED! LAUGH AT THIS!

AJARN'S VIKING TEMPER WAS AS EXPLOSIVE AS KARL'S!

BY THE HAMMERER, I ALLOW NO MAN TO DO THAT TO ME! YOUR FALL WAS AN ACCIDENT. DRAW YOUR SWORD!

AS KARL DID SO, AJARN'S ANGER COOLED AND HE REMOUNTED HIS HORSE...

YOU ARE MY CHIEFTAIN—AND MORE LIKE A BROTHER THAN A COMRADE. IT WOULD BE WRONG FOR US TO FIGHT. ENJOY YOUR HUNT. I RETURN TO THE SETTLEMENT!

IT WAS WITH A STRANGE FEELING OF UNEASINESS THAT KARL WATCHED HIS FRIEND LEAVE...

THREE MAGPIES CIRCLE ABOVE AJARN. THEY ARE AN OMEN OF EVIL. SHALL I RIDE AFTER HIM? NO... BETTER TO LET HIM COOL OFF.

WHILE KARL FORCED HIMSELF TO CARRY ON WITH THE HUNT, AJARN AT LAST REACHED THE SETTLEMENT—TO BE GREETED WITH CRIES OF ALARM...

AJARN, SOMETHING IS WRONG. WE SEE FLAMES IN THE DISTANCE!

THAT IS NO CAUSE FOR FEAR. IT IS ONLY A WOODLAND FIRE CAUSED BY SOME CARELESS PERSON.

THEN GAZE AT THE SIGN OF THE SMOKE—AND *KNOW FEAR!* DOOM AND DESTRUCTION ARE NEAR. WHY DOES KARL NOT RETURN?

BECAUSE HE HUNTS—AND HIS TEMPER IS BAD. CALM YOURSELF, CRONE! YOU LET A SUMMER BLAZE ROB YOU OF YOUR WITS!

BUT THE FLAMES WERE FROM NO WOODLAND FIRE. WEIRDLY-DRESSED RAIDERS WERE PLUNDERING WITH RUTHLESS FEROCITY!

FEAR SEEMED TO PARALYSE THE VIKING DEFENDERS...

WE ARE DOOMED! 'TIS USELESS TO FIGHT SUCH DEMONS!

IF ONLY OUR CHIEF WERE HERE!

ONE WOUNDED VIKING CRIED OUT IN FURY AT THE LEADER OF THE RAIDERS...

KARL THE VIKING WILL BRING VENGEANCE UPON YOU! YOU AND YOUR DEVILS FROM THE FAR SEAS WILL PAY IN BLOOD!

AH— I HAVE HEARD OF THIS KARL—AND OF HIS COMRADE, AJARN. BUT NEITHER IS A MATCH FOR ME —EL SARID THE MERCILESS!

AND DOWN SWEPT EL SARID'S SWORD

I WILL VISIT THEIR SETTLEMENT—THEY SHALL BE THE NEXT TO DIE!

THE DISTANT FLAMES BEGAN TO DIE AWAY, BUT THE SMOKE COULD STILL BE SEEN. AGAIN THE WISE-WOMAN WARNED AJARN.

IT IS A SIGN OF DOOM! MANY OF US WILL NEVER LIVE TILL NIGHTFALL! AN ENEMY APPROACHES!

IN KARL'S ABSENCE, AJARN ASSUMED COMMAND OF THE VIKINGS...

CLOSE THE GATES! MAN THE DEFENCES! SHOULD THE WISE-WOMAN BE RIGHT, THE ENEMY WILL MEET KEEN VIKING STEEL!

SOON THE WALLS AND RAMPARTS BRISTLED WITH WATCHFUL DEFENDERS. SUPERSTITIOUS MEN GAZED DOWN AT THE WATERS OF THE FIORD...

I FEEL UNEASY. THOSE THREE MAGPIES ARE AN OMEN OF ILL-LUCK!

THEY SAY KARL AND AJARN HAVE QUARRELLED. THAT ALSO BODES ILL! THE FATES MAY HAVE DIVIDED THEM FOR SOME TERRIBLE REASON!

AJARN, TOO, SHARED THE SAME FOREBODINGS...

THOUGH I SEE NO DANGER, I BELIEVE WHAT THE WOMAN SAID. THE AIR HOLDS A MENACE. HOW I WISH THAT KARL WOULD RETURN!

SOME MILES AWAY, KARL WAS CLOSING IN ON THE STAG HE HUNTED...

NOW! TONIGHT AJARN AND I WILL FEAST ON VENISON AND LAUGH AT THE WAY WE QUARRELLED!

HIS AIM WAS DEADLY, BUT A SUDDEN GUST OF WIND SWAYED A BOUGH AND —

BY THE HAMMER OF THOR, THE THROW IS DEFLECTED!

THE SEVERED BRANCH TWISTED AND FELL TO THE GROUND. AT THE SAME INSTANT SUNLIGHT BLAZED THROUGH THE CLOUDS...

THE BRANCH FORMS AN ARROW POINTING BACK TO THE SETTLEMENT! IT IS A WARNING FROM THE GODS FOR ME TO RETURN!

FRENZIEDLY KARL MOUNTED HIS HORSE AND URGED IT INTO A GALLOP!

WHAT CAN BE HAPPENING? PERHAPS IT IS SOMETHING TO DO WITH AJARN. IF HARM COMES TO HIM, THE BLAME WILL BE MINE!

MEANWHILE, THE VESSELS OF THE NORTH AFRICAN RAIDERS MOVED TOWARDS THE SETTLEMENT...

EL SARID THE MERCILESS, LEADER OF THE RAIDERS, HAD HEARD OF KARL AND AJARN.

IT IS THE TURN OF THE NORSE PLUNDERERS TO BE PLUNDERED! THEY SHALL LEARN THAT THE FAME OF THEIR FURY IN BATTLE IS STILL SECOND TO MINE!

THE GREAT DHOWS WERE BEACHED...

PUT ON YOUR HYENA AND JACKAL SKINS! THEY WILL STRIKE TERROR IN THE HEART OF OUR ENEMIES!

WITHIN THE SETTLEMENT THE ALARM HAD BEEN GIVEN...

AJARN, ARE THEY ANIMALS OR MEN? THEY LAND LIKE A PACK OF WILD BEASTS!

THEY—THEY ARE DEVILS! THEY CANNOT BE MEN!

THE BLOOD-CURDLING HOWLS OF A JACKAL PACK MINGLED WITH THE LAUGHTER OF HYENAS!

YAI-EEE! YAI-EEE!

DESPERATELY AJARN SOUGHT TO QUELL THE SUPERSTITIOUS FEAR OF THE VIKINGS.

FOOLS, THEY MUST BE MEN WEARING SKINS! DRAW YOUR BOWS AND WAIT TILL THEY COME WITHIN BOWSHOT. BE THEY MEN OR BEASTS, THEY WILL DIE WHILE TRYING TO ASCEND THE SLOPE!

BUT THE RAIDERS MADE NO ATTEMPT TO DRAW CLOSER. INSTEAD, STRANGE CONTRAPTIONS WERE LANDED...

PREPARE THE CATAPULTS! LOAD THEM WITH THE FIRE WHICH CAN BURN BENEATH WATER

A FLAME WAS PUT TO A MIXTURE OF SULPHUR, NITRE, NAPTHA AND ASPHALT. THEN—

TAKE AIM! FIRE SHALL BE ONLY THE FIRST OF THE TERRORS WE'LL UNLEASH ON THEM!

AT EL SARID'S COMMAND, DEADLY MISSILES OF FLAME WERE UNLEASHED FROM THE GIANT CATAPULTS...

FIRE! LET KARL'S VIKINGS FEEL THE HEAT OF EL SARID'S FURY!

IN KARL'S ABSENCE, AJARN WAS IN CHARGE OF THE GRIMLY DETERMINED YET SUPERSTITIOUS DEFENDERS...

FLIGHT YOUR SHAFTS! THE PLUNDERING CURS HOPE TO CONQUER US BY TERROR. IT IS NOT THE FIRST TIME WE HAVE SEEN BURNING PITCH!

BUT THE MISSILES, KNOWN AS "GREEK FIRE", WERE MADE OF MORE THAN ORDINARY PITCH. THEIR TERRIBLE POWERS OF DESTRUCTION WERE CAUSED BY A MIXTURE OF NITRE, SULPHUR AND INFLAMMABLE NAPTHA...

KEEP YOUR HEADS! IT IS MADNESS TO PANIC! FETCH WATER TO FIGHT THE BLAZE!

WITH THE CHOKING FUMES, WHICH ENVELOPED THE FIRE-FIGHTERS CAME A NEW TERROR

THE PITCH STILL BURNS UNDER WATER! THE FLAMES CANNOT BE QUENCHED!

IT IS DEMON FIRE!

REACHING A DESPERATE DECISION, AJARN HACKED A GAP IN THE STOCKADE AT THE REAR OF THE SETTLEMENT.

WOMEN AND CHILDREN ARE TO ESCAPE TO THE WOODS! THE REST OF US WILL STAY TO FIGHT ON TILL THE DEATH!

MEANWHILE, THE SAVAGE INVADERS, CLAD IN THE SKINS OF HYENAS AND JACKALS, STORMED FORWARD...

USE THE SHIELD TRICK! MY MAGIC WILL GUARD YOU!

THE POLISHED SHIELDS, GLITTERING LIKE MIRRORS, REFLECTED THE BRIGHT RAYS OF THE SUN...

CRIES OF FEAR ROSE FROM THE PARTIALLY DAZZLED VIKING BOWMEN!

AAH! THE ATTACKERS HAVE CHANGED INTO WILD BEASTS! WE CANNOT FIGHT DEVILS!

BY ODIN, WHAT'S THE MATTER WITH THE FOOLS?

FURIOUSLY AJARN AND OTHER WARRIORS CLIMBED THE DEFENCES...

COWARDS, THE INVADERS ARE ORDINARY MEN! THE SKINS THEY WEAR CANNOT CHANGE THEM TO BEASTS. HAS FEAR DRIVEN YOU OUT OF YOUR WITS?

THEN THE BLINDING RAYS FROM A SHIELD STRUCK AJARN. AT THE SAME TIME, THE SCENE AHEAD SEEMED TO CHANGE...

NO! IT CANNOT BE! SOMETHING MUST BE WRONG WITH MY MIND...

WHAT AJARN THOUGHT HE SAW WERE NO LONGER MEN! HOWLING CRIES BEAT IN HIS EARS!

LIKE THE REST OF HIS MEN, AJARN LEAPT BACK TO THE GROUND. THE SPIRIT OF THE VIKINGS HAD BROKEN!

THE FORCES OF EVIL ARE ENGULFING US. WE ARE DOOMED! WITHOUT KARL'S LEADERSHIP THERE IS NO HOPE!

FLEE! FLEE!

KARL ALTHOUGH MILES AWAY, HAD AN INSTINCTIVE FEELING OF APPROACHING DISASTER...

MY PEOPLE AND AJARN ARE IN DANGER! I MUST REACH THEM BEFORE IT IS TOO LATE!

REMORSE AND FEAR MADE KARL SPARE NEITHER HIMSELF NOR HIS MOUNT...

WYRD, WEAVER OF DESTINY, HELP ME TO BE IN TIME! I WOULD DIE FOR MY PEOPLE!

HE SAW THE DISTANT SMOKE AND FLAME.

IT IS THE SETTLEMENT! MY RETURN IS TOO LATE!

AT THAT MOMENT, EL SARID'S RAIDERS SMASHED THROUGH THE GATES...

PLUNDER AND KILL! THE PREY IS YOURS, MY BROTHERS!

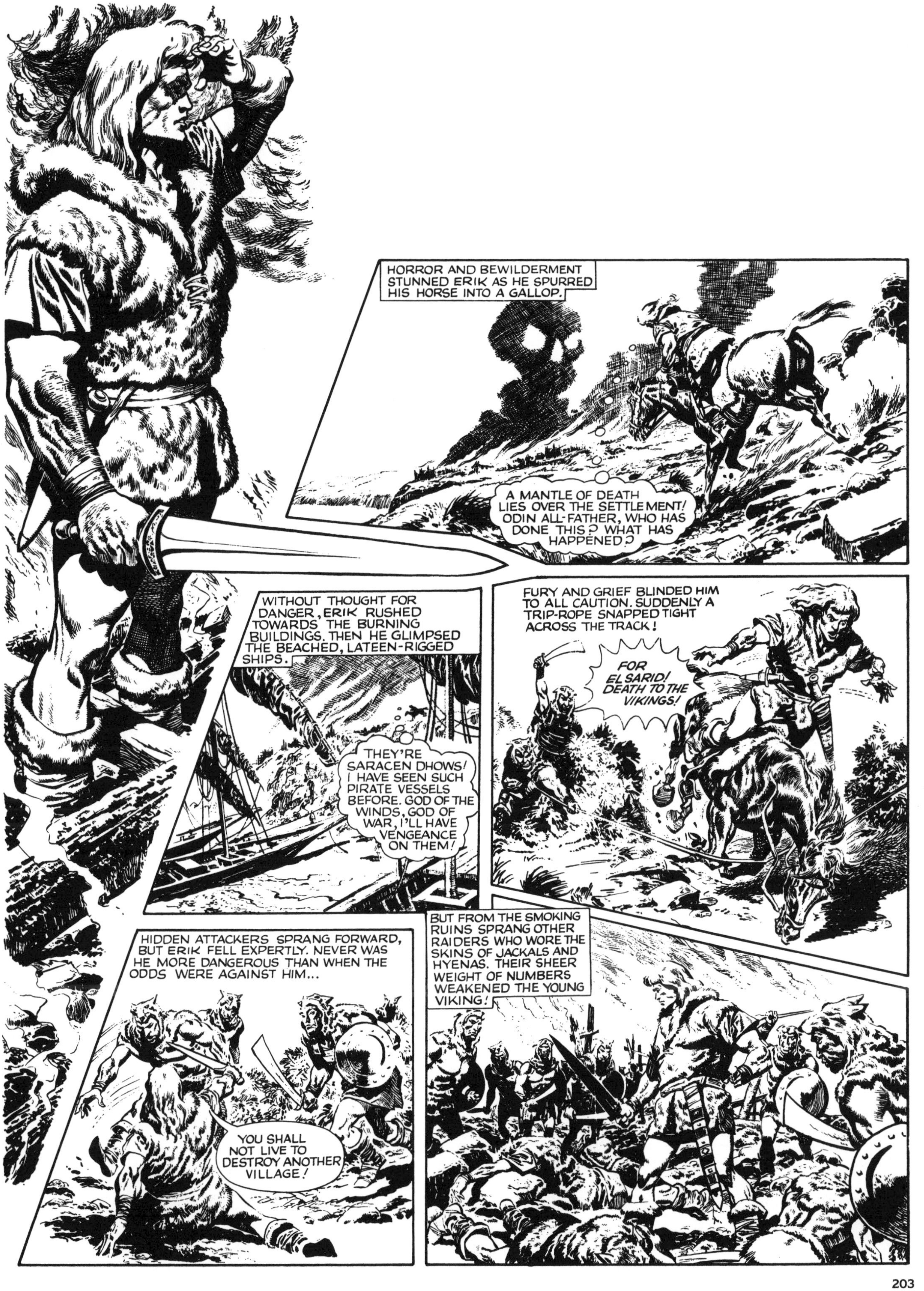

HORROR AND BEWILDERMENT STUNNED ERIK AS HE SPURRED HIS HORSE INTO A GALLOP.
A MANTLE OF DEATH LIES OVER THE SETTLEMENT! ODIN ALL-FATHER, WHO HAS DONE THIS? WHAT HAS HAPPENED?
WITHOUT THOUGHT FOR DANGER, ERIK RUSHED TOWARDS THE BURNING BUILDINGS. THEN HE GLIMPSED THE BEACHED, LATEEN-RIGGED SHIPS.
THEY'RE SARACEN DHOWS! I HAVE SEEN SUCH PIRATE VESSELS BEFORE. GOD OF THE WINDS, GOD OF WAR, I'LL HAVE VENGEANCE ON THEM!
FURY AND GRIEF BLINDED HIM TO ALL CAUTION. SUDDENLY A TRIP-ROPE SNAPPED TIGHT ACROSS THE TRACK!
FOR EL SARID! DEATH TO THE VIKINGS!
HIDDEN ATTACKERS SPRANG FORWARD, BUT ERIK FELL EXPERTLY. NEVER WAS HE MORE DANGEROUS THAN WHEN THE ODDS WERE AGAINST HIM...
YOU SHALL NOT LIVE TO DESTROY ANOTHER VILLAGE!
BUT FROM THE SMOKING RUINS SPRANG OTHER RAIDERS WHO WORE THE SKINS OF JACKALS AND HYENAS. THEIR SHEER WEIGHT OF NUMBERS WEAKENED THE YOUNG VIKING!

BEFORE KARL COULD BE KILLED, HOWEVER, A COMMANDING VOICE RANG OUT!

STOP! HE IS THE CHIEFTAIN. I WANT HIM ALIVE. DO NOT HARM HIM!

WE HEAR YOU, EL SARID!

KARL WAS DRAGGED INTO WHAT HAD ONCE BEEN HIS SETTLEMENT.

I, EL SARID THE MERCILESS, KNOW WHO YOU ARE. WE HAVE LOOTED, KILLED, AND TAKEN PRISONERS. GAZE WELL ON THE RESULTS OF DEFEAT!

THE SIGHT OF ONE OF THE CAPTIVES MADE KARL STRUGGLE DESPERATELY.

AJARN!

HE IS ANOTHER TROPHY I WILL SHOW TO MY PEOPLE WHEN I RETURN HOME. DRAG THEM TO THE SHIPS!

BROKENLY AJARN TURNED TO HIS LEADER...

KARL FORGIVE ME THAT WE, YOUR WARRIORS, COULD NOT BEAT BACK THESE FIENDS. POWERS OF EVIL SERVE EL SARID. NO LIVING HUMAN CAN DEFEAT HIM!

THE PLIGHT OF HIS FRIEND GAVE KARL STRENGTH TO TEAR HIMSELF FREE!

LET HIM GO! EL SARID, HAVE YOU COURAGE ENOUGH FOR A CHALLENGE? SNEERING CRAVEN, I'LL FIGHT YOU FOR AJARN'S FREEDOM!

EL SARID'S ANSWER WAS THE LAST KARL EXPECTED!

GIVE THE FOOL HIS SWORD! IF KARL DEFEATS ME, AJARN GOES FREE!

SKILL, SPEED AND SAVAGERY WERE EQUAL. HATRED FLARED, STEEL SPARKED ON STEEL!

THE BURNISHED SHIELD OF EL SARID REFLECTED THE LIGHT OF SUN AND FIRE. KARL PAUSED, TEMPORARILY DAZZLED.

LOOK AT ME, VIKING! LOOK— AND KNOW FEAR!

EL SARID'S EYES NO LONGER SEEMED HUMAN. IT APPEARED TO KARL THAT A TERRIBLE CHANGE TOOK PLACE!

HE—HE TURNS INTO A BEAST! MY—MY EYES—

KARL'S SENSES WERE REELING. HE FELT HIMSELF DRIVEN BACKWARDS...

HEAT! I FEEL FLAMES CLOSE ABOUT ME!

COMPLETELY DAZED, KARL STEPPED BACK INTO THE FLAMING RUINS OF A COLLAPSING HOUSE...

WIDE-EYED WITH HORROR, AJARN AND THE OTHER CAPTIVES WATCHED EL SARID DRIVE KARL BACK INTO THE BLAZING BUILDING...

DIE, VIKING DOG!

BY THE GODS — THE ROOF IS ABOUT TO FALL IN!

FIRE-WEAKENED TIMBERS GAVE WAY—AND KARL WAS BENEATH THEM! EL SARID LAUGHED GRIMLY AS THERE CAME A SHUDDERING CRASH!

THE FOOL DARED TO CHALLENGE ME. HE PAYS FOR THAT MADNESS!

AJARN COULD ONLY STARE DUMBLY. HE SCARCELY FELT THE VIOLENT HANDS OF THE GUARDS...

TO THE SHIPS WITH THEM! WE SAIL BACK HOME IN TRIUMPH!

KARL, GREATEST OF THE VIKINGS, IS DEAD. ALL HOPE DIES WITH HIM!

SOON THE LATEEN-RIGGED DHOWS, LADEN WITH CAPTIVES AND BOOTY, DIPPED AWAY FROM THE SCENE OF DESTRUCTION. AJARN WATCHED IN BROKEN-HEARTED DISMAY...

BETTER THAT I HAD PERISHED TOO. ONLY THE GODS KNOW WHAT NOW LIES AHEAD!

BUT KARL WAS NOT DEAD! INSIDE THE HOUSE WHERE HE HAD COLLAPSED WAS A NARROW SHAFT WHICH LED DOWN TO SPRING WATER...

HIS RETREATING STEPS HAD CARRIED HIM OVER THE BRINK OF THE WELL!

THE YOUNG VIKING CHIEFTAIN, WOUNDED AND BARELY CONSCIOUS, STILL STRUGGLED GRIMLY FOR LIFE...

I MUST KEEP—KEEP TREADING WATER! BY SOME WITCHCRAFT EL SARID DEFEATED ME. I MUST LIVE—TO RESCUE THOSE CAPTIVE VIKINGS AND WREAK VENGEANCE ON EL SARID!

SHEER WILL-POWER ALONE GOVERNED KARL'S PAIN-WEARY BODY...

...MUST REACH THE TOP! BUT THE FEVER — I BURN WITH FEVER—!

MEANWHILE, THOSE WHO HAD TAKEN TO THE WOODS TO SEEK REFUGE FROM THE RAIDERS BEGAN TO RETURN. SUDDENLY—

HERE —QUICK! BRING ROPE! SOMEONE IS ALIVE!

KARL, MORE DEAD THAN ALIVE, MANAGED TO TIE THE ROPE ROUND HIS BODY, AND SOON—

IT IS KARL! RAISE HIM GENTLY!

HE STILL LIVES! OUR CHIEFTAIN HAS NOT PERISHED!

FOR MANY DAYS KARL LAY IN A DELIRIUM, SKILFULLY NURSED BY A WISE-WOMAN...

HIS DREAMS TORTURE HIM. HE HAS LOST AJARN AND MANY OF HIS FRIENDS. BUT SUCH A CHIEF AS KARL NEVER ADMITS TO DEFEAT!

IN HIS FEVER KARL SAW THE FACE OF HIS ENEMY, EL SARID THE MERCILESS...

THEN, AT LAST—

ODIN, GOD OF WAR, GOD OF THE NINE RUNES, I WILL HUNT EL SARID TO THE ENDS OF THE EARTH. I SWEAR TO RESCUE MY PEOPLE AND DEAL WITH EL SARID. HE WILL NOT BEAT ME AGAIN!

KARL'S DETERMINATION BURNED AS FIERCELY AS HAD THE FLAMES OF THE SETTLEMENT. WEEKS WERE SPENT IN RALLYING A FLEET AND MEN FROM THE CLANS...

... OUR VIKING COMRADES HAVE BEEN TAKEN TO NORTH AFRICA. WHO WILL JOIN ME TO HUNT EL SARID TO HIS LAIR?

WE WILL, KARL! LET US FIGHT WITH YOU!

SHIPS WERE STOCKED AND REFITTED...

WYRD, WEAVER OF DESTINY, GUIDE US! GRANT THAT I SHALL NOT FAIL MY PEOPLE AGAIN!

THE VIKING FORCE SAILED! WHAT LAY AHEAD?

EL SARID, KARL SEEKS YOU! YOUR POWERS OF WITCHCRAFT SHALL NOT SAVE YOU THIS TIME!

HUNDREDS OF MILES AWAY, EL SARID HAD A FORE-BODING OF DANGER. HE POURED WINE INTO A BLACK DISH...

I MUST READ THE SIGNS IN THE BOWL. *WHAT I SEE WILL TELL ME WHETHER KARL HAS SURVIVED!*

206

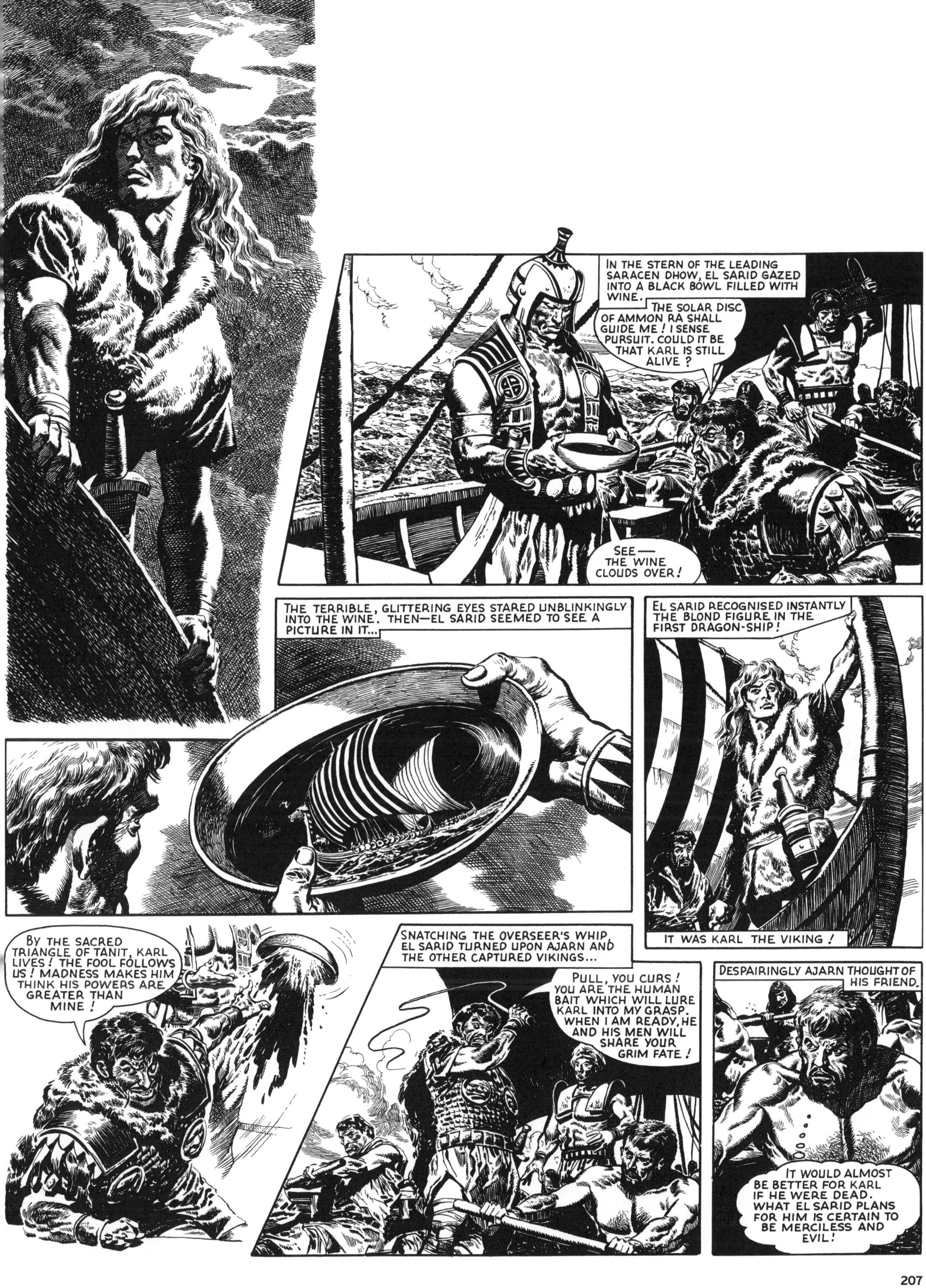

IN THE STERN OF THE LEADING SARACEN DHOW, EL SARID GAZED INTO A BLACK BOWL FILLED WITH WINE.
THE SOLAR DISC OF AMMON RA SHALL GUIDE ME! I SENSE PURSUIT. COULD IT BE THAT KARL IS STILL ALIVE?
SEE— THE WINE CLOUDS OVER!
THE TERRIBLE, GLITTERING EYES STARED UNBLINKINGLY INTO THE WINE. THEN—EL SARID SEEMED TO SEE A PICTURE IN IT...
EL SARID RECOGNISED INSTANTLY THE BLOND FIGURE IN THE FIRST DRAGON-SHIP!
IT WAS KARL THE VIKING!
BY THE SACRED TRIANGLE OF TANIT, KARL LIVES! THE FOOL FOLLOWS US! MADNESS MAKES HIM THINK HIS POWERS ARE GREATER THAN MINE!
SNATCHING THE OVERSEER'S WHIP EL SARID TURNED UPON AJARN AND THE OTHER CAPTURED VIKINGS...
PULL, YOU CURS! YOU ARE THE HUMAN BAIT WHICH WILL LURE KARL INTO MY GRASP. WHEN I AM READY, HE AND HIS MEN WILL SHARE YOUR GRIM FATE!
DESPAIRINGLY AJARN THOUGHT OF HIS FRIEND.
IT WOULD ALMOST BE BETTER FOR KARL IF HE WERE DEAD. WHAT EL SARID PLANS FOR HIM IS CERTAIN TO BE MERCILESS AND EVIL!

BUT KARL AND HIS VIKINGS, UNAWARE OF THEIR ENEMY'S KNOWLEDGE, CONTINUED THEIR VOYAGE DURING THE FOLLOWING WEEKS. IN THE BAY OF BISCAY THEY FOUGHT AGAINST A TERRIBLE STORM.

KEEP BALING! DON'T GIVE UP!

THE WATERS SHOW THEIR FURY!

FRESH MEAT SUPPLIES BEGAN TO RUN OUT...

WE HAVE ONLY ONE PIG LEFT!

THEN START FISHING! FISH WELL—OR WE SHALL STARVE!

EVENTUALLY THEY PASSED THE ROCK OF GIBRALTAR. THEN —

KARL, THE WATER CASKS ARE EMPTY!

WE MUST RAID A COASTAL VILLAGE FOR STORES!

THE VIKINGS MADE MANY RAIDS ON THE NORTH AFRICAN COAST TO REPLENISH THEIR DEPLETED STORES...

FOR ODIN! VIKING STEEL IS OUR STRENGTH!

BENEATH A BLISTERING SUN THE DRAGON-SHIPS SAILED ON...

KARL, WHERE DO WE MAKE FOR? HOW DO YOU KNOW WHERE EL SARID MAY BE FOUND?

I FOLLOW MY INSTINCT. THE GODS OF VALHALLA WILL GIVE ME A SIGN!

AT THAT MOMENT THE FIN OF A MONSTER SHARK ROSE FROM THE WARM WATERS AHEAD...

ODIN ALL-FATHER ANSWERS ME! WE MUST FOLLOW YONDER FISH! IT IS THE OMEN I SOUGHT!

IT WAS NIGHT WHEN THE GUIDING FIN, ONE OF MANY, AT LAST SANK FROM VIEW...

WHAT NOW? WE ARE CLOSE IN TO THE COAST!

HAVE PATIENCE, SWEYN, DARKNESS GIVES US SAFETY FROM OUR ENEMIES!

THE MOON, IN FULL BRILLIANCE, BROKE THROUGH TO REVEAL A GLITTERING TEMPLE...

LOOK, KARL! I HAVE HEARD OF THAT TEMPLE. IT IS THE TEMPLE OF JUPITER AMMON, WHERE THE GREEK TRADERS GO TO LISTEN TO THE WISDOM OF THE ORACLE!

I, TOO, HAVE HEARD OF THE ORACLE. IT IS SAID TO TELL MEN WHATEVER THEY MOST NEED TO KNOW. I NEED TO DISCOVER HOW TO FIND EL SARID!

KARL STRIPPED OFF HIS ARMOUR.

COMRADES, IT WOULD BE MADNESS FOR US ALL TO RISK LANDING. I WILL SWIM ASHORE TO SPEAK WITH THE ORACLE AND LEARN ITS WISDOM!

KARL, I'LL COME WITH YOU — THOUGH I FEAR DEATH MAY LIE AHEAD!

KARL AND HIS COMPANION, SWEYN, POISED TO DIVE FROM THE VIKING DRAGON-SHIP...

THE ORACLE WITHIN THE GREEK TEMPLE WILL TELL US WHERE TO SEEK EL SARID AND HIS CAPTIVES. SHOULD WE FAIL TO RETURN, YOU WILL KNOW WE ARE DEAD!

MAY THE GODS PROTECT YOU, KARL!

SOUNDLESSLY THE TWO MEN VANISHED OVERBOARD, BUT THEY ATTRACTED A NUMBER OF GRIM FORMS WHICH SLID SAVAGELY THROUGH THE WATERS TOWARDS THEM...

SHARKS! KARL — BEWARE!

FRENZIEDLY KARL AND SWEYN STRUCK OUT FOR THE SHORE. THEY SENSED RATHER THAN HEARD THE COMMOTION BEHIND THEM...

KILL THE DEVIL-FISH — QUICK!

ARROWS STRUCK ONE OF THE WHITE KILLERS, AND THE SCENT OF ITS BLOOD MADE THE OTHER SHARKS TURN TOWARDS IT...

THE DIVERSION LASTED JUST LONG ENOUGH FOR THE GASPING, EXHAUSTED SWIMMERS TO REACH SAFETY...

THE BRUTES ARE CANNIBALS! THEIR GREED SAVED US!

BUT WHAT LIES AHEAD MAY BE FAR WORSE, SWEYN!

EERILY THE TEMPLE OF JUPITER AMMON GLEAMED IN THE PALE MOONLIGHT. KARL BATTLED AGAINST SUPERSTITIOUS FEAR...

I WONDER IF THE GREEK GODS OF THE ORACLE WILL HELP US? WE ARE NORTHMEN — PERHAPS THEY WILL EVEN TURN AGAINST US!

LIKE SHADOWS THEY MOVED INTO THE APPARENTLY DESERTED TEMPLE. SWEYN SAW A WELL OPENING IN THE FLOOR...

YONDER IS THE ORACLE, KARL! YOU CALL YOUR QUESTIONS INTO THE MOUTH OF THE WELL—— AND THE ANSWERS COME BACK!

MAY THE ANSWER BE THE RIGHT ONE!

KARL REACHED THE MOUTH OF THE WELL. THEN ——

O GREAT ONE, I AM KARL THE VIKING. THOR GUIDED ME TO YOU. WHERE MAY I FIND EL SARID THE MERCILESS? HE AND HIS CURS HOLD AJARN AND OTHERS OF MY PEOPLE!

UNKNOWN TO THE VIKINGS, FROM A GALLERY HIGH ABOVE, TWO SWARTHY FACES GAZED DOWN...

I KNOW THE TONGUE OF THE NORTHMEN. THESE FOOLS SEEK EL SARID! MORE OF THEIR MEN MUST BE AROUND!

EL SARID WOULD PAY US WELL IF WE COULD DELIVER THEM INTO HIS HANDS.

THE CHANCE ONLOOKERS BEGAN TO CREEP FROM THE GALLERY...

WE'LL WARN THE CREWS OF ALL DHOWS MOORED BY THE RIVER. THE VIKINGS WILL MEET AN ONSLAUGHT FROM ALL SIDES!

PERHAPS IT WAS KARL'S IMAGINATION, BUT SUDDENLY A WHISPERING VOICE SEEMED TO FLOAT FROM THE WELL...

VIKING, BEWARE OF TREACHERY! THERE ARE THOSE IN THE TEMPLE WHO PLAN YOUR DESTRUCTION!

UPON HEARING THE WORDS OF WARNING, KARL MOVED WITH THE SPEED OF A JUNGLE BEAST AND SAW THE TWO ARABS...

HALT THEM, SWEYN! THEY MUST NOT GET AWAY!

THE SPIES' ESCAPE WAS PREVENTED BY KARL HURLING HIS SWORD IN THEIR PATH!

NOW CLOSE WITH THE JACKALS!

NEXT MOMENT, SCIMITARS GLITTERED IN THE LIGHT OF THE OIL LAMPS!

DIE, ENEMIES OF EL SARID!

STEEL RANG AGAINST STEEL!

THE SOUNDS CARRIED TO THE BANKS OF THE NILE...

SOMETHING STRANGE GOES ON IN THE TEMPLE! FOLLOW ME, COMRADES! BY THE HORNED LIZARD, I FEEL THAT DEATH IS HUNTING TONIGHT!

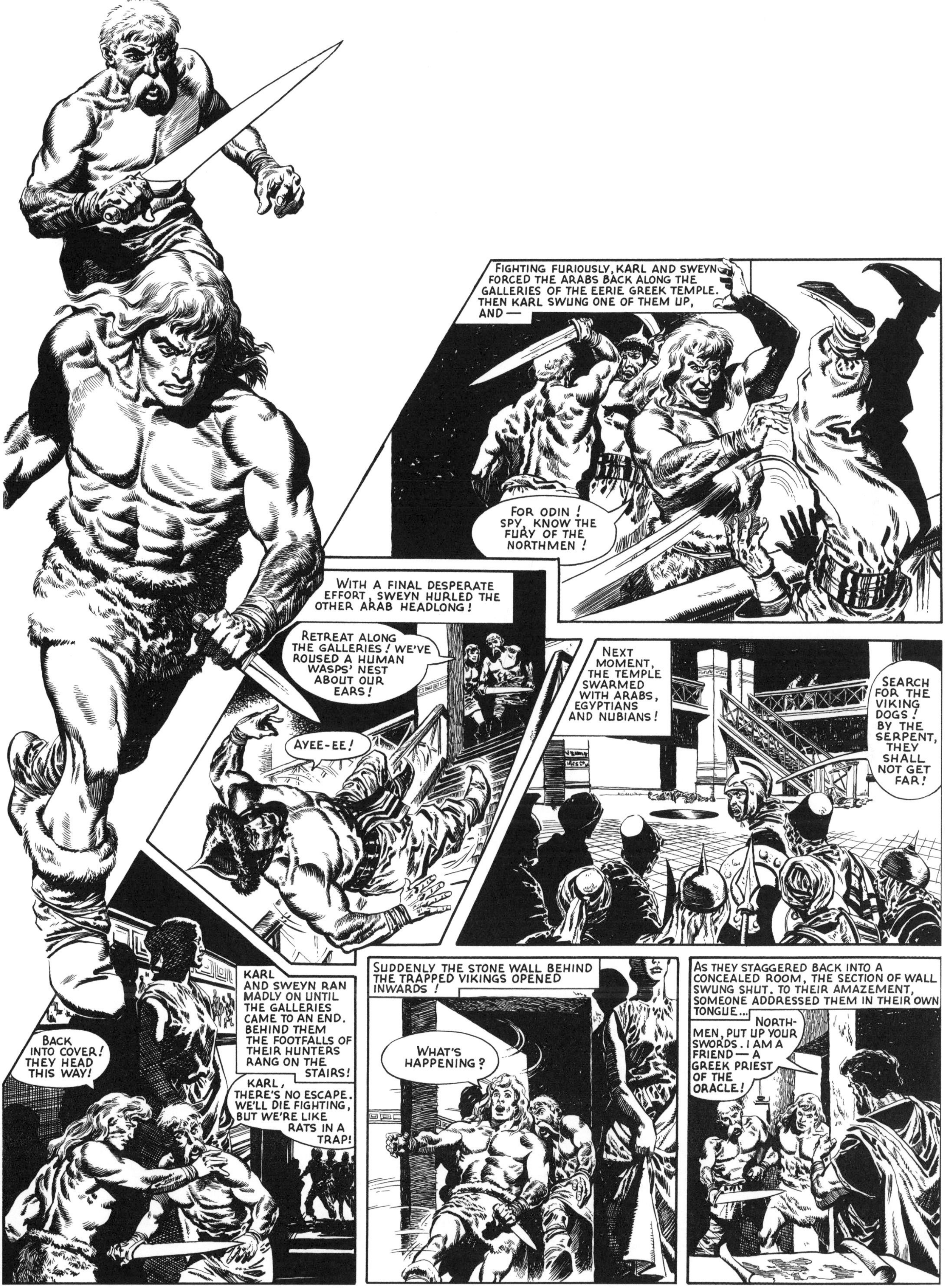
FIGHTING FURIOUSLY, KARL AND SWEYN FORCED THE ARABS BACK ALONG THE GALLERIES OF THE EERIE GREEK TEMPLE. THEN KARL SWUNG ONE OF THEM UP, AND —
FOR ODIN! SPY, KNOW THE FURY OF THE NORTHMEN!
WITH A FINAL DESPERATE EFFORT, SWEYN HURLED THE OTHER ARAB HEADLONG!
RETREAT ALONG THE GALLERIES! WE'VE ROUSED A HUMAN WASPS' NEST ABOUT OUR EARS!
AYEE-EE!
NEXT MOMENT, THE TEMPLE SWARMED WITH ARABS, EGYPTIANS AND NUBIANS!
SEARCH FOR THE VIKING DOGS! BY THE SERPENT, THEY SHALL NOT GET FAR!
KARL AND SWEYN RAN MADLY ON UNTIL THE GALLERIES CAME TO AN END. BEHIND THEM THE FOOTFALLS OF THEIR HUNTERS RANG ON THE STAIRS!
BACK INTO COVER! THEY HEAD THIS WAY!
KARL, THERE'S NO ESCAPE. WE'LL DIE FIGHTING, BUT WE'RE LIKE RATS IN A TRAP!
SUDDENLY THE STONE WALL BEHIND THE TRAPPED VIKINGS OPENED INWARDS!
WHAT'S HAPPENING?
AS THEY STAGGERED BACK INTO A CONCEALED ROOM, THE SECTION OF WALL SWUNG SHUT. TO THEIR AMAZEMENT, SOMEONE ADDRESSED THEM IN THEIR OWN TONGUE...
NORTH-MEN, PUT UP YOUR SWORDS. I AM A FRIEND — A GREEK PRIEST OF THE ORACLE!

I HEARD YOU CALL ON THE GODS TO TELL YOU WHERE EL SARID MAY BE FOUND. NOW THE ORACLE ANSWERS YOU! THIS MAP WILL SHOW YOU THE WAY TO EL SARID'S KINGDOM OF EVIL!

THE PRIEST LED THE VIKINGS ALONG AN UNDERGROUND TUNNEL...

GREEK, WHY SHOULD YOU HELP US?

I, TOO, HATE EL SARID! HE IS A FIEND — A MAN WITHOUT MERCY. I AM HOPING YOUR POWER PROVES GREATER THAN HIS!

THE TUNNEL AT LAST CAME TO AN END...

KARL! YONDER ARE OUR SHIPS!

GREEK, I WILL REMEMBER YOUR KINDNESS. I WILL REPAY IT BY DESTROYING EL SARID!

KARL'S SOFT CALL, LIKE THAT OF AN OWL, BROUGHT ONE OF HIS WAITING SHIPS ALONGSIDE...

KARL! SWEYN! WE HAD ALMOST GIVEN YOU UP

THE GODS ANSWERED ME. I LEARNT WHAT I NEEDED TO KNOW!

KARL STUDIED THE MAP. LATER, WITH OARS MUFFLED, THE SLEEK SHIPS FOLLOWED THE WESTERN BANKS OF THE NILE...

KEEP TO THE SHADOWS! IF WE ARE CHALLENGED, THERE CAN BE NO TURNING BACK. WE MUST REACH THE KINGDOM OF EL SARID — OR DIE!

DAY AFTER DAY, THE VIKINGS TRAVELLED ON WITHOUT CHALLENGE. THEY PASSED THE CARAVAN TRAILS AND OLD ROMAN MILESTONES...

AS A BLINDING, MERCILESS SUN BEAT DOWN ON THE ROWERS, KARL'S CONFIDENCE STEADILY INCREASED...

WE FOLLOW THE ROUTE TAKEN BY EL SARID'S DHOWS. MEN OF MANY RACES HAVE SEEN US, BUT WE HAVE NOT BEEN ATTACKED. BY THE RUNES, PERHAPS THE SUN BLINDS THEM INTO THINKING WE ARE TRADERS!

I WISH I COULD BELIEVE THAT! IT SEEMS *TOO* QUIET!

THE RIVER FORKED, THEN ITS WATERS GREW MUDDIER AND DARKER. DENSE JUNGLE STRETCHED OUT ON EITHER SIDE OF THE CROCODILE-INFESTED WATER...

THE VERY AIR SMELLS OF EVIL. STRANGE BEASTS AND REPTILES LURK EVERYWHERE!

HAVE NO FEAR—I TRUST THE GREEK PRIEST AND HIS MAP. WE'LL GO ON, SWEYN!

SWEYN'S DOUBTS GREW STRONGER STILL WHEN THE MAP INDICATED A MUDDY, SOUR-REEKING TRIBUTARY...

KARL, THE RIVER IS BLOCKED BY VEGETATION. NO DHOWS COULD HAVE SAILED BEYOND THIS POINT. THE GREEK HAS BETRAYED US!

FROM HIGH ABOVE, AN UNSEEN FIGURE WATCHED THE DISTANT SHIPS...

MY MASTER, EL SARID, SAID THE WHITE FOOLS WOULD COME. IF THEY KNEW WHAT HE HAS PLANNED FOR THEM, THEY WOULD BE HAPPY TO DIE NOW!

When it seemed impossible to sail any farther, Karl ordered his men to steer for the bank...

I SWEAR OUR MAP HAS NOT BETRAYED US. WE NEAR THE KINGDOM OF EL SARID! WE ARE GUIDED BY THE POWER OF THE GODS!

BY THE RUNES, I HOPE KARL IS RIGHT!

Karl noticed great tunnels in the tall grass...

BEACH THE SHIPS AND FOLLOW THOSE PATHS. PERHAPS THEY ARE MAN-MADE. WHERE OTHERS CAN TREAD, SO CAN WE!

The lurking crocodiles were a hideous menace. Grimly the warriors hacked a way through them...

THE SKIN OF THE BRUTES IS LIKE ARMOUR, BUT VIKING STEEL IS TOO KEEN FOR THEM!

Later, even Karl felt uneasy as he led the way along the strange tunnels...

I THINK THAT NO MEN COULD HAVE MADE THESE PATHS — UNLESS THEY MOVED ON ALL FOURS!

Suddenly a churning sound came from the river. A monstrous, enormous shape surfaced and emerged from the water!

KARL! A DEMON PURSUES US!

IT IS THE CREATURE THAT MADE THE TUNNELS!

At sight of the men in its tunnel, the great hippopotamus uttered a bellow of fury. Next moment —

FIGHT, VIKINGS! ODIN GIVE US STRENGTH!

KARL STRUCK WITH THE JAVELIN, WHICH SNAPPED LIKE A STRAW!

THE WOUND WAS ENOUGH TO MAKE THE ANIMAL TURN. LEAVING ITS HUMAN ENEMIES, IT PLUNGED BACK TOWARDS THE VIKINGS' VESSELS.

HAMMER OF THOR! THE CREATURE VENTS ITS HATRED ON OUR SHIPS!

SEE! OTHER MONSTERS APPEAR!

GREAT RAM TUSKS STOVE THROUGH THE STOUT TIMBERS!

THEY SINK OUR SHIPS! THE FORCES OF EVIL SERVE EL SARID AND BRING DOWN A CURSE UPON US!

KARL, NOW WE ARE WITHOUT MEANS OF RETREAT!

MEANWHILE, FROM AFAR, GREAT HORNS SENT OUT MOURNFUL, BLOOD-CHILLING NOTES...

COWARDS, WE HAVE BEEN GIVEN A SIGN THAT WE ARE NOT TO TURN BACK! ODIN HIMSELF DRIVES US ON TO SEEK EL SARID AND RESCUE OUR COMRADES!

THOSE SOUNDS RACKED THE NERVES OF THE VIKINGS, YET THEY GRIMLY PRESSED ON...

GHOSTS AND DEMONS SURROUND US...

THEN WE FACE THEM. THERE IS NO TURNING BACK!

STRANGE RUINS AND TOMBS CAME INTO VIEW. A MERCILESS HEAT ADDED TO THE VIKINGS' DISCOMFORT...

YOU MAY BE RIGHT, SWEYN. WE WILL GROUP TOGETHER IN CASE OF ATTACK!

KARL, IT LOOKS LIKE A SACRED CLEARING. I SENSE DANGER!

BUT WHAT FOLLOWED HELD THE VIKINGS ROOTED TO THE SPOT IN HORROR...

WYRD, WEAVER OF DESTINY, PROTECT US! GIANT MONSTERS LEAD THE ATTACK!

NEVER BEFORE HAD THE VIKINGS SEEN ELEPHANTS, LET ALONE MET THEM IN BATTLE. DESPERATELY THEIR ARCHERS OPENED FIRE.

FLIGHT YOUR SHAFTS! TO RUN WILL MEAN DEATH!

WE'LL BE CRUSHED LIKE ANTS!

AS THE MASSIVE ANIMALS BORE DOWN ON THE TRAPPED VIKINGS, A NUBIAN SHOUTED A HOARSE COMMAND...

FOR EL SARID! DON'T KILL THE WHITE DOGS—CAPTURE THEM! THEY SHALL PAY WITH THEIR LIVES LATER!

EVEN THE STOUT HEARTS OF THE VIKINGS TREMBLED BEFORE THE ONSLAUGHT OF THE MASSIVE BEASTS. KARL'S SMALL FORCE WAS OUTNUMBERED AND TRAPPED

KARL, WE ARE DOOMED! NOTHING HALTS THE TERRIBLE MONSTERS!

WE FACE CAPTIVITY— OR DEATH!

KARL CRIED ALOUD TO THE SKIES IN DESPAIR

ODIN! GOD OF THE WINDS, GOD OF WAR, ARE WE TO BE TRAMPLED LIKE ANTS?

KARL SHUDDERED AS THE WIND ROSE AS IF IN ANSWER

ODIN SPEAKS! SEE— MY BLADE BURNS LIKE FIRE! IT IS A SIGN! IT TELLS ME WHAT TO DO!

WITH STEEL AND FLINT KARL LIT A TORCH AND SET FIRE TO THE NEARBY PARCHED FERNS AND GRASSES

SMOKE AND FLAME SHALL BE OUR BARRICADE!

THE ELEPHANTS TRUMPETED SHRILLY IN FEAR AS THE WALL OF HEAT RACED TOWARDS THEM. THE GREAT BEASTS TURNED, SCATTERING THE SCREAMING MEN IN THEIR PATH

THEIR FIRST CHARGE HAS BEEN ROUTED!

VIKINGS, CLIMB ABOVE THE SMOKE! WE'LL MAKE OUR STAND WITH OUR BACKS TO THE ROCK!

KARL'S WARRIORS CLAWED THEIR WAY UP THE CLIFF. FROM BELOW ROSE A THROBBING OF DRUMS

THEY ADVANCE AGAIN! MAKE FOR THAT IDOL!

BY THE RUNES, THEY HAVE COURAGE. I FEAR WE'LL NEVER LIVE TO FREE AJARN AND OUR BROTHERS FROM SARID THE MERCILESS

THE VIKINGS FLUNG THEMSELVES INTO COVER. THEN KARL HAD A SUDDEN IDEA.

SWEYN, CLIMB INTO THE IDOL! YOU SPEAK THE TONGUE OF THESE PEOPLE. A MAN'S VOICE COULD BOOM LIKE THUNDER FROM THAT MOUTH!

SWEYN LISTENED TO THE PLAN KARL EXPLAINED — AND, A FEW MOMENTS LATER —

BACK, YOU SONS OF JACKALS! THE WHITE INVADERS ARE PROTECTED BY MY POWER. LEAVE BEFORE MY VENGEANCE DESTROYS YOU!

THE GOD TALKS!

SUDDEN TERROR GRIPPED THE PRIMITIVE SOLDIERS...

IT IS MAGIC!

THE GODS WILL DESTROY US!

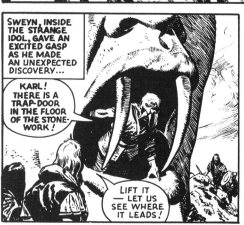

SWEYN, INSIDE THE STRANGE IDOL, GAVE AN EXCITED GASP AS HE MADE AN UNEXPECTED DISCOVERY...

KARL! THERE IS A TRAP-DOOR IN THE FLOOR OF THE STONE-WORK!

LIFT IT — LET US SEE WHERE IT LEADS!

AFTER SEVERAL ATTEMPTS THE FLAT STONE WAS LEVERED FROM POSITION...

SEE—A PASSAGE RUNS THROUGH THE ROCK! LIGHT TORCHES! THIS COULD BE A WAY OF ESCAPE!

IN A SINGLE FILE THE WARY VIKINGS DESCENDED. THEY WERE GREETED BY DANK AIR, SOUR WITH THE PRESENCE OF GIANT BATS...

AUGH! IT SMELLS LIKE A TOMB!

AFTER WHAT SEEMED A LIFETIME, FRESH AIR WELLED IN FROM AHEAD...

THE PASSAGE ENDS! MOVE WARILY! I SENSE THAT WE ARE NEAR EL SARID!

THE SCENE THAT FINALLY MET THEIR GAZE MADE KARL CATCH HIS BREATH...

THE DHOW SHIPS OF EL SARID! THEN THE WHITE CITY ABOVE IS HIS CAPITAL WHERE AJARN AND THE OTHERS ARE CAPTIVES!

MEANWHILE, WITHIN THE CITY, EL SARID WAS WAITING.

LIGHT THE OIL! I FEEL UNEASY. KARL APPROACHES — YET NOT IN THE WAY I HAD PLANNED!

I CALL ON THE POWERS OF DARKNESS TO REVEAL MY ENEMY! SHOW ME WHERE HE IS!

ERIK APPEARS! DEMONS OF CAHANNAB, HOW NEAR IS MY ENEMY? SHOW US MORE THAT WE MAY RECOGNISE WHERE HE IS!

BUT BEFORE THE PICTURE COULD CHANGE, THE OIL LAMP SUDDENLY BURST INTO FLAMES!

MASTER, STRANGE POWERS PROTECT ERIK! HIS GODS STRIKE TO SAVE HIM!

EYES GLEAMING FANATICALLY, EL SARID SHOUTED TO THE SKIES...

I CALL ON THE DEVOURER OF MOUNTAINS! ROUSE MY FOUR-FOOTED SUBJECTS! SEND THE PACKS OUT TO HUNT AND DESTROY ERIK! IF I CANNOT MEET HIM ALIVE, LET ME SEE HIM DEAD!

FROM THE DISTANT JUNGLE THE SNARLING OF JACKALS AND THE SCREAMING LAUGHTER OF HYENAS ANSWERED. THE PACKS, WITH FOAM-FLECKED MOUTHS, STARTED TO GATHER...

MEANWHILE, ERIK AND HIS VIKINGS GAZED ACROSS AT THE KINGDOM OF EL SARID HIGH ABOVE THEM...

IN THAT WHITE CAPITAL EL SARID HOLDS OUR FELLOW VIKINGS! ERIK, WE ARE FEW IN NUMBER. WHAT DO YOU PLAN?

WE'LL JOURNEY UNTIL WE FIND A PLACE, BEYOND THE VIEW OF OUR ENEMIES, WHERE THE RIVER MAY BE FORDED. OUR ONE CHANCE OF RESCUING THE CAPTIVES LIES IN TAKING EL SARID BY SURPRISE!

FOLLOWING KARL'S INSTRUCTIONS, THE VIKINGS MADE A JOURNEY WHICH TESTED EVERY OUNCE OF THEIR ENDURANCE. THEN AT LAST—

THERE'S OUR CROSSING! A BROKEN CAUSEWAY OF ROCKS!

KARL LED THE WAY OVER THE PERILOUS CROSSING. RUSHING WATERS SWEPT AWAY ANY MAN WHO JUMPED SHORT...

NEXT COMMENCED THE GRIM, WEARYING RETURN TOWARDS EL SARID'S CAPITAL...

KARL, THE GROUND GROWS HOTTER BENEATH OUR FEET!

WE CANNOT STOP! WE MUST REACH THE CITY!

THE HEAT INCREASED. THE AIR AHEAD SHIMMERED, FORMING A MIRAGE...

KARL, WHAT MADNESS IS THIS? THE CITY OF EL SARID COMES TO MEET US!

THE GROUND SEEMS TO BOIL!

EVEN KARL HESITATED...

IT IS ONLY A REFLECTION — A TRICK OF THE AIR!

EVEN SO, IT IS DEATH TO ADVANCE, KARL! THE AIR MIGHT BURN US ALIVE!

THE PACKS OF HYENAS AND JACKALS WERE CLOSING IN BEHIND THE VIKINGS. IT WAS AS IF THEY KNEW THAT KARL'S PATH WAS BARRED.

THE CRIES OF THE BEASTS DREW NEARER...

LISTEN, KARL! WE ARE HUNTED! MAY ODIN PROTECT US!

SAVAGELY THE MASSED PACKS SWEPT FROM COVER AND ATTACKED...

STAND SHOULDER TO SHOULDER, MY COMRADES! FORM UP TO MEET THE BRUTES! DRIVE THEM BACK WITH ARROWS AND SWORDS!

ANIMAL AFTER ANIMAL DIED IN ITS TRACKS, YET THE MADDENED PACK STILL CAME ON.

THESE ARE NO ORDINARY BEASTS — THEY ARE DEMONS! WE'LL BE TORN TO SHREDS!

IN DESPERATION KARL MADE A DECISION...

WE'LL CROSS THE BURNING GROUND AND MEET WHATEVER FATE HOLDS IN STORE! IF WE ARE TO DIE, THEN THE BEASTS WILL BE DESTROYED WITH US!

KARL AND HIS VIKINGS WERE FORCED TO RETREAT INTO A VOLCANIC REGION WHERE THE HOT EARTH SCORCHED THEIR FEET!

MAKE FOR THE BURNING GROUND! FIGHT A REARGUARD ACTION! IF WE ARE TO DIE FROM HEAT, WE'LL SEE THAT THESE BRUTES DIE ALSO!

THE WARRIORS' FLASHING BLADES CHECKED THE SAVAGE ATTACKERS BUT —

KARL, THE VERY GROUND IS ON FIRE! WE SHALL PERISH IF WE GO ON!

WE ARE DOOMED EITHER WAY. THE PACKS PREPARE FOR A LAST RUSH!

AGAIN THE JACKALS AND HYENAS SURGED FORWARD. BUT AS THEY DID SO, HIDDEN GEYSERS — SPRINGS OF HOT WATER — ERUPTED AMONG THEM!

YELPING CRIES OF TERROR RANG FROM BEHIND THE VIKINGS, THEN —

BY THE HAMMERER, THE BEASTS RUN FOR THEIR LIVES!

OUR FEAR OF THE HOT GROUND WAS FOR NOTHING! ODIN HAS SAVED US!

THE PARTY PRESSED ON UNTIL THEY WERE AGAIN HACKING THEIR WAY THROUGH THICK JUNGLE. HIGH ABOVE WAS THE WALLED CITY OF EL SARID...

KEEP GOING, MY BROTHERS! THERE MUST BE NO REST UNTIL NIGHT-FALL!

BUT THE VIKINGS HAD NOT PASSED UNNOTICED. TELLTALE SIGNS WARNED THE CITY'S WATCHFUL GUARDS!

SEE — ANIMALS FLEE FROM THE PATH OF THE INVADERS!

WE MUST WARN EL SARID! THE ENEMY WILL THEN MARCH TO THEIR DOOM!

As darkness came, the vikings decided to rest for the night...

LIGHT NO FIRES! ONLY BY CUNNING AND SURPRISE WILL WE EVER BREAK THROUGH EL SARID'S DEFENCES. LET NOTHING GIVE OUR PRESENCE AWAY!

When the sun rose, the weary party pressed on beneath huge wasps' nests!

IT IS IMPOSSIBLE FOR US TO PENETRATE SUCH A FORTRESS. HAD WE TWENTY TIMES OUR NUMBER WE WOULD STILL BE TOO WEAK!

DO NOT WORRY, SWEYN! WE'LL WAIT UNTIL FATE GIVES US A CHANCE!

Meanwhile, Karl's friend Ajarn and the other captives were held in the city's deep dungeons!

AT LEAST WE LIVE TO SEE THE START OF ANOTHER DAY. BUT ONLY THAT DEMON EL SARID KNOWS HOW IT WILL END FOR US!

SILENCE! I CAN HEAR SOMEONE COMING!

The door was unlocked and hurled open. El Sarid the merciless stared contemptuously at the helpless prisoners...

FREE THEM! TAKE THEM OUT IN CHAINS THROUGH THE STREETS. AT LAST I CAN PUT THEM TO GOOD USE!

WHAT DEVILRY IS HE PLANNING?

Ajarn knew the worst once he and the prisoners were in the open...

YOU ARE THE BAIT WHICH WILL DELIVER KARL INTO MY HANDS. HE AND THE POOR FOOLS WITH HIM SHALL BE MADE TO SHOW THEMSELVES!

While the shields of El Sarid's troops reflected the sun dazzlingly into the eyes of the prisoners, El Sarid used his hypnotic powers.

YOUR TONGUES WILL NO LONGER MOVE TO GIVE SPEECH. YOU WILL OBEY ONLY MY ORDERS. YOU SHALL NOT WARN KARL IN ANY WAY!

GUARDS, STRIKE OFF THEIR ANKLE CHAINS! ROPE THEM LOOSELY TOGETHER, AND THEN LEAD THEM OUT THROUGH THE CITY GATES. I THINK KARL AND HIS VIKINGS ARE NEAR ENOUGH TO SEE THEM!

With only a light escort the hypnotised prisoners were taken out through the gates!

Karl and his concealed followers watched tensely, their hopes rising!

DOGS, WE WILL FREE YOUR HANDS SO THAT YOU CAN TEAR BACK THE GRASS FROM THE CITY WALLS! DO AS YOU'RE TOLD — OR BE LASHED TILL YOU DROP!

Behind the gates crouched the armed hordes of El Sarid...

KARL IS CERTAIN TO ATTEMPT A RESCUE. THEN WE WILL FALL ON HIM, LIKE THE WAVES OF THE SEA!

CROUCHED IN COVER, KARL'S VIKINGS SAW THE PRISONERS BEING SET TO WORK OUTSIDE EL SARID'S CITY WALL. THE SCENE ROUSED THEM TO FURY!

KARL, IN ONE SWIFT RUSH WE CAN OVERPOWER THE MEN WHO GUARD OUR COMRADES! LET US ATTACK!

AN INSTINCT FOR DANGER WARNED KARL TO RESTRAIN HIS ANGRY WARRIORS...

FOOLS, KEEP YOUR WITS! EL SARID'S EVIL IS ONLY MATCHED BY HIS CUNNING. WE MUST BEWARE OF A TRAP!

THE VIKINGS STARED IN BEWILDERMENT, FOR KARL SUDDENLY CLIMBED TO WHERE GREAT NESTS OF WASPS WERE HANGING...

BY THE HAMMERER, I HAVE AN IDEA! DIG CLAY WITH YOUR SWORDS AND PASS IT UP TO ME!

HAS KARL GONE MAD?

KARL SEALED EACH ENTRANCE HOLE WITH THE SOFT CLAY!

THE NESTS, WITH THEIR SEETHING INHABITANTS SAFELY TRAPPED, WERE THEN CUT FREE AND PASSED DOWN!

HANDLE THEM GENTLY — THE WASPS ARE OUR ALLIES. LISTEN CAREFULLY TO WHAT WE WILL DO...

MEANWHILE, WITHIN THE CITY, EL SARID AND HIS FORCES WERE WATCHING THE PRISONERS WHO HAD BEEN HYPNOTISED TO MAKE THEM POWERLESS TO WARN KARL!

AT ANY MOMENT KARL AND HIS VIKINGS WILL ATTEMPT TO RESCUE THE PRISONERS. I WANT KARL'S FORCE TO BE CAPTURED ALIVE, FOR WHEN THEY DIE IT WILL BE VERY SLOWLY!

AT THAT INSTANT KARL'S VIKINGS LAUNCHED AN ATTACK!

UGH!

MAY ODIN GUIDE OUR ARROWS!

EL SARID'S GUARDS WERE CUT DOWN AS THE RAIDERS REACHED THE PRISONERS AND SEVERED THEIR BONDS!

KARL IS HERE, AJARN! FOLLOW US AND BE FREE!

THEN THE CITY GATES WERE FLUNG WIDE OPEN, AND EL SARID AND HIS HORDE POURED OUT WITH HOWLS OF TRIUMPH!

KARL HAS ENTERED THE TRAP! SURROUND THEM! THEY HAVE NO HOPE OF ESCAPE!

BUT KARL AND A SECOND PARTY OF VIKINGS PLUNGED FORWARD. THEY CARRIED THE WASPS' NESTS IN SLINGS MADE FROM VINES.

SEND EACH SHOT RIGHT INTO EL SARID'S FORCES!

THE SLINGS WHIRLED, AND EACH MISSILE SPED WITH ALL THE STRENGTH THE THROWERS COULD MUSTER!

WE HAVE A MILLION WINGED ALLIES! EL SARID, TASTE THEIR FURY!

THE NESTS BURST AMONGST EL SARID'S HORRIFIED FOLLOWERS. INFURIATED SWARMS WERE SET FREE!

RETREAT! RETREAT!

WE'LL BE STUNG TO DEATH!

AGONISING ATTACKS BY THE WASPS TURNED EL SARID'S FORCE INTO A SCREAMING RABBLE. AT THE SAME TIME KARL SHOUTED TO THE VIKING PRISONERS!

MAKE FOR THE PATH WHICH LEADS TO THE SHIPS! THE GODS GIVE US OUR CHANCE!

EL SARID'S FLEET OFFERED A WONDERFUL MEANS OF ESCAPE. KARL'S MEN HURRIED ALONG A MOUNTAIN TRAIL TO THE BOATS' MOORINGS!

FIGHT YOUR WAY THROUGH, MY BROTHERS! WE MUST REACH THE VESSELS AND SET SAIL FOR FREEDOM!

DESPERATE VIKINGS HURLED THEM-SELVES AT THE GUARDS OF A MULE TRAIN WHO SOUGHT TO STOP THEM!

MEET VIKING STEEL!

THEY SEEK TO FLEE FROM EL SARID! HALT THEM!

THE CONFUSION CAUSED BY THE WASPS COULD NOT LAST FOR EVER. EL SARID AT LAST REGAINED CONTROL. HIS EYES GLITTERED WITH FURY!

THE VIKINGS WILL NOT GET FAR! WE'LL BE ON THEM BEFORE THEY CAN SAIL! AND THEN THEY SHALL SUFFER DOUBLE TORTURE!

THE GUARDS OF A MULE TRAIN, WHICH WAS ON ITS WAY TO EL SARID'S STRONGHOLD, FOUGHT SAVAGELY TO HALT THE ESCAPING VIKINGS!

DRIVE THE CURS BACK TO EL SARID!

BUT WHIRLING STEEL CUT THE GUARDS DOWN AS KARL SHOUTED AN URGENT COMMAND...

KEEP GOING! GET THROUGH TO THE SHIPS!

THE VIKINGS, WITH THE CAPTIVES THEY HAD FREED, STORMED ON TOWARDS THE LIGHTLY-MANNED DHOWS...

WELL DONE, MY BROTHERS! NOW SEIZE THE TWO LARGEST VESSELS!

THE ARABS WHO WERE GUARDING THE SHIPS STOOD NO CHANCE AGAINST THE FURY OF THE VIKINGS...

THROW THE FIENDS INTO THE WATER!

FOR ODIN!

MEANWHILE, EL SARID AND HIS HORDES POURED LIKE A RIVER OF HATE IN PURSUIT...

USE THE SHIELD TRICK! KARL AND HIS VIKINGS WILL SOON BE IN OUR HANDS!

THE POLISHED SHIELDS OF THE TERRIBLE PURSUERS DAZZLINGLY REFLECTED THE SUN!

CRIES OF FEAR ROSE FROM SOME OF KARL'S MEN. TEMPORARILY BLINDED BY THE LIGHT, THEY WERE FALLING UNDER THE INFLUENCE OF EL SARID'S HYPNOTISM!

KARL! SOMETHING DEVILISH IS HAPPENING! *OUR ATTACKERS ARE NO LONGER HUMAN!*

WHAT THE VIKINGS THOUGHT THEY SAW WAS FRIGHTENING ENOUGH TO ROB THEM OF REASON!

BUT KARL ALREADY KNEW THE DANGER —

FOOLS, DO NOT GAZE AT THEIR SHIELDS! EL SARID USES A TRICK TO WORK WITCH-CRAFT ON YOUR MINDS. BY THE HAMMERER, I WILL SHOW YOU A WAY TO DEFEAT HIM!

IN ONE DHOW WAS A GIANT CATAPULT USED IN WARFARE BY EL SARID'S RAIDERS. IT HURLED A MIXTURE OF NITRE, SULPHUR AND INFLAMMABLE NAPTHA...

EL SARID USED THIS DEVICE AGAINST MY SETTLEMENT! NOW IT SHALL BE HIS TURN TO MEET THE TERRIBLE FIRE WHICH CAN BURN BENEATH WATER!

KARL WORKED THE RELEASE HANDLE...

TRY YOUR WITCHCRAFT ON THIS, EL SARID!

CRIES OF HORROR BURST FROM THE DESCENDING HORDES...

AA-ARGH!

THE INFLAMMABLE MIXTURE SET FIRE TO TINDER-DRY VEGETATION...

EL SARID, LET US RETREAT! OUR CITY WILL BE THREATENED UNLESS WE CAN PUT OUT THE FIRE!

EL SARID HAD NO CHOICE BUT TO AGREE. THOUGH HATRED FOR KARL ALMOST CHOKED HIM, HIS FIRST THOUGHT WAS THE SAFETY OF HIS STRONGHOLD!

CLOSE THE GATES! FORM TEAMS TO EXTINGUISH ALL SPARKS WHICH COME IN! I WILL CALL ON OTHER POWERS TO CAUSE KARL'S DESTRUCTION!

MEANWHILE, THE VIKINGS WERE STEERING THE CAPTURED DHOWS FROM THE BANK!

PULL! PULL! RAISE THE SAILS!

THE FIRE DRIVES EL SARID'S DEMONS TO SEEK SAFETY!

EL SARID MOUNTED TO THE TOP OF A TOWER, AND EVIL SEEMED TO RADIATE FROM HIM!

AMMON RA, I CALL UPON YOU TO CHANGE THE COURSE OF THE WIND! LET FIRE CUT OFF MY ENEMIES' RETREAT! THE BLAZE THEY STARTED SHALL DELIVER KARL INTO MY HANDS!

TRIUMPHANT VIKINGS TOILED TO GET THE SHIPS UNDER WAY...

EL SARID AND HIS FOLLOWERS ARE BUSY SAVING THEIR CITY FROM THE FIRE. THE GODS HAVE GIVEN US THIS CHANCE TO ESCAPE!

THE SPEEDY DHOWS WERE SKILFULLY MANOEUVRED, BUT A BARRIER OF DENSE GREENERY LOOMED UP AHEAD...

KARL, THE RIVER IS BLOCKED! WE ARE TRAPPED!

THE VEGETATION MUST BE SOME FORM OF TRICKERY! EL SARID SAILED IN, SO WE CAN SAIL OUT! STEER INTO IT! USE YOUR AXES!

BOWS RAMMED THE SEEMINGLY IMPENETRABLE WALL OF JUNGLE GROWTH!

IT STARTS TO GIVE! SWING YOUR STEEL!

IT NOW BECAME APPARENT THAT THE BARRIER WAS MERELY CAMOUFLAGED NETS AND CREEPERS. SLOWLY THE DHOWS BEGAN TO FORCE A WAY THROUGH...

IT DOES NOT STOP US! THIS TIME EL SARID'S DECEPTION HAS FAILED!

MEANWHILE, EL SARID—A FIGURE OF EVIL—STOOD AT THE TOP OF A TOWER...

AMMON RA, LET THE WIND DRIVE THE FLAMES TO CUT OFF MY ENEMIES! BY THE DEMONS OF CAHANNAB, I COMMAND YOU!

THEN, AS IF BY SOME GRIM ACT OF CHANCE, THE WIND GATHERED STRENGTH AND CHANGED DIRECTION. NO LONGER WERE THE FLAMES FANNED TOWARDS THE CITY!

AMMON RA ANSWERS! MY POWERS ARE GREATER THAN KARL'S!

WITH INCREDIBLE SPEED A TIDAL WAVE OF FLAME LICKED THROUGH PARCHED GRASS AND BAMBOO!

TERRIFIED ANIMALS BOLTED BEFORE THE FIERY MENACE!

AN INFERNO OF HEAT REACHED OUT ACROSS THE RIVER...

THE FIRE RACES US! THE BEASTS SEEK THE SAFETY OF THE WATER!

BLAZING LEAVES, CARRIED BY HEAT EDDIES, STARTED NEW FIRES!

SOAK THE TIMBERS AND SAILS WITH WATER! BEAT OUT ALL SPARKS FALLING ABOARD! TO HALT NOW WILL BE FATAL!

FEAR-CRAZED JUNGLE BEASTS ADDED TO THE PERIL OF THE VIKINGS AND SLOWED THE DHOWS' PROGRESS!

KARL CLIMBED ALOFT TO BEAT OUT A SMOULDERING SAIL!

ABOVE THE TREMENDOUS SOUND OF THE BLAZE KARL HEARD A DESPAIRING CRY FROM BELOW!

SMOKE DIMS THE LIGHT OF THE SUN! KARL, WE CANNOT SEE TO NAVIGATE THE RIVER!

THE HULL JARRED WARNINGLY AGAINST FLOATING DEBRIS.

TAKE IN SOME SAIL! USE POLES TO TEST THE DEPTH OF WATER! IF WE RUN AGROUND WE ARE DOOMED!

EL SARID AND HIS MEN, WHO KNEW THE RIVER BETTER THAN KARL, DID NOT FACE THE SAME HANDICAP...

PURSUE! WE SHALL SOON OVERTAKE THE VIKINGS, AND THEN REVENGE SHALL BE MINE!

AT LAST THE VIKINGS DREW CLEAR OF THE FIRE, WHICH WAS NOW BEGINNING TO BURN ITSELF OUT...

THE SMOKE CLEARS! WE CAN SEE TO NAVIGATE KARL! BY THE HAMMERER, IT IS SAFE TO MAKE GREATER SPEED!

BUT KARL WAS LOOKING AT AJARN AND THE OTHER FREED CAPTIVES. SOMETHING ABOUT THEIR APPEARANCE MADE HIM UNEASY...

AJARN, MY OLD FRIEND, YOU DO NOT SPEAK! WHAT HAS HAPPENED? YOU ARE LIKE A MAN IN A DREAM!

AJARN'S EYES SHOWED HE UNDERSTOOD, BUT, WHEN HE TRIED TO SPEAK, NO SOUND CAME FROM HIS LIPS...

THE TERRIBLE TRUTH DAWNED ON KARL...

THE WITCHCRAFT OF EL SARID HAS ROBBED OUR RESCUED BROTHERS OF SPEECH! HIS ACCURSED POWER STILL HOLDS THEM!

EL SARID'S EVIL IS EVEN GREATER THAN WE THOUGHT!

THE DHOWS BEGAN TO GLIDE BENEATH AN ARCHWAY OF GREENERY!

O KARL, WHAT CAN WE DO TO BEAT EL SARID?

MY CUNNING MUST MATCH HIS! HE SHALL BE FORCED TO RETURN THE POWER OF SPEECH TO THOSE HE HAS CURSED. LISTEN! THIS IS MY PLAN...

WE ACTED LIKE FOOLS TO UNDERESTIMATE EL SARID! EVEN THIS ESCAPE IS TOO EASY. AS LONG AS HE IS LIVING, HE AND HIS FOLLOWERS WILL NEVER GIVE UP!

AFTER KARL HAD SWIFTLY EXPLAINED HIS PLAN, HIS ACTIONS GREW STRANGE...

KARL, COME BACK! IT IS MADNESS! YOUR PLAN WILL NEVER WORK!

DO AS I ORDER! MY WAY IS THE ONLY HOPE OF DEFEATING EL SARID. FOR IT IS CERTAIN THAT HE ALREADY PURSUES US!

VERY WELL! WE SHALL OBEY AND DO AS YOU COMMAND!

MEANWHILE, EL SARID'S LARGE FORCE SPED THROUGH THE AREA OF SMOKE...

KARL CANNOT BE FAR AHEAD. OUR KNOWLEDGE OF THE RIVER PREVENTS THE SMOKE SLOWING OUR SPEED!

IT WAS NOT LONG BEFORE THE ARCHWAY OF VEGETATION WAS REACHED.

EL SARID! SEE, WE OVERTAKE THE VIKINGS! THERE ARE THE TWO SHIPS!

THE TRIUMPHANT PURSUERS SAW A TEMPTING SIGHT...

THE FOOLS HAVE RUN AGROUND! NOW THEY CANNOT ESCAPE US!

WE OUT-NUMBER THE VIKINGS TWENTY TO ONE!

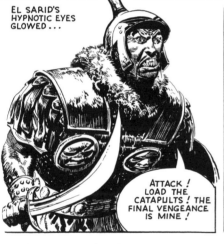

EL SARID'S HYPNOTIC EYES GLOWED...

ATTACK! LOAD THE CATAPULTS! THE FINAL VENGEANCE IS MINE!

THERE WAS A SLIGHT MOVEMENT AMONGST THE LOFTY GREENERY. KARL WAS THERE!

EL SARID GROWS CARELESS! HE SHALL QUICKLY LEARN HIS MISTAKE!

TOO LATE EL SARID GLIMPSED THE FIGURE WHICH HURTLED TOWARDS HIM...

IT IS THE VIKING CHIEFTAIN!

KARL'S FEET CRASHED INTO EL SARID'S CHEST!

WITH STUNNING FORCE EL SARID WAS DASHED INTO THE WATER, AND KARL PREPARED TO FOLLOW HIM...

IF I FAIL WE ARE DOOMED!

CRIES OF SHOCKED FURY CAME FROM THE CREW OF THE LEADING SARACEN DHOW

THE VIKING HAS ATTACKED EL SARID! FOR THAT HE SHALL DIE!

ALTHOUGH EL SARID, WEIGHED DOWN BY ARMOUR, WAS ALMOST UNCONSCIOUS, KARL'S POWERFUL ARM KEPT HIM AFLOAT

ODIN, GIVE ME STRENGTH ENOUGH TO REACH THE BANK WITH HIM. FOR, IF MY PLAN IS TO SUCCEED, I NEED THIS HUMAN DEVIL ALIVE!

THEN, AS KARL DRAGGED HIS RECOVERING ENEMY TO SAFETY —

SHOUT! TELL YOUR FOLLOWERS TO RETURN TO THEIR SHIPS! MY DAGGER IS AT YOUR THROAT! DISOBEY AND YOU DIE!

GO BACK! I AM HELD HOSTAGE! HARKEN, YOU FOOLS!

CONFUSION GRIPPED THE LEADERLESS FORCE

WE HAVE NO CHOICE BUT TO DO AS WE ARE COMMANDED!

ONLY EL SARID'S WITCHCRAFT CAN SAVE HIM!

TRIUMPHANTLY KARL DROVE HIS PRISONER FORWARD

ON! MY VIKINGS AWAIT US! AS YOU VALUE YOUR LIFE, MAKE NO TREACHEROUS MOVE!

THE SAILS OF THE CAPTURED DHOWS AGAIN CRACKED IN THE BREEZE

KARL'S PLAN HAS SUCCEEDED! QUICK, TAKE HIM AND THE HOSTAGE ABOARD!

EL SARID'S FLEET DARE MAKE NO MOVE!

WILLING HANDS DRAGGED THE TWO MEN ABOARD

EL SARID, ORDER YOU'R MEN TO RETREAT!

VIKING, BE WARNED! YOU WILL LIVE TO REGRET THIS

BUT, FOR THE MOMENT, EL SARID COULD ONLY OBEY, AND HE ORDERED HIS FLEET TO TURN BACK

WE HEAD FOR THE SEA! HEAD FOR OUR HOMELAND!

THE TWO DHOWS, ONE WITH EL SARID ABOARD, SAFELY NEARED THE MOUTH OF THE NILE

FREEDOM LIES AHEAD!

KARL TURNED TO THE STRANGELY QUIET PRISONER

NOW, EL SARID, I COMMAND YOU TO USE YOUR WITCHCRAFT TO RETURN THE POWER OF SPEECH TO MY FRIENDS WHOM YOU CAPTURED

SO BE IT!

THE GLOWING, HYPNOTIC EYES OF EL SARID STARED AT AJARN AND THE OTHER RELEASED PRISONERS

YOUR TONGUES LOOSEN! YOU ARE FREED FROM YOUR SILENCE!

WILD JOY OVERWHELMED AJARN AND HIS COMPANIONS

KARL, WE CAN SPEAK! WE CAN SPEAK! AT LAST I CAN GIVE THANKS FOR OUR RESCUE

LET US DRINK TO IT! SWEYN, BRING REFRESHMENT FROM BELOW

SWEYN HAD OBEYED WHEN EL SARID SOFTLY CALLED HIS NAME

SWEYN! I, TOO, AM PARCHED. BE MERCIFUL — LET ME DRINK!

DRINK, THEN! I AM NO TYRANT

SWEYN STOOPED — AND EL SARID'S EYES BLAZED INHUMANLY. IT SEEMED TO THE HYPNOTISED VIKING THAT THE PRISONER WAS GROWING IN SIZE

SWEYN, CUT ME FREE! THEN PASS ME YOUR SWORD!

WOODENLY, LIKE A MAN IN A DREAM, THE VIKING BEGAN TO SEVER THE SARACEN'S BONDS

KARL GREW CARELESS! IT SHALL BE HIS FINAL MISTAKE!

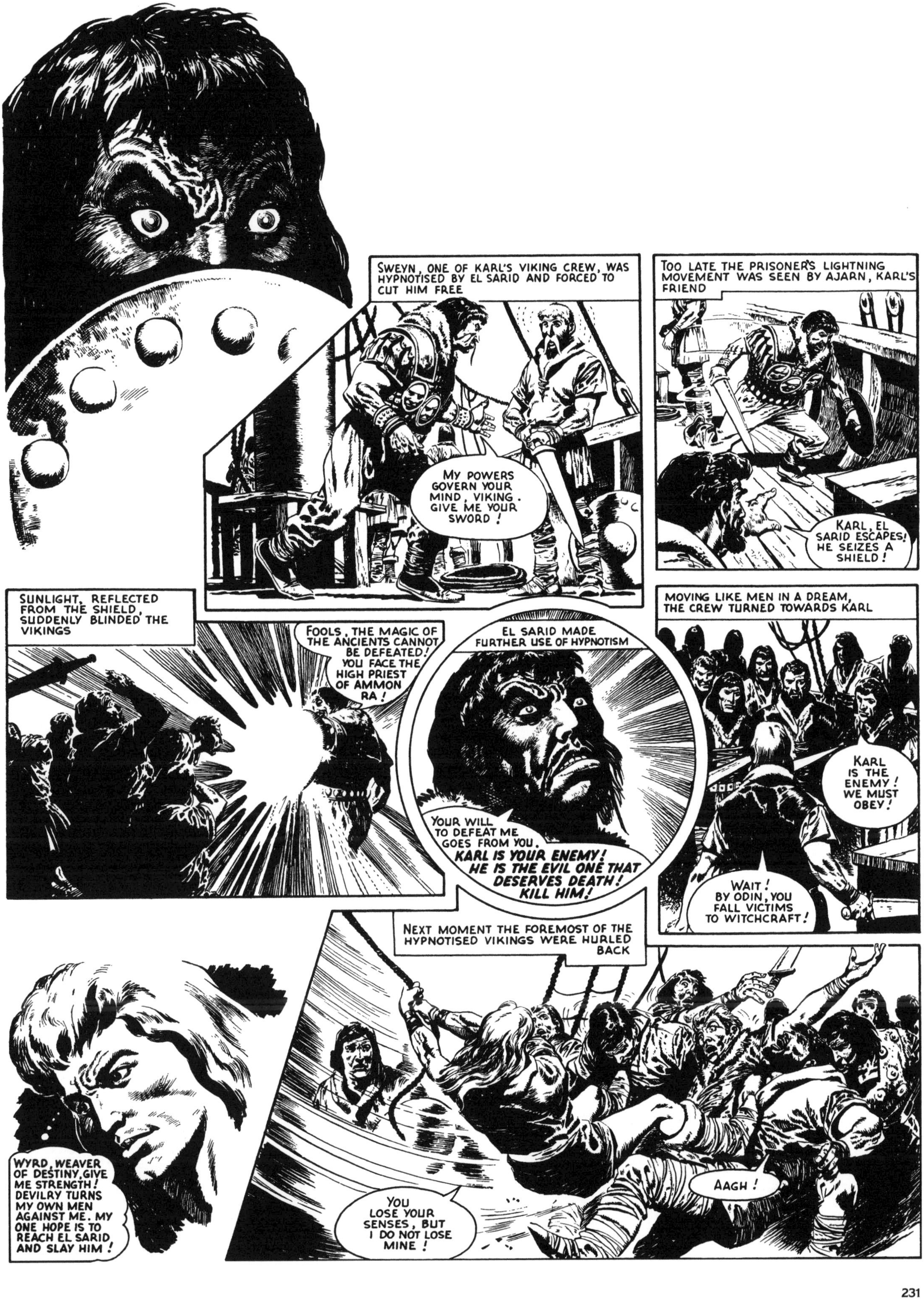

SWEYN, ONE OF KARL'S VIKING CREW, WAS HYPNOTISED BY EL SARID AND FORCED TO CUT HIM FREE
MY POWERS GOVERN YOUR MIND, VIKING. GIVE ME YOUR SWORD!
TOO LATE THE PRISONER'S LIGHTNING MOVEMENT WAS SEEN BY AJARN, KARL'S FRIEND
KARL, EL SARID ESCAPES! HE SEIZES A SHIELD!
SUNLIGHT, REFLECTED FROM THE SHIELD, SUDDENLY BLINDED THE VIKINGS
FOOLS, THE MAGIC OF THE ANCIENTS CANNOT BE DEFEATED! YOU FACE THE HIGH PRIEST OF AMMON RA!
EL SARID MADE FURTHER USE OF HYPNOTISM
YOUR WILL TO DEFEAT ME GOES FROM YOU. KARL IS YOUR ENEMY! HE IS THE EVIL ONE THAT DESERVES DEATH! KILL HIM!
MOVING LIKE MEN IN A DREAM, THE CREW TURNED TOWARDS KARL
KARL IS THE ENEMY! WE MUST OBEY!
WAIT! BY ODIN, YOU FALL VICTIMS TO WITCHCRAFT!
NEXT MOMENT THE FOREMOST OF THE HYPNOTISED VIKINGS WERE HURLED BACK
WYRD, WEAVER OF DESTINY, GIVE ME STRENGTH! DEVILRY TURNS MY OWN MEN AGAINST ME. MY ONE HOPE IS TO REACH EL SARID AND SLAY HIM!
YOU LOSE YOUR SENSES, BUT I DO NOT LOSE MINE!
AAGH!

KARL MOVED WITH TIGERISH SPEED AND AGILITY

TURN, EL SARID! YOU ARE NOT YET MASTER OF THIS SHIP!

VIKING COURAGE WAS BEHIND KARL'S WHIRLING BLADE.

VIKINGS ABOARD THE SECOND DHOW, MANNED BY THE REMAINDER OF KARL'S MEN, STARED AGHAST

THERE IS MUTINY! KARL'S CREW HAS GONE MAD!

NO— LOOK! IT IS THE WORK OF EL SARID! WE MUST STOP THEM!

A SHOWER OF ARROWS HALTED THE HYPNOTISED VIKINGS

KEEP THE MUTINEERS BACK! THEY ARE VICTIMS OF WITCHCRAFT!

A CLEVER TWIST FORCED EL SARID OVER THE SIDE OF THE SHIP

AA-EEEEH!

A BLOW SENT KARL'S SWORD FLYING FROM HIS GRASP, BUT HE MANAGED TO GRAB EL SARID'S SWORD-ARM

YOUR STEEL MISSES! NOW LEARN FROM A VIKING!

SHARKS SWIRLED, AND THE TYRANT'S POWERS OF HYPNOTISM DIED WITH HIM

THE HYPNOTISED VIKINGS, RETURNING TO NORMAL, RECALLED NOTHING OF WHAT HAD JUST HAPPENED

KARL, WHAT HAS TAKEN PLACE? THOSE ARROWS — THAT CRY?

HAVE NO FEAR! EL SARID IS DEAD! HIS WITCHCRAFT IS NO MORE!

AHEAD LAY THE OPEN SEAS TO FREEDOM—AND THE VIKINGS' HOMELAND. THE MENACE OF EL SARID AND HIS PIRATES WAS FINISHED!

EL SARID'S FINAL CRY MARKED THE DEATH OF HIS WITCHCRAFT! ASK NO MORE QUESTIONS. INSTEAD, LET US THINK OF WHAT OUR NEXT ADVENTURES MAY BE!

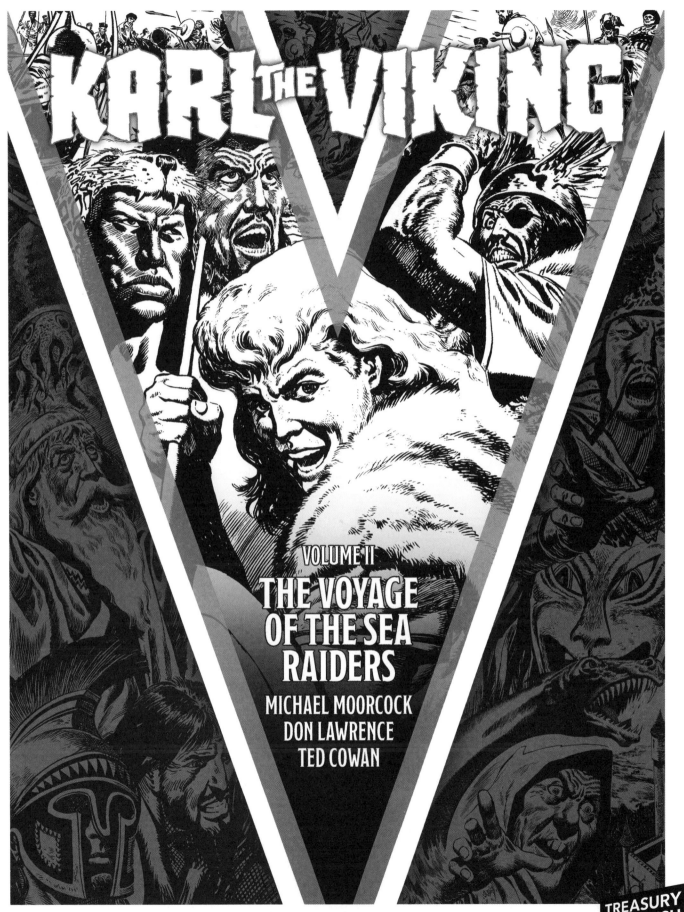

KARL THE VIKING

VOLUME II
THE VOYAGE OF THE SEA RAIDERS

MICHAEL MOORCOCK
DON LAWRENCE
TED COWAN

COMING JANUARY 2023
ISBN: 978-1-78618-658-4

TREASURY
OF BRITISH
COMICS

THE RISE AND FALL OF

THE TRIGAN EMPIRE

MIKE BUTTERWORTH · DON LAWRENCE

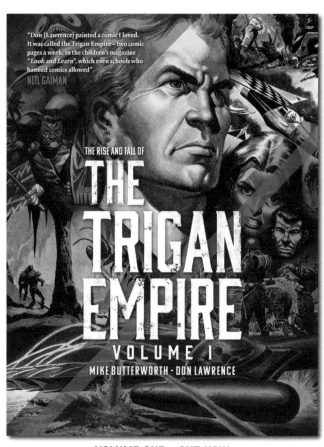

"Don [Lawrence] painted a comic I loved. It was called the Trigan Empire – two comic pages a week, in the children's magazine "Look and Learn", which even schools who banned comics allowed"
NEIL GAIMAN

THE RISE AND FALL OF
THE TRIGAN EMPIRE
VOLUME I
MIKE BUTTERWORTH · DON LAWRENCE

VOLUME ONE • OUT NOW
ISBN: 978-1-78108-755-8

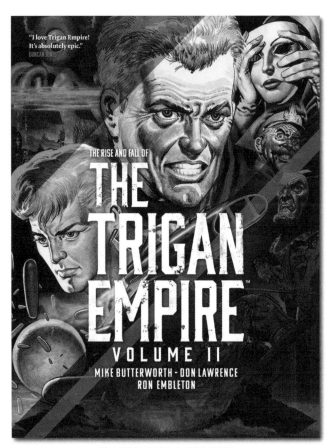

"I love Trigan Empire! It's absolutely epic."
DUNCAN JONES

THE RISE AND FALL OF
THE TRIGAN EMPIRE™
VOLUME II
MIKE BUTTERWORTH · DON LAWRENCE
RON EMBLETON

VOLUME TWO • OUT NOW
ISBN: 978-1-78108-775-6

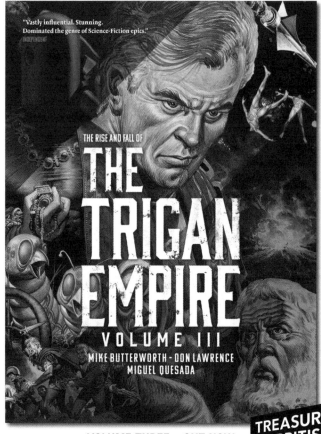

"Vastly influential. Stunning. Dominated the genre of Science-Fiction epics."
INDEPENDENT

THE RISE AND FALL OF
THE TRIGAN EMPIRE
VOLUME III
MIKE BUTTERWORTH · DON LAWRENCE
MIGUEL QUESADA

VOLUME THREE • OUT NOW
ISBN: 978-1-78108-932-3

TREASURY OF BRITISH COMICS

TED COWAN   JERRY SIEGEL   REG BUNN

THE SPIDER'S
SYNDICATE OF CRIME

OUT NOW
ISBN: 978-1-78108-905-7

TREASURY
OF BRITISH
COMICS

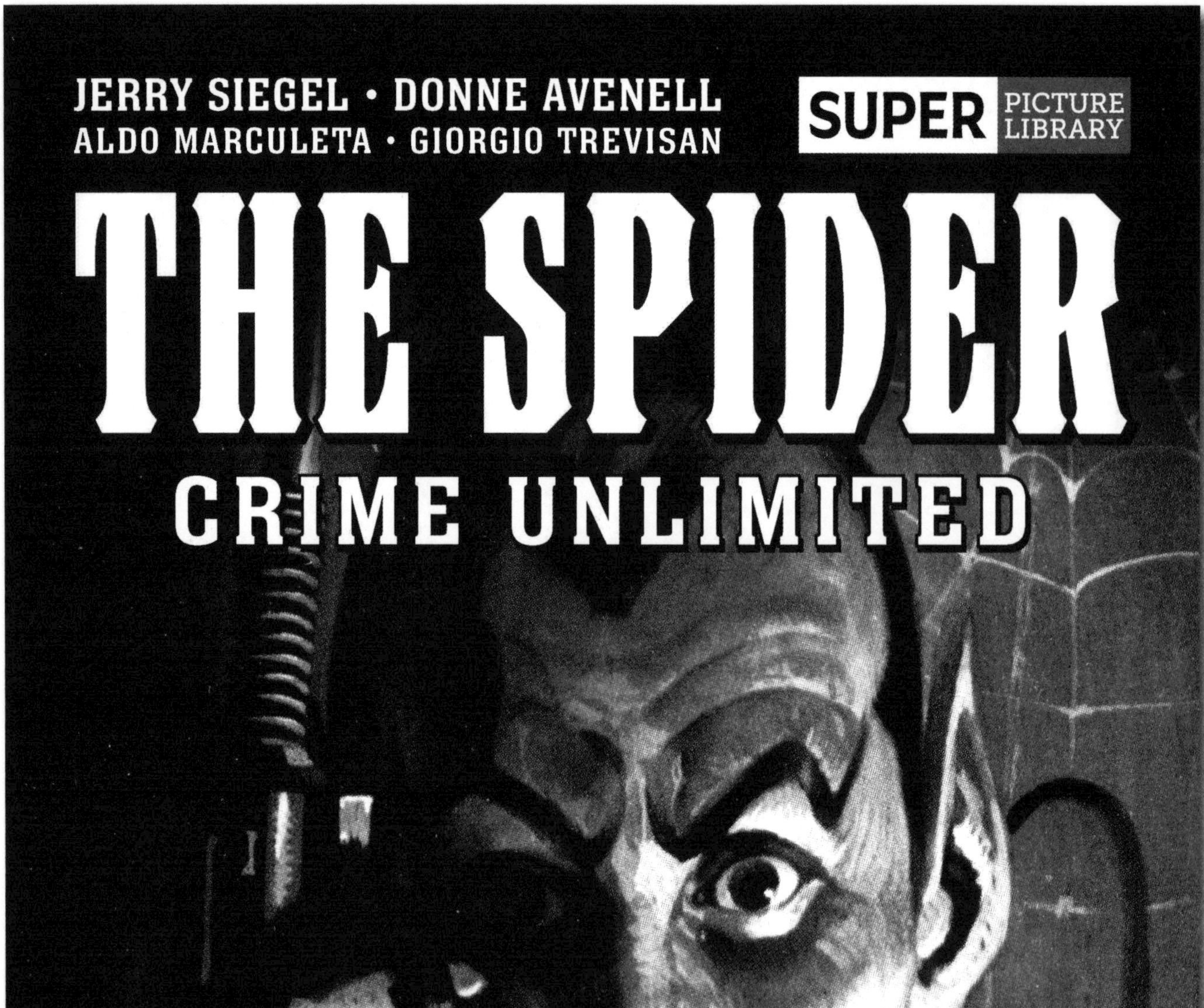

JERRY SIEGEL • DONNE AVENELL
ALDO MARCULETA • GIORGIO TREVISAN

SUPER PICTURE LIBRARY

THE SPIDER
CRIME UNLIMITED

COMING 2022
ISBN: 978-1-78618-465-8

TREASURY OF BRITISH COMICS

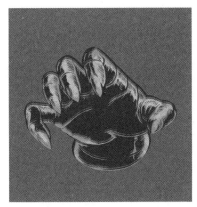  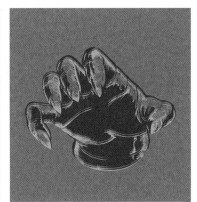

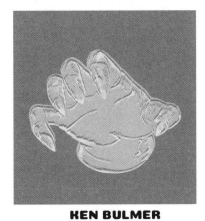  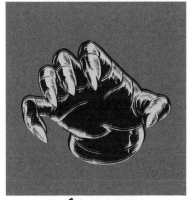

THE STEEL CLAW
Invisible Man

 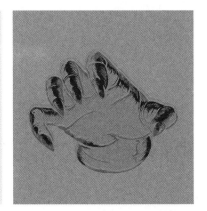

KEN BULMER

JESÚS BLASCO

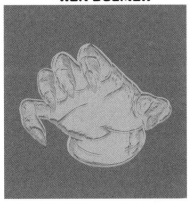 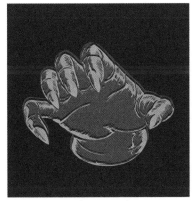 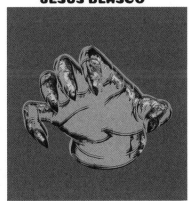 

OUT NOW
ISBN: 978-1-78108-906-4

TREASURY
OF BRITISH
COMICS

TOM TULLY • JESÚS BLASCO

SUPER PICTURE LIBRARY

THE STEEL CLAW
THE COLD TRAIL

COMING 2022
ISBN: 978-1-78618-659-1

TREASURY OF BRITISH COMICS

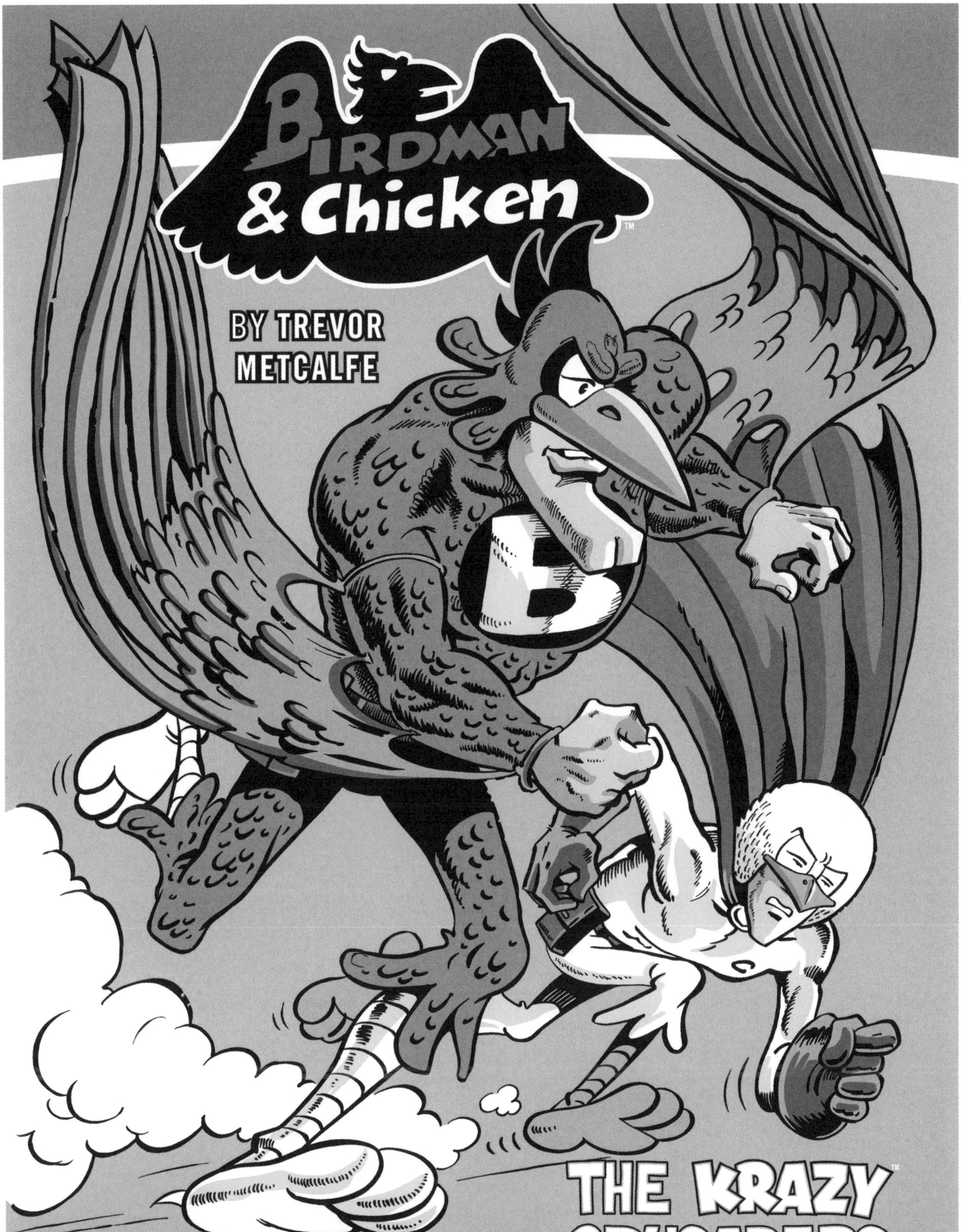
BIRDMAN & Chicken
BY TREVOR METCALFE
THE KRAZY CRUSADERS

ISBN: 978-1-78618-492-4

THE HOUSE OF DOLMANN

TOM TULLY
ERIC BRADBURY

FROM THE PAGES OF
VALIANT

COMING 2022
ISBN: 978-1-78618-491-7

TREASURY
OF BRITISH
COMICS